America's West

The American West has influenced important national developments throughout the twentieth century, not only in the cultural arena but also in economic development, in political ideology and action, and in natural resource conservation and preservation. Using regionalism as a lens for illuminating these national trends, *America's West: A History, 1890–1950* explores this region's history and its influence on the rest of America. Moving chronologically from the late nineteenth to the mid-twentieth century, David Wrobel examines turn-of-the-century expansion, the Progressive Era, the 1920s, the Great Depression and the New Deal, World War II, and early Cold War years. He emphasizes cultural and political history, showing how developments in the West frequently indicated the future direction of the country.

David M. Wrobel is a native Londoner who came to the United States for graduate school in 1985 and never left. He is the author of *Global West, American Frontier* (2013, winner of the Western Heritage Award for nonfiction), *Promised Lands* (2002), and *The End of American Exceptionalism* (1993) and is currently working on "John Steinbeck's America: A Cultural History, 1930–1968." David is a past president of the Pacific Coast Branch of the American Historical Association and of Phi Alpha Theta, the National History Honor Society, and is a frequent collaborator with K–12 teachers across the country.

Cambridge Essential Histories

Cambridge Essential Histories is devoted to introducing critical events, periods, or individuals in history to students. Volumes in this series emphasize narrative as a means of familiarizing students with historical analysis. In this series, leading scholars focus on topics in European, American, Asian, Latin American, Middle Eastern, African, and World History through thesis-driven, concise volumes designed for survey and upper-division undergraduate history courses. The books contain an introduction that acquaints readers with the historical event and reveals the book's thesis; narrative chapters that cover the chronology of the event or problem; and a concluding summary that provides the historical interpretation and analysis.

Editors

General Editor: Donald T. Critchlow, Arizona State University

Other Books in the Series:

Edward D. Berkowitz, *Mass Appeal: The Formative Age of the Movies, Radio, and TV*
Howard Brick and Christopher Phelps, *Radicals in America: The U.S. Left since the Second World War*
Sean P. Cunningham, *American Politics in the Postwar Sunbelt*
Ian Dowbiggin, *The Quest for Mental Health: A Tale of Science, Medicine, Scandal, Sorrow, and Mass Society*
John Earl Haynes and Harvey Klehr, *Early Cold War Spies: The Espionage Trials that Shaped American Politics*
James H. Hutson, *Church and State in America: The First Two Centuries*
Maury Klein, *The Genesis of Industrial America, 1870–1920*
John Lauritz Larson, *The Market Revolution in America: Liberty, Ambition, and the Eclipse of the Common Good*
Wilson D. Miscamble, *The Most Controversial Decision: Truman, the Atomic Bombs, and the Defeat of Japan*
Charles H. Parker, *Global Interactions in the Early Modern Age, 1400–1800*
Stanley G. Payne, *The Spanish Civil War*
W. J. Rorabaugh, *American Hippies*
Smith, Jason Scott, *A Concise History of the New Deal*

America's West

A History, 1890–1950

DAVID M. WROBEL
University of Oklahoma

CAMBRIDGE
UNIVERSITY PRESS

University Printing House, Cambridge CB2 8BS, United Kingdom

One Liberty Plaza, 20th Floor, New York, NY 10006, USA

477 Williamstown Road, Port Melbourne, VIC 3207, Australia

4843/24, 2nd Floor, Ansari Road, Daryaganj, Delhi – 110002, India

79 Anson Road, #06–04/06, Singapore 079906

Cambridge University Press is part of the University of Cambridge.

It furthers the University's mission by disseminating knowledge in the pursuit of education, learning, and research at the highest international levels of excellence.

www.cambridge.org
Information on this title: www.cambridge.org/9780521192019
DOI: 10.1017/9781139022439

First published 2017

Printed in the United States of America by Sheridan Books, Inc.

A catalogue record for this publication is available from the British Library

ISBN 978-0-521-19201-9 Hardback
ISBN 978-0-521-15013-2 Paperback

For my mother, Evelyn, with everlasting love and gratitude, from the Southern Great Plains to Southwest London

Contents

Figures

Maps

Acknowledgments

I am grateful to Donald Critchlow for inviting me to write a book for Cambridge's Essential Histories series, to Deborah Gershenowitz and Lew Bateman for their editorial guidance, and to Eric Crahan, who, with Don, shepherded the work through the initial proposal stage. The formal readers of the proposal – along with Robert Johnston and Andy Fry – all provided helpful feedback; Andy was kind enough to read a draft of the whole manuscript. Many thanks to David Chappell, Bill Deverell, Janet Fireman, Keith Gaddie, Robert Goldberg, Rob Griswold, Anne Hyde, Robert Johnston, Paula Petrik, Greg Schneider, David Tanenhaus, and Jay Taylor, who each read portions of the manuscript. Their feedback was invaluable.

While working on *America's West*, I benefited from supportive institutional colleagues and administrators at two universities. My thanks go to the History Departments – faculty, staff, and students – at the University of Nevada Las Vegas (UNLV) and the University of Oklahoma (OU), and especially to my OU department chair, James S. Hart. I am grateful to the faculty and staff of the OU Libraries, including the Western History Collections, for their support. I am also indebted to another group of excellent scholars and staff, and especially to Peter Blodgett, the H. Russell Smith Foundation Curator of Western Manuscripts, at my periodic intellectual home away from home, the Huntington Library, where much of the work on the book was done.

I have had the good fortune in recent years to teach a graduate readings colloquium titled The West and America both at UNLV and at OU and another titled West, Nation, World at OU. I am grateful to the historians who kindly agreed to conference call or videoconference with us, and to the students for their contributions to those courses, and thus to my thinking about this book. In addition, a number of outstanding OU History graduate students provided research support: Courtney Buchkoski, Derek Donwerth, Jeff Fortney, Alistair Fortson, Dustin Mack, Alexandra Mogan, and Jesus Perez – my deepest thanks to you all.

At OU, I have the time and resources to research, reflect, and write, and to balance the responsibilities of scholarship with those of teaching and service, in no small part because of the generosity of the Merrick Family Foundation in funding my position; I am deeply appreciative of the Merricks' support for and interest in my work.

Most importantly, as I worked on *America's West*, I have had the love and support of my wife, Janet, my children, Davey, Ethan, and Miranda, and my mother, Evelyn.

Introduction: The West and America

America developed its West in the nineteenth century, but the West, to no small degree, developed America in the first half of the twentieth. *America's West* tells the story of the West against the backdrop of national developments from the last decade of the nineteenth century through the first half of the twentieth.[1] The West has been and remains culturally, economically, politically, geographically, and demographically dynamic, distinct, and diverse. It has also served as the source of important trends in the cultural arena, in political thought and action at both ends of the ideological spectrum, in economic development, and in natural resource conservation and preservation. While the West was not always at the leading edge of major changes during this period, frequently the region indicated the directions in which the nation was moving and continues to do so into the present.

This book treats the West as a single region but is attentive to the significant demographic, cultural, physiographic, and economic differences among the West's subregions: the Southern Plains (from Texas to Kansas), the Northern Plains (from Nebraska to North Dakota), the Southwest (primarily Arizona and New Mexico), the Pacific Northwest (Oregon, Washington, and Idaho), California, the Great Basin (Nevada and Utah), and the Rocky Mountain West (Colorado, Montana, and Wyoming).[2] Western writer Wallace Stegner emphasized that there were

[1] A later companion study will examine the West and the nation from the mid-twentieth to the early-twenty-first century.

[2] This volume's regional definition – from the Plains to the Pacific, and including Alaska and Hawaii, departs from that of Richard W. Etulain and Michael P. Malone, *The American*

"many Wests" and "trying to make a unanimous culture out of them would be a hopeless job . . . like wrapping five watermelons."[3] Yet, the West persists as a coherent regional entity for Americans and people around the world, even with its varied subregions, and despite the supposed flattening weight of corporate influence – chain motels, restaurants, and big-box stores – as well as the changes resulting from immigration and interregional migration.

America's West emphasizes the western region's transformation from the 1890s through the 1940s as well as the West's impact on the nation. In the popular imagination, not to mention school and college textbooks, western history remains largely confined to the nineteenth century; it is a story of mountain men, pioneers, gold rushes, wagon trains, homesteading, transcontinental railroads, cowboys, cattle drives, and Indian wars. By the late nineteenth century, the region was becoming increasingly modernized through vast federal subsidies and massive private financing from outside the region, which together tied the West into an increasingly modern, urban, and industrial national economy. The West's transformation continued in the first half of the new century and was just as important to the national story as its earlier history, but those later developments are less well known.[4]

The West's population was negligible in 1900 when roughly 10 million people lived west of the Mississippi River out of a national population of some 76 million, a little over 13 percent.[5] Yet by 1950, close to 35 million of the United States's 152 million residents, or almost 23 percent, lived in the area stretching from the second tier of trans-Mississippi western states to the Pacific Coast, and including the territories of Alaska and

West: A Modern History, 1900 to the Present (Lincoln: University of Nebraska Press, 1997), which does not include the noncontiguous Wests. Earl Pomeroy's *The American Far West in the Twentieth Century* (New Haven, CT: Yale University Press, 2008) covers the same region, but with the exclusion of Texas.

3 Wallace Stegner and Richard Etulain, "On Western History and Historians," in *Conversations with Wallace Stegner on Western History and Literature* (Salt Lake City: University of Utah Press, 1983), 145–166, quotation on 156.

4 Patricia Nelson Limerick's observations concerning the absence of the twentieth-century West in textbooks, in "The Case of the Premature Departure: The Trans-Mississippi West and American History Textbooks," *The Journal of American History* 78 (March 1992): 1380–1394, reprinted in Limerick, *Something in the Soil: Legacies and Reckonings in the New West* (New York: W. W. Norton, 2000), 92–105, still ring true.

5 Of those 10 million residents of the West in 1900, more than three-quarters lived in just 5 of the region's 19 states and territories: Texas, 3,049,000; California, 1,485,000; Kansas, 1,470,000; Nebraska, 1,066,000; and Oklahoma, 790,000. See *Historical Statistics of the United States*.

Hawaii. The trend has not abated. By the start of the twenty-first century, roughly 100 million of the nation's 282 million residents, about 35 percent, resided between the Plains and the Pacific. Today the percentage is higher still.[6]

American politics reflected the country's demographic tilt west. The region was home to the nation's president (either as birthplace or state of residence) for most of the years from 1953 to 2016. Moreover, the West's shift away in the last third of the twentieth century from the liberal orientation nurtured during the Progressive Era, New Deal, and Great Society years, had much to do with the influence of western conservative forces pushing back against federal social programs and regulation of private business. That conservative ascendancy was halted in the 2008 and 2012 presidential elections, partly because of new demographic realities most evident in the West. In 2005, Texas joined California, Hawaii, and New Mexico as one of the nation's four majority minority states, and by 2013 California's Hispanic population outnumbered its white population; Texas is trending in the same direction.[7] With the issues of border security and immigration at the forefront of contemporary political debates between the Democratic and Republican parties, it is likely that the changing demography of the West will continue to influence national elections.

These contemporary developments grew out of changes in the first half of the twentieth century, when western states worked hard to attract new residents and lobbied the federal government to make massive infrastructural investments in the region. The war against Mexico and subsequent seizure of half of that nation's territory in 1846–1848, and the conquest, displacement, and confinement of Native peoples across the West during and after the Indian Wars in the second half of the nineteenth century, are disturbing and well-known developments. Less known is the vital role of the federal government during World War II and the Cold War in expending tens of billions of dollars in subsidies to finance massive new industrial infrastructure and military bases across the region, thereby creating the nation's largest regional landscape of war. The federal government had played a central role in nineteenth-century western frontier development by underwriting railroad building, homesteading, and the conquest and control of indigenous peoples. And Washington, DC, continued to shape the region just as dramatically in the twentieth century through

[6] The 2017 figure is almost 36 percent.

[7] The District of Columbia is also majority minority.

massive dam construction projects and water initiatives. A series of mineral booms in California, Colorado, Nevada, and other far western states from the mid to the late nineteenth century altered the region's landscape and economy. Those extractive transformations continued throughout the twentieth century in the form of copper, coal, uranium, and precious metals mining from the Great Plains to the West Coast.

Furthermore, nearly a century and a half after the establishment of the first national park (Yellowstone, 1872), approximately half of the land mass of the 13 far western states (including Alaska and Hawaii) remains "America's West" – publicly owned and federally managed parks, forests, preserves, and recreation areas that play a vital role in defining the region for both the nation and the world. And today, after a century and a half of efforts by the national government to manage those public lands, western local interests continue to push back in the courts and in local and state legislatures against the very notion of federal landownership, as they have since the 1890s. The Sagebrush Rebellion of the 1970s and 1980s, and the more recent armed standoffs between federal agents and local rancher Cliven Bundy and his supporters in southwestern Nevada (2014), and at the Malheur National Wildlife Refuge in Southeast Oregon (2016), involving Bundy's sons and various militia members, are reminders of the deep anger and resentment of some westerners toward the government. Secessionist movements, by 11 counties mostly in northeast Colorado and by Siskiyou County in northern California in 2013, also reflect tensions against federal regulations in the rural West as well as intrastate divides between rural regions and urban/suburban centers. However, these confrontational moments and "independence" movements are a departure from the long tradition of more constructive western efforts at the local level to bend federal policies toward regional needs.

Popular conceptions of the geographic West have shifted over time. For example, the West for the characters in F. Scott Fitzgerald's *The Great Gatsby* (1925) is not San Francisco, Los Angeles, or Denver, but Chicago, where, in 1893, the entertainer William F. ("Buffalo Bill") Cody celebrated the Wild West of yesteryear before millions of spectators and the academic Frederick Jackson Turner declared that the frontier had closed. During the first half of the twentieth century the Great Plains states were generally considered western – Texas being the partial exception, with its amalgam of southern political institutions and western culture. *America's West* includes the Plains states, from the Dakotas to Texas, along with 11 of the 13 states of the US Census West; Alaska and Hawaii, which both gained statehood in 1959, receive only limited coverage.

The book's opening chapter examines the 1890s, when the nation was in the grip of a depression and witnessed violent strikes by labor unions and equally violent responses from the police, National Guard units, and private militias. A widespread rebellion of farmers against bankers, merchants, and railroads profiting from their labor led to takeovers of state governments in the South and Midwest. Mob attacks on former slaves and their descendants, as well as their systematic segregation, economic oppression, and political disenfranchisement, characterized race relations in the so-called New South. Concerns over immigration, particularly the influx of people from Southern and Eastern Europe, were pervasive across the Northeast and Midwest, along with accompanying fears of urban overcrowding and disease. Violent repression and formal exclusion of the Chinese, and an assault on Native American cultures and landholdings, characterized the West. Political corruption was rampant across the nation. Such developments contributed to a growing sense of crisis over the nation's future. The notion that the western frontier was closing helped explain both the ominous domestic developments and the push toward overseas empire through the conquest of foreign peoples in Asia, the Caribbean, Latin America, and the Pacific.

The first two decades of the new century, encompassing the administrations of Theodore Roosevelt (1901–1909), William Howard Taft (1909–1913), and Woodrow Wilson (1913–1921), are treated in Chapters 2 and 3. In many respects the West was more progressive than the nation in this period. Women's suffrage, for example, came to the region ahead of the nation, and political reforms designed to make the electoral and legislative systems more responsive to the will of the people were particularly popular. However, conservative pushback against the more liberal developments of the era also found some powerful beachheads in the West. Chapter 4 examines 1920s cultural conflicts as they manifested across the region, particularly the Red Scare, the second Ku Klux Klan, and a series of racially motivated policies directed at westerners of color. The Klan proved to be a major force in parts of the West, including the Southern Plains and the Pacific Coast, and controlled numerous state legislatures in the region during the first half of the decade.

The next two chapters focus on the pivotal decade of the 1930s. Chapter 5 charts the New Deal's impact on the West, especially its massive public works projects, work relief initiatives, and conservation measures. By most accounting, westerners benefited more from the 1930s federal programs than residents of any other region. Chapter 6 highlights the fortunes of the West's peoples of color during the Depression decade, including minority rights and labor initiatives. The chapter also explores the role of New Deal photographers and independent writers in exposing the plight of migrant agricultural workers in the West.

Chapter 7 addresses the massive demographic, political, and economic changes wrought by the rapidly expanding defense industry that accompanied World War II and the first years of the Cold War. Chapter 8 explores the theme of "the Good War" against the backdrop of racially motivated policies that continued to characterize the region, most lamentably in the rounding up of loyal Japanese and Japanese American citizens residing on the West Coast and their confinement in camps in the Intermountain West. The study closes with the rebirth of American exceptionalist thinking grounded in selective memory of the American frontier experience, as the Cold War began to take shape in the late 1940s.

By the middle of the twentieth century, the West's population had increased by more than 400 percent since 1890, while the national rate during those six decades was about 250 percent. The West had become an even more remarkably diverse, multiracial region whose residents had come north from Mexico, east from the Pacific World, west from Europe and the eastern United States, as well as south from Canada. The region had also become a hydraulic landscape, reengineered with electricity-generating dams on all its major rivers to provide power, flood control, and a reliable water supply to arid and semiarid lands. The West was a martial landscape dotted with military bases, weapon testing ranges, including nuclear test sites, and secret laboratories. Additionally, the region was a metropolitan landscape – the most urbanized population of any American region – distinguished by wider spaces between its population centers than was the case in other parts of the country and larger distances between home and work, owing to so much of the West's urban and suburban infrastructure having developed during the automobile age. More than ever before, the West's dramatic natural landscapes (military sites aside!) had become a cherished set of increasingly popular public landscapes, often featuring comfortable amenities to enhance the visitor experience, but protected from unregulated development and resource extraction.

These major transformations had occurred over the course of a single lifetime.[8] For a child in the 1890s who had reached old age by 1950,

8 Life expectancy in the United States was about 40 years in 1890 and around 65 years by 1950.

the West, distinctive natural features aside, would surely have seemed more thoroughly changed and less readily recognizable than any other American region. And, as it developed during this period, the dynamic West in turn played a major role in shaping the course of the nation's history.

I

Frontier, Region, Nation, and Crisis

> There has never been a time in our history when we were without an "East" and a "West," but the novel day when we shall be without them is now in sight. As the country grows it will inevitably grow more homogenous... and we shall at last be one people.
>
> – Woodrow Wilson, "The Making of the Nation," 1897[1]

At the Wake of the Frontier

As the United States entered the final decade of the nineteenth century, the West was at the forefront of the national consciousness. The first two installments of future president Theodore Roosevelt's triumphalist multivolume account of frontier expansion, *The Winning of the West* (4 vols., 1889–1896), appeared in 1889, and the final stages of a process of national expansion into the West that had begun a century and a half earlier seemed to be closing. In the opening pages of his study, Roosevelt placed himself and other late-nineteenth-century western pioneers in the tradition of Daniel Boone and other legends of the late-eighteenth- and early-nineteenth-century frontier: "We... established civil government, and put down evil-doers, white and red, on the banks of the Little Missouri... exactly as did the pioneers who a hundred years previously built their log-cabins beside the Kentucky." But Roosevelt's tone was cautionary as well as congratulatory, and he referred anxiously in 1889 to the "fast vanishing frontier life of the present."[2]

[1] Woodrow Wilson, "The Making of the Nation," *Atlantic Monthly* LXXX (1897): 4.

[2] Theodore Roosevelt, *The Winning of the West, Volume I: From the Alleghenies to the Mississippi, 1769–1776* (New York: G. P. Putnam's Sons, 1889), xiv.

Seven years later, in the closing lines of the fourth and final volume of *The Winning of the West*, Roosevelt brought the story of frontier expansion up to 1807 with the explorations of Meriwether Lewis and William Clark and of Zebulon Pike. He concluded that as Thomas Jefferson's administration approached its end, "much yet remained to be done before the West would reach its natural limits, would free itself forever from the pressure of outside foes, and would fill from frontier to frontier with populous commonwealths of its own citizens." But the implication was clear: nine decades after the journeys of Lewis and Clark and Pike, the filling of those frontiers was complete, those natural continental limits reached.

Native peoples were confined to reservations in the wake of the Indian Wars that had been fought from the 1860s through the 1880s. The Dawes Act (1887) championed assimilation of indigenous peoples into the national mainstream and opened tens of millions of acres of their lands to non-Indian settlement. Those developments seemed to herald the end of an era of frontier expansion into the West. This moment of transition played out most dramatically on the Southern Great Plains. The first of the Oklahoma land rushes took place in the central part of the territory in April 1889 as 50,000 people raced to stake their claims to 160-acre homesteads on 1.9 million acres of Indian land. A year later, the Oklahoma Territory was created. Subsequent land rushes in 1891, 1892, 1893, and 1895 opened up 12 million additional acres of Iowa, Sac, Fox, Pottawatomie, Shawnee, Arapaho, Cherokee, and Kickapoo lands, with 2 million additional acres distributed by lottery to settlers in 1901.[3]

The government was breaking its earlier promises of Indian sovereignty in the Oklahoma Territory, which dated back to the removal of the Five Civilized Tribes from the southeastern United States in the 1830s. Congressional deference to the land hunger of a growing white population was the new order of the day. Meanwhile, 800 miles to the north, at Wounded Knee, in the new state of South Dakota, the final large-scale violent encounter of the Indian Wars took place in late December 1890. The confrontation between the Seventh Cavalry and Lakota Sioux Indians resulted in approximately 180 Indian deaths; more than half were women and young boys and girls. Oglala Sioux leader Black Elk, reflecting on

[3] W. David Baird and Danney Goble, *Oklahoma: A History* (Norman: University of Oklahoma Press, 2008), 141–162; and Charles Robert Goins and Danney Goble, eds., *Historical Atlas of Oklahoma*, 4th ed. (Norman: University of Oklahoma Press, 2006), 142–148.

the event some four decades later, recalled, "I can still see the butchered women and children lying heaped and scattered along the crooked gulch as plain as when I saw them with young eyes."[4] US troop losses in the engagement numbered 25, mostly victims of "friendly fire" resulting from inept troop formations. The casualty toll suggests a massacre rather than a battle, and the awarding of the Medal of Honor to some of the soldiers was a travesty added to the tragedy.[5]

Whatever label we apply today to this awful moment in the national past, Wounded Knee quickly came to symbolize the end of a period of intense warfare in the West beginning in the early 1860s between Indian peoples and American and recently arrived European settlers, state and territorial militias, and federal forces. Two weeks before Wounded Knee, Indian Police had murdered the famous Sioux leader Sitting Bull on the Standing Rock River Reservation, north of Pine Ridge. Sitting Bull, who had participated in William F. (Buffalo Bill) Cody's Wild West performances in the summer of 1885, had recently returned to the reservation, and the US military feared he was about to leave again, this time to join the Ghost Dance, an indigenous cultural revival movement, ignited by the vision of Nevada Paiutes shaman Wovoka, that was spreading across the Plain and the Far West. In late March 1891, just a few months after Wounded Knee, Cody secured the release of 23 of the 27 Ghost Dancers who had been arrested and imprisoned at Fort Sheridan in Illinois in the wake of the terrible carnage. Cody then employed the men in his show, which was about to depart for a yearlong tour of Europe, and advertised them as "the worst Indians engaged in the Wounded Knee fight." Sitting Bull's participation in Cody's performances, along with that of the recently imprisoned Ghost Dancers – all ostensible representatives

[4] John G. Niehardt and Black Elk, *Black Elk Speaks: Being the Life Story of a Holy Man of the Oglala Sioux* (1932; repr., Albany: State University of New York Press, 2008).

[5] For more on Wounded Knee, see Heather Cox Richardson, *Wounded Knee: Party Politics and the Road to an American Massacre* (New York: Basic Books, 2010), which emphasizes the immediate aftermath of the 1890 midterm elections and argues that the massacre was a direct outgrowth of the Republican Party's needs to secure the support of South Dakota for the 1892 election. See also Jerome Greene, *American Carnage: Wounded Knee, 1890* (Norman: University of Oklahoma Press, 2014); Jeff Ostler, *The Plains Sioux and US Colonialism, from Lewis and Clark to Wounded Knee* (New York: Cambridge University Press, 2004); and Robert M. Utley, *The Last Days of the Sioux Nation*, 2nd ed. (1963; repr., New Haven, CT: Yale University Press, 2004).

of an indigenous savagery conquered by white American civilization and willingly engaged in the reconstructed narrative of their own defeat – served as another milestone marking of the end of the frontier era.[6]

When white Americans envisioned the West in the 1890s, the recent memory of the Indian Wars, the prospects for settlement of Indian lands, and a growing nostalgia for Indians – a sentiment that emerged in the wake of their conquest and demographic decline – were all a part of the picture. The Census of 1890 recorded a figure of fewer than 250,000 Native Americans, down from more than 400,000 in 1850. Native peoples had not only been vanquished; according to popular perception, and demographic evidence, they seemed to be vanishing.[7] The nation appeared to be in the midst of a great moment of change, and the recently conquered West, the nation's newest region, was now growing up with the country. In a mere eight months, from November 1889 to July 1890, a massive swath of the Northwest, comprising the Dakota, Idaho, Montana, Washington, and Wyoming Territories, transitioned into six new states. The nation's rapidly developing railroad network reached into every corner of the West. Yet, in the very process of maturing, it seemed that America was losing something important.

The fencing in of much of the formerly open range after the brutal winter of 1886–1887 signaled the end of the era of the great cattle drives that had begun a generation earlier in 1866. Half of Roosevelt's cattle in the Dakotas were killed by the blizzards; the figure reached 90 percent for some cattle herds in the northern West.[8] At the very moment that western mythmakers were creating the legend of the quintessential western character – the cowboy – technological innovations rendered him largely irrelevant to the economic life of the region. Concurrently, another of the iconic figures of the Old West, the homesteader, faced terrible conditions. The drought of 1893 forced farmers to abandon their properties in western Kansas and Nebraska, some of them heading back East to try to start over, and some painting signs on their wagons declaring

[6] Richardson, *Wounded Knee*, 294.

[7] For more on this theme, see Patrick Brantlinger, *Dark Vanishings: The Discourse on the Extinction of Primitive Peoples, 1830–1930* (Ithaca, NY: Cornell University Press, 2003); and Brian Dippie, *The Vanishing American: White Attitudes and US Indian Policy* (1982; repr., Lawrence: University Press of Kansas, 1991).

[8] Philip McFarland, *Mark Twain and the Colonel: Samuel L. Clemens, Theodore Roosevelt, and the Arrival of a New Century* (Lanham, MA: Roman and Littlefield, 2012), 125.

"In God we trusted, in Kansas we busted." Their failure suggested the end of an era of frontier promise. Ironically, some of the western counties of those two states have lower populations today than they did at the end of the 1880s and qualify as "frontier" counties according to the 1890 Census Bureau definition of fewer than two people per square mile.[9]

By the 1890s, the "myth of superabundance" of natural resources had exploded in the wake of extensive clear-cutting of forests and the consequent impact on watersheds.[10] Late in his second term in 1897, President Grover Cleveland had asked Gifford Pinchot to draw up a comprehensive plan for management of the western forest reserves. In 1898, Cleveland's successor, William McKinley, appointed Pinchot chief of the US Division of Forestry. The old century closed and the new one began with a "conservation ethic" driving natural resource policy rather than the motive of unbridled profit making without concern over consequences for the natural environment. There was a growing understanding that resources needed to be utilized more carefully and that systematic reforestation needed to accompany timber harvesting to ensure the long-term needs and natural health of the nation. Large-scale irrigation efforts were another part of the conservationist agenda, and Salt Lake City, Denver, Los Angeles, and California's Central Valley were among the major beneficiaries of this initiative in the 1890s.

In addition to the developing conservationist ethic, an emerging preservationist movement advocated the maintenance of American wilderness in its supposed natural, primordial state as a restorative for the soul of the nation. "Wilderness" is a cultural construct, the invention of people rather than an identifiable and tangible physical state or stage of nature.[11] Nonetheless, the overriding concern that the frontier landscape was disappearing and that something essential to the maintenance of the American character was being lost prompted a preservationist push that resulted in the addition of California's Sequoia and Yosemite National Parks in 1890 and Washington's Mount Rainier in 1899.[12]

9 See Dayton Duncan, *Miles from Nowhere: Tales from America's Contemporary Frontier* (New York: Viking, 1993).

10 Stewart L. Udall, *The Quiet Crisis* (New York: Holt, Rinehart, and Winston, 1983), 54.

11 William Cronon, "The Trouble with Wilderness," in *Uncommon Ground: Toward Reinventing Nature*, ed. William Cronon (New York: W. W. Norton, 1995), 69–90.

12 For more on the theme of wilderness preservation and national parks creation, see Roderick Nash, *Wilderness and the American Mind*, 5th ed. (New Haven, CT: Yale University Press, 2014).

The superintendent of the US Census reinforced this sense of change in the nation's physical landscape when he declared the official end of the American frontier in 1890, noting that the frontier line was so broken up by isolated bodies of settlement in the Far West that the Census Bureau would no longer use the term "frontier." Homesteading would in fact not reach its high point until the second decade of the twentieth century, as settlers continued to move into many parts of the northern West. Nonetheless, to many American observers at the beginning of the 1890s, it seemed that the frontier epoch was ending and a new postfrontier era was beginning. The young historian Frederick Jackson Turner famously declared at the end of his 1893 essay "The Significance of the Frontier in American History" that the first period of the nation's history had closed.[13] Turner was one of many contemporary American intellectuals whose observations about the end of an era framed a disturbing question: if the frontier was the wellspring of American democracy, individualism, nationalism, and a distinctive, pragmatic national character, then what would happen to the nation and its citizens in the wake of the frontier's passing?

If, as Turner and others insisted, the intermingling of people from various northwestern European nations on the frontier had forged a composite American type and character, then what fate awaited that new American race without a frontier? Southern and eastern Europeans who were ostensibly less assimilable than their earlier arriving immigrant counterparts were flooding into the country. Would the new waves of Catholic and Jewish immigrants, many hailing from peasant backgrounds and authoritarian societies, submerge the democratic and individualistic American mainstream with their alien and collectivist ideologies? Should the government restrict the flow of those new huddled masses or even bar them completely to ensure the maintenance of national health?

Nativists called for restrictive immigration policies to "keep America American" in the 1890s. Concerns over the closing frontier and the nation's diminished capacity for assimilation helped shape their thinking. At times the frontier argument was nothing more than a convenient cloak to cover over blatant racism against non-Nordic Europeans. No such veiling was necessary when it came to anti-Asian sentiment. In 1892, Congress renewed the Chinese Exclusion Act, which originally passed in

[13] Frederick Jackson Turner, "The Significance of the Frontier in American History," in *Annual Report of the American Historical Association for the Year 1893* (Washington, DC: Government Printing Office, 1894), 199–227.

1882 and was the first US immigration legislation that explicitly banned any group based on race, national origin, and socioeconomic class – the law applied to laborers, not all Chinese. White labor unions, including the Knights of Labor, were among the strongest supporters of the original and renewed legislation, which moved forward on a veritable wave of thoroughly dehumanizing and undemocratic rhetoric in Congress. The exclusion act was renewed again in 1902, without a time limit.[14]

Growing concerns over urban crime, decay, and disease accompanied nativist claims about the unassimilability of immigrants from Southern and Eastern Europe and from Asia. Had America's rapidly growing cities come to approximate their European counterparts, such as London and Paris, where glittering wealth and crushing poverty existed together in conspicuous proximity? In 1889, Jane Addams led an intrepid and altruistic group of women reformers in the founding of Hull-House, the Chicago settlement house project that would become the single most impressive example of amateur social work in the nation's history.[15] Jacob Riis's disturbing nonfiction account of poverty on New York's Lower East Side, *How the Other Half Lives*, appeared at the beginning of the 1890s. Stephen Crane's novel *Maggie: A Girl of the Streets* (1893, 1896) charted the tragic descent of a young New York woman from lower-class squalor and destitution into presumed prostitution and death. Addams's initiative and these popular works of journalism and fiction underscored the stark reality of urban decay in the very shadows of fabulous new urban wealth. When Jack London's gripping and disturbing sociological account of the abominable conditions in London's East End, *The People of the Abyss* (1903), appeared early in the new century, readers surely found the conditions in those metropolises of the New World and the Old, New York and London, to be more alike than dissimilar.

By the 1890s, the Jeffersonian myth of the noble yeoman farmer as the bedrock of American democracy had suffered a substantial battering. Writer Hamlin Garland painted a heartbreaking picture of failed homesteading dreams in his 1891 chronicle of life on the Prairie, *Main Travelled Roads*. In the preface to his novel *Jason Edwards* (1892), Garland angrily

[14] Elliott Young, *Alien Nation: The Chinese Migration in the Americas from the Coolie Era through World War II* (Chapel Hill: University of North Carolina Press, 2014), 103.

[15] Toynbee Hall, a settlement house in London's East End, founded in 1884 to help alleviate the impoverished conditions in one of that city's most notorious slums, provided the inspiration for Addams.

proclaimed, "Free land is gone. The last acre of available farm land has passed into private or corporate hands. The nation has squandered the inheritance of the unborn as well as the living."[16] The stark realities of agricultural failure and the horrors of the modern American urban and industrial present seemed to have suffocated Jefferson's agrarian dream. In 1787, Jefferson had written to James Madison, declaring, "Our governments will remain virtuous... as long as they are chiefly agricultural; and this will be as long as there shall be vacant lands in any part of America." Jefferson added, ominously, "when they [the people] get piled upon one another in large cities, as in Europe, they will become corrupt as in Europe, and go to eating one another."[17] Jefferson was referring to violent struggle among people rather than to literal cannibalism, and indeed, conditions for the lower classes in the tenements of America's urban slums, and growing class conflict and industrial violence resulting from the nation's rapid pace of industrialization, suggested that the Jeffersonian nightmare had become the national reality.

The closed-frontier fears of the 1890s, like most concerns over demographic, cultural, and economic change, were not always rational. The process of "filling up" the vast conquered region from the Plains to the Pacific was actually just beginning. Nevada aside, the population of all the western states continued to increase in the 1890s, and while the rate of growth was much slower than in the 1880s, the Far West (the region west of the Plains states) saw a population increase of 27.3 percent, well exceeding the national average of 20.7 percent for the decade (Figure 1.1). The economic depression from 1893 to 1897 certainly slowed the pace of migration, and the Central Plains states – Kansas and Nebraska – experienced next to no population growth at all. The Southern Plains states of Oklahoma and Texas fared much better demographically, growing by 27.5 percent and nearly 48 percent, respectively, with Texas topping 3 million residents by 1900. In addition, more land was homesteaded between 1900 and 1920 in the United States (virtually all of it in the West) than in the entire period from the passage of the Homestead Act in 1862 to the end of the nineteenth century.

[16] Hamlin Garland, *Main Travelled Roads* (Boston: Arena, 1891); and Garland, *Jason Edwards: An Average Man* (Boston: Arena, 1892), v.

[17] For the Jefferson quotation, see Gilbert Chinard, *Thomas Jefferson: The Apostle of Americanism* (Boston: Little, Brown, 1929), 80–82. See also James C. Malin, *The Contriving Brain and the Skillful Hand in the United States* (Ann Arbor, MI: Edwards Brothers, 1955); and H. A. Washington, ed., *The Writings of Thomas Jefferson* (Washington, DC: Taylor and Maury, 1854), 2:332.

State/Decade	1850	1860	1870	1880	1890	1900
Alaska	NA	NA	NA	NA	NA	NA
Arizona	NA	NA	9,658	40,440	88,243	122,931
California	92,597	379,994	560,247	864,694	1,213,398	1,485,053
Colorado	NA	34,277	39,864	194,327	413,249	539,700
Hawaii	NA	NA	NA	NA	NA	NA
Idaho	NA	NA	14,999	32,610	88,548	161,772
Kansas	NA	107,206	364,399	996,096	1,428,108	1,470,495
Montana	NA	NA	20,595	39,159	142,924	243,329
Nebraska	NA	28,841	122,993	452,402	1,062,656	1,066,300
Nevada	NA	6,857	42,491	62,266	47,355	42,355
New Mexico	61,570	93,516	91,874	119,565	160,282	195,310
North Dakota	NA	NA	2,405	36,909	190,983	319,146
Oklahoma	NA	NA	NA	NA	790,391	1,167,155
Oregon	12,093	52,465	90,923	174,768	317,704	413,536
South Dakota	NA	4,837	11,776	98,268	348,600	401,570
Texas	212,592	604,215	818,579	1,591,749	2,235,527	3,048,710
Utah	11,380	40,273	86,786	143,963	210,779	276,749
Washington	1,201	11,594	23,955	75,116	357,232	518,103
Wyoming	NA	NA	9,118	20,789	62,555	92,531

FIGURE 1.1 Population of the western states and territories, 1850–1900.

The phenomenon of homesteading, then, not only continued to characterize the West after the presumed closing of the frontier in 1890; it in fact expanded. Moreover, by the time the homesteading process first began, during the Civil War, industrialization and urbanization characterized life and labor in the West just as readily as homesteading did. The arrival of industry and cities did not mark the end of the frontier era of agrarian settlement. Indeed, mineral rushes in California, Colorado, Nevada, and other far western states ensured that cities and industry, along with cultural and racial diversity, were often the first significant markers of "American" arrival, not the hardy white agrarian disciples of the Jeffersonian and Turnerian visions. The city and the surrounding rural areas coexisted, even if more often in conflict than harmony.

Still, closed-frontier concerns were widespread and contributed significantly to the sense of crisis that developed during the 1890s. The processes of urbanization and industrialization, and the race for colonies, were under way in Britain, France, Germany, and other European nations, and the wielders of power and influence in all of them subscribed to notions of national exceptionalism. Yet, Manifest Destiny, the frontier heritage, and the idea of the West as the most American part of America (as the British visitor Lord James Bryce declared in his 1888 book *The American Commonwealth*) together struck a chord in the national imagination. There was something powerful, too, in the increasingly common perception during the 1890s that the frontier was the wellspring of so much that was distinctive about the United States, and that it was now disappearing. This perception added even greater urgency to the heated debates over immigration, urbanization, industrialization, agrarian protest, and overseas expansion. Furthermore, some Americans viewed the terrible economic depression of 1893–1897, which severely damaged both the agrarian and industrial sectors, as a direct and quite immediate consequence of the closing of the frontier.

To make matters worse, acute sectional tensions persisted beyond the end of Reconstruction and into the 1880s and 1890s, with Republicans deriding the Democrats as the party of former slaveholders and Democrats reminding white Southern voters that the Republican Party had directed the federal occupation and alleged oppression of the South during and after the Civil War. The West emerged as a sort of measure of national health at a critical moment. The prognosis in the 1890s was not good. For many writers, thinkers, and policy makers, the decade's myriad problems seemed to confirm the passing of the first great epoch of American history – the age of frontier opportunity. Deteriorating urban conditions for the working and nonworking poor, including large numbers of new immigrants and new American migrants from farming regions, and growing levels of industrial conflict further contributed to the sense of crisis.

Federal troops and state and local militias clashed with striking workers across the nation, from Homestead, and Lattimer, Pennsylvania, to Cripple Creek, Colorado, and Coeur d'Alene, Idaho. In Cripple Creek, in 1894 the Populist Governor Davis Waite, in a marked departure from standard government practice, ordered the National Guard to protect workers, led by the new Western Federation of Miners (WFM), from antilabor forces. However, the more common scenario during the decade involved the mobilization of state and federal forces against striking workers. In Lattimer, in 1897, hired deputies shot 19 un-armed Slavic strikers, mostly in the back. Labor violence across the West, and particularly in Colorado and Idaho, suggested that the western frontier panacea, the haven for homesteading, was home to the same industrial strife that marred the landscape of the Northeast and Midwest. Meanwhile, "armies" of the unemployed and destitute converged on the nation's capital seeking support from the federal government: Coxey's Army marched from Ohio; Kelly's Army, trekked from California; and Hogan's Army commandeered a train from Montana.[18]

[18] Carlos A. Schwantes, *Coxey's Army: An American Odyssey* (Lincoln: University of Nebraska Press, 1985).

Tensions over the New Immigration, pervasive political corruption, growing economic dislocation and maldistribution of wealth, a deplorable wave of lynching of African Americans in the South, the growth of urban slums, and horrifying industrial violence: this was America as the century drew to its end. The social fabric was unraveling, and the country was almost certainly in greater crisis, in more imminent danger of falling apart during the 1890s, than at any other time since – including the years of the Great Depression.

Two additional important factors helped to shape the perfect storm of crisis in the 1890s: agrarian radicalism and imperialism. Growing tensions between the agrarian and industrial sectors exacerbated fears over America's postfrontier future and led to the emergence of the "Populist" or People's Party in 1892. Southern and western farmers faced high railroad shipping rates, expensive fees charged by middlemen and grain elevator companies, high tariffs, and, consequently, high debt levels. The federal government's tight money policies added to farmers' woes. The Omaha Platform of 1892 articulated a very clear set of demands designed to address these concerns. The Populists insisted on the coining of silver at a rate of 16:1 to gold (about four times its actual value of approximately 65:1 at the time, but in fact a return to silver's traditional value) and the abandonment of high tariff policies. They argued that movement away from the gold standard would bring about inflation and thereby reduce the actual value of farmers' debts and that lower tariffs would help secure overseas markets and higher prices for their goods, as well as reduced prices for certain European products, including needed agricultural machinery.[19]

The Populist platform also included a subtreasury plan to enable farmers to borrow money from the federal government at low interest rates and store crops in government grain elevators as collateral until favorable market conditions developed. Taking private banks and grain elevators out of the equation would allow farmers to manage market forces rather than being the victims of economic circumstances beyond their control. In addition, the platform called for government ownership of the railroads, and telephone and telegraph lines, and for a graduated income tax, and a wide range of direct democracy reforms designed to give ordinary people a larger voice in political decision making. The Omaha Platform was

[19] The 16:1 ratio of silver to gold had been in place prior to its removal by the Republicans, who essentially killed the silver standard in the Coinage Act of 1873.

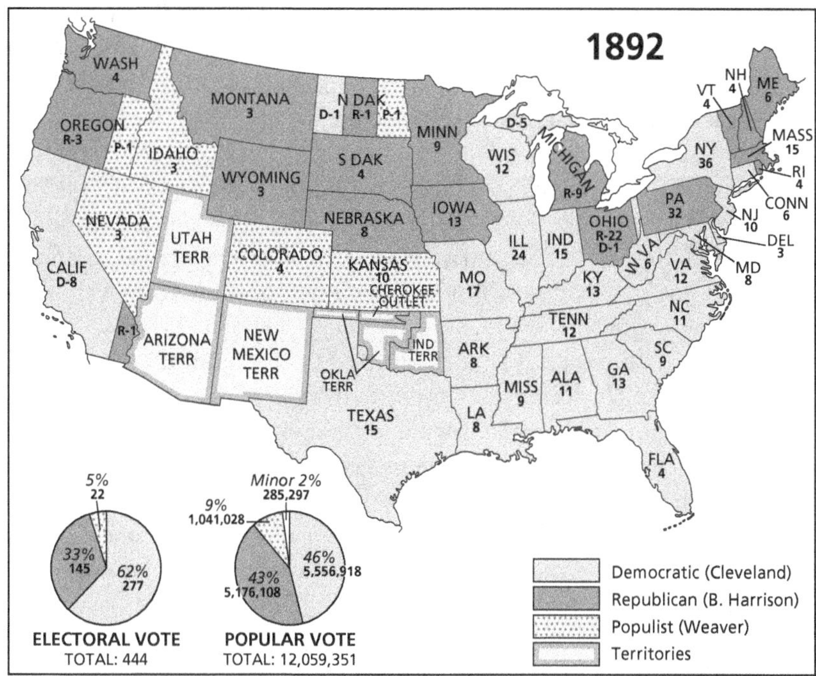

MAP 1.1 Electoral map, 1892.

a clear articulation of the economic conditions crippling the agrarian South and West, was directed at the business and banking interests of the Northeast, and embodied a clear and practical prescription for restoring the health of the agrarian sector. The party's presidential candidate, James B. Weaver of Iowa, received more than a million votes in the 1892 election (about 8.5 percent of the popular vote) and won a majority in Kansas and North Dakota, as well as in Colorado, Idaho, and Nevada, where silver mining and agrarian interests coalesced (Map 1.1). Silver at 16:1 was as attractive to silver mining companies and investors, and to mine workers, as it was to farmers.

"Are the People of the West Fanatics?" the title of an 1895 article in the reformist Boston-based magazine *The Arena* asked. The author, J. K. Miller, in response to increasing condemnation of the Populists by the Republican Party and the business interests it represented, offered a strong defense of the western region and Populists' economic agenda. He explained that western calls for currency inflation were eminently logical, fair, and democratic and that it was the Eastern corporate interests that were out of touch with the national character.[20] Despite Miller and others' best efforts, business interests in the buildup to the 1896 national election continued to paint westerners' criticisms of national fiscal and tariff policy as dangerously radical and un-American.

In the 1896 campaign the Republican Party presented the Nebraska Democrat William Jennings Bryan, the "fusion" candidate of both the People's Party and the Democratic Party, as a thoroughgoing radical determined to lead the country away from a bright industrial future and down the paths of socialism and anarchy. Theodore Roosevelt, then police commissioner of New York City, in a major political speech at the Chicago Coliseum in October, referred to the pending "crisis of the fate of America."[21] Roosevelt denounced Bryan as the advocate not of "a government of the people, for the people and by the people" but of "a government by a mob, by the demagogue for the shiftless and disorderly and the criminal and semicriminal." The Populist and "Popocrat" leaders, Roosevelt proclaimed, were seeking to "overturn our existing civilization," and he implored his audience to "set your faces against that spirit of lawless mob violence which could in the end produce nothing but anarchy; anarchy the handmaiden and sure herald of tyranny." For good measure, Roosevelt added that the Bryan forces were "repudiating everything which has made the name [America] a symbol of hope among nations," seeking to "substitute a crazy fabric, patched up from the worn-out theories of every European dreamer and European agitator."[22]

Such deep fears of agrarian radicalism among eastern and Midwestern corporate interests and their Republican allies, combined with agrarian anger over the partnership between American industrial and banking interests and the federal government which resulted in tight money policies and high tariffs, together resulted in a 79.3 percent voter turnout in the 1896 election, a figure that has not been surpassed in any American

[20] J. K. Miller, "Are the People of the West Fanatics?," *The Arena* XIII (June 1895): 92–97, quotations on 93. For a similar position, see Charles S. Gleed, "The True Significance of Western Unrest," *Forum* (October 1893): 251–261.

[21] "The Menace of the Demagogue," Speech before the American Republican College League, Chicago, IL, October 15, 1896. Clipping (source and date unknown) from author's scrapbook for 1896, in Theodore Roosevelt, Campaigns and Controversies, The Works of Theodore Roosevelt, National ed., Col. XIV (New York: Charles Scribner's Sons, 1926), 258–74, quotation on 272.

[22] Ibid., 26 and 273. The "of the people, for the people, by the people" segment of the speech is also quoted in McFarland, *Mark Twain and the Colonel*, 59.

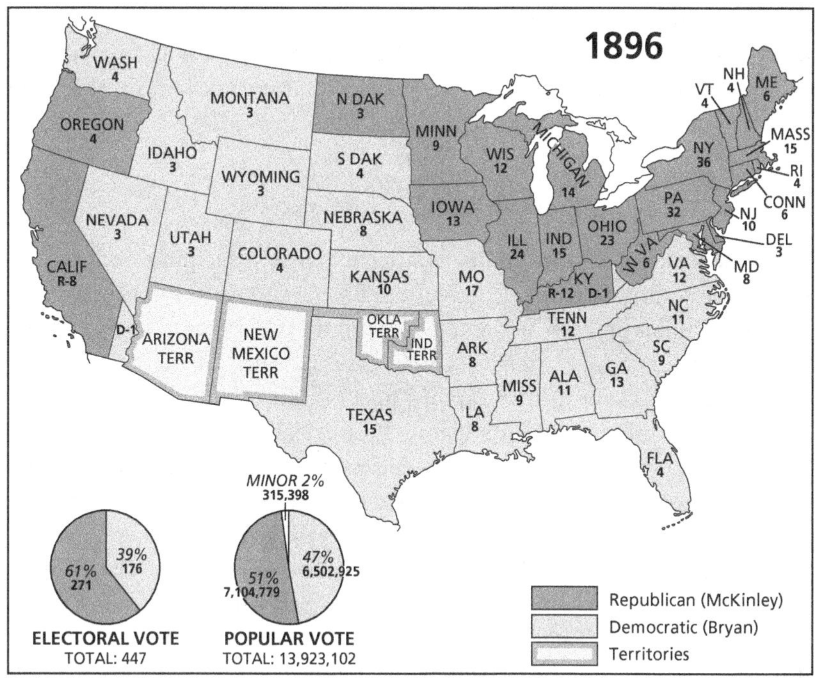

MAP 1.2 Electoral map, 1896.

election since.[23] Bryan received nearly 47 percent of the vote to McKinley's 51 percent (Map 1.2). The Republicans maintained the significant congressional gains they had made in the 1894 midterm elections, and those majorities would hold until 1910. While California, Oregon, and North Dakota went for McKinley, Bryan won the rest of the western and southern states.[24] Western town dwellers tended to support McKinley, while the region's farmers favored Bryan; the rural and urban Wests were hardly united.

Most significantly though, the 1896 election showed how deeply divided the industrializing Northeast and Midwest were from most of the rest of the country, and those regional divisions seemed to confirm the

[23] Voter turnout rates were exceeded in 1876 (81.8 percent) and 1880 (79.4 percent), nearly matched in 1884 (77.5 percent), and matched in 1888 (79.3 percent). The sectional tensions of 1896 between the agrarian and industrial sectors of the economy approximated in intensity those of the late- and post-Reconstruction elections.

[24] Regarding electoral politics, this study defines the West as the region stretching westward from the second tier of trans-Mississippi western states (North Dakota to Texas) to the Pacific Coast, and including Alaska and Hawaii after they received statehood in 1959.

worst closed-frontier fears about the nation's future. McKinley's defeat of Bryan and the forces of agrarian America suggested that a new, more urban and industrial future, a postfrontier future marked by lessening agrarian political influence, was beginning.

Expansion and Exceptionalism

With the process of contiguous frontier expansion seemingly coming to its natural terminus at the shores of the Pacific Ocean and the great interior West filling up with settlers, where would the energy that had fueled US growth for more than a century, since the birth of the nation, now be directed? Without further expansionist initiatives, would the relatively young nation start to lose its vigor? Would new generations of Americans no longer imbued with the hardy pioneering spirit be doomed to an existence less rugged, manly, and self-reliant than that of their frontiering forbears? Future president Theodore Roosevelt, along with many others, expressed this gendered fear and lauded the benefits of "The Strenuous Life" in 1899 as the United States occupied the Philippines. Was the US military presence in the Philippines evidence that the nation was now seeking new frontiers overseas to compensate for the closed space of the American continent and to provide outlets for the pent-up energies of its expansionist people? Advocates of overseas empire certainly hoped so.

However, in reaching beyond its continental limits, would the United States depart from the model of Manifest Destiny, which imagined the North American continent as a body or a skin that the nation would naturally, providentially, and inevitably grow into, from sea to shining sea? To expand beyond those supposed foreordained boundaries of its body might be to depart from Jefferson's notion of an "empire of liberty."[25] If the nation were to seek overseas conquests to keep the expansionist process and spirit alive, would it not then be treading the same imperial path as the European nations from which it so ardently sought to distinguish itself? Would noncontiguous expansion sustain American exceptionalism, or undermine it?

The debate over expansion and empire became increasingly heated as the United States went to war with Spain in the wake of the explosion on board the USS *Maine* in Havana Harbor in February 1898. The victorious war lasted just three and a half months during the spring and summer

[25] Jefferson first used the term "empire of liberty" in 1780.

of 1898, but the great debate over American imperialism continued to rage during the nation's brutal suppression of Filipino resistance from 1899 to 1902. During those years, more than 200,000 Filipino civilians died from famine, disease, or violence, along with approximately 20,000 Filipino combatants and more than 4,000 US troops.[26] For most anti-imperialists, the acquisition of a Pacific and Caribbean empire (Cuba, Wake, Guam, Hawaii, Puerto Rico, and the Philippines) was a stark and unnatural departure from the story of contiguous expansion westward over the North American landscape. For most imperialists, though, it was a natural and appropriate continuation of a process that dated back at least to the American annexation of the Republic of Texas and the war against Mexico, and then continued with the Indian Wars.[27]

Norton Parker Chipman, Commissioner of the California Supreme Court, writing in the *Overland Monthly and Out West Magazine* in January 1900, encapsulated the imperialist position. He described the march of white settlement to the Alleghenies as the "years of apprenticeship" that "bred a race of self-reliant men, trained and equipped with a pioneer experience, a confidence, and a courage." Chipman proclaimed that the subsequent "conquer[ing of] three thousand miles of wilderness in less than a hundred years" was the prelude to a larger story about to unfold. He asked why this "rugged pioneer, the sturdiest character in all history" should "exhaust his vitality... and lose his enterprise on reaching the bold shores of the Pacific." Assuming that "the son [was] still equal to the sire," the nation's imperialist course was set. If the United States did not follow its natural path, then the present generation was not the equal of its pioneering predecessor. Chipman thus encouraged the nation to continue to expand and thereby preserve its manhood.[28]

[26] Casualty figures for the US occupation of the Philippines remain highly contested; the numbers provided here are drawn from George C. Herring, *From Colony to Superpower: U.S. Foreign Relations since 1776* (New York: Oxford University Press, 2008), 329.

[27] Walter Nugent, in *Habits of Empire: A History of American Expansion* (New York: Alfred A Knopf, 2008), pushes the chronology of national expansion back into the late eighteenth century; see also Richard H. Immerman, *Empire for Liberty: A History of American Imperialism from Benjamin Franklin to Paul Wolfowitz* (Princeton, NJ: Princeton University Press, 2010).

[28] N. P. Chipman, "Territorial Expansion – II: The Philippines – The Oriental Problem," *Overland Monthly and Out West Magazine* XXXV (January 1900): 23–32, quotations from 27. See also Chipman's "Territorial Expansion: The Philippines – The Oriental Problem," *Overland Monthly and Out West Magazine* XXXIV (December 1889): 491–502.

Anti-imperialists disagreed and viewed such calls for manly militarism as evidence that some of America's leaders had not yet matured into adulthood. The philosopher and pragmatist William James complained that Theodore Roosevelt "gushes over war as the ideal condition for human society," implying that in all his brimming enthusiasm for battle and empire, Roosevelt was like a child.[29] Others, such as William Jennings Bryan, in a speech accepting the Democratic Party's nomination for president in August 1900, emphasized how the nation's new imperial course violated its republican principles. Advocating that the Philippines be turned over to self-rule, Bryan declared, "Better a thousand times that our flag in the Orient give way to a flag representing the idea of self-government than that flag of this republic should become the flag of an empire!"[30] Such arguments failed to win the day.

The stronger voices in the foreign policy debate were those of imperialists such as Chipman; Indiana senator Albert J. Beveridge, advocating "The March of the Flag" in September of 1898; and Roosevelt, heralding the benefits of "The Strenuous Life" and the pioneer spirit. And there was President McKinley, who, at least according to popular legend, informed the public that he had gone down on his knees and prayed to "Almighty God for light and guidance" and that divine authority had directed him to keep the Philippines.[31] Beveridge insisted that America's past was "a glorious... history of a multiplying people who overran a continent in half a century." To the American critics of national expansion who insisted that "all just government derives its authority from the consent of the governed," Beveridge replied that such strictures only applied "to those who are capable of self government" and went on to add, "We govern Indians without their consent, we govern our territories without their consent, we govern our children without their consent."[32]

29 William James to the editor, *Springfield Republican*, June 4, 1900, quoted in Howard K. Beale, *Theodore Roosevelt and the Rise of America to World Power* (Baltimore: Johns Hopkins University Press, 1956), 37. See also Kim Townsend, *Manhood at Harvard: William James and Others* (New York: W. W. Norton, 1997); and Evan Thomas, *The War Lovers: Roosevelt, Lodge, Hearst and the Rush to Empire, 1898* (Boston: Little, Brown, 2010).

30 William Jennings Bryan, Democratic National Convention acceptance speech, Indianapolis, IN, August 8, 1900.

31 See Lewis L. Gould, *The Spanish-American War and President McKinley* (Lawrence: University Press of Kansas, 1982), 108–110, for more on the apocryphal nature of this story.

32 Albert Beveridge, "The March of the Flag," campaign speech, September 16, 1898, available at: http://legacy.fordham.edu/halsall/mod/1898beveridge.asp accessed February 6, 2016.

Westward continental expansion and Pacific and Caribbean expansion were chapters of the same story, as was the matter of administration of conquered peoples, whether in the nation's contiguous Far West or on its new island possessions. For Beveridge, Cuba's "15,000,000 acres of forest unacquainted with the ax," along with "the riches of the Philippines," were fruits of empire not to be passed over; they were natural benefits of keeping alive the frontier of expansion.[33]

Visions of Regional Diversity and Homogeneity

Founded in 1833 and incorporated in 1837, Chicago was very much a western city throughout the whole of the nineteenth century. The city's growth in the 1890s, from 1.1 million residents to nearly 1.7 million, was staggering. But Chicago seemed to be ground zero for the growing class conflict and industrial violence of the era. In 1886, a bomb thrown in the city's Haymarket Square during a labor demonstration killed seven policemen and sparked a riot that left several civilians dead and more than a hundred police and civilians wounded and cast the specter of radicalism and anarchism over the city and its large foreign-born population. The 1900 Census showed that more than three-quarters of Chicagoans were first- or second-generation immigrants – foreign-born or the children of immigrants.

Prospects seemed brighter when the city hosted the World's Columbian Exposition, or World's Fair, from May through the end of October 1893 and approximately 27 million people visited a city that had been home to mere hundreds just 60 years earlier. A testament to the nation's technological prowess, the Machinery and Electricity buildings were among the most impressive and popular attractions, and the Fair was a celebration of progress in the four centuries since Columbus's arrival in the New World. But the fair also looked back to the frontier past. Turner first presented his frontier thesis there, suggesting the frontier served as a safety valve that provided people an opportunity to start over again in the wide-open spaces of the agrarian West, thereby helping to prevent urban and industrial discontent in the East. Turner made the story of the nation's newest region the foundational narrative for the entire United States and made the moving western frontier the embodiment of the nation's highest ideals. Yet, he mentioned three times in the essay that the frontier no longer

[33] Ibid.

existed and declared that its passing marked a moment of monumental significance.[34]

Cody performed his Wild West exhibition in an arena constructed just outside of the fairgrounds, and approximately 6 million people attended over the course of the six months. And the Boone and Crockett Club, cofounded by Theodore Roosevelt, constructed a small frontier hunter's log cabin in the fair grounds in honor of the nation's pioneers and as a reminder of the enduring American frontier spirit. Roosevelt explained that the cabin was furnished "exactly as such cabins are now fitted out in the wilder portions of the great plains and among the Rockies, wherever the old-time hunters still exist... The bleached skull and antlers of an elk were nailed over the door outside; the head of a buffalo hung... inside; and the horns of other game... were scattered about."[35]

But it was in this shining new metropolis of the West, during the following summer, 1894, that workers in the company town of Pullman went on strike and were joined by more than a quarter-million members of Eugene Debs's short-lived American Railway Union. Industrial violence exploded during the Pullman Strike, with President Cleveland sending in federal troops to break it up; 30 workers lost their lives. The postfrontier nightmare, the shutting of the safety valve, seemed to be unfolding.

At the turn of the new century, Woodrow Wilson – whom Turner had met several years earlier while in graduate school at Johns Hopkins University – welcomed the end of that earlier American age in an 1897 essay in the *Atlantic Monthly* titled "The Making of the Nation." He looked forward, in the absence of the frontier, to a nation without an East and a West and, even as the wounds of the Civil War slowly healed, to a nation without a North and a South. "As the country grows," Wilson wrote, "it will inevitably grow more homogenous," and that homogeneity would be a healthy development.[36] Turner fretted for the rest of his life over the nation's postfrontier future. Wilson, by way of contrast, reveled in the prospect of a frontierless and sectionless nation.

By the second decade of the twentieth century, Turner had come to see the nation's regional diversity as its salvation. When President Wilson

[34] For Turner and the larger landscape of intellectual and popular concern over the presumed closing of the frontier, see David M. Wrobel, *The End of American Exceptionalism: Frontier Anxiety from the Old West to the New Deal* (Lawrence: University Press of Kansas, 1993).

[35] Theodore Roosevelt and George Bird Grinnell, eds., *American Big-Game Hunting: The Book of the Boone and Crockett Cub* (New York: Forest and Stream, 1893), 334–335.

[36] Wilson, "The Making of the Nation," 4.

was in Versailles negotiating the peace treaty after World War I, Turner offered his model of the United States as a nation comprising diverse yet complementary regions ("fit rooms for a worthy house," he called them), as a blueprint for war-torn postwar Europe.[37] Wilson may not have even seen the document, but if he had, he would most likely have rejected it out of hand. His conception of patriotism during the war privileged the notion of 100 percent Americanism and rejected the idea of "hyphenated Americanism" (Italian-American, Irish-American, etc.). Unlike Turner, Wilson's thinking about the nation and its constituent regional parts derived from his understanding of regional homogeneity and cultural conformity as healthful and of heterogeneity as harmful.

Thus, in the 1890s, a generation before the shadow of global war fell across Europe, the future president of the American Historical Association, Turner, and the future president of the United States, Wilson, both contemplated, in very different ways, the nation's future and the place that the West would play in it. For Turner, the West would remain different. The region's heightened democratic tendencies, nurtured by the frontier's advance, would continue to roll back, in wavelike fashion across the continental expanse, from West to East, rejuvenating the nation generations after the frontier had closed. That was Turner's hope, and he clung to it stubbornly. He found the alternative vision of a frontierless democracy and the consequent end of American exceptionalism deeply concerning and spent the second half of his career worrying whether the nation would come to mirror its European progenitors as its democratic foundations crumbled.[38] Turner hoped that the differences among American regions would prove complementary and constructive, not caustic and contentious.

[37] For the "fit rooms in a worthy house" quotation see Frederick Jackson Turner, "Sections and Nation," *Yale Review* 12 (October 1922): 1–21, reprinted in Frederick Jackson Turner, *"The Significance of the Frontier in American History" and Other Essays*, ed. by John Mack Faragher (New York: Henry Holt, 1994), 181–200, quotation on 200. Turner's friend and Harvard University colleague Charles Homer Haskins had presented to the American delegation in Paris in December 1918 Turner's memo titled "International Political Parties in a Durable League of Nations," in which Turner suggested that a system of European-wide political parties could effectively mirror the American system of national political parties and, thereby, work across regional lines in a large geographic area and help ensure peace in war-ravaged Europe. See also Turner's "The Significance of the Section in American History," *Wisconsin Magazine of History* 8 (March 1925): 255–280, republished in Turner, *"The Significance of the Frontier,"* 201–224.

[38] The second half of Turner's career, from around 1910 until his death in 1932, was marked by a deep anxiety deriving from his perception that the frontier had closed.

Wilson's vision was optimistic, too, at least in his estimation: a maturing postfrontier nation cleansed of divisive tendencies, devoid of ethnic and regional tensions, and bound in common purpose – a nation capable of leading the world toward its democratic future. But from the perspective of the early twenty-first century, where we more commonly herald the advantages of regional and cultural diversity and highlight the dangers of uniformity, Turner's vision seems the more prescient. There may be no United States of Europe to parallel the United States (as Turner proposed), but there is a European Union, which has tried since the 1950s to promote economic cooperation and stability in the region.

That is the starting point for this examination of America's West. Westward expansion had been a central part of the national narrative throughout the nineteenth century. The 1890s seemed to be a moment of great change in the grand sweep of American history – a decade of growing crisis for a newly postfrontier democracy. Would the future witness the Turnerian vision of the West as one fit and distinctive room for a worthy national house made stronger by the diversity of its parts? Or would the Wilsonian vision of a newly deexceptionalized West, homogenized into the larger unified nation, become the reality in the new century? Would the West become a mere reflector and imitator of national trends in the first half of the twentieth century, or would it retain a distinct regional identity and be a wellspring of innovation? Would the West follow the nation's lead or lead the nation?

2

The Rise of a Leader and a Region

> Be progressive. A great democracy has got to be progressive, or it will soon cease to be either great or a democracy.[1]
>
> – Theodore Roosevelt, Colorado, August 29, 1910

A Western President

Theodore Roosevelt's *The Winning of the West* (4 vols., 1889–1896) had charted the course and proclaimed the beneficent legacy of American martial triumph on the frontier. His powerful rhetoric in his writings and speeches helped promote the nation's fin-de-siècle imperialist ventures. His own courageous, and carefully publicized, military actions, leading his regiment of Rough Riders in the Battle of San Juan Hill in July 1898 – the most significant nonnaval engagement of the Cuban campaign – helped to forge a positive public memory of the Spanish–Cuban–American War, even as concerns over the Philippine occupation began to emerge. Roosevelt was the living embodiment of eastern gentility hardened by western frontier virtue, and the most popular figure in America at the turn of the twentieth century. Like a latter-day Andrew Jackson after the Battle of New Orleans, Roosevelt after San Juan Hill seemed to capture the hopes and ambitions of the nation.

But Roosevelt was not universally loved and lauded in America in 1900, and certainly not by the anti-imperialists, who loathed and at

[1] Theodore Roosevelt, "The Nation and the States," speech to the Colorado Legislature, August 29, 1910, in Theodore Roosevelt, *The New Nationalism* (New York: Outlook, 1911), 34–38, quotation on 37.

times ridiculed his martial enthusiasms, or by the big business interests that vehemently opposed his progressive regulatory tendencies. A war hero with an established record of public service, Roosevelt had won the New York gubernatorial election after returning home from that "splendid little war," as Secretary of State John Hay called it. After a successful term governing the nation's most populated and powerful state, he accepted the Republican Party's nomination for vice president in June 1900. This resulted from the lobbying efforts of friends and supporters who genuinely wished to advance his career, and those of opponents anxious to get him out of the governor's office. The anti-Roosevelt forces feared that his ongoing reform agenda would do further damage to big business interests in the state of New York and that the governorship would serve as a springboard to a successful presidential run in 1904.

The vice presidency was considered a relatively unimportant position at the time, which is curious considering that four US presidents had died in office since 1841. The documentary photographer and progressive reformer Jacob A. Riis remarked in an August 1900 promotional pamphlet for the Republican ticket, "The Vice-Presidency is not going to kill Theodore Roosevelt. It will take a good deal more than that to do it." Riis was almost certainly referring to TR's political career rather than his life.[2] Still, with McKinley content to wage a sedate front porch campaign from his home in Canton, Ohio, Roosevelt embraced the campaign trail in 1900 with the enormous energy and enthusiasm that had come to characterize his public persona. Perhaps he was already laying the foundations for his own 1904 campaign, ensuring, even before he entered the office, that the vice presidency would not kill his career.

Roosevelt's travels from July to October 1900 took him across the Midwest, the Great Plains, and the Rocky Mountains on a whistle-stop tour covering more than 21,000 miles and 24 states, delivering 673 speeches in 567 towns (at the rate of 8 to 10 per day) to an estimated 3 million people in total; roughly 1 in every 25 Americans and more than 1 in 4 of the West's residents heard him speak during those few months.[3] A popular campaign slogan described the Republican ticket as

[2] Jacob A. Riis, "Document No. 116: Theodore Roosevelt," Republican National Committee, New York; reprinted by permission from the *American Monthly Review of Reviews* (August 1900), 4-page pamphlet, quotation on 4, in Henry E. Huntington Library Rare Book Collection (Hereafter HEH RB), #42603.

[3] For more on TR's role in the campaign, see Edmund Morris, *The Rise of Theodore Roosevelt* (New York: Coward, McCann, and Geoghegan, 1979), 729–732; Philip McFarland, *Mark Twain and the Colonel: Samuel L. Clemens, Theodore Roosevelt, and the*

comprising "William McKinley, a Western man [an Ohioan] with Eastern ideas; and Theodore Roosevelt, an Eastern man with Western characteristics." Popular opinion identified the former cowboy/rancher, president of the Civil Service Commission, New York assemblyman, New York City police commissioner, heroic wartime colonel, and state governor as the quintessential American man of action, and Roosevelt played to that perception. In a defining statement of the campaign, he declared, "Four years ago the nation was uneasy because at our very doors an American island was writhing in hideous agony under a worse than medieval despotism... We drew the sword and waged the most righteous and brilliantly successful foreign war that this generation has seen." It proved an effective response to the rhetoric of the anti-imperialist William Jennings Bryan, who headed the Democratic Party ticket again, as he had in 1896.

The fresh memory of the glorious victory over Spain, along with the general economic prosperity that accompanied McKinley's first term, helped the incumbent president to marginally increase his portion of the popular vote, from 51 percent in 1896 to 51.6 percent in 1900 (Map 2.1). But more significant, that prosperity took the steam out of the free-silver movement and the Republican ticket pulled in six additional western states – Washington, Wyoming, Utah, South Dakota, Kansas, and Nebraska – over McKinley's 1896 haul. The vice president's campaigning in the West surely helped. The former Confederate South, including its westernmost state, Texas, remained solidly Democratic, and the western states of Colorado, Idaho, Montana, and Nevada also voted for Bryan. But the Great Plains, from Kansas to North Dakota, and the Pacific Coast, from Washington to California, along with Wyoming and Utah in the lightly populated Inter-Mountain West, went for the McKinley/Roosevelt ticket. Oklahoma, New Mexico, and Arizona were still territories. The Republicans even won a narrow victory in Bryan's home state of Nebraska and in his hometown of Lincoln.[4]

The 1900 election did not have the same momentous feel as 1896, when the very future of the nation had seemed to hang in the balance as the forces of silver and gold clashed for the first time. The Republican campaign in 1900 effectively contrasted the economic health of the nation under McKinley with the devastating depression, as well as agrarian

Arrival of a New Century (Lanham, MD: Rowman and Littlefield, 2012), 23–27; and H. W. Brands, *T. R.: The Last Romantic* (New York: Basic Books, 1997), 399–404.

4 McFarland, *Mark Twain and the Colonel*, 62. McFarland notes that Bryan even lost his home precinct.

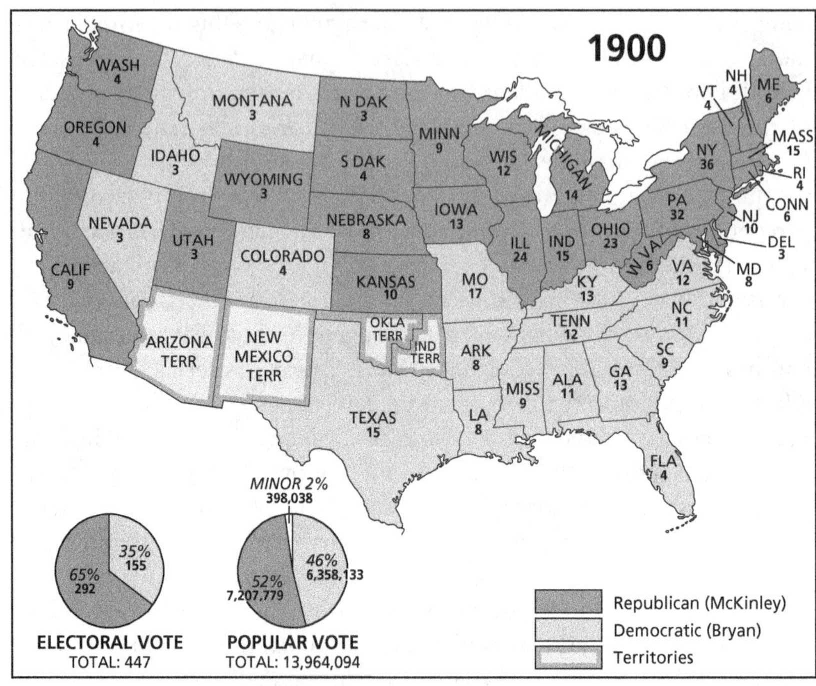

MAP 2.1 Electoral map, 1900.

radicalism that had accompanied the Grover Cleveland years. One of the most memorable campaign posters declared "Prosperity at Home, Prestige Abroad" and depicted McKinley held aloft on a gold coin by a group of workers and businessmen together, advancing the interests of "Commerce and Civilization." McKinley's reelection seemed secure from the outset, and voter turnout was down to around 75 percent (still remarkably high compared with contemporary figures – 57.1 percent in 2008, 54.9 percent in 2012, and 57 percent in 2016). Nonetheless, the 1900 election marked the largest Republican victory since President Ulysses S. Grant's reelection in 1872, and the West was clearly trending toward the Grand Old Party.[5]

At the start of the campaign season, when it had become clear that Roosevelt would secure the vice presidential nomination, wealthy Ohio businessman, US senator, and chair of the Republic Party National Committee Marcus A. Hannah had declared in frustration, "There's only one

[5] The nickname was first applied to the Republican Party right after the 1888 election.

life between this madman [Roosevelt] and the Presidency."[6] In the wake of McKinley's assassination in September 1901 by anarchist Leon Czolgosz, Hannah, who was seated on the funeral train with his old friend's coffin, on the way to Washington, DC, confided to another friend that he had asked the president at the Republican convention in Philadelphia "if he realized what would happen if he should die. Now Look! That damned Cowboy is President of the United States!"[7] Roosevelt, the New Yorker, with his experience in the 1880s of ranching, hunting, and seeking physical and psychic rejuvenation in the West; his standing as a popular writer of frontier histories; and his growing sensibilities as both a conservationist of western natural resources and a preservationist of western landscapes, might well be considered the nation's first modern western American president; at 42 years of age, he was also the nation's youngest.[8]

Reflecting on those first moments as chief executive in his autobiography (published in 1913), Roosevelt made a point of emphasizing that Abraham Lincoln's Republican Party was founded "as the radical progressive party of the Nation" but, as it combated radicalism in the 1890s, had "moved into the hands not merely of the conservatives but of the reactionaries; of men who... distrusted anything that was progressive and dreaded radicalism." Roosevelt explained that he had made sincere efforts to work with the Republican leaders in Congress but was gradually forced by necessity to forgo cooperation and appeal directly "to the people." Because of his efforts, Roosevelt contended, "the Republican Party became once more the progressive and indeed the fairly radical Progressive Party of the Nation."[9] Like all autobiographers, the former president remembered the past selectively and in his own best interests. But on the matter of his party's trajectory, he was not too far off the mark. For all the deep contradictions of reform agendas in the first two

[6] Quoted in Morris, *The Rise of Theodore Roosevelt*, 724.

[7] McFarland, *Mark Twain and the Colonel*, 144.

[8] For the connections between Roosevelt's writing about the western frontier and the shaping of his western outlook, see Michael L. Collins, *That Damned Cowboy: Theodore Roosevelt and the American West, 1883–1898* (New York: Peter Lang, 1989), especially 91–109. Roosevelt's *The Life and Times of Thomas Hart Benton* (New York: Houghton Mifflin, 1887) and *Ranch Life and the Hunting Trail* (1889) were published prior to the appearance of the first volumes of *The Winning of the West* in 1889. Roosevelt was not the first president to have spent any significant time west of the Mississippi River; Ulysses S. Grant had done so prior to his presidency.

[9] Theodore Roosevelt, *"The Rough Riders," and "An Autobiography"* (1913; repr., New York: Library of America, 2004), 607–608 and 608–609.

decades of the twentieth century, it was on balance an age of progressive reform. Under his leadership, an influential, albeit minority reformist block developed within the Republican Party, and Roosevelt emerged as an activist progressive president. Moreover, the western states proved to be a central force in many of the reform movements, and some of the more radical initiatives, of the period.

On December 3, 1901, seven weeks after President McKinley was assassinated in Buffalo, New York, President Roosevelt addressed Congress for the first time. His remarks included attention to immigration, urban conditions, circumstances of wage workers and farmers, regulation of corporations, administration of the nation's new territorial possessions, and, in one of the lengthiest sections of the speech, the outlining of a conservationist agenda and with it a plan for the irrigation of the semiarid West. It was a bold vision designed to positively alter the relationships between the government and the American people, capital and labor, corporations and the public, cities and their residents, and the citizenry and its lands and landscapes, thereby securing a "Square Deal" for all. In the immediate aftermath of Roosevelt's speech, a group of western representatives, led by representative Francis G. Newlands of Nevada, began drafting the important Newlands Reclamation Act.

Also, in February 1902, just a few months into his administration, Roosevelt instructed the Department of Justice to begin antitrust proceedings against the Northern Securities Company, a New Jersey corporation which controlled the Northwest's three major railroads, the Northern Pacific, Great Northern, and Chicago, Burlington, and Quincy, which operated from Minnesota and Wisconsin in the upper Midwest to North Dakota, Montana, Idaho, Oregon, and Washington in the northern West, and was doing so in a clearly monopolistic fashion. In taking this bold and controversial step, the new president was going head to head with four of the nation's most powerful corporate leaders, E. H. Harriman, James J. Hill, J. P. Morgan, and John D. Rockefeller. And later that year, the new president confronted corporate power again, intervening in the United Mineworkers (UMW)-led strike of anthracite coal miners in Pennsylvania. In so doing, he reversed previous federal tradition by siding primarily with the workers. In classic pragmatic progressive fashion, Roosevelt established a fact-finding commission and then took its findings seriously, subsequently brokering a deal that improved the miners' economic conditions – a 10 percent pay increase and reduction in the working day from 10 to 9 hours – though union recognition was not extended to the UMW. Roosevelt also managed to push through the Elkins Act (1903), which increased federal regulation of the nation's railroads. He was making good on his Square Deal promises

Meanwhile, the president's conservation agenda began to gain momentum. On March 14, 1903, Congress authorized five federal projects, under the Newlands Act, including the Shoshone Dam in Wyoming (opened in 1910) and the Theodore Roosevelt Dam on the Salt River, near Phoenix, Arizona. The project, begun in 1906 and completed in 1911, provided water for irrigation, flood control, and hydroelectric power, turning the Phoenix area into a major agricultural region. The Elephant Butte Dam and Reservoir on the Rio Grande, built from 1910 to 1916, ensured that El Paso had the water supply necessary for its growth.

On April 1, 1903, just a couple of weeks after these land reclamation initiatives officially began, and a little more than 18 months after entering the White House, President Roosevelt embarked on another tour of the West, traveling "fourteen thousand miles through twenty-five states, visiting nearly 150 towns and giving an estimated two hundred speeches" in just two months.[10] On April 8, a week into the tour, just as he rode off for a two-week sojourn in Yellowstone National Park with the naturalist John Burroughs, Roosevelt received news that the Eighth Circuit Court in St. Louis had upheld his suit against the Northern Securities Company.[11] Roosevelt also spent a few days and nights camping at Yosemite, with renowned nature writer and preservationist John Muir. The two men clearly reveled in each other's company, and Roosevelt's appreciation for the natural world certainly grew under Muir's tutelage. Nonetheless, the president's preservationist ideals were circumscribed by his and his chief forester Gifford Pinchot's more utilitarian conservationist tendencies. Roosevelt and Pinchot would later clash with Muir over one of the great environmental issues of the day: the controversy during 1907–1913 over whether to flood the Hetch Hetchy Valley to ensure a water supply for the growing city of San Francisco. But that rift was still several years away. In the meantime, Roosevelt helped to develop some western lands, through the Newlands Act, while withdrawing other lands from settlement, including more than 30 million acres of forest reserves that he, with his chief conservationist and close friend Pinchot, set aside on federal lands, much to the chagrin of pro-development westerners.

[10] For Roosevelt's western tour, see Edmund Morris, *Theodore Rex* (New York: Random House, 2001), 214–235; and H. W. Brands, *T. R.: The Last Romantic* (New York: Basic Books, 1997), 471–476.

[11] Morris, *Theodore Rex*, 219.

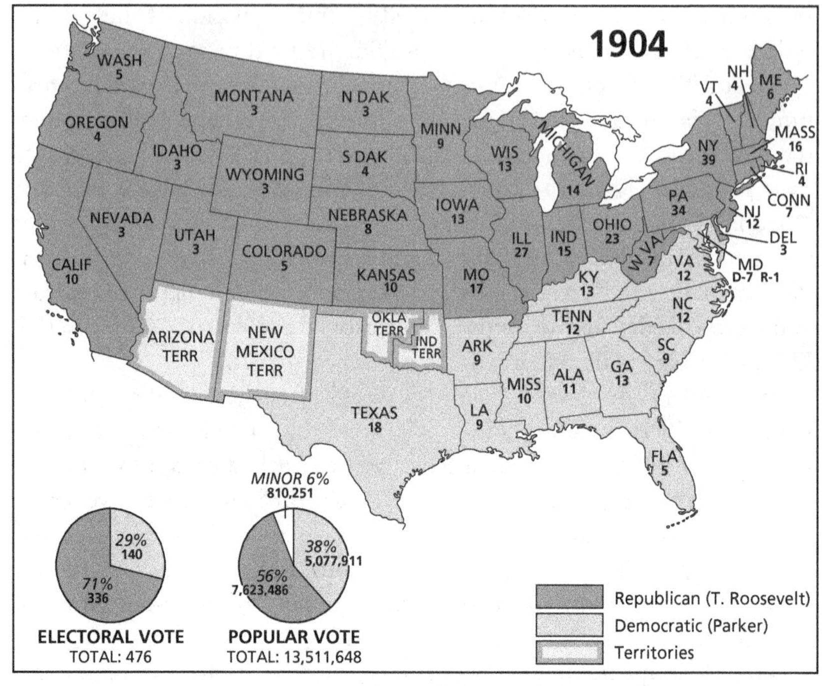

MAP 2.2 Electoral map, 1904.

Roosevelt's popular policies helped secure a landslide election victory in 1904 (Map 2.2). A largely ineffective Democratic opponent, Alton B. Parker, facilitated that effort. With 57.4 percent of the popular vote (almost 6 percentage points higher than McKinley's total in 1900) and a popular vote tally of over 7.6 million to Parker's mere 37.6 percent and 5 million, the election was a resounding mandate for Roosevelt's progressive agenda. The 1904 election also confirmed Roosevelt's popularity in the West. Roosevelt won a total of 32 states nationwide, including every state from the Great Plains to the Pacific, aside from Texas. On the eve of the election he had felt uneasy about his chances in some of those states (particularly Colorado, Montana, and Nevada), but in the wake of his momentous victory Roosevelt wrote to his son Kermit declaring, "The only states that went against me were those in which no free discussion is allowed and in which fraud and violence have rendered the voting a farce," adding with no small pride, "I have the greatest popular majority and the greatest electoral majority ever given to a candidate for President."[12] An enormously popular president, except in the old Confederate South (and even there he had made gains over McKinley's tally in 1900), Roosevelt was also a progressive, environmentally enlightened, and activist one, and a western one, too, attentive to the needs of the region and popular with a significant majority of its residents. His administration coincided with an impressive period of economic and demographic growth across the West.

The New West

As the twentieth century dawned a chorus of western boosters from the Great Plains to the California Coast and all places in between sang the praises of the "New West," presenting to prospective settlers the nation's youngest region as a land of frontier-sized opportunities but devoid of the dangers and demands of the old frontier. While many American intellectuals lamented the passing of the frontier phase of American history and were anxious over the ostensibly unfolding crisis of a frontierless democracy, promoters of western lands, towns, and investment opportunities found myriad benefits in the frontier's newfound absence. They insisted that in the wake of the privations of conquest and early settlement, western places had become true wonderlands, a set of thoroughly safe, tamed, modern, progressive, prosperous, postfrontier Wests. Boosters invariably presented the gleaming future as an already established fixture of the western landscape – not a set of hopeful dreams, but one of established and uncontestable facts about economic progress, cultural and educational infrastructure, and unparalleled natural climate and fertility.[13] Most western towns – from Bismarck, Boise, and Spokane in the northern West to Fresno and Amarillo in the Greater Southwest – while comparatively undeveloped, nonetheless presented themselves as

[12] Theodore Roosevelt to Kermit Roosevelt, from the White House, November 10, 1904, and October 26, 1904 (in which he articulated his doubts about capturing all the western states), in *Letters to Kermit from Theodore Roosevelt, 1902–1908*, ed. with an introduction and preface by Will Irwin (New York: Charles Scribner's Sons, 1946), 84–85, 77–81.

[13] For early-twentieth-century western promotion, see David M. Wrobel, *Promised Lands: Promotion, Memory and the Creation of the American West* (Lawrence: University Press of Kansas, 2002), 51–74. For the frontier concerns boosters countered, see Wrobel, *The End of American Exceptionalism: Frontier Anxiety from the Old West to the New Deal* (Lawrence: University Press of Kansas, 1993).

emerging regional metropolises destined soon to rival San Francisco and Denver.[14]

Western urban realities provided a more sobering picture than the boosters' heady visions. The nation in 1900 was home to a total of 38 cities with more than 100,000 residents, but the West could boast only a mere handful of them. San Francisco led the region with nearly 343,000 residents, Denver had about 134,000, and Los Angeles and Omaha were just over the 100,000 mark. Still, while the booster visions were clearly exaggerated, as the crisis of the 1890s subsided and the new century began, the New West clearly was on the rise. By 1910, San Francisco's population had passed 400,000, Los Angeles more than tripled in size to over 300,000, and Denver's exceeded 200,000. Portland, Oakland, Seattle, Dallas, Houston, San Antonio, and Salt Lake City also experienced tremendous growth. The urban West was on the rise (Figure 2.1).[15]

The nationwide economic downturn of the mid 1890s had reduced the number of European immigrants coming to the United States and had the overall effect of decelerating the pace of migration into the West. Between 1891 and 1900 approximately 3.7 million new immigrants entered the country. However, in the period from 1901 to 1910, the figure more than doubled, reaching 8.8 million. The much-improved national and fast-growing western regional economies of the early Progressive period both contributed to and benefited from an increase in the numbers of immigrants coming into the country and the pace of westward migration. Not surprisingly, given the tremendous urban growth in the Bay Area and in Los Angeles County, California led the way in western demographic growth. The Golden State's increase from 1.2 million to just below 1.5 million in the 1890s was not insignificant, but the addition of nearly 900,000 people in the 1900s, taking the population to nearly 2.4 million, was nothing short of remarkable. The West's other demographic giant, Texas, also saw impressive growth in the 1890s, from 2.3 million to over 3 million, and that pace was sustained in the 1900s with the population reaching nearly 3.9 million by 1910.

[14] See Carl Abbott, "All Roads Lead to Fresno," in *How Cities Won the West: Four Centuries of Urban Change in Western North America* (Albuquerque: University of New Mexico Press, 2008), 1–15, especially 8.

[15] "Selected Western Cities and Their Populations, 1900–1950," in Richard W. Etulain, *Beyond the Missouri* (Albuquerque: University of New Mexico Press, 2006), 306. For the national figure, see John Milton Cooper Jr., *Pivotal Decades: The United States, 1900–1920* (New York: W. W. Norton, 1990), 1.

City	1850	1860	1870	1880	1890	1900
San Antonio	3,396	8,235	12,256	20,550	37,673	53,321
Houston	2,396	4,845	9,382	16,513	27,557	44,633
Galveston	4,117	7,307	13,818	22,248	29,084	37,789
Austin	2,000	3,494	4,428	11,013	14,575	22,258
Dallas	250	2,000	4,500	10,358	38,067	42,638
El Paso		428	764	736	10,338	15,906
Oklahoma City					4,151	10,037
Santa Fe	4,846	4,635	4,765	6,635	6,185	5,603
Albuquerque		1,203	1,307	2,315	3,785	6,238
Phoenix			240	1,708	3,152	5,544
Tucson	400	915	3,224	7,007	5,150	7,531
Los Angeles	1,610	4,385	5,728	11,183	50,395	102,479
San Francisco	34,870	56,802	149,473	233,959	298,997	342,782
Sacramento	6,820	13,785	16,283	21,240	26,386	29,282
Oakland		1,442	10,500	34,555	48,682	66,960
San Jose	3,500	4,579	9,089	12,567	18,060	21,500
Portland	821	2,868	8,293	17,577	46,385	90,426
Tacoma			73	1,098	36,006	37,714
Seattle			1,107	3,533	42,837	80,671
Boise			995	1,899	2,311	5,957
Helena			3,106	3,624	13,834	10,770
Fargo			400	2,693	5,664	9,589
Sioux Falls			1,000	2,164	10,177	10,266
Omaha		1,883	16,083	30,518	140,452	102,555
Lincoln			2,441	13,003	55,154	40,169
Leavenworth		7,429	17,873	16,546	19,768	20,735
Kansas City				3,200	38,316	51,418
Topeka		759	5,790	15,452	31,007	33,608
Denver		4,749	4,759	35,629	106,713	133,859
Cheyenne			1,450	3,456	11,690	14,087
Salt Lake City	6,157	8,236	12,854	20,768	44,843	53,531
Virginia City (NV)	2,345	7,048	10,917	6,433	2,695	
Reno			1,035	1,302	3,563	4,500

FIGURE 2.1 Population of western cities, 1850–1900. Data from Richard W. Etulain, *Beyond the Missouri: The Story of the American West* (Albuquerque: University of New Mexico Press, 2006), 247.

The pattern of growth was similar across most of the West. New Mexico, Colorado, Wyoming, North Dakota, South Dakota, Oregon, and Washington all experienced solid population growth in the 1890s, followed by a considerably higher pace of increase in the 1900s. Arizona, Idaho, Montana, and Utah all made consistently strong demographic gains over both decades. Oklahoma, partly because of the multiple land rushes and lotteries of Indian lands, reached a population of close to 800,000 by 1900, achieved statehood in 1907 (in the wake of the federal government's dissolution of the sovereign governments of the Five Civilized Tribes) and then more than doubled in size to over 1.65 million by 1910. Kansas and Nebraska, both hard hit by drought and economic depression in the 1890s saw next to no growth during that decade and only minimal growth in the 1900s; but those two Plains states were the major exceptions to the regional trend.

The West was expanding demographically in the 1890s (albeit generally at a slower rate than in the 1880s), and the pace picked up significantly in the first decade of the new century. The population of the western states generally expanded at a much higher rate than the nation, which itself saw a quite impressive increase over the decade from 63 million to 76 million (or about 20 percent). By 1900, approximately 11 million people resided in the West, up from around 8 million in 1890 (a 37.5 percent increase).[16] The West's population was increasing as a percentage of the national population: the region was home to 14.5 percent of Americans in 1890, over 15 percent in 1900, and close to 18 percent in 1910. Although the West housed just three of the nation's 25 most populated states in 1900 (Texas, ranked sixth; California, twenty-first; and Kansas, twenty-second), a decade later Texas had moved up to fifth, California had jumped to twelfth, Kansas remained twenty-second, and Oklahoma, with its massive in-migration during the 1900s, had entered the list (at number 23).

A series of legislative initiatives, new agricultural methods, and other favorable factors facilitated settlement of the western states and territories. The Newlands Act used funds from the sale of public lands to finance large-scale irrigation projects for homesteaders working standard 160-acre tracts and willing to organize themselves into irrigation districts. The act led to the creation of the US Reclamation Service (which was moved into the Department of the Interior in 1907 and renamed the US Bureau of Reclamation in 1923) and the damming of most western rivers to make semiarid parts of every western state "bloom like a rose," as regional promoters liked to declare. One observer, writing in *Outlook* in 1903, described the "independent, powerful, proud, modern West [as] the World's inexhaustible food garden" – hyperbole to be sure, though the West was beginning to emerge as an important agricultural region, partly because of the Newlands Act.[17] Moreover, the Newlands Act continued the well-established tradition of federal underwriting of western settlement, evidenced decades earlier in the Homestead Act and the huge grants to railroad companies.

[16] US Census Bureau.

[17] William R. Lighton, "Where Is the West?," *Outlook* 74 (July 18, 1903): 702–704; quotation on 704.

In addition, the Kincaid Act (1904) provided for 640-acre homesteads in western Nebraska, and the Enlarged Homestead Act (1909) doubled the homestead size to 320 acres, promoting a new wave of settlement in North Dakota, eastern Montana, eastern Oregon, and other semiarid parts of the West. In 1912, the mandated period for "proving up" homesteaded land was reduced from five years to three, providing a further boost to small farmers. Later, the Stock Raising Homestead Act (1916) increased homesteads to 640 acres in some semiarid regions to enable cattle raising as a supplement to farming. Irrigation and dry-land farming techniques involving deep plowing to preserve soil moisture, the use of new agricultural machinery, rising crop prices, a largely healthy national economy, along with ample rainfall, and the extensive promotional efforts of railroads and state and local chambers of commerce and immigration bureaus all combined in the early twentieth century, with the various expansions of the Homestead Act, to promote agricultural settlement in the West. During the nearly four decades from 1862 to 1900, 1.4 million homesteaders filed claims; a million more did so just in the years 1900 to 1913. The year 1913 was the peak year for homesteading, and 1910–1920 the biggest decade, based on the number of acres successfully proven up and transferred from the federal government to sole proprietors. The homesteader's frontier remained very much open a generation after the Census Bureau announced the western frontier officially closed.[18]

However, as the federal government adjusted the size of homesteads in the early twentieth century, it also retained control over valuable western timber and grasslands, hydroelectric dam sites, and subsurface mineral rights. The larger homesteads usually comprised marginal land that was subject to severe drought and often proved unsustainable over the long term. Economic conditions and climate remained favorable in the semiarid West during the comparatively wet years of the first decade and a half of the century, but then drought set in across parts of the West, and its effects were often devastating. To take one tragic example, eastern Montana's new wave of hopeful homesteaders suffered six straight years of drought from 1916 to 1922. By that date, a full three-quarters of those who had arrived since 1909 – attracted in no small part by the massive advertising campaign undertaken by James J. Hill's Great Northern Railroad, and the Chicago, Milwaukee, and St. Paul Railway – had left. One colorful illustration from 1910 featured a stream of gold coins shooting up out of the ground as a hardy yeoman farmer trailed his plow across

[18] Nugent, *Into the West*, 131–132.

the land. Montana homesteaders, recalling the terrible drought years, offered a considerably grimmer set of images.[19] The story of western agricultural expansion in the first two decades of the century was hardly one of universal growth and good fortune across all parts of the West. But the general trend was certainly positive in most of the region for most of the period. The West produced an increasing portion of the nation's food during the Progressive Era, and increased demand prompted by the collapse of the European agricultural economies during the Great War sustained agrarian growth to around 1920 in most parts of the region.[20]

During the war, the US Food Administration, directed by Herbert Hoover, provided generous subsidies to farmers to ensure that the nation's military and domestic consumption needs were met, along with those of the nation's allies. Production of grain, fruit, and vegetables in California doubled during the war years and accounted for fully one-third of the food grown in the United States. Federal incentives enabled the mass expansion of the cotton industry in California's Imperial Valley, too. On the Great Plains, farmers responded to the positive economic conditions by expanding their land holdings, and buoyed by favorable weather conditions, they enjoyed huge harvests. The shipbuilding and infant aircraft industries on the Pacific Coast also received a massive boost from federal contracts after American entry into the war.[21]

A boom in extractive industries was another vital factor in the West's early-twentieth-century growth. The end of the nineteenth century saw the spectacular Klondike Gold Rush in the Yukon region of northwestern Canada (1896–1899) and the start of the Nome, Alaska Gold Rush (1899–1909). But dramatic as these events were, and much as they recalled the heralded Gold Rush days of old, from California (1848–1855) to Coeur d'Alene, Idaho (1884), they belied the new realities of the New West. Precious metals mining would certainly continue to the present in California, Colorado, Idaho, Nevada, Utah, and South Dakota, but it became a large-scale corporate venture in all those places rather than the purview of small groups and lone pioneering prospectors. On the eve of the Great War, the West was producing 90 percent of the

[19] Ibid., 192; see also Jonathan Raban, *Bad Land: An American Romance* (New York: Pantheon, 1996). The image in question appears on the front cover of *Montana* (Chicago, Milwaukee, and St. Paul Railway, c.1910).

[20] Gerald Nash, *The American West in the Twentieth Century: A Short History of an Urban Oasis* (New York: Prentice Hall, 2003), 26.

[21] Gerald Nash, *The Federal Landscape: An Economic History of the Twentieth-Century West* (Tucson: University of Arizona Press, 1999), 14–15, 16–17.

nation's copper and most of its lead and other heavy metals. These new extractive economies of scale took a considerable toll on the environmental well-being of the West's landscapes, not to mention the health of the workers.

Serious environmental consequences also accompanied the expanding copper and oil industries, which proved especially important to the growth of the West and the nation in this era. Arizona, Montana, Nevada, and Utah were the centers of copper extraction, while California, Oklahoma, and Texas became the booming sites of oil production, collectively accounting for 70 percent of the nation's output by 1910. A decade earlier the western states had accounted for less than 10 percent of national oil production. The copper and oil industries grew at an even greater pace in the second decade of the new century because of the expansion of the automobile and electrical utilities industries, and the pace of extraction and production increased significantly once the United States began to gear up for the war.[22] However, it is important to note that the oil boom was uneven across the West and the states that benefited the most in terms of revenue tended to be the ones that retained control of most of their mineral royalties, such as Oklahoma and Texas. Meanwhile, the states that contained more public land, including California, were less well positioned because of federal control of subsurface mineral rights. Manufacturing was a less impressive sector of the western economy in this period, and the region was largely reliant on eastern goods, but even that started to change as the region's population continued to grow and a regional banking infrastructure began to develop.

While hardly yet a region of booming metropolises, or an industrial behemoth to rival the Northeast and Midwest, the West was characterized by significant growth in the urban, extractive industrial, and agricultural sectors and was certainly a land of spectacular scenic attractions from the Rockies to the Pacific Coast. Meanwhile, rapidly expanding railroad networks were integrating the West and America, turning a formerly isolated region into a vital part of the growing national economy. All parts of the West were more readily accessible to migrants and to tourists than ever before. A 1909 article in the *New York Times* on the explosion in railroad travel to the West declared "passenger travel to the Pacific Coast is the heaviest in the history of American transcontinental railroading"; it was not a particularly long history yet, to be sure, but still a useful marker of western regional growth. Passengers could journey from New York to

[22] Etulain, *Beyond the Missouri*, 312–313.

San Francisco and back on the fastest trains for $107.25 and could make the trip for as little as $88. These were large sums if translated into today's money, but considerably less than early-twentieth-century Americans had previously paid for transcontinental travel. Railroads had transformed the westward migration process in myriad ways, enabling people to reach new jobs, town lots, and homesteads more easily and quickly and turning increasing numbers of tourists – who were being encouraged to forgo European trips and "see America first" – into potential future western residents.[23]

The rapid expansion of America's automobile culture in the period also facilitated western economic and demographic expansion. As late as 1904, only 154,000 miles of the nation's 2,152,000 miles of rural roads (a mere 7 percent or so) were surfaced, and generally very poorly with gravel mix and a binding agent. The primitive nature of the nation's roadways prompted the development of a "Good Roads" movement, promoted initially by bicyclists and bicycle manufacturers, but increasingly after 1903 by the emerging automobile industry. There were less than 10,000 automobiles in the United States at the turn of the century, but nearly 500,000 a decade later, close to 2.5 million by 1915, and well over 9 million cars and trucks by 1920.[24] As those numbers skyrocketed, the pressures for improvement and expansion of the nation's road infrastructure increased, to the benefit of all American regions, but particularly the developing West.

Notably, the automobile became a vehicle not just for transportation around and to the West but also for promotion of the region, as writers of various quality and renown in the first two decades of the century recorded their western travels in books and popular magazines. Among the more famous was etiquette aficionado Emily Post's engaging 1916 account *By Motor to the Golden Gate*.[25] Such publications encouraged eastern car owners to test their own pioneering mettle on western automotive frontiers, or, at the very least, to make packaged excursions to parts of the region, such as the Southwest, where railroad travel was combined with automotive "detours" in luxury vehicles, to encounter presumably vanishing Indian cultures and experience various natural wonders.

[23] Marguerite P. Shaffer, *See America First, Tourism and National Identity, 1880–1940* (Washington, DC: Smithsonian Institution Press, 2001).

[24] The figures for roads and automobiles are from Peter Blodgett, ed., *Motoring West*, vol. 1, *Automobile Pioneers, 1900–1909* (Norman, OK: Arthur H. Clark, 2015), 21–22.

[25] Emily Post, *By Motor to the Golden Gate* (New York: Appleton, 1916). For an excellent sampling of these western automotive accounts from the first decade of the century, see Blodgett, *Motoring West*, vol. 1.

The West, the nation's most rapidly developing region, was also characterized by racial and ethnic diversity on a scale generally far greater than in the nation. Fully 11.7 million immigrants entered the United States between 1871 and 1900, and another 14.5 million between 1900 and 1920. Many of these millions headed directly to ethnic enclaves in East Coast and Midwestern metropolises. But significant numbers soon made their way to the Plains and points farther west.[26] The proportion of foreign-born in the US population was between about 14 percent and 15 percent from 1890 to 1910, while in the West, the figure was over 25 percent in 1890 and remained over 20 percent in 1900 and 1910.[27] North Dakota had the highest number of foreign-born residents in the nation in 1890, with close to 45 percent, while Montana (ranked third), Nevada (fourth), Arizona (fifth), and California (eighth) all topped 30 percent. North Dakota still had a foreign-born population of over 35 percent in 1900, leading the nation. Montana, California, and Nevada placed among the top 10 states nationally in this category in both 1900 and 1910.[28]

Cultural diversity was not necessarily viewed as a benefit by all observers. For example, the popular writer Emerson Hough, in a major series on the settlement of the West in *Century Illustrated Magazine* in 1902, bemoaned the fact that in just the last two months of the nineteenth century, "fifty-seven thousand foreigners were brought to this country to be made over into Americans." Regretting the presence of "Croatians, Slavs, Armenians, Bohemians, Ser[b]ians, Montenegrins, Dalmatians, Bosnians, Herzegovinians, Moravians, Lithuanians, Magyars, Jews, Syrians, Turks, [and] Slovaks" among that number, Hough expressed his concern that "many of these immigrants from lower Europe linger in the cities of the West, and do not become a part of the agricultural communities." Instead, they become "parasites." He explained that during the earlier eras of western settlement, which had preceded transcontinental railroad travel, the process of getting to the "old West" was a demanding one that "begot character, grew mighty individuals [through]

[26] Figures are provided in David A. Gerber, *American Immigration: A Very Short Introduction* (New York: Oxford University Press, 2011), 35. For more detail on the migration of various ethnic groups into the West, see Elliott Barkan, *From All Points, America's Immigrant West: 1870s–1952* (Bloomington: Indiana University Press, 2007); and Nugent, *Into the West*.

[27] The figures here are for the Census Bureau Western Region (comprising the Mountain and Pacific West states).

[28] Campbell Gibson, *American Demographic History Chartbook: 1790–1910*, available at: www.demographicchartbook.com/Chartbook/images/chapters/gibson12.pdf.

its long and devious trails, its constant stimulus and challenge," but "the days of the adventurers are gone." Hough ominously added, "There is no land of the free. America is not American. Food must digest before it can be flesh and blood, and our population must digest before it can be called American."[29] Hough's fears were widespread, and he expressed them in less overtly racist terms than many of his American contemporaries. They rested on the idea that the frontier was no longer present as a force to Americanize immigrants and on the prevalent notion that the new immigrants were literally less white and less Protestant and thus less easily assimilated into the nation than the earlier waves of immigration from Northern and Western Europe – primarily Britons, Germans, Scandinavians, and French.

In addition to its large European immigrant populations, the West at the turn of the new century was (and remains) home to most of the United States's Native American nations, most of its Hispanic and Asian populations, and a steady migration of African Americans from the Old South heading to the promised lands of the Plains states (particularly Texas and Oklahoma) and the Pacific Coast (most notably Los Angeles, San Francisco, and Seattle). The West was the nation's most demographically dynamic and diverse region in the early twentieth century; however, the intersections of race and reform brought lamentable consequences (as we will see in Chapter 3). The West was arguably, by all measures collectively considered, one of the country's more progressive regions during the Progressive Era. Certainly, when it came to matters of managing the environment, the West stood at the leading edge of reform initiatives.

The Western Environment

As the nation's most arid, and thus environmentally challenging, region, it is no great surprise that the West led the nation in both conservationist and preservationist efforts in the early twentieth century. Most of the spectacular natural landscapes that environmentalists wanted to preserve were in the West. Roosevelt secured passage of the National Monuments Act (1906) – which preserved natural sites of special scientific interest such as Muir Woods in California and Mount Olympus National Monument in Washington State (which became Olympic National Park in 1938) –

[29] Emerson Hough, "The Settlement of the West: A Study in Transportation, III: Across the Waters," *Century Illustrated Magazine* 63 (January 1902): 355–418, quotations on 362.

along with various wildlife protection acts. Moreover, during the first two decades of the twentieth century, a total of 12 new national parks were created, 11 of them in the region (broadly defined here to include Alaska and Hawaii): Crater Lake, Oregon (1902), Wind Cave, South Dakota (1903), Mesa Verde, Colorado (1906), Glacier, Montana (1910), Rocky Mountain, Colorado (1915), Hawaii Volcanoes (1916), Lassen Volcanic, California (1916), Denali, Alaska (1917), Haleakala, Hawaii (1919), Grand Canyon, Arizona (1919), and Zion, Utah (1919). Most of that expansion of the park system came in the latter part of the Progressive Era, and the only period since that has seen results comparable to 1915 to 1919 is the Jimmy Carter administration, 1977–1981, when 12 new national parks were created.

The National Park Service was created in 1916 and charged with the complicated task of both "conserv[ing] the scenery and the natural and historic objects and the wild life contained therein" and at the same time "provid[ing] for the enjoyment of the same in such a manner that will leave them unimpaired for the enjoyment of future generations."[30] Concurrently providing for both protection and use would prove a delicate balancing act for the Park Service throughout the twentieth century, and continues to do so today. In addition to the parks, vast reserves of publicly owned forest lands were protected by the executive branch from unregulated extraction by timber interests, and all unpatented coal and oil lands, water power, and potential irrigation sites were also withdrawn from settlement. But what amounted to federal protection for the larger public good in the eyes of some (particularly the leaders of government regulatory agencies such as the Forest Service) was viewed as inexcusable federal overreach by residents of western states who were losing control of their natural resources.

Not surprisingly, regional growth during the Progressive Era, particularly in urban centers, precipitated conflicts between preservationists and conservationists, and between urban and rural dwellers. The Hetch Hetchy debate pitted the needs of Bay Area urban development (in the wake of the terrible San Francisco Earthquake of 1906) against those of wilderness protection in Yosemite National Park, more than 150 miles away. Much to John Muir's dissatisfaction, Congress in 1913 approved the damming and flooding of the Hetch Hetchy Valley (the dam was completed a decade later). The outcome of the Hetch Hetchy

[30] See National Park Service Organic Act, available at: www.nps.gov/grba/learn/management/organic-act-of-1916.htm accessed July 20, 2015.

controversy seemed to be a clear victory for the conservationist emphasis on a utilitarian approach to resource use over the preservationist dedication to preventing development of pristine areas in Yosemite National Park. However, Muir and other preservationists' impassioned articulation of the need to sustain the national soul through protection of wild nature resonated with the American public over the long term and helped promote that major expansion of the park system in the late Progressive Era.[31]

The same year that Congress sealed the fate of the Hetch Hetchy Valley, William Mulholland, superintendent of the Los Angeles Department of Water and Power, did the same for the Owens Valley when his plans for Los Angeles growth materialized with the opening of the Los Angeles Aqueduct. LA City leaders had started buying up lands in the Owens Valley in the early years of the century, and the 233-mile long aqueduct was constructed between 1905 and 1913. Owens Lake and the Owens Valley had been pumped dry by 1924, but by then LA's long-term water needs had already been guaranteed by the Colorado River Compact of 1922.[32] Here powerful urban interests prevailed over weaker rural ones, and the outcome was the provision of a liquid foundation for LA's surging demographic growth in the second and third decades of the century. Notably, LA had previously benefited from congressional approval in the 1890s of federal funding for the construction of the Port of Los Angeles (built between 1899 and 1907).

The West was generally enthusiastic about President Roosevelt's reclamation initiatives, which provided federal funding for development at the state and local level, and generally raised land values tremendously in the regions that were to be irrigated and the cities that were to be supplied with water. However, western business interests and politicians were largely and often vehemently opposed to federal regulation of the timber and mining industries, championing the principle of local control of regional resources. The process of withdrawing forest lands had begun with Presidents Benjamin Harrison, Grover Cleveland, and William McKinley in the late 1880s and 1890s; they had collectively preserved more than 40 million acres. There was some western resistance to withdrawals by Cleveland, but it was with Roosevelt's forest

[31] For Hetch Hetchy, see Robert W. Righter, *The Battle over Hetch Hetchy: America's Most Controversial Dam and the Birth of American Environmentalism* (New York: Oxford University Press, 2005).

[32] For more on the Los Angeles Aqueduct, see Norris Hundley, *The Great Thirst: Californians and Water – A History*, rev. ed. (Berkeley: University of California Press, 2001).

reserve initiatives that the western pushback against federal conservation and preservation programs began to gain steam, and continues into the present.

Roosevelt worked hard early in his first term to try to keep the western states on board with his environmental agenda, which included both conservationist and preservationist initiatives. The president's thoughts on the matter were clear. He wanted western resources to be developed with a careful eye to future needs. This agenda included federal support for the irrigation of arid lands; for the remaining arable public lands to be transferred only to homesteaders and never to corporate farming or industrial interests; for due attention to be paid to water quality and other public health issues related to natural resource development; and finally, for the nation's most sublime scenic areas to be preserved for the enjoyment of present and future generations of Americans and not opened up for corporate development. This embodied a clear environmentalist vision, one anchored at the intersection of preservation and conservation, and one that was not just ahead of its time in the early 1900s, but far more progressive than that subscribed to by many contemporary senators and house members. Indeed, Roosevelt understood the regional resources and related land management issues as well as the ecological fragility of western lands and landscapes better than any president before him, and perhaps better than any president since, perhaps excepting his younger relative Franklin D. Roosevelt.

Emerson Hough's 1908 article in the popular publication *Everybody's Magazine*, "The Slaughter of the Trees," warned the American public of the cataclysmic dangers that would accompany continued clear-cutting of the nation's forests. German American Rudolf Cronau extended Hough's message to all the nation's natural resources that same year in his book *Our Wasteful Nation*. Such works were in part inspired by the efforts of Roosevelt and his chief forester Gifford Pinchot and contributed to the nation's developing conservationist ethos, which Roosevelt and Pinchot effectively tapped into.[33] Following a precedent set by Cleveland, who had withdrawn the "Washington's Birthday Reserves in 1897," Roosevelt in 1909 bypassed congressional legislation that prohibited any further setting aside of forested western lands. In one of the most controversial steps of his entire administration, the president reserved 16 million additional

[33] For discussion of Cronau and Hough, see Ian Tyrell, *Crisis of the Wasteful Nation: Empire and Conservation in Theodore Roosevelt's America* (Chicago: University of Chicago Press, 2015), 3–4.

acres by bold executive action right as his term was about to expire. He delighted in the creation of these "midnight reserves" just as effusively as opponents of the measure, many of them pro-development western politicians, angrily damned his actions; Roosevelt later recalled that they "turned handsprings in their wrath."[34] During his administration Roosevelt successfully withdrew more than 100 million forested acres of the public domain (an area the size of the entire state of California), along with the reservation of subsurface minerals.

Roosevelt's dedication to conservationist initiatives and use of executive authority set a precedent for protective efforts by subsequent presidents, including Carter's actions and Bill Clinton's setting aside of nearly 2 million acres of southern Utah plateau and canyon lands under the Antiquities Act to create Grand Staircase–Escalante National Monument in 1996, much to the consternation of Utah's own congressional delegates. Indeed, we are left to wonder whether the nation's remarkable system of national parks, forests, monuments, recreation areas, and other federally managed lands – a system that has served as an inspiration to other countries across the globe – would have developed so impressively without the massive impetus provided by Roosevelt's deep familiarity with and affinity for the West's dramatic landscapes.

A little more than four years prior to his controversial appropriation of those additional forest lands, Roosevelt, thrilled at his massive electoral victory in 1904 and aware that he had served out virtually all of McKinley's second term, announced that he would not run again for president in 1908. He emphasized that two terms was enough for any chief executive. By early 1908, Roosevelt was confident that his vice president, the eminently capable and experienced William Howard Taft, would continue his conservationist legacy in the White House. Roosevelt, the youngest former president in the nation's history (just 50 years of age), within just a few months of departing the office, had left the political arena far behind and was traveling across British East Africa and the Belgian Congo with his son Kermit on a major safari expedition. Together, father and son killed more than 500 large game animals (including elephants, rhinoceroses, giraffes, lions, and zebras); one cartoonist depicted the continent's animals hiding in a tree when the Roosevelt expedition arrived. But in Roosevelt's absence from the United States, political trouble was brewing in the conservation arena.

34 Theodore Roosevelt, *An Autobiography*, 662; in the volume Roosevelt provides a full accounting of his conservation achievements, 651–682.

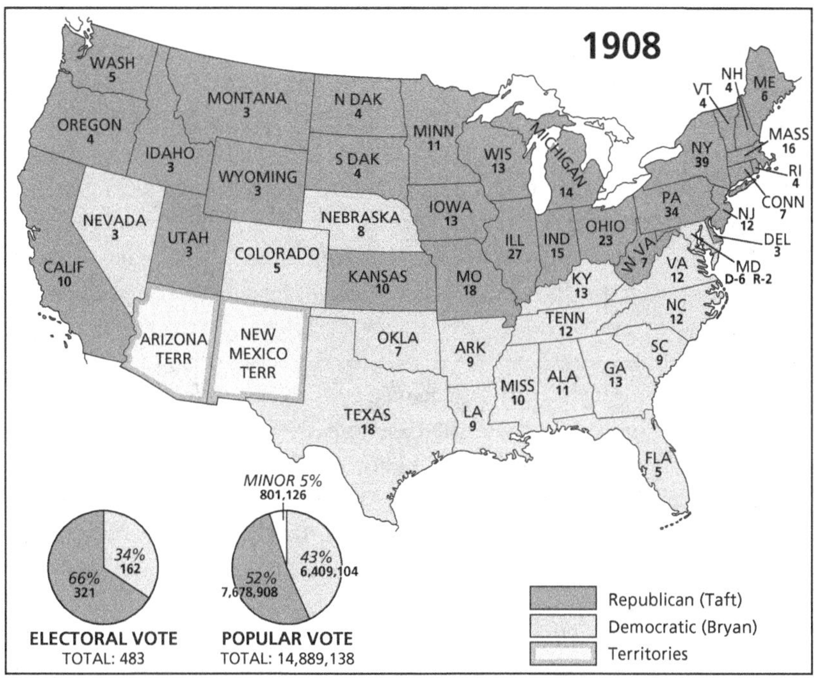

MAP 2.3 Electoral map, 1908.

Taft won the 1908 election comfortably (with just under 52 percent of the popular vote) against third-time candidate William Jennings Bryan. But Taft's victory was markedly less impressive than Roosevelt's in 1904 against Alton B. Parker; his popular vote total was a million and a quarter lower than Roosevelt's. Moreover, Taft fared considerably less well in the West than Roosevelt had done in the previous election, when Texas, in keeping with the solidly Democratic South, was the only state in the whole region that went Democratic. In 1908, Bryan won the Plains states of Texas, Oklahoma, and Nebraska, as well as Colorado and Nevada. Taft secured the Pacific Coast, from California to Washington, along with Idaho, Montana, Wyoming, the Dakotas, Utah, and Kansas (Map 2.3). It was actually Roosevelt's reputation that was bolstered by the election results, and with Taft and Bryan's lackluster performances, he remained the nation's most popular political figure.[35]

Early in Taft's term, Pinchot, still the chief forester in the Department of Agriculture, had begun to fall afoul of the new administration. Taft,

[35] See Cooper, *Pivotal Decades*, 119–121.

to the chagrin of progressive and conservation minded Republicans, had appointed Richard A. Ballinger as the first secretary of the Interior Department, which oversaw the federal lands, including the US Forest Service, which Pinchot had transferred over to Interior in 1905. Ballinger, the former mayor of Seattle (1904–1906), who had served as commissioner of the public lands (1907–1908) during Roosevelt's administration, butted heads with Pinchot, and resigned from that position. When claims to some Alaskan coalfields were investigated and approved by Ballinger in 1909, Pinchot opposed the decision. Pinchot insisted the claims were fraudulent, thus implying that Ballinger was corrupt, and then launched an investigation into Ballinger's earlier actions as land commissioner. Pinchot lobbied hard against Ballinger until Taft forced him to resign from his position. Taft had personally reviewed the case and decided Ballinger was innocent of all charges and ordered Pinchot to end his investigation; when he refused to do so, Taft saw no alternative but to fire him. Ballinger eventually stepped down from his position to help relieve some of the pressure on the president from conservationist-minded Republicans.

The so-called Ballinger–Pinchot Affair highlighted the environmental politics of the era. Conservationists presented the controversy, rather inaccurately, as a classic case of special interests colluding with government officials to exploit the public lands. This was exactly how Pinchot described matters to Roosevelt, sending copies of correspondence and other documents relating to the controversy to him in Africa and presenting Taft as a concerted enemy of conservation. Pinchot even traveled to Italy in the spring of 1910 to meet with his friend and present his case. Taft, while not a crusader for natural resource conservation on the scale of his predecessor, did withdraw a significant amount of public land from development, along with subsurface mineral rights and waterpower sites. Nonetheless, the Ballinger–Pinchot Affair, which occupied the public's attention for a full year starting in the summer of 1909, incensed Roosevelt and was a major contributing factor in his decision to seek the nomination of the Republican Party for the next election.[36] As the incumbent, Taft controlled crucial parts of the nomination process and was duly selected at the Republican nominating convention in 1912. That decision precipitated Roosevelt's formation of the Progressive or "Bull Moose" Party, a movement led by western progressives, that

[36] For more on the Ballinger–Pinchot controversy, see Claus M. Naske and Herman E. Slotnick, *Alaska: A History* (Norman: University of Oklahoma Press, 2011), 150–151, and Cooper, *Pivotal Decades*, 155–157.

effectively split the Republican vote, and ultimately resulted in the election of Woodrow Wilson.

The 1912 election was, for those interested in the clash of actual ideas and policies, one of the most fascinating contests in the nation's modern history. The Democrat Wilson ran as a Progressive on an antimonopoly platform, the New Freedom, designed by Louis Brandeis. Roosevelt's New Nationalism program emphasized federal regulation of large corporations in the public interest, rather than plain trust busting, and was designed in part by Progressive theorist Herbert Croly and social reformer Jane Addams, and included women's suffrage. Taft, having alienated progressive forces within the Republican Party, many of whom were westerners who he had tried to purge in the 1910 midterm elections, was forced to appeal to the party's conservative, big business–oriented base. Socialist Party leader Eugene Debbs rounded out the field in 1912, offering a program considerably more radical than even Roosevelt's wide-ranging array of proposed social justice reforms.

In the end, the Republican split created too wide a chasm for Roosevelt to overcome, and Wilson won the election easily with 6.3 million votes to TR's 4.2 million; Taft finished third with 3.5 million. Eugene Debbs pulled in a remarkable 900,000 votes, roughly 6 percent of the total, the most ever for a Socialist candidate in the United States. Voter turnout was down to 59 percent, a massive drop from 1896, and a significant decline even from the 65.4 percent rate in 1908. Wilson secured most of the western states in the Plains and Intermountain regions, excepting South Dakota, which went for TR. Roosevelt also won California and Washington, while Taft won only Utah. Debbs received no popular majorities in any of the western states, though he did better in the region than in any other part of the country (Map 2.4).[37] Although environmental issues played no significant part in the election campaign itself, which revolved largely around the issue of corporate regulation, it was an environmental controversy in Alaska, the West's "last frontier," that had precipitated the Republican division and paved the way for Wilson's victory.

The election was Roosevelt's last great moment on the national scene. During the campaign, he was shot in the chest in Milwaukee, Wisconsin, right before he took the stage. He asked the crowd to be as quiet as possible and explained that the bullet had passed through the 50-page copy of his speech and was lodged in his chest. He then proclaimed, "It takes more than that to kill a bull moose," and proceeded to deliver the

[37] Cooper, *Pivotal Decades*, 187–188.

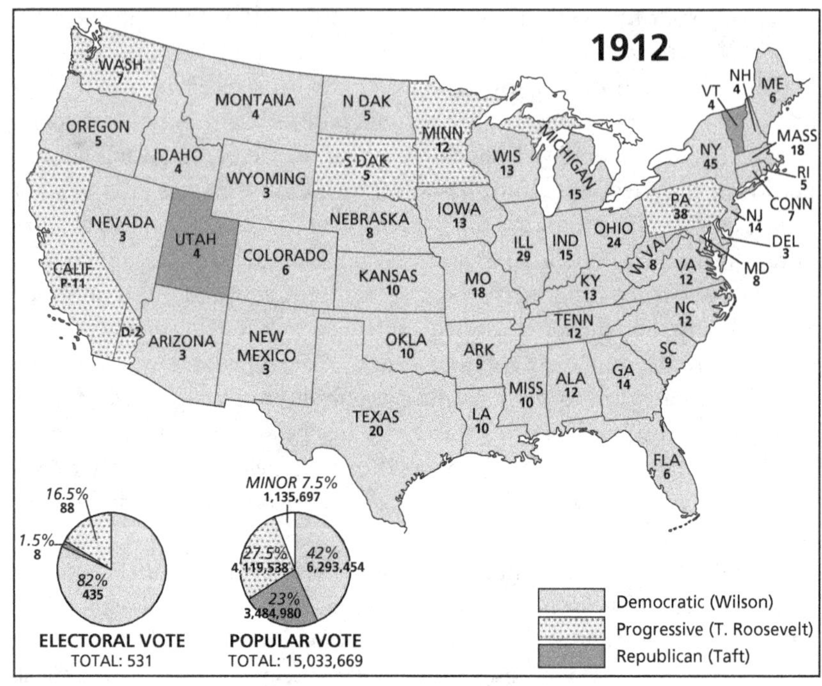

MAP 2.4 Electoral map, 1912.

speech.[38] The high drama that had accompanied Roosevelt's entry onto the national stage after the Battle of San Juan Hill was still very much in evidence 15 years later. Theodore Roosevelt dominated the first 12 years of the twentieth century to a degree that no single figure would for another generation, when another Roosevelt began his presidency. His rise to prominence played out together with the emergence of the New West.

[38] Edmund Morris, *Colonel Roosevelt* (New York: Random House, 2010), 245–246.

3

Progressive Reform, Progressive Intolerance

> We watched from our rock shelter while the militia dragged up their machine guns and poured a murderous fire into the arroyo from a height by Water Tank Hill above the Ludlow depot. Then came the firing of the tents... what looked like a blazing torch waved in the midst of militia a few seconds before the general conflagration swept through the place.
>
> – Godfrey Irwin, eyewitness to the Ludlow Massacre, April 1914

Progressive Motivations and Variations

The term "Progressivism" encompassed a broad array of reform efforts in the early twentieth century. The diverse goals of reformers included direct democracy measures such as women's suffrage; the initiative, referendum, recall, secret ballot, and direct election of US senators; anticorruption and antimonopoly measures; social justice campaigns to increase safety in the workplace, provide worker compensation for injury, restrict child labor, impose limits on the length of the working day and week, provide childcare, improve housing for the working poor, and assist and Americanize new immigrants; moral crusades such as prohibition and antiprostitution efforts; more careful stewardship of natural resources; and racially motivated movements such as immigration restriction, alien land laws, eugenics, segregation, and disenfranchisement of racial minorities, which were based on fear and yet brashly claimed to be progressive.

Those wide-ranging, sometimes conflicting, and even paradoxical efforts constituted the full range of organized responses to the rapid urbanization, industrialization, and immigration, with all its accompanying cultural diversity, that had transformed the nation in the late nineteenth century. The sweeping scale and speed of these changes was jarring, the consequences for American society were often alarming, and the spectrum of proposed solutions was broad and often contradictory.[1]

Gilded Age and Progressive Era modernization, urban, industrial, and demographic growth, and the massive push toward business consolidation, especially between 1897 and 1903, resulted in the accumulation of truly massive fortunes and accompanying political power by a relative handful of corporate giants, along with low wages and long working days and weeks, and astonishingly high levels of workplace injuries and fatalities, among the growing blue-collar workforce. Around 1 million workers were wounded and somewhere between 25,000 and 35,000 died in US workplaces in the year 1900 alone. Such figures approximated the awful human consequences of war rather than the natural by-products of industrial progress and testified to the shameful lack of consideration for workplace safety in industrializing America, when compared to industrializing European nations.[2] In addition to the endangered adult workers, children labored in textile mills, factories, and mines. These awful circumstances precipitated industrial conflict and class polarization. The volatile mix of conditions at the turn of the century also included endemic corruption in both political parties at every level from the national to the local. In addition, many Americans saw the New Immigration as a massive threat to the national body politic. It was in this vast landscape of change and uncertainty that self-described reformers emerged to try to eradicate the various ills they felt were afflicting the nation.

Some of these reformers were motivated by concerns over their own social standing in a changing America, while others, many with specialized professional training, wished to make the nation more orderly and efficient and, in doing so, to find a fitting place for themselves at the vanguard of American social, economic, and political structures. Social control of an increasingly diverse and lower-class populace in apparent need of Americanization and moral uplift was the chief motivating factor for some reformers. Meanwhile, others, perhaps even the majority of self-defined progressives, were driven by a genuine altruistic desire to improve lives. Most wished to smooth off the roughest edges of industrial

[1] For a useful introduction to the historiography of Progressivism, including the motivations of progressive reformers see Eugene E. Leach, "1900–1914," in *A Companion to 20th-Century America*, ed. Stephen J. Whitfield (Malden, MA: Blackwell Publishing, 2004).

[2] John Fabian Witt, *The Accidental Republic: Crippled Workman, Destitute Widows, and the Remaking of American Law* (Cambridge, MA: Harvard University Press, 2004).

capitalism (not abandon the entire system) and to make it more humane, and to render American politics less corrupt and more democratic. Some reformers were also driven by moral and evangelical principles, and often by an accompanying cultural myopia. Unfortunately, just as in earlier and later periods, there were those who imagined themselves as progressives and certainly sought to improve society in ways they saw as important but who were clearly inspired by unenlightened racist fears and animosities.

Progressivism as a movement in America made no sense, and yet simultaneously made complete sense. Its apparent contradictions – social justice and social control, cultural empathy and base racism, Christian moralism and patently un-Christian disregard for the rights of others – merely represent the predictable array of responses to a perceived state of acute crisis and may well have been no more wide ranging than those of any other period in the nation's modern history. Added to the lack of uniformity that marked the reform initiatives themselves and the reformers' motivations, there were also major regional variations that further complicate efforts to evaluate the record of reform in the West.

At the turn of the new century, the Northeast, Mid-Atlantic, and Midwest were characterized in no small part by a WASP–New Immigration divide, and anti-immigration crusaders and eugenicists in those regions laid claim to the mantle of Progressivism as they sought to preserve the health of the nation and the Nordic race. In the South, a biracial, black–white fault line dominated, and virulent racists such as Mississippi's James K. Vardaman and South Carolina's "Pitchfork Ben" Tillman won their respective state governorships and US Senate races in the late nineteenth and early twentieth centuries campaigning for what they called a more progressive South. That "progressive" South featured increased funding for education and other social services, regulation of railroads and other corporations, and the implementation of direct primaries and various additional direct democracy reforms typical of the progressive agenda nationwide. Vardaman, Tillman, and like-minded southern progressives, however, also proposed financing their reform initiatives in part through reduction in funding for black education and contended that advanced learning was not suited to people destined only to perform field labor and other physical tasks. Vardaman and others like him also believed their vision for regional progress could only be achieved via strict segregation and disenfranchisement of the black population and that these undemocratic measures would ensure harmonious race relations. Vardaman openly advocated the benefits of lynching to emphasize to the African American population its proper place in southern society. Therefore, reform in the South rested on deep and dangerous racist foundations.[3]

Meanwhile, a range of cultural divides characterized the West's various subregions. The northern West, composed of the Dakotas, Montana, and Wyoming, was home to a large foreign-born population, comprising both new immigrant Southern and Eastern Europeans as well as those from Northern and Western Europe and Native peoples, including the Sioux, Blackfeet, Northern Cheyenne, Eastern Shoshone, and Northern Arapaho. The remaining interior parts of the West that bordered neither the Pacific nor Mexico (Colorado, Utah, and Nevada) were also marked by a diversity of European ethnicities and a significant Native presence, including Paiutes, Western Shoshone, and Utes. The Pacific Northwest states of Oregon and Washington had a similar European ethnic presence, an Asian one, and several Native nations, including the Umatilla and Klamath in Oregon and the Colville, Puyallup, Spokane, and Yakama in Washington. Idaho also had a significant Native presence, including the Northern Shoshone and Bannock, Nez Perce, and Cour d'Alene.

The Greater Southwestern region stretching from the California Coast to the Southern Plains was even more racially diverse than those areas to its north. Newly arrived white Americans dominated California. In 1910, fully 60 percent of the state's population was born in the Midwest, but California was also home to the nation's largest Hispanic and Asian populations as well as a wide array of Native peoples.[4] Anglo, Hispanic, and Native American (primarily Navajo, Apache, and Pueblo) constituted the distinctive "tricultural" landscape of the Southwest. The Hispanic presence in the US–Mexican borderlands region stretching from California to Texas expanded rapidly in the second decade of the century as more than a million Mexicans fled the violence and economic dislocation that accompanied their nation's revolution. In the 1890s and early 1900s, Oklahoma's rapidly expanding nexus of white Americans, recent European immigrants primarily from Britain, Ireland, and

[3] William A. Link, *The Paradox of Southern Progressivism, 1880–1930* (Chapel Hill: University of North Carolina Press, 1997); and Jack Temple Kirby, *Darkness at the Dawning: Race and Reform in the Progressive South* (Philadelphia: Lippincott, 1972).

[4] Kevin Starr, *Inventing the Dream: California through the Progressive Era* (New York: Oxford University Press, 1985), 236. Today there are 109 federally recognized Indian tribes, over 100 federal reservations, and more than 40 additional groups seeking tribal recognition from the government; see Benjamin Madley, *An American Genocide: The United States and the California Indian Catastrophe* (New Haven, CT: Yale University Press, 2016), 348.

Germany, in addition to African American migrants seeking a promised land far away from the "progressive" South, arrived in the most culturally diverse Native region in the nation. Oklahoma Indian Territory was home to the Five Civilized Tribes – Cherokee, Chickasaw, Choctaw, Creek, and Seminole – who were removed there during the 1830s and 1840s from the Southeast, and to various other nations, who were relocated there in subsequent decades, including the Kiowa, Comanche, and Pawnee.

In addition to their diverse geography and demography, the West's various regions featured a broad range of economic foundations and disparate levels of urbanization. Parts of the West were certainly more progressive in some regards than others, and more progressive than the nation at large; other parts were not. Wallace Stegner was right about the difficulty of trying to make a regional whole from the West's varied parts, whether during the Progressive Era or in any other period. These subregional differences and sometimes conflicting types of reform initiatives and motivations make it difficult to determine whether the West was more progressive than the nation. However, an examination of the various kinds of progressive initiatives including direct democracy reform, social justice initiatives, and examples of western intolerance and injustice that adopted the moniker of Progressivism can highlight where the region's constituent parts led the nation and where they lagged behind.

The Democratic West

Western women were the first women in the nation to secure the right to vote; indeed, women's suffrage is the clearest example of the Progressive Era West leading the nation. Wyoming led the way in 1869 when the tiny territorial legislature granted women the vote by a narrow margin, partly because of the hope that suffrage would attract more female settlers to the underpopulated region. When Wyoming achieved statehood in 1890, suffrage was in place, although no women participated in drafting the state constitution. Utah followed in 1870, albeit through an unusual set of circumstances that had to do with the protection of the Mormon practice of plural marriage rather than democratic reform. Alliances with the Populists facilitated women's efforts to secure suffrage in Colorado (1893) and Idaho (1896). When Utah became a state in 1896, it did so with suffrage in place and with strong Populist support. But for all the impressive gains of the early Populist Era, the succeeding years, from 1897 to 1910, were labeled the "doldrums" by western women's suffrage reformers as they continued to seek change across the rest of the region

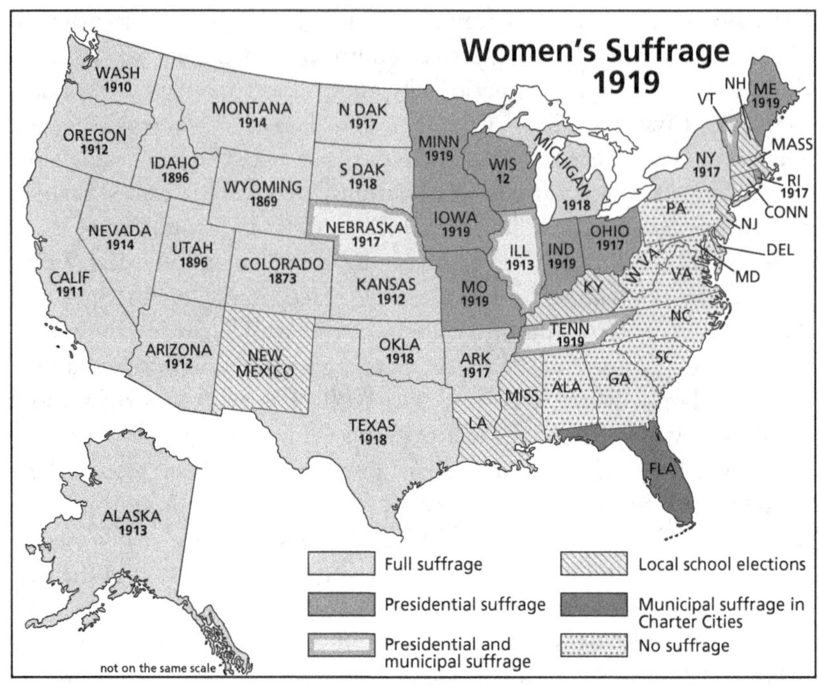

MAP 3.1 Women's suffrage, 1919. From the National Education Association, http://cdn3.vox-cdn.com/uploads/chorus_asset/file/783754/trowbridge2_1.0-fig 05_031.0.jpg.

in an unsupportive political environment marked by Republican Party congressional dominance.

Then, during the second decade of the new century, as the Socialist Party under *Eugene v. Debs*, a more reform-oriented Democratic Party under Woodrow Wilson, and Theodore Roosevelt's Progressive Party shook up the political mainstream, suffrage reformers regained the opportunity to leverage their cause. Women in Washington State (1910), where voting rights had been in place from 1883 to 1887 (during the territorial era), California (1911), Arizona, Kansas, and Oregon (all 1912), Alaska Territory (1913), Montana and Nevada (1914), all secured their suffrage rights before every single nonwestern state but one (Illinois, 1913). Oklahoma and South Dakota women earned the right to vote in 1918. During that eight-year period, the only nonwestern states besides Illinois to grant suffrage ahead of the ratification of the Eighteenth Amendment were New York (1917) and Michigan (1918) (Map 3.1).

The only western states that failed to grant women suffrage in advance of the constitutional amendment were Nebraska and North Dakota, where women could at least vote for president in advance of national ratification, and New Mexico and Texas, where they could not. In fact, Texas voters narrowly rejected women's suffrage in May 1919, a mere five weeks before the state legislature approved the Nineteenth Amendment. A total of 12 nonwestern states (including Illinois, Michigan, and New York) permitted women to vote in presidential elections in advance of the constitutional amendment, but aside from Illinois, even that privilege was not conferred on women anywhere outside of the West until 1917. Nine western states had instituted women's suffrage before a single state from outside the region did so. Simply put, while the ideology of women's suffrage was anchored in the East, its first political successes were in the West.

Women's relentless activism in pushing the suffrage agenda and placing bills before state legislatures again and again, their alliances with progressive farm and labor groups, and the comparatively fluid nature of party politics in the West help explain why suffrage came first to the region. Women arrived in the West with their gender baggage intact, but over time, and because of the social and environmental conditions they faced, they cast off that baggage and lobbied for suffrage with greater energy and commitment than women in other regions. Also important was the belief of western men that western women deserved the right to vote. However, Republican Party hegemony across most of the West after the 1896 election through the end of the first decade of the century worked against suffrage. Indeed, the Republicans popularized the notion that suffrage had been gained in Colorado and Idaho in the 1890s through alliances with radical groups such as Populists, socialists, and anarchists, thereby tainting the suffragists as radical by association. Such opposition helps explain why suffrage did not come even sooner to most of the West.[5]

In fact, the suffrage struggle hit major roadblocks in many western states before eventually achieving success. Montana women struggled for a whole generation from 1895 to secure suffrage, with no bill making

[5] Rebecca Mead, *How the Vote Was Won: Woman Suffrage in the Western United States, 1868–1914* (New York: New York University Press, 2004), and Mead, "Pioneers at the Polls: Woman Suffrage in the West," in *Votes for Women: The Struggle for Suffrage Revisited*, ed. Jean H. Baker (New York: Oxford University Press, 2002), 90–102.

its way out of the state legislature for a popular vote until 1914, when a narrow victory was won.[6] In Oregon, the movement's most charismatic and influential advocate, Abigail Scott Duniway, battled for nearly three decades, starting in the mid 1880s, with her own brother and editor of *The Oregonian* Harvey Scott. Oregon voters defeated the suffrage measure five times before narrowly passing it in 1912. Suffrage was also voted down several times in both Washington and California in this same period before it eventually passed in both states, in 1910 and 1911, respectively.[7] In fact, when California women gained the vote in 1911, it was only by a razor-thin margin and despite the *LA Times*'s concerted opposition, including warnings that family life and female morality would degenerate.[8] In many parts of the West, the opposition to reform not only came from those proclaiming to uphold moral standards but also from those made nervous by moral reformers. Thus, suffrage debates became entangled with the politics of temperance and prohibition, with some voters fearing that most enfranchised women, imbued as they were with the spirit of moral uplift, would vote to abolish alcohol.[9]

The Women's Christian Temperance Union (WCTU) was founded in New York in 1873 to combat alcohol abuse and its deleterious impact on women, children, and home life. By 1881 the first western chapters of the organization were in place in California and Oregon. Alcohol abuse seems to have been an even larger problem across the West in the late nineteenth century than in the nation a whole, in no small part because of the heavy rates of in-migration, the demographic preponderance of males over females, and the generally unsettled state of society. In response, the WCTU spread rapidly across the region in the last two decades of the century, and its members pushed for numerous reforms beyond prohibition of alcohol, including more favorable marriage, divorce, and property laws for women and higher teacher salaries (women dominated the profession). The WCTU was particularly active in California, Oregon, Kansas, and North Dakota, but the organization's efforts were stymied by the lack of

[6] Paula Petrik in *No Step Backward: Women and Family on the Rocky Mountain Mining Frontier, 1865–1900* (Helena: Montana Historical Society Press, 1987), recounts the experiences of three generations of Montana women in moving the state toward suffrage.

[7] For suffrage in Oregon, see Robert D. Johnston, *The Radical Middle Class: Populist Democracy and the Question of Capitalism in Progressive Era Portland* (Princeton, NJ: Princeton University Press, 2003), 147–152.

[8] Starr, *Inventing the Dream*, 259.

[9] Shannon D. Smith, "The Rise of Western Women to National Stature in the Early Twentieth Century," in *The World of the American West*, ed. Gordon Morris Bakken (New York: Routledge, 2011), 448–473, especially 456–457.

women's political power; stopping the production, sale, and consumption of alcohol required legislation, and without the vote, women could lobby and protest but not directly affect policy. Thus, fears about the motives of enfranchised women were not unfounded, and opposition to the movement slowed it down.[10]

Nonetheless, delayed as suffrage was in the West, it became a reality well ahead of the nation and before any other American region. The general success of suffrage in the West also helped lay the foundations for western women to enter the political arena ahead of women in other parts of the country. One of the leading lights of the California suffrage campaign, Katherine Philips Edson, became a part of Hiram Johnson's administration in 1912 and rose to the position of executive director of the California Division of Industrial Welfare, becoming the first woman in the state's history to hold a high-profile position in the state government.[11] That same year, Mary W. Howard became the first elected woman mayor in the country, in the southern Utah town of Kanab, where she headed an all-female town council. Most famously, Jeanette Rankin, who spearheaded the fight for suffrage in Montana, became the first woman elected to the US Congress in 1916. Nearly a decade later, Miriam "Ma" Ferguson of Texas and Nellie Taylor Ross of Wyoming became the first female governors in the nation, and the following year, Bertha Landes of Seattle became the first woman mayor of a large city.

Western women reformers had also made their mark in the presuffrage era. In 1907, on the eve of statehood and more than a decade before full women's suffrage came to Oklahoma, schoolteacher and newspaper writer Kate Bernard was elected to the new office of commissioner of charities and corrections, becoming the first woman in the nation elected to a statewide position. In addition to being an important advocate for prison reform, Bernard lobbied successfully for worker rights, built a farmer–worker coalition, and managed to ensure the prohibition of child labor in the state constitution; she was considered the Jane Addams of the Sooner State.[12] Lamentably, when Bernard sought to expand the work of her commission on behalf of the poor, the new state's political hierarchy slashed her budget. "Our Good angel Kate's" efforts were fleeting but

[10] Sheila McManus, *Choices and Chances: A History of Women in the U.S. West* (Wheeling, IL: Harlan Davidson, 2011), 172–175.

[11] Starr, *Inventing the Dream*, 259.

[12] Walter Nugent, *Progressivism: A Very Short Introduction* (New York: Oxford University Press, 2010), 66.

underscored the vital role of newly empowered women in Progressive Era social justice reform.[13]

Women's suffrage was part of a broader movement of "direct democracy" reforms introduced in the Progressive Era to enhance the people's power to effect change. Progressive reformers, and the historians who wrote about them in the first decades after the end of the Progressive Era, viewed society in dualistic terms, pitting "the people," in whose inherent wisdom they generally had great faith, against "the interests," the monopolistic corporations and banks that reformers felt needed to be regulated or broken up. Reformers believed this goal could be achieved through expanding the involvement of ordinary people in the political arena. If fully informed by reformers of the unfair and corrupt systems that adversely affected them, ordinary citizens would push politically to correct those problems. Various direct democracy reforms were introduced in the early twentieth century to enhance the people's power to effect change.

Again, the West, as with women's suffrage, was generally at the leading edge of reform and an example to the nation in participatory government. These initiatives were fueled by a greater level of anti-institutionalism and by the comparative weakness of traditional political party structures in the West. Additionally, western direct democracy efforts were responses to the control that major corporations exerted over state politics. Mining companies such as Anaconda in Butte, Montana, and Phelps-Dodge in Bisbee, Arizona, dominated those towns and had enormous influence at the state level. The Union Pacific and Burlington Railroads had enormous influence over Nebraska's political institutions, and the Southern Pacific Railroad virtually controlled the California state legislature. Western progressives placed great faith in direct democracy reforms as a tool for curbing corporate influence. The breakthroughs tended to come at the local level first, as reform mayors displaced corrupt machine governments, most notably in Denver, Seattle, and San Francisco. Building on these local reform foundations, several western states became important pace setters.

Oregon Populist-Progressive, and later Republican Party leader William S. U'Ren, a lawyer, religious mystic, and, briefly, a Hawaiian sugarcane plantation manager, was among the most memorable direct democracy crusaders. In 1889, U'Ren came to Oregon, where he soon

[13] W. David Baird and Danney Goble, *Oklahoma: A History* (Norman: University of Oklahoma Press, 2008), 177–178.

campaigned for the Australian, or secret, ballot, which was adopted in 1891. Five years later he was elected to the state house of representatives as a Populist but served just a single term (1897–1899). But by the beginning of the new century, U'Ren had organized a new coalition, the People's Power League, that reshaped Oregon's political system, making it one of the most progressive in the nation. The "Oregon System" comprised the initiative, the referendum, and the recall. The initiative enabled citizens to petition to get issues on the ballot, thus bypassing the state legislature. The referendum provided the electorate the opportunity to vote yes or no on bills that were passed by the state legislature. The recall empowered citizens to vote elected officials out of office before the expiration of their terms, thereby holding them accountable to the public will. The initiative and referendum were in place in Oregon as early as 1902 and the recall by 1908. Oregon also passed a law in 1908 ensuring that the state's voters elected their US senators rather than having them chosen by the state legislature, thus helping to pave the way for the Seventeenth Amendment in 1913.

Oregon's Pacific Northwest neighbors Idaho and Washington were slower to implement the initiative, referendum, and recall, but all three measures were in place by 1912 in both states. California adopted them by 1911.[14] Most of the Plains States followed suit during the Progressive Era: North Dakota instituted the initiative, referendum, and recall; South Dakota and Nebraska instituted the initiative and referendum, but not the recall; the initiative and referendum both failed in Kansas, but the state did adopt the recall.[15] Notably, a Kansan House representative, Joseph L. Bristow (R), introduced the revised resolution in 1911 that facilitated the Seventeenth Amendment. Direct democracy measures were popular in Montana. The first state to institute the Australian ballot, in 1889, Montana's voters overwhelmingly approved the initiative and referendum in 1906. Voters did the same in Colorado in 1910 and added the recall provision in 1912. Nevada was another bastion of western direct democracy, establishing the referendum in 1904, direct primary elections

[14] For more on U'ren and the Oregon System, see Johnston, *The Radical Middle Class*, 115–137. For direct democracy in the Pacific Northwest, see Carlos A. Schwantes, *The Pacific Northwest: An Interpretive History* (Lincoln: University of Nebraska Press, 1989); and William Robbins and Katrine Barber, *Nature's Northwest: The North Pacific Slope in the Twentieth Century* (Tucson: University of Arizona Press, 2011), 50–53.

[15] North Dakota also held the nation's first presidential preference primary, in March 1912, voting overwhelmingly for Wisconsin Progressive Robert La Follette over the hopeful Republican nominees – Roosevelt and the incumbent Taft.

in 1909, and the initiative and the recall in 1912.[16] Utah, however, proved largely unreceptive to direct democracy measures, and in Wyoming, the "Equality State," no such provisions were in place until 1968.[17]

The southwestern states of Arizona and New Mexico followed different courses to direct democracy reform. Arizona entered the Union in February 1912, but only after scrapping a controversial constitutional provision for voter recall of judges, thereby gaining President Taft's support for statehood. Nonetheless, the state's progressive constitution provided for the initiative and referendum, and the recall of elected officials was soon added to it. The very first initiative measure in the state was for women's suffrage. Moreover, labor forces, in alliance with Arizona's pro-labor inaugural governor George W. P. Hunt, took full advantage of these reform opportunities to push back against the state legislature and protect worker rights, despite the lobbying efforts of the copper industry.[18] New Mexico statehood came in January 1912, but with no initiative and no recall.[19] Direct democracy measures also failed to gain traction in Texas.[20]

New Mexico, Texas, Utah, and Wyoming were exceptions to the western trend. Taken together, the direct democracy movement was more successful in the West than in any other region during the Progressive Era. The legacy of those developments is complicated, however, even convoluted. Today, of the nine states that have full recall provisions enabling the recall of all elected officials, five are in the West: Washington, Oregon, Montana, North Dakota, and Colorado. And every state from the Plains to the Pacific, with the sole exception of Utah (which does now have the initiative), currently allows for at least limited recall of officials. No other region of the country is as committed to direct democracy in state government as the West. These measures are far more a feature of the political right's activities today than those of the left, and not uncommonly are

[16] Though, notably, there were no initiatives introduced in Nevada for six years after voters approved the measure.

[17] In Nevada, the initiative and referendum narrowly failed on a technicality, despite a huge popular majority favoring the measures, and there was no recall either. The initiative and referendum passed in Utah as early as 1900 but were not implemented, and there was no recall provision there either.

[18] Richard W. Etulain and Michael P. Malone, *The American West: A Modern History, 1900 to the Present*, 2nd ed. (Lincoln: University of Nebraska Press, 2007), 63.

[19] The popular referendum was embedded in the New Mexico constitution, but that measure was never used during the Progressive Era.

[20] Texas voters narrowly rejected a constitutional amendment providing for the initiative and referendum processes in 1914 and had no recall provision.

central to corporate-financed efforts to unseat progressive incumbents and undo progressive policies. Originally designed as tool for "the people" to oppose "the interests," direct democracy has ironically become more often a tool of "the interests" in limiting the rights of labor, immigrants, and other groups seeking government protection.

Despite this antiprogressive legacy, many parts of the West in the early twentieth century were models of progressive possibility. Galveston, Texas, in the wake of the hurricane and tidal wave that killed more than 6,000 people and destroyed much of the city's infrastructure in 1900, eradicated corrupt municipal government structures and replaced them with functional models of professional administration and representative democracy. Other western cities, including Denver, Seattle, and San Francisco (which experienced a terrible earthquake in 1906 that left more than 3,000 residents dead and most of the city's population homeless), became models of municipal reform.[21] Moreover, western reformers' efforts to regulate corporations in the public interest were helped by the presence of a mobilized and more fully enfranchised electorate. Indeed, direct democracy initiatives facilitated many of the social justice reforms instituted in the region. In addition, these new measures weakened both Democratic and Republican party structures and, in doing so, reflected and nurtured the comparative lack of party loyalty that characterized western politics.[22]

Western Social Justice

The political power of the Southern Pacific Railroad (or SP, as it was known) over the California state legislature was a barrier to substantive reform at the state level in the first decade of the century. Dubbed "the Octopus" in the early 1890s and made infamous by Frank Norris in his influential 1901 muckraking novel of the same name, the SP had been relentless in its pursuit of economic advantage by controlling the levers of state political power. Significant reforms were enacted in California's major cities during the early 1900s. Physician and reformer Dr. John Randolph Haynes and other members of the state's emerging professional class cemented the foundations for statewide reform with the

[21] Michael P. Malone and F. Ross Peterson, "Politics and Protests," in *The Oxford History of the American West*, ed. Clyde Milner III, Carol A. O'Connor, and Martha Sandweiss (New York: Oxford University Press, 1994), 501–533, esp. 506–507.

[22] Richard White, *"It's Your Misfortune and None of My Own": A New History of the American West* (Norman: University of Oklahoma Press, 1991), 382.

establishment of the League of Lincoln–Roosevelt Republican Clubs in 1907. The organization devoted itself to fighting the SP for control of the state and, together with the successful passage of the direct primary law in 1909, the league laid the groundwork for victory in the 1910 election.

In San Francisco, Hiram Johnson rose to political prominence in 1906 as the prosecuting attorney in municipal corruption trials. Drawn to his anticorporate agenda, progressive Republicans selected him as their gubernatorial candidate in 1910; California voters agreed and duly elected Johnson. As he developed a reform agenda for California, Johnson sought the advice of three leading Progressives, ex-president Theodore Roosevelt, Wisconsin senator and former governor and congressman Robert La Follette, and muckraking journalist and Socialist Lincoln Steffens. Their advice helped Johnson design the program that he took into the 1911 legislative session where he secured the initiative, the referendum, and the more radical recall. He also signed into law an eight-hour working day for women, increased the regulatory power of the state railroad commission to rein in the SP by ensuring fair rates, secured a worker compensation/employer liability measure, in addition to anti–child labor legislation, pensions for senior citizens and schoolteachers, various conservation measures, and free public school textbooks. Theodore Roosevelt declared that these efforts constituted "the most comprehensive program of constructive legislation ever passed at a single session of any American legislature."[23] Roosevelt was technically correct, although the entire slate of reforms that La Follette instituted in Wisconsin in the early twentieth century was more comprehensive than even California's reform record.

Johnson served as governor from 1911 to 1917, helped form the Progressive Party in 1912 and ran as Roosevelt's vice presidential candidate, and later served in the US Senate from 1917 to 1945. Under his direction, the state became a model for social justice reform. For example, by 1913, California's newly formed Commission on Immigration and Housing was hard at work, under the direction of Simon Julius Lubin, providing sanitary facilities and schools for the state's migrant agricultural workers and their families, who had been subjected to truly horrendous labor and

[23] Earl Pomeroy, *The Pacific Slope: A History of California, Oregon, Washington, Idaho, Utah, and Nevada* (New York: Alfred A. Knopf, 1965), 204; and Mowry, *The California Progressives* (Berkeley: University of California Press, 1951), 133–157. For a good introduction to reform efforts in the Golden State, see William Deverell and Tom Sitton, eds., *California Progressivism Revisited* (Berkeley: University of California Press, 1994).

living conditions. In addition, the 1914 legislative session further augmented the state's progressive mantle, establishing a minimum wage for women and children. The expanded California social welfare system, first instituted during the Progressive Era, made the state one of the national leaders in addressing the needs of disadvantaged citizens throughout much of the century.[24]

There were serious limits to California's pro-labor program, however. In fact, the state's broad coalition of reform-minded activists feared and demonized big labor almost as much as they did the big corporations. In the same 1914 session that saw so many progressive gains, voters rejected the 8-hour day for all workers and the 6-day, 48-hour week maximum. The state government, along with newspapers such as the vehemently antilabor *LA Times*, enthusiastically championed a pro–big business, open shop climate in the state. California's mix of strong liberal and conservative impulses was well established by the early twentieth century and remains a core characteristic of the state today, a century later.

Under U'Ren's guidance, Oregon, like California, was at the cutting edge of socially progressive labor legislation, and in some respects ahead of its southern neighbor by several years, pushing through a law in 1903 providing for a maximum 10-hour working day for women. The US Supreme Court upheld the measure in 1908 in the influential *Muller v. Oregon* case. Louis Brandeis served as the attorney for the state and presented his famous "Brandeis Brief," comprising voluminous statistical evidence concerning the harmfulness of extended working days for women's health. These detrimental effects included increased numbers of workplace accidents, particularly later in the working day, and increased stillbirths suffered by pregnant employees. His approach was a classic example of emerging legal pragmatism, or sociological jurisprudence, that emphasized facts over legal precedent, and viewed the law as something that evolved to meet changing social conditions. This inherently reformist ideology was starting to supersede constitutional conservatism, an approach that dominated the late nineteenth century, opposed social justice reform, and provided generous protections for corporations from the regulatory efforts of states and municipalities. Brandeis returned to the Supreme Court on Oregon's behalf again in 1914 to successfully defend the state's creation of an Industrial Welfare Commission with the authority to establish minimum wages for women. Brandeis fought for

[24] Starr, *Inventing the Dream*, 234–235, 257–258.

these kinds of regulations on behalf of working people across the country, but his journey as a social justice reformer had begun in Oregon.

Influenced by developments in Oregon, Washington had a strong coalition of labor and farmer organizations and middle-class progressive reformers which organized into an influential pressure group, the Joint Legislative Committee. In 1910–1911, Washington reformers pushed through an impressive array of social justice reforms, including child labor laws, the eight-hour day for women, minimum wage levels for women and children, and worker's compensation.[25] In contrast, Idaho, though home to Republican senator William E. Borah, a significant Progressive force in the US Senate, where he served from 1907 to 1940, made few advances in the arena of social justice reform, partly because Borah was generally unsupportive of progressive reform at the state level.

Kansas was not as committed to social justice reform as California, Oregon, or Washington but did adopt a worker's compensation law and passed legislation in 1905 to keep children under the age of 14 out of factories, meatpacking houses, and mines; in 1909, the state raised the age to 16 for work in those hazardous occupations. The Texas legislature in 1907 expanded the state's antitrust programs and created a bureau of labor statistics, empowered to gather the necessary data to advocate for decent working conditions and compensation. In the early 1910s, the Texas legislature also provided for limitations on women's working hours, restrictions on child labor, improvements in workplace safety, and workers' compensation as well as reform of its brutal penal system.

The landscape of social justice reform was less enlightened in other parts of the Plains. South Dakota passed no legislation on behalf of worker rights. The Nebraska legislature passed a minimum wage law in 1913 but never enforced it and then repealed it in 1919. While Oklahoma enacted meaningful provisions against child labor in 1910, voters overturned a bill from the state legislature in 1913 providing for the health and safety of mine workers and rejected a comprehensive worker compensation amendment in 1916. North Dakota saw little social justice reform until the spectacular ascendancy of the Non-Partisan League in 1915. This organization of disaffected farmers imbued with socialist doctrines seized control of the legislature and governor's office that year, augmented its majority in the 1918 elections, and implemented workers' compensation and a graduated income tax.

[25] Schwantes, *The Pacific Northwest*, 275; and Robert E. Ficken and Charles P. LeWarne, *Washington: A Centennial History* (Seattle: University of Washington Press, 1988), 81.

In the Rocky Mountain West, Wyoming adopted worker compensation laws in 1914, during the reform governorship of Joseph M. Carey (1911–1915). In Montana, the eight-hour workday for public works projects, as well as mills, smelters, and underground mines, was enacted as early as 1904.[26] Colorado voters instituted an eight-hour workday for women workers in 1912, along with the same provision for underground miners and those working in smelters and coke ovens. In 1914 Coloradans voted to relieve employees from assuming risk of injury or death in workplaces, though that year was memorable more for the terrible massacre of striking coal miners and their families at Ludlow. In neighboring Utah, maximum hour legislation in 1911 and minimum wage standards were instituted in 1913, but only for women and child laborers. Between 1909 and 1912, the Nevada legislature instituted the eight-hour day for more dangerous occupations, along with workers' compensation, and the office of mine inspector was created to oversee safety standards.

In the Southwest, Arizona's pro-labor Governor George Hunt pushed child labor legislation through the legislature in 1912, and the state was the first to institute old age pensions – nine years ahead of Montana, Nevada, and Pennsylvania. But the new state's voters proved less committed to worker needs and in 1916 rejected an amendment that would have regulated hazardous workplaces and occupations, provided for worker's compensation for injuries, and established an Industrial Accident Board. Arizonans also resoundingly rejected an initiative to establish a Department of Labor and, two years later, overwhelmingly defeated an amendment providing for worker's compensation for those in hazardous occupations and creating an Industrial Accident Fund. New Mexico's record was even less impressive; child labor and worker compensation legislation did not go into effect there until the 1920s.

The West in 1910 was home to only 36 of the nation's 413 social settlement houses, including 22 in California, 8 in Texas, and 4 in Colorado. That number represented only 8.7 percent of the total, but that was hardly surprising given that the region, for all its rapid urban growth, still had far fewer large cities than the Northeast or Midwest.[27] Indeed, the presence of these settlement houses, important centers of social support for the urban working poor and jobless, in the three western states

[26] That same year, 1904, Montana voters rejected a bill providing for worker compensation in extrahazardous industries.

[27] Robert A. Woods and Albert J. Kennedy, *Handbook of Settlements* (New York: Charities Publication Committee/Russell Sage Foundation, 1911).

that housed the region's largest cities, when considered together with the legislative activity in those states and across much of the rest of the region, suggests that social justice reform was a truly significant part of the West's reform landscape. Another western progressive landmark was the work of Judge Benjamin Barr Lindsey in creating Denver's juvenile court in 1901, which became a model for the nation in developing a juvenile justice system. Overall, the West's achievements in social justice reform were less impressive than advances in political democracy, but they were certainly on a par with achievements in the Mid-Atlantic, Northeast, and Midwest, and more extensive than those in the South.

Western Injustice

Concurrent with these efforts across much of the West to secure direct democracy and social justice reform, there were numerous examples of cultural intolerance and social injustice. For all the rhetoric lauding the benefits of giving greater voice to "the people" and all the legislation that ensured their voices and opinions would matter, popular mainstream conceptions in the West of who "the people" were could be quite limited. Furthermore, measures that are better described as manifestations of social control than as social justice may have characterized the West even more markedly than the nation during the period. Perhaps the most striking and disturbing example was manifest in eugenic pseudo-science-inspired sexual sterilization statutes, which were applied to the mentally challenged and sometimes to habitual criminals. Such legislation was more readily embraced in the western states than in any other region during the Progressive Era. Of the first 16 states in the country to enact such measures between 1907 and 1917, fully half were western: Washington (1909), California (1909), Nevada (1912), North Dakota (1913), Kansas (1913), Nebraska (1915), Oregon (1917), and South Dakota (1917). Montana (1923), Idaho (1925), Utah (1925), Arizona (1929), and Oklahoma (1931) later followed course. From the early twentieth century through the 1960s, California led the nation in the numbers of people sterilized.[28] More politically significant and wide reaching, though, than the movement to limit the reproductive capacity of some human bodies

[28] J. H. Landman, *Human Sterilization: The History of the Sexual Sterilization Movement* (New York: Macmillan, 1932), 291–293; and Natalia Molina, *Fit to Be Citizens? Public Health and Race in Los Angeles, 1879–1939* (Berkeley: University of California Press, 2006), 147.

was the movement to limit what people could ingest into their bodies. Moreover, the two movements – eugenics and prohibition – were both part of the larger Progressive obsession with hygiene: clean government, streets, homes, and water supplies, as well as clean gene pools, bodies, and bloodstreams.

Supporters of prohibition were most likely to reside in the South and the West.[29] Indeed, voters and politicians in those regions effectively imposed the Eighteenth Amendment and the Volstead Act, which codified the new constitutional reality, on the rest of the nation. Between January 1915 and November 1917 – that is, before the Eighteenth Amendment was put up for ratification by states at the beginning of 1918 – Arizona (1915), the Pacific Northwest states of Oregon, Washington, and Idaho (all in 1916), as well as the Plains states of Kansas and Nebraska (both in 1917) and South Dakota (1916), the Mountain states of Colorado and Montana (both in 1916), and Utah (1917) had all enacted prohibition by popular vote or legislative action. Nevada, New Mexico, North Dakota, Oklahoma, and Texas all imposed statewide restrictions on alcohol prior to the amendment, though all still allowed for its legal purchase. Things were different in California, where voters rejected prohibition by defeating initiated prohibition amendments to the state constitution in 1914, 1915, 1917, and 1918. Indeed, among the western states where women were enfranchised prior to 1919, only California and Wyoming opposed prohibition and remained unrestrictedly "wet" prior to the constitutional amendment. The fears of wet opponents of women's suffrage were to some degree realized: there was a direct causal relationship between suffrage and prohibition in much of the West; western women did tend to vote against alcohol.

The regional lodestone of Great Plains prohibition was the state of Kansas, where the indefatigable axe-wielding, barrel-busting Carry Nation led the charge in preserving the perceived moral integrity of the Sunflower State, which had been dry since 1880. The West was clearly at the leading edge of the prohibition movement, and along with the South, the region was responsible for drying up the country as a whole, through the efforts of the WCTU and the Anti-Saloon League. Prohibition in the West, just as in the rest of the nation, reflected an urban–rural divide, concerns over industrial efficiency and family abuse, and, to some degree, the cultural fears of the white Anglo-Saxon Protestant (WASP)

[29] Michael E. Parrish, *Anxious Decades: America in War and Depression, 1920–1941* (New York: W. W. Norton, 1992), 97.

American mainstream that became magnified as the nation diversified demographically.

Prohibition would probably not have become the law of the land had the movement's highlighting of racial and ethnic stereotypes – of Irish whiskey drinkers, German beer swillers, Eastern European vodka toasters, Greek and Italian winos, and alcohol-aroused African Americans and other racial minority groups – not resonated so strongly with older-stock Americans. The West may not have been as fractured by the ethnocultural divides that characterized the political arenas of the Northeast and Midwest, but the region was at the leading edge of prohibition.[30] Prohibition in turn, on the national level, certainly was a manifestation of the cultural conflicts and racial and ethnic tensions that developed as the American populace became increasingly diverse. But prohibition efforts proved merely the tip of the iceberg when it came to cultural injustice and intolerance in the West.

Japanese migrants, coming from Hawaii as well as mainland Japan, began arriving in West Coast cities in significant numbers at the start of the new century, finding work as laborers and truck farmers, and starting in 1910, Japanese women began arriving as picture brides. Around 24,000 Japanese resided in the nation in 1900, but by 1910, that figure had tripled to over 72,000 and grown to 110,000 by 1920. The vast majority of Japanese in the United States resided on the West Coast, from Seattle to Southern California, though some moved into the Inter-Mountain West.[31] While the Chinese immigration restriction legislation of 1882, 1888, and 1892, and a series of violent anti-Chinese race riots across the West in the 1880s, had limited their demographic growth, the Chinese still outnumbered the Japanese in the region in the early twentieth century.[32] Add to this demographic montage the many Native peoples, whose populations were increasing in number after the demographic nadir of 1890 to 1900, as well as African Americans fleeing the Jim Crow South, and it becomes evident that the Progressive Era West was the nation's most racially diverse region.

30 White, in *"It's Your Misfortune,"* 359–362, emphasizes that the West was less ethnoculturally fractured than those other regions.

31 Nugent, *Into the West*, 165–167.

32 Contemporaries referred to the 1882 legislation as the "Chinese Restriction Act"; full exclusion was not enacted until 1888; see Beth Lew-Williams, "Before Restriction Became Exclusion: America's Experiment in Diplomatic Immigration Control," *Pacific Historical Review* 83 (February 2014): 24–56.

Unfortunately, from the Great Plains to the Pacific Coast, manifestations of cultural intolerance marred notions of the West as a promised land for all. In fact, early-twentieth-century American boosters presented the northern West as a wonderland *of* whiteness, claiming the region was largely untainted by the presence of peoples of color. Meanwhile, promoters depicted California and the Southwest as wonderlands *for* whiteness – places where the presence of racial diversity could not be denied but where Native Americans and Hispanics were thoroughly subservient and white Europeans could enjoy complete dominance.[33] Regional promoters in Southern California made the "Spanish fantasy past" a feature of their efforts, constructing a romantic Californian and Native American backdrop for the city and presenting it to the public in the form of parades such as La Fiesta de Los Angeles, which began in the mid 1890s, and the massively popular *Mission Play*, which opened in 1912. The city was thoroughly dominated by Anglos, while its growing Mexican population was thoroughly marginalized and had no place in the colorful booster books and posters full of radiant sunshine, oranges, and roses.[34]

Western race relations were considerably more complicated and fraught than the boosters' visions suggested. For example, antimiscegenation laws to prevent the marriage of blacks and whites were enacted in Oklahoma (1897), Montana, North Dakota, and South Dakota (all in 1909), and Wyoming (1913). Such laws were already long established in Arizona, California, Colorado, Idaho, Nebraska, Nevada, Oregon, and Utah prior to the Progressive Era. In this unfortunate category of legislative activity, the West did not lead the nation, but it certainly failed to depart from national trends. The West in this period was distinctive in its combination of exclusion of most minorities from the political process and its simultaneous inclusion of women.[35]

[33] Wrobel, *Promised Lands*, 173–176. This was much in line with how British cultural propaganda presented the subject populations of India and other colonies around the globe.

[34] William Deverell, "Privileging the Mission over the Mexican: The Rise of Regional Identity in Southern California," in *Many Wests: Place, Culture, and Regional Identity*, ed. David M. Wrobel and Michael C. Steiner (Lawrence: University Press of Kansas, 1997), 235–258; and William Deverell and Douglas Flamming, "Race, Rhetoric, and Regional Identity: Boosting Los Angeles, 1880–1930," in *Power and Place in the North American West*, ed. Richard White and John M. Findlay (Seattle: University of Washington Press, 1999), 117–143.

[35] See White, *"It's Your Misfortune,"* 353.

In 1900, Progressive reformer and Stanford sociology professor Edward Ross and San Francisco's Mayor James Duval Phelan spoke at the nation's first anti-Japanese rally, an event sponsored by the city's Labor Council. Both the professor and politician applied the same arguments that had been leveled for decades against the Chinese, insisting the Japanese were unassimilable and willing to work for such low wages that they undercut white labor. Ross and Phelan prophesied the standard doomsday scenarios if the Japanese menace was not dealt with, invoking the lesson of the fall of Rome to underscore the presumed threat to American democracy. Thus, the city's leaders helped generate the heightened anti-Japanese sentiment that would escalate in 1905 and 1906 and develop into an anti-Japanese riot in 1907 as civic leaders and white residents sought to segregate Japanese students in the city's schools. President Roosevelt brokered the "Gentleman's Agreement" with Japan that year to diffuse the tensions, and the school board eventually agreed to abandon its segregation program once Japan placed tighter restrictions on emigration to the United States.[36]

Anti-Japanese sentiment continued to develop, however, as Japanese immigrants bought or leased land in California, Oregon, and Washington and quickly established themselves as vital contributors to the agricultural economies of those states. Japanese intensive farming techniques proved so effective that on just 1 percent of California's agricultural lands, they were responsible for fully 10 percent of the value of the state's agricultural production. White Californians, led by Governor Hiram Johnson, responded with the passage of the Webb–Henry Act, or Alien Land Law, a statute specifically designed to limit Japanese leasing and purchasing of land. In 1920, through a referendum and with a 3–1 majority, Californians further narrowed the opportunity for Japanese leasing and landholding. The Nisei, those Japanese who were American-born, had circumvented the law by leasing land themselves and by having their Issei (Japanese-born) parents transfer lands to them, but the 1920 law curtailed those practices.[37] Washington's residents passed similar legislation in 1921, and Oregon's voters followed the same path of intolerance in 1923.

[36] Kevin Starr, *Embattled Dreams: California in War and Peace, 1940–1950* (New York: Oxford University Press, 2002), 41–42.

[37] Valerie J. Matsumoto, *Farming the Home Place: A Japanese American Community in California, 1919–1982* (Ithaca, NY: Cornell University Press, 1983), 25; and Nugent, *Into the West*, 168.

Interestingly, while Californians were closing loopholes to the original 1913 anti-Japanese law and thereby demonstrating their intolerance of racial diversity, D. W. Griffith was filming his second historical epic in the nation's emerging moviemaking capital, Hollywood. Griffith's massively successful and influential 1915 film *The Birth of a Nation*, based on Thomas Dixon's 1905 novel *The Clansman: An Historical Romance of the Ku Klux Klan*, had presented a deeply racist, pro-Klan vision of the Reconstruction Era South. Largely in response to criticism that *The Birth of a Nation* was racist, a wounded Griffith decided to chronicle and critique the long human history of intolerance from Ancient Babylon to the American present to promote a spirit of cultural tolerance. The resulting 1916 film *Intolerance*, however, turned out to be a resounding critical and commercial failure, and it marked the beginning of Griffith's decline, just as *The Birth of a Nation* had marked the start of Hollywood's remarkable ascendancy.[38]

For all the social justice and direct democracy reforms of the Progressive Era, it was a time of deep racial and cultural divides. From the Texas legislature's introduction of the poll tax in 1902, which effectively disenfranchised large numbers of African American voters, and Theodore Roosevelt's court-martialing of an entire regiment of black troops (167 soldiers in total) who had been falsely accused of starting a riot in Brownsville, Texas, to the alien land laws later passed in the Pacific Coast states, the West was at least as much a landscape of intolerance as one of progress.[39] In the wake of the real racial failings of Reconstruction and the so-called New South, black southerners moved to the North and the West (including Kansas, Colorado, Oklahoma, and the Pacific Coast) in large numbers to improve their circumstances. The railroads played a vital role in bringing African Americans to the West. While the region's promised lands generally failed to fully live up to black boosters' halcyon visions, the New West's cities, towns, and farmlands did provide black migrants a higher quality of life and freedom than they had known, and they developed thriving neighborhoods and established newspapers that helped build community.[40] Thus the black leader

[38] Starr, *Inventing the Dream*, 302–308.

[39] The Texas poll tax was of course as much a manifestation of the race-based policies of the Progressive South as those of the Progressive West.

[40] Nell Irving Painter, *Exodusters: Black Migration to Kansas after Reconstruction* (New York: W. W. Norton, 1976); Quintard Taylor, *In Search of the Racial Frontier: African Americans in the American West, 1528–1900* (New York: W. W. Norton, 1998), and *The Forging of a Black Community: Seattle's Central District from 1870 through the*

W. E. B. Du Bois, founding editor of the NAACP's journal *The Crisis*, declared in July 1913 that "nowhere in the United States was the Negro so well and beautifully housed." But the following month, Du Bois cautioned his readers that Los Angeles was "not Paradise," though it was nonetheless a great improvement over the Jim Crow South.[41]

The demographic and agricultural growth of the West had particularly adverse consequences for Native Americans. In the post-Reconstruction era, the federal government backed away from its efforts to regulate southern race relations, essentially enabling systematic segregation, disenfranchisement, and violent repression. Meanwhile, the government pursued a policy of assimilation through the Dawes Severalty Act, Indian boarding schools, and growing restrictions of cultural practices. The legislation was implemented among most Native nations in the West, though not in Oklahoma and Indian Territory. Native Americans acquired individual ownership of formerly tribal holdings through the Dawes Act, but surplus lands were subsequently opened to white settlement. With the Supreme Court's unanimous decision in *Lone Wolf v. Hitchcock* (1903), Congress was given the power to "abrogate the provisions of an Indian treaty." Within just a few years of the court's sweeping ruling, additional Indian lands were made available to settlers on the Rosebud (South Dakota – Sioux), Uintah (Utah – Northern Ute), Crow (Montana), Flathead (Montana – Salish and Kootenai), and Wind River (Wyoming – Eastern Shoshone and Northern Arapaho) reservations. In 1908, nearly 3 million additional acres on the Standing Rock (North and South Dakota – Sioux) and Cheyenne River (South Dakota – Sioux) reservations were secured for white settlers. Millions more acres were opened to leasing by non-Natives during the Progressive Era.[42] The dissolution of the sovereign governments of the Five Civilized Tribes in eastern Oklahoma began in 1898 with the Curtis Act, which mandated the termination

Civil Rights Era (Seattle: University of Washington Press, 1994); Albert Broussard, *Black San Francisco: The Struggle for Racial Equality in the West, 1900–1954* (Lawrence: University Press of Kansas, 1993); Douglas Flamming, *Bound for Freedom: Black Los Angeles in Jim Crow America* (Berkeley: University of California Press, 2005); Tiya Miles and Sharon P. Holland, eds., *Crossing Waters, Crossing Worlds: The African Diaspora in Indian Country* (Durham, NC: Duke University Press, 2006).

41 W. E. B. Du Bois, *The Crisis*, July 1913, quoted in Josh Sides, *L.A. City Limits: African American Los Angeles from the Great Depression to the Present* (Berkeley: University of California Press, 2003), 11; and W. E. B. Du Bois, "Colored California," *The Crisis* (August 1913): 192–193, cited in Deverell and Flamming, "Race, Rhetoric, and Regional Identity," 131.

42 See Frederick Hoxie, *A Final Promise: The Campaign to Assimilate the Indians, 1880–1920* (Lincoln: University of Nebraska Press, 1984).

of tribal governments by the spring of 1906; this was "the most important instance of Indian land loss in the twentieth century."[43]

Federal acquiescence to the segregation and disenfranchisement of African Americans in the South and the federal policy of assimilation of Native peoples in the West seem at first glance to be antithetical positions; the impulse behind them was not so dissimilar, however. In both cases the government was essentially abandoning a sizeable minority population in an entire region of the country to the will of the political and racial majority. African Americans, so the misguided reasoning went, with the Thirteenth, Fourteenth, and Fifteenth Amendments in place, had the legal foundations to fend for themselves in the South. Likewise, Native Americans, with the Dawes Act and its accompanying pathway to assimilation in place, could do the same in the West without special protections from the federal government. Politicians and reformers favoring the dispossession of Indians argued that the very example of white farmers working the land that Native peoples had formerly owned would facilitate the Americanization process through positive example. When western politicians introduced their plans for opening additional Native lands, they received easy approval in Congress and, predictably enough, an enthusiastic response from settlers and local businessmen.[44]

At the time of the passage of the Dawes Act in 1887, Native American nations owned 138 million acres of land in the United States (an area as large as the entire states of Nevada and Colorado combined). By 1934, when the Indian New Deal began the process of restoring Indian lands to tribal ownership, Native landholdings had been reduced by almost two-thirds, to around 48 million acres. Thus the Dawes Act, regardless of the motivations of its many proponents, that ran the spectrum from genuine humanitarian concern to base land hunger and racism, facilitated a land grab of truly massive proportions. Developments in the Progressive Era West proved as devastating for Native peoples as those in the Progressive Era South did for African Americans.

Meanwhile another of the great migrations into the West further exacerbated racial tensions in the region. The whole Progressive Era, and particularly the decade 1910 to 1920, saw a massive influx into Texas, the Southwest, and California, especially into the cities of El Paso, San Antonio, Tucson, and San Diego, of more than 1 million Mexicans – about 10 percent of that nation's population – fleeing their country's

43 Donald L. Parman, *Indians and the American West in the Twentieth Century* (Bloomington: Indiana University Press, 1994), 52.

44 Hoxie, *A Final Promise*, 165.

violent revolution. Anti-Hispanic sentiment was a well-entrenched feature in this region prior to the Mexican Revolution.[45] In fact, the poll tax instituted in Texas in 1902 was directed not only at that state's African American population but also at its Tejano, or Mexican heritage, residents. Furthermore, Mexican American populations in New Mexico and Texas were losing their lands in Anglo-dominated courts in this period; many were forced into farm tenancy, mining, and other wage labor.

Amid the revolutionary turmoil in the region, a group of Tejano leaders met in the South Texas town of San Diego in late February 1915 to organize a revolt. They did so in response to repressive Anglo-Texan dominance and with support from Mexican president Venustiano Carranza. Their bold agenda, laid out in the "Plan de San Diego," was to free the Southwest's people of color from Texas to California – Mexicans, as well as Indians and African Americans – from US rule, restore the lands to their original occupants, and remove all "North Americans" from the region. Raids from Mexico into Texas began that July, numbered around 30 in total, and generally included dozens of participants and occasionally as many as a hundred. The raids resulted in the killing of 21 white Texans and precipitated a wave of repressive violence by the Texas Rangers and local Anglo vigilantes against Tejano communities across the southern part of the state. That response was facilitated by the support of Mexican forces after October 1915, when President Wilson extended recognition to the Carranza administration.

The Plan de San Diego itself was uncompromisingly harsh. It included the provisions that "every North American over 16 years of age shall be put to death; and only the aged men, the women, and the children shall be respected; and on no account shall the traitors to our race be spared or respected." Although the document's creators and the forces that mobilized amounted to only a tiny fraction of the border region's Tejano and Mexican populations, the brutal and systematic reprisals carried out by North Americans resulted in the death of at least several hundred Tejanos, according to federal records. The number of Tejanos and Mexicans killed, however, may have been as high as 5,000, resulting in the ethnic cleansing of some parts of the region.[46]

[45] Etulain, *Beyond the Missouri: The Story of the American West* (Albuquerque: University of New Mexico Press, 2006), 308.

[46] Benjamin Heber Johnson, *Revolution in Texas: How a Forgotten Rebellion and Its Bloody Suppression Turned Mexicans into Americans* (New Haven, CT: Yale University Press, 2003), 1–3. For a fuller discussion, with emphasis on the manipulation of the movement by Carranza, see Charles H. Harris III and Louis R. Sadler, *The Plan*

The border violence continued when Mexican revolutionary leader Pancho Villa launched a raid on Columbus, New Mexico, in March 1916, prompting President Wilson to send a US expedition across the border to apprehend Villa. It was in the context of these border tensions, and the recent US military incursion into Mexico, that the German government sought a Mexican declaration of war against the United States, promising that Mexico would, once its northern neighbor was defeated, reacquire the southwestern lands it had lost after the Mexican–American War. The Zimmermann Telegram from the German foreign secretary Arthur Zimmermann to the German ambassador in Mexico created a storm of controversy in the United States after its interception in January 1917 and helped lead the country into World War I.

While the West's record in social justice reform measured up well with such efforts in other regions, by the second decade of the new century, the intolerance of the West's majority white population toward peoples of color found its own parallel in an increasing intolerance for organized labor and leftist ideologies and their adherents. If western progressives had been more fully committed to helping workers during the years leading up to American entry into the war, there would have been less opportunity for radical elements to take up their cause.[47] Founded in 1893, the radical Western Federation of Miners (WFM) pushed for worker rights in the Inter-Mountain West, most notably in Cripple Creek, Colorado during 1903–1904, and in 1905, the even more radical Industrial Workers of the World (IWW), or "Wobblies," developed out of the WFM and waged the struggle nationwide. The IWW was particularly active in the West and participated in strikes that turned violent from the hop fields of California's Central Valley (1913), to the copper mines of Butte, Montana, and Bisbee, Arizona, (1917), the lumber mills of Evergreen (1916), and the forests of Centralia, Washington (1919).

From 1915, the Nonpartisan League pushed its radical pro-farmer, anticorporate socialist agenda in North Dakota and achieved its greatest success in 1918, sweeping the state elections and implementing a good deal of its program. Oklahoma, with its large numbers of exploited and impoverished tenant farmers, by 1908 was home to the largest socialist party in the nation and by 1910 comprised roughly 10 percent of the

de San Diego: Tejano Rebellion, Mexican Intrigue (Lincoln: University of Nebraska Press, 2013). The text of the document is available at: www.digitalhistory.uh.edu/disp_textbook.cfm?smtid=3&psid=3692 accessed January 11, 2016.

47 Malone and Peterson, "Politics and Protests," 510.

party's membership nationwide. Five socialist representatives and one senator were elected to the state legislature in 1914.[48] In short, radical solutions to the real needs of working people manifested more readily in the West than nationwide, and the region experienced some of the most memorable farmer and labor organizing efforts of the era, as well as its most violent striking and strikebreaking.

The most tragic of these labor conflicts played out in spring 1914 in the town of Ludlow, Colorado, where roughly 900 striking coal miners and family members, representing a dozen different nationalities, were camped out in a tent city. On April 20, 1914, after one side or the other fired a single shot, the Colorado National Guard, company guards and hired militia, occupying the high ground above the arroyo housing the striking workers and their families, rained machine gun and rifle fire down on them. In the accompanying chaos, tents and buildings caught on fire. Eleven children, two women, five miners, and one militia guard perished. The striking miners retaliated with a spree of violence over the next 10 days, killing 10 strikebreakers and company guards. In response to the worsening crisis, Wilson sent in federal troops. From September 1913 into December 1914, the Great Coalfield War, as the protracted struggle in Ludlow and the surrounding area became known, cost at least 75 and perhaps as many as 100 lives, including strikers, their family members, strikebreakers, and guards. Ludlow left a greater human toll than any other strike in the nation's history.[49]

World War I and the American West

By the end of the conflict in the Colorado coalfields, the Great War in Europe had been raging for months. Once the United States committed itself to the Allied cause in April 1917 and the Wilson administration mobilized to ensure 100 percent Americanism on the home front, the radical responses to the needs of small farm owners, farm laborers, and industrial workers across the West were themselves met with a

[48] H. Wayne Morgan and Anne Hodges Morgan, *Oklahoma: A Bicentennial History* (New York: W. W. Norton, 1977), 98–99; and White, *"It's Your Misfortune,"* 377.

[49] Thomas Andrews, *Killing for Coal: America's Deadliest Labor War* (Cambridge, MA: Harvard University Press, 2008), 1–19; and Duane A. Smith, *Rocky Mountain Heartland: Colorado, Montana, and Wyoming in the Twentieth Century* (Tucson: University of Arizona Press, 2008), 31. Godfrey Irwin's eyewitness account of the event can be found at: http://historymatters.gmu.edu/d/5737/ accessed January 11, 2016.

powerful conservative backlash. Federal and state agencies and private citizen groups, including the American Legion, clamped down on radicalism in no uncertain terms. The Committee on Public Information (CPI), led by Denver progressive and former police commissioner George Creel, helped create a wave of hyperpatriotism and reactionary intolerance of any ideas or activities that might threaten the war effort.

When the United States entered the war in April 1917, the West was the region least favorable to the war effort, closely followed by the Midwest. Both regions were home to significant numbers of German Americans and former residents of the Austro-Hungarian Empire in higher concentrations than in the nation at large; members of these groups tended to view the war as a capitalist conflict and the working classes as its primary victims. Two years earlier, Wilson's secretary of state, William Jennings Bryan, concerned that Wilson had placed the nation on a path to war, resigned after the president's strongly worded response to Germany following the sinking of the *Lusitania* (May 1915). Bryan became an active opponent of American military intervention. As the American war effort escalated and the CPI's activities ramped up, voices such as Bryan's were drowned out by the wave of hyperpatriotism, and the West seemed to display levels of intolerance toward labor, leftism, ethnic diversity, and German Americans that exceeded those in the nation at large. Statutes in South Dakota and parts of Nebraska, Oklahoma, and Texas suppressed the teaching of the German language in grade schools; German books were removed from school libraries, German language newspapers were shut down by "patriotic" groups, and enrollments in German classes at institutions of higher education such as the University of Colorado and the University of Oklahoma plummeted. German Americans were persecuted across the Great Plains, and hundreds of pacifist Mennonites fled the Plains states of Oklahoma, Kansas, and Nebraska for Canada. There was a push to change North Dakota's capital's name from Bismarck to something more American, but the North Dakota populace resisted it.[50]

The Bolshevik Revolution in Russia in early November 1917 further sparked the fires of reaction in the United States, and radical thinkers

[50] Todd M. Kerstetter, *Inspiration and Innovation: Religion in the American West* (Malden, MA: Wiley Blackwell, 2015), 178; and Christopher Capozzola, *Uncle Sam Wants You: World War I and the Making of the Modern American Citizen* (New York: Oxford University Press, 2008), 191–192.

and activists were readily targeted as revolutionary agents. The government's Bureau of Investigation (created in 1908 and renamed the Federal Bureau of Investigation, FBI, in 1935) clamped down on the IWW's strike-organizing efforts during the war, raided its offices across the West, and arrested between 150 and 200 members, including its leaders "Big Bill" Haywood and Elizabeth Gurley Flynn. IWW leader Frank Little suffered a worse fate; he was lynched by a vigilante mob in Butte. Western business interests took advantage of the atmosphere of nationalistic fervor to brand striking workers as traitors, and local authorities actively cooperated in the suppression of labor.

The nation's worst mass violation of worker civil liberties took place in July 1917 in the mining region of Bisbee, Arizona, during the heightened fear and distrust of immigrants from south of the border in the wake of the Zimmerman Telegram. The previous month, more than half the 4,700 workers at the Copper Queen mine, including many of Mexican origin, joined an IWW-led strike against the Phelps-Dodge Corporation. The Cochise County sheriff, Henry E. Wheeler, deputized 2,000 men from the Citizens Protective League, an organization comprising business leaders and members of the local middle class and men from the Workmen's Loyalty League, a group consisting of nonstriking workers along with hundreds of Pinkerton detectives. The sheriff even deputized the president of Phelps-Dodge. The large civilian force rounded up the strikers and family members, transported them to a local baseball field, forced 1,200 of them onto a train at gunpoint, and "deported" them to the New Mexico desert town of Hermanas.[51]

The following month in southeastern Oklahoma's Canadian River Valley, an antidraft movement comprising perhaps as many as 1,000 African American and white tenant farmers as well as Creeks and Seminoles took up arms and planned to march to the nation's capital to lobby against the Wilson administration's war policy. Local sheriffs and militia forces quickly put down the Green Corn Rebellion, so named for the food the marchers planned to eat along the way. The threatened rebellion led to systematic reprisals against the Socialist Party in Oklahoma, essentially eradicating the organization in the state. The western states also took the lead in creating criminal syndicalism laws to prosecute any antiwar

[51] Capozzola, *Uncle Sam Wants You*, 126–127; and Kathleen Benton-Cohen, *Borderline Americans: Racial Division and Labor War in the Arizona Borderlands* (Cambridge, MA: Harvard University Press, 2009).

activities or language; Montana's Sedition Act became the model for the national law enacted in 1918.[52]

The West, in many respects, had been the nation's most progressive region in the early twentieth century; however, during and immediately after World War I, the region stood in the forefront of America's reactionary turn. The swiftness of the shifting political tide was evident in the collective federal, state and local response to the Seattle General Strike in early February 1919. Across the city, 60,000 workers joined the action. Local and national newspapers portrayed the stand-off as a showdown between Americanism and Bolshevism. Pressured by the police, thousands of newly hired deputies, federal forces, the press (which helped shape the public's rejection of the general strike as a legitimate labor tactic), the city's mayor, Ole Hanson, and the more moderate American Federation of Labor, ended the strike in a mere six days. The short-lived Seattle General Strike was a far cry from Colorado's extended Coalfield War a half decade earlier.

In the wake of the Seattle strike, the Socialist Party, the IWW, and other radical groups across the West were effectively undermined by the coordinated response of government officials and conservative vigilante groups. Labor activity in general was easily dismissed as radical and unpatriotic in the atmosphere of hyper-Americanism that pervaded the postwar period. In November 1919, the governor of Kansas, Arthur Capper, encouraged the American Legion to break a coal strike. By the end of that year the recently reborn Ku Klux Klan, characterized by its strong antialien and antiradical emphases, had added perhaps 100,000 new members.[53] Theodore Roosevelt, who had protected the rights of labor during the United Mine Workers Strike, became one of the most vocal champions of the conservative response to labor radicalism in those years.[54]

Coda: TR Returns

In late 1913, little more than a year after his failed 1912 presidential campaign, Theodore Roosevelt undertook one of the most remarkable

[52] Etulain and Malone, *The American West*, 76–80; and Baird and Goble, *Oklahoma*, 182–183.

[53] Robert K. Murray, *The Red Scare: A Study in National Hysteria, 1919–1920* (1955; repr., New York: McGraw-Hill, 1964), 57–66.

[54] Capozzola, *Uncle Sam Wants You*, 212.

adventures of his life. With the West explored and largely settled, he sought challenges on untamed frontiers to parallel his experiences in the Dakotas in the 1880s. In February 1914, he and his son Kermit began a journey of almost 1,000 miles through the Brazilian rainforest, down the uncharted Rio da Dúvida, the River of Doubt, as part of a joint American–Brazilian expeditionary party. Roosevelt suffered a serious leg wound and coronary stress; delirious with fever, he asked to be left behind, to improve the others' chances of survival. Kermit refused and inspired his father to keep going. The expedition doctor performed surgery without anesthetic on Roosevelt's infected leg, probably saving his life, as well as his limb, and the explorers eventually reached safety. During the 3-month ordeal Roosevelt lost 57 pounds and remarked that he lost 10 years off his life.

Roosevelt had hoped to secure the Republican Party nomination in 1916 and run against Wilson. This would have been the ultimate triumph for Roosevelt: with the world at war, he imagined himself a new Lincoln, leading the nation through its darkest hours. But it was not to be. Roosevelt had no more influence over the Republican nominations process in 1916 than he had in 1912. Charles Evans Hughes, a Supreme Court justice and former governor of New York, secured the nomination.[55] Wilson won the election, partly on the promise of keeping the nation out of war, partly because he earned the backing of labor through his support of the Adamson Act guaranteeing the eight-hour day to interstate railroad workers, and because his 1916 income tax bill rallied support in the South and West. Many residents of the South and West viewed the income tax as redressing the regional economic imbalance of national tariff policy that favored the manufacturing regions of the Northeast and Midwest. One additional factor in the campaign was Hughes's perceived snub of Hiram Johnson, California's popular reformist governor, which may have swung the state's vote to Wilson. With California, the Republicans would have won the Electoral College. The incumbent president secured 49 percent of the vote to Hughes's 46 percent, a 600,000-vote majority, and the Democrats won the entire South and all the western states aside from Oregon and South Dakota (Map 3.2). The 1916 election was quite a reversal from 1904, when Roosevelt had won all the western states excepting Texas.

Roosevelt had advocated American entry into World War I long before Wilson's declaration, and he started labeling pacifists as un-American, but he largely withheld criticism of the president while requesting permission

[55] Brands, *T.R.*, 763–769.

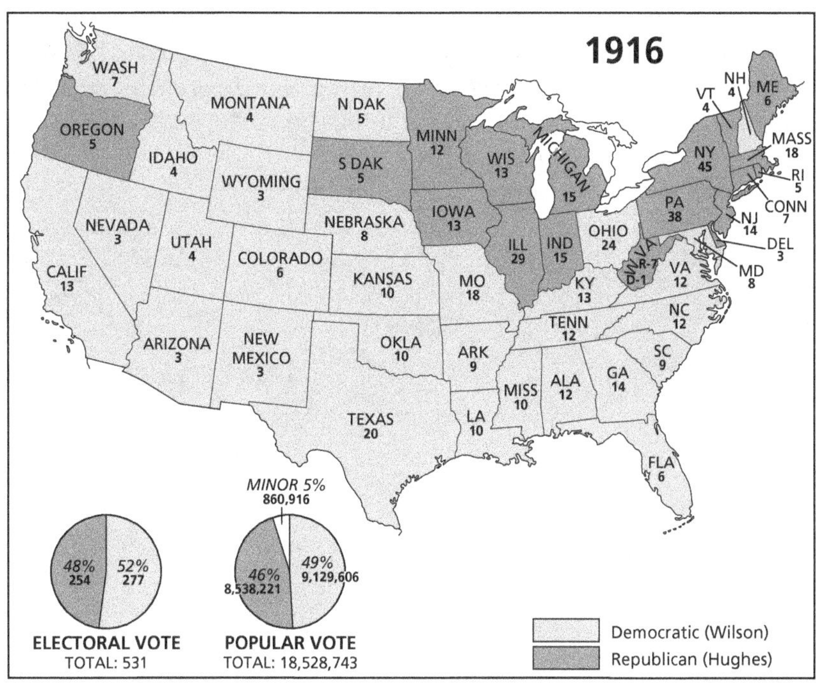

MAP 3.2 Electoral map, 1916.

to raise and lead a regiment of volunteers as he had done in Cuba two decades earlier. The administration turned down his offer, and the ex-president began deriding Wilson in a regular editorial column for the *Kansas City Star*. Roosevelt lambasted the president for not dealing more harshly with those who dissented against the war or disrupted the national economy and for failing to conduct the war mobilization effort more vigorously.[56] He later denounced the Nonpartisan League, centered in his beloved North Dakota, the site of his former ranching and hunting sojourns, as "Bolshevistic."

Roosevelt, the era's most prominent figure, both in America and across the globe, had encapsulated the promise of Progressivism as the new century dawned and had brought much of that promise to fruition, shaping the national reform agenda in vital ways. But by the time his remarkable life ended on January 6, 1919, Roosevelt had become as much a voice

[56] Ibid., 773–789. See also Theodore Roosevelt, *"America and the World War," and "Fear God and Take Your Own Part," in Works of Theodore Roosevelt*, XVIII (New York: Charles Scribner's Sons, 1926).

of reactionary, "100 percent Americanism" as any of the political and economic conservatives who had abhorred his reform agenda. The West had also shifted from its position at the apex of reform to one at the nadir of reaction. In the nation and in the West, the reform spirit that had sparked so much change in the first two decades of the century had largely dissipated.

4

Regional Growth and Cultural Conflict

The thought that Kansas should have a government beholden to this hooded gang of masked fanatics, ignorant and tyrannical in their ruthless oppression, is what calls me... into this disgraceful but necessary task.

– *Emporia Gazette* editor William Allen White, launching his gubernatorial campaign, 1924

Retraction and Growth

Once the Great War ended and the European nations began to recover and reestablish their agricultural sectors, the market for American farm exports contracted alarmingly. Unfortunately, a decline in production levels did not accompany this acute drop in demand, and consequently, prices for American crops fell and the farm sector sank into a serious depression in the early 1920s. The West was particularly impacted by these new economic realities, since many of the region's farm owners had responded to rising commodity prices during the Progressive Era and the war years by augmenting their landholdings and investing heavily in new agricultural machinery. Cotton slumped by more than half from the peak wartime price of 35 cents per pound to just 16 cents by 1920; corn plummeted by nearly two-thirds, from $1.50 to just 52 cents.[1] Even though agricultural prices picked up slightly after 1921, they remained low throughout the decade, and that new market reality combined with rising indebtedness proved devastating in some parts of the

[1] David M. Kennedy, *Freedom from Fear: The American People in Depression and War* (New York: Oxford University Press, 1999), 17.

region throughout the 1920s and 1930s. For those living in the West's agricultural regions, the depressed economic conditions of the early to mid 1930s were a continuation of those of the 1920s.

National tariff policy made the situation even worse for American farmers. The Underwood Tariff of 1913 had passed Congress with strong support from the West, the South, and President Wilson and reduced rates considerably. However, the outbreak of war in Europe the following year disrupted regular trade patterns; it is thus difficult to determine the impact of the Underwood Act. The war years had been particularly good ones for the American farm sector, but that changed once the Republicans regained control of Congress in the 1920 election. The Emergency Tariff Act of 1921 and the Fordney–McCumber Tariff Act of 1922 raised tariff rates across the board, generally benefiting American manufacturers and adversely impacting farmers. Since foreign countries responded to higher tariff rates in the United States by raising tariff rates on the commodities the United States was trying to export, overseas markets for the nation's agricultural goods contracted significantly.

The farm sector pushed back against the downturn in prices with a plan designed to restore "parity" with the other sectors major of the economy (e.g., heavy industry and manufacturing). Parity, in the estimation of agricultural producers, essentially meant a restoration of the commodity price levels of the prewar and war years (though those levels were unusually high). Oregon senator Charles McNary and Iowa representative Gilbert Haugen introduced a bill into Congress designed to raise prices on agricultural goods. The plan was to have the federal government pay farmers at the higher parity price for as much of their produce as was needed to meet domestic demand and then dump the surplus on overseas markets at the lower world market price. As the bill worked its way through Congress, however, the costs of the program were shifted from the farm sector to the transportation and processing companies.[2]

The McNary–Haugen Bill that emerged amounted to a massive set of subsidies for farmers, financed by the government and other sectors of the economy. Coolidge vetoed the measure twice, much to the frustration of the agrarian sector in general, and the West, where more than 70 percent of US House representatives and more than three-quarters of senators from the region had voted for the bill in 1927.[3] The president

[2] Michael E. Parrish, *Anxious Decades: America in War and Depression, 1920–1941* (New York: W. W. Norton, 1992), 86–88.

[3] In the House, 52 of 73 western representatives voted for the bill, 19 voted against, and two abstained; in the Senate, 26 of 34 voted in favor, and 7 against, with 1 abstention.

was probably right to do so, since the bill's constitutionality – forcing one sector of the economy to directly subsidize another – was questionable, as was the plan to dump surpluses overseas. This was much easier said than done during a time of tariff restrictions and when agricultural surpluses were becoming the norm globally. Most significantly, though, the McNary–Haugen Bill did nothing to discourage farmers from creating further surpluses; in fact, by subsidizing a high domestic price for American farm goods, the federal government would have encouraged them to produce more. Coolidge offered no alternative plan to help American farmers, and their circumstances continued to worsen in the 1920s. This trend was evident in much of the West's agrarian sector.[4]

Nonetheless, as the farm sector declined and the western homesteading boom ended across most parts of the West in the immediate postwar years, the center of the national population continued to move in a westerly direction. As the extractive sector of the western industrial economy – including coal and oil – expanded in the 1920s, the strong demand for labor meant that wages were higher than in the East.[5] The region's towns and cities attracted new migrants in extraordinarily large numbers, including tens of thousands of former rural dwellers escaping the agricultural depression. Commenting on these trends as they developed, historian John Carl Parish wrote in 1926 about "The Persistence of the Westward Movement" and correctly predicted that the region would continue to become home to an increasing proportion of the national population. Parish also offered the remarkable statistic that the growth of even the massive metropolises of the East and Midwest had been dwarfed in the period from 1890 to 1920 by that of two West Coast cities: Seattle, which had increased by a 636 percent, and Los Angeles, which had grown by 1,044 percent, over those three decades.[6]

Los Angeles County saw the most impressive growth in the nation during the 1910s and 1920s. Between 1910 and 1930 the national population grew by a healthy 33.5 percent; meanwhile, the population of the Census West (which excludes the Plains states) grew at the even more impressive rate of 53.8 percent, adding more than 3.5 million new residents. However, California's population increased during these two decades by 138.7 percent, and Los Angeles County's by a staggering

4 Parrish, *Anxious Decades*, 86–88.

5 William G. Robbins, *Colony and Empire: The Capitalist Transformation of the American West* (Lawrence: University Press of Kansas, 1994), 152.

6 John Carl Parish, "The Persistence of the Westward Movement," *The Yale Review* XV (April 1926): 461–477, esp. 467.

State/Decade	1900	1910	1920	1930	1940	1950
Alaska	NA	NA	NA	NA	NA	NA
Arizona	122,931	204,354	334,162	435,573	499,261	749,587
California	1,485,053	2,377,549	3,426,861	5,677,791	6,907,387	10,586,223
Colorado	539,700	799,024	939,629	1,035,791	1,123,296	1,325,089
Hawaii	NA	NA	NA	NA	NA	NA
Idaho	161,722	325,594	431,866	445,866	524,873	588,637
Kansas	1,470,495	1,690,949	1,769,257	1,880,999	1,801,028	1,905,299
Montana	243,329	376,053	548,889	537,606	559,456	591,024
Nebraska	1,069,300	1,192,214	1,296,372	1,377,963	1,315,834	1,325,510
Nevada	42,335	81,875	77,407	91,058	110,247	160,083
New Mexico	195,310	327,301	360,350	423,317	531,818	681,187
North Dakota	319,146	577,056	646,872	680,845	641,935	619,636
Oklahoma	790,391	1,657,155	2,028,283	2,396,040	2,336,434	2,233,351
Oregon	413,536	672,765	783,389	953,786	1,089,684	1,521,341
South Dakota	401,570	583,888	636,547	692,849	642,961	652,740
Texas	3,048,710	3,896,542	4,663,228	5,584,715	6,414,824	7,711,194
Utah	276,749	373,351	449,396	507,847	550,310	688,862
Washington	518,103	1,141,990	1,356,621	1,729,205	1,901,974	2,005,552
Wyoming	92,531	145,965	194,402	225,565	250,742	290,529

FIGURE 4.1 Population of the western states, 1900–1950.

338 percent, fully 10 times the national rate. In fact, LA County's population increase of 1.7 million in this period nearly equaled the increase of 1.77 million in the remainder of the Census West (excluding California). By 1920, Los Angeles had become the West's largest city, with a population of nearly 577,000, about 70,000 more than San Francisco; LA County had around 936,000 residents by this date. But most of the meteoric LA County growth came during the 1920s, when the population increased by an average of more than 124,000 people each year, many coming from the Midwestern states of Iowa, Illinois, and Ohio, of white European extraction, and a good number of them retirees and quite socially conservative. In fact, Los Angeles had the highest proportion of residents over the age of 45 of the nation's 10 largest cities. By 1930, the City of Los Angeles had approximately 1.24 million residents, which

City	1900	1910	1920	1930	1940	1950
Albuquerque	6,238	11,020	15,157	26,570	35,449	96,815
Billings	3,221	10,301	15,000	16,380	23,261	31,824
Boise	5,957	17,358	21,393	21,544	26,130	34,393
Cheyenne	14,087	11,320	13,829	17,361	22,474	31,935
Colorado Springs	21,085	29,078	30,105	33,237	36,789	45,472
Dallas	42,638	92,104	158,976	260,475	294,734	434,462
Denver	133,859	213,381	256,491	287,861	322,412	415,786
El Paso	15,906	39,279	77,560	102,421	96,810	130,485
Fargo	9,589	14,331	21,961	28,619	32,580	38,256
Fort Worth	26,688	73,312	106,482	163,447	177,662	278,778
Houston	44,633	78,800	138,276	292,352	384,514	596,163
Kansas City, KS	51,418	82,331	101,177	121,857	121,458	129,533
Las Vegas	25	945	2,304	5,165	8422	24,624
Los Angeles	102,479	319,198	576,673	1,238,048	1,504,277	1,970,358
Oakland	66,960	150,174	216,261	284,063	302,163	384,575
Oklahoma City	10,037	64,205	91,295	185,389	204,424	243,504
Omaha	102,555	124,096	191,601	214,006	223,844	251,117
Phoenix	5,544	11,134	29,053	48,118	65,414	106,818
Portland	90,426	207,214	258,288	301,815	305,394	373,628
Reno	4,500	10,867	12,016	18,529	21,317	32,497
Salt Lake City	53,531	92,777	118,110	140,267	149,934	182,121
San Antonio	53,321	96,614	161,379	231,542	263,854	408,442
San Diego	17,700	39,578	74,361	147,995	203,341	334,287
San Francisco	342,782	416,912	506,676	634,394	634,536	775,357
San Jose	21,500	28,946	39,642	57,651	68,457	95,280
Seattle	80,671	237,194	315,312	365,583	368,302	467,591
Sioux Falls	10,266	14,094	25,202	33,362	40,832	52,696
Spokane	36,484	104,402	104,437	115,514	122,001	161,721
Tucson	7,531	13,193	20,292	32,506	35,752	45,454
Tulsa	1,390	18,182	72,075	141,258	142,157	182,740
Wichita	24,671	52,450	72,217	111,110	114,966	168,279

FIGURE 4.2 Western urban growth, 1900–1950. Data from Richard W. Etulain, *Beyond the Missouri: The Story of the American West* (Albuquerque: University of New Mexico Press, 2006), 306.

was nearly double the size of San Francisco, and the city's population accounted for just 56 percent of the county, which had become home to over 2.2 million residents[7] (Figures 4.1 and 4.2).

During the 1920s, Southern California also attracted more than a quarter of a million people from the southwestern states of Arkansas, Missouri, Oklahoma, and Texas. Mostly lower-middle-class, conservative, evangelical Protestants, they were refugees from a depressed regional agricultural economy and precursors of an even larger exodus from the

[7] Walter Nugent, *Into the West: The Story of Its People* (New York: Alfred A. Knopf, 1999), 219; and Michael P. Malone, *The American West: A Modern History, 1900 to the Present*, 2nd ed. (Lincoln: University of Nebraska Press, 207), 81.

region in the following decade.[8] They provided the demographic foundations for one of Southern California's most important movements during the decade: religious revivalism. Aimee Semple McPherson put the spectacle back into religious services as she espoused her Four Square Gospel in LA's 5,000-plus seat Angelus Temple from 1922 to 1926, and on the radio. She disappeared in 1926 and, when she reemerged several weeks later, claimed to have been kidnapped; some reporters claimed she was having an affair. The Reverend Robert P. ("Fighting Bob") Shuler offered less in the way of showmanship – he considered McPherson a "charlatan" – but he provided plenty of traditional fiery Methodist opposition to alcohol, evolution, movies, jazz music, prostitution, and other purported sins, which enabled him to dominate LA's moral landscape throughout the decade. As some Hollywood movies pushed cultural boundaries in the 1920s, Shuler waged a holy war from his pulpit in LA's Trinity Methodist Church and, between 1926 and 1932, from his radio station KGEF to push them back into their ostensibly rightful place. In this way, Southern California seemed to encapsulate the cultural extremes of the 1920s, and nowhere more so than Hollywood, which charted new cultural horizons and simultaneously championed old ones in the form of the western, with its clearly delineated boundaries of right and wrong as white Americans "civilized" the West.[9]

Whether drawn to the Hollywood high life or the high road of plain folk evangelicalism, or motivated by the need to escape from racist violence and revolutionary turmoil, as was respectively the case for African Americans exiting the South and Mexicans fleeing their country, people poured into the Golden State in unprecedented numbers during the 1920s. California's population grew to nearly 5.7 million by 1930, only about a million less than the other Census West states, from the Pacific Coast to the Rockies, Great Basin, and Southwest combined. The trend has continued, and California's 2017 population of just under 40 million far

[8] Carol L. Higham and William H. Katerberg, *Conquests and Consequences: The American West: From Frontier to Region* (Wheeling, IL: Harland Davidson/Cody, WY: Buffalo Bill Historical Center, 2009), 303–304.

[9] For more on Shuler and McPherson, see Matthew Avery Sutton, *Aimee Semple McPherson and the Resurrection of Christian America* (Cambridge, MA: Harvard University Press, 2007); James N. Gregory, *The Southern Diaspora: How the Great Migrations of Black and White Southerners Transformed America* (Chapel Hill: University of North Carolina Press, 2005), 225–226; and Gerald Nash, *The American West in the Twentieth Century: A Short History of an Urban Oasis* (2003; repr., Albuquerque: University of New Mexico Press, 1985), 86–87.

exceeds that of the rest of the Census West, which totals approximately 30 million.[10]

The six Plains states also saw significant growth between 1910 and 1930, with Texas increasing in size from 3.9 million in 1910 to just below 4.7 million in 1920, and to more than 5.8 million by the start of the depression decade. Oklahoma in 1910 had a very slightly lower population than its northern neighbor Kansas: 1.66 million compared to 1.69 million; but by 1920 Oklahoma's population exceeded 2 million, while Kansas reached only about 1.77 million. By 1930 the Sooner State was up to nearly 2.4 million, in part because of the state's oil boom, with Kansas lagging well behind at 1.88 million. The Northern Plains states of Nebraska, North Dakota, and South Dakota experienced limited growth during the 1910s and 1920s, reaching just under 1.4 million and around 680,000 and 690,000, respectively, by 1930. Clearly Texas was the demographic giant of the Plains, with a population only about a million less than the region's other five states combined. Today Texas's demographic primacy is even more pronounced: its 28.5 million residents nearly triple the combined population of around 10.5 million on the rest of the Plains, from Oklahoma to North Dakota.[11]

The West's growth in the 1920s, whether on the Southern Plains or across the Far West, was increasingly in the urban and industrial sectors. Houston's population almost doubled from 1910 to 1920, reaching 138,000, and then more than doubled again by 1930, reaching over 292,000. Dallas's growth rate was almost as impressive, nearly tripling in size between 1910 and 1930. Overall, Texas's rate of urban population growth in the 1920s was an impressive 58 percent. Oklahoma City grew with the state's oil boom; the city had 64,000 residents when the state capitol moved there in 1910, 91,000 by the start of the 1920s, and over 185,000 by 1930. San Diego matched that pace, increasing from under 40,000 residents in 1910 to 148,000 by 1930. Oakland, Denver, San Francisco, and Seattle all experienced impressive demographic growth, too. The trend was consistent across the region – the urban West was on the rise. Other regions, most notably the Midwest, Mid-Atlantic, and Northeast, housed larger cities but did not see urban growth rates to match those in the West (Figure 4.2).

[10] US Census Bureau, and http://worldpopulationreview.com/states/ (accessed May 16, 2017). The Census West does not include Texas and the other Great Plains states.

[11] US Population by State from 1900, available at: www.demographia.com/db-state1900.htm accessed July 23, 2015.

For all its regional variations, the demographic and economic horizons of the 1920s West revealed a decidedly bifurcated appearance. Much of the region's agrarian sector was in a deep economic downturn long before the Great Depression began. As the homesteading era ended, the West and the nation began a now century-long process of contraction in the number of family-owned farms as people sold up and moved to towns and cities. Yet concurrent with that rural decline, the West's population continued to increase at a nation-leading pace, and the urban, industrial extractive, and commercial sectors of the western economy soared in the 1920s (Figure 4.2). The Texas Panhandle town of Borger exemplified the demographic changes and the explosive growth in extractive industry in the 1920s West. The surrounding land had been largely unpopulated since the removal to Oklahoma of the Comanches, Kiowas, Southern Cheyennes, and Arapahos after the Red River War (1874). Oil was discovered there in March 1926, and the newly founded town of Borger went from virtually zero population to around 45,000 in the space of just 90 days. Thomas Hart Benton's famous "Regionalist" painting "Boomtown" (1927–1928) (see book cover) depicted Borger in its moment of transformation, capturing, as the artist described it, the "expansive grandeur" of western expansion, showing "the peoples' behavior, their actions on the opening land," along with the "mighty anarchic carelessness of our country," exemplified in a "great, wasteful, extravagant burning of resources for momentary profit."[12]

Borger exemplified both the promise and the fragility of western boom economies.[13] The West was still hampered to a significant degree in the 1920s by its economic dependence on extractive industry, with its perennial boom and bust cycles, and Northeastern capital. The region's manufacturing sector remained relatively undeveloped, and by decade's end, railroads were still carrying roughly three tons of cargo eastbound from the West for every ton that traveled westbound from the East.[14] However, claims that the West was a mere colony of the East at this late stage in its development are overstated. California's factories had doubled their output between 1914 and 1919, and that growth escalated further in the 1920s. Concurrently, the West's own entrepreneurs were beginning to establish home grown banking systems. San Franciscan A. P. Giannini's

[12] Emily Ballew Neff et al., *The Modern West: American Landscapes, 1890–1950* (New Haven, CT: Yale University Press, 2006), 216–219.

[13] Borger's population was around 13,000 in 2017.

[14] Nash, *The American West in the Twentieth Century*, 89.

Bank of Italy – later Bank of America (1930) – played a key role in providing the capital for California's economic expansion, as did Joseph Sartori in Southern California. Also, as metropolitan Southern California grew and expanded in the 1920s, the region attracted the large automakers and tire manufacturers and their subsidiary assembly plants.[15]

With all the contiguous western territories admitted to statehood by 1912, the entire western region could flex its economic and political muscle to a degree well beyond its relative population. Between 1864 and 1912, 13 new states had entered the union, all of them former western territories. With lightly populated states such as Nevada (77,000 in 1920), Wyoming (194,000), Arizona (334,000), New Mexico (360,000), and Idaho (432,000) collectively providing 10 of the nation's 96 Senators and representing a total combined population of less than 1.4 million of the nation's 100 million residents, the West was exceedingly well represented in Congress. If we add the somewhat higher populated states of North and South Dakota (647,000, and 637,000, respectively, in 1920), Montana (549.000), and Utah (449,000) to the mix we see that a total of 18 western senators (nearly one-fifth of the total membership) represented a little less than 3.8 million Americans in 1920, less than 4 percent of the total population.[16] Because of the Republicans' refusal to reapportion representation in the House based on the 1920 census, the West's demographic growth was not fully reflected in that chamber. However, western influence in the Senate more than compensated during the decade. With California's former governor Hiram Johnson serving in the Senate from 1917 to 1945, Nebraska's George Norris from 1913 to 1945, and Idaho's William Borah from 1907 to 1940, the economic needs of the West were being carefully protected by influential progressive leaders who encouraged federal initiatives that benefited the region.[17] There were certainly some colonial dimensions to the relationship between America and its West – and more specifically the West and the old Northeast – yet, the nation's bicameral legislative system ensured that the regional tail often had the bargaining power to wag the national dog.

Certain federal policies in the 1920s proved particularly advantageous to the West. For example, the vast wide-open spaces between the region's

[15] Etulain and Malone, *The American West*, 48–49; and White, *"It's Your Misfortune and None of My Own": A New History of the American West* (Norman: University of Oklahoma Press, 1991), 46.

[16] State population figures from Demographia, available at: www.demographia.com/db-state1900.htm accessed September 3, 2015.

[17] White, *"It's Your Misfortune,"* 383.

new mushrooming metropolitan centers became more easily traversable in the wake of the passage of the Federal Highway Act of 1921, which provided 50/50 matching funds to states to build a network of graded, hard-surfaced, two-lane roads. A million miles of new roads in the western states resulted from this initiative during the 1920s. California led the way and by the end of the decade accounted for fully 10 percent of the 23 million cars and trucks in the nation; the rest of the West accounted for about another 10 percent.[18] Like railroads during the preceding generations, improved roads, along with the mass production of affordable automobiles (most notably Ford's Model T), introduced potential new residents to the West's cities, as well as visitors to its grandest natural spectacles. The ease of accessibility that marked the automobile age, along with NPS director Steven Mather's coordinated promotional efforts, led to a spike in national park visitation. In 1910, less than 200,000 people visited the parks, but by 1920, the figure had risen to 920,000, and it tripled again by 1930, reaching a figure of 2,775,000 – and most of those nationally designated natural wonders were in the West.[19] In 1922 Secretary of Commerce Herbert Hoover negotiated the Colorado River Compact, securing agreement on water use from the states that bordered the river (excepting Arizona). Four years later, Congress approved construction of the Boulder Dam on the southern Nevada–northeastern Arizona line to provide irrigation, flood control, and hydroelectric power. The federal landscape was becoming increasingly evident across the West throughout the 1920s, in advance of the massive stimulus the government provided during the following decade.[20]

Meanwhile, the West was also becoming a leader in cultural production as the film industry, centered in Hollywood, exploded in size and significance; 90 percent of the nation's motion pictures were made there in the 1920s.[21] Westerns proved to be one of the industry's staple and most successful genres throughout the decade and often revolved around clear moral dichotomies: good versus evil battling for the soul of the nation in the Old West, its newest, most unsettled region. Unfortunately, in the arenas of political thought and culture, the West also saw significant reactionary growth on the foundations of injustice and intolerance that had developed in the Progressive Era and during World War I.

[18] Nash, *The American West in the Twentieth Century*, 88. [19] Figures ibid., 44.

[20] Nash, *The Federal Landscape: An Economic History of the Twentieth-Century West* (Tucson: University of Arizona Press, 1999), 19.

[21] Nash, *The American West in the Twentieth Century*, 103.

Cultural Fault Lines

All American decades have been marked by conflicts between groups separated by race, religion, socioeconomic status, and social practice. The 1920s were not unique in this regard; yet, there may be no other decade since the Civil War and Reconstruction that has been more completely defined by its cultural fault lines. Prohibition was one of the four Progressive Era reform initiatives that resulted in constitutional amendments; women's suffrage, the income tax, and the direct election of senators were the others. However, and despite the moral earnestness of many of its leaders and followers, the prohibition movement was a clear example of the imposition of white Anglo-Saxon Protestant (WASP) values on a nation comprising increasing numbers of new and non-WASP citizens. Immigrant groups resented prohibition as an assault on individual liberties and on their very cultures.[22] The Eighteenth Amendment and its enforcing legislation the Volstead Act remained in effect until 1933. The 1920s were thus defined in no small part by the cultural tensions that accompanied prohibition, and it was the South and the West that drove the prohibitionist crusade and turned the nation "dry."

But the fractures that prohibition wrought were the mere tip of the iceberg when it came to manifestations of cultural conflict in the 1920s. The antiradical and antilabor crusades of the decade were often fueled by anti-immigrant rhetoric. That animus against the New Immigration, and against Asian immigrants, was manifested and codified in the passage of the Emergency Immigration Act of 1921 and the National Origins Quota Act of 1924. The former reduced the number of immigrants allowed into the country annually to 350,000 and placed a yearly cap of 3 percent of the number of foreign-born from any given country, based on the 1910 Census. The 1924 legislation went further still and amounted to an even more blatant effort to discriminate against new immigrants from Southern and Eastern Europe by reducing the annual immigration limit to 150,000 and setting the per country limit at 2 percent for all nations outside of the Western Hemisphere. The 1924 act determined those quota numbers based not on the newly available 1920 Census but on the 1890 Census, which reflected significantly lower numbers of new immigrants. The act also established an Asiatic Barred Zone, which almost completely

[22] For more on the prohibition movement's emphasis on immigrant and African American communities, see Lisa McGirr, *The War on Alcohol: Prohibition and the Rise of the American State* (New York: W. W. Norton, 2015).

eradicated Asian immigration into the nation. The quotas were not applied to Latin American countries, including Mexico, in part because of the lobbying efforts of western agricultural interests seeking to maintain a steady supply of cheap labor.[23]

Eugenic pseudoscientists helped to nurture the climate that enabled the passage of blatantly race-based immigration laws. Most influential of all was Madison Grant, who had also played an important role in the conservation movement during the Progressive Era, helping to create the New York Zoological Society, as well as McKinley (now Denali) National Park in Alaska and Glacier National Park in Montana. Calls for the preservation of American "wilderness" and of the animal and bird life that inhabited those undeveloped spaces were inextricably linked in the minds of Grant and many other self-labeled progressives of the day to preservation of the white race. Grant's book *The Passing of the Great Race* (1916) proved particularly popular and influential in the 1920s; Lothrop Stoddard's *The Rising Tide of Color: The Threat Against White World Supremacy* (1920), and Henry Pratt Fairchild's *The Melting Pot Mistake* (1926) were among the other important eugenics tracts of the era. When compared to extreme Eugenicist demands – including calls for the sterilization and segregation of non-Nordics in America to prevent further impurification of the Nordic race through miscegenation – the crusade to restrict the entry of new immigrants into the nation seemed relatively moderate. Anti-immigration laws sailed through Congress on a wave of WASP anxiety over the changing color and culture of the nation.[24] Thus the old immigrant stock white majority in the United States in the early to mid 1920s defined the nation by what and who it was not. The process would prove detrimental to the interests of those seeking to flee conditions in Southern and Eastern Europe and other parts

[23] David A. Gerber, *American Immigration: A Very Short Introduction* (New York: Oxford University Press, 2011), 42–42. Rachel St. John, in *Line in the Sand: A History of the Western U.S.–Mexico Border* (Princeton, NJ: Princeton University Press, 2011), 181, provides slightly higher figures of 387,803 for the 1921 act and 186,437 for the 1924 legislation. For more on Asian immigration to the US in this period, see Erika Lee and Judy Yung, *Angel Island: Immigrant Gateway to America* (New York: Oxford University Press, 2010).

[24] For more on Grant, see Jonathan Peter Spiro, *Defending the Master Race: Conservation, Eugenics, and the Legacy of Madison Grant* (Lebanon, NH: University of Vermont Press/University Press of New England, 2009); and Christine Bold, *The Frontier Club: Popular Westerns and Cultural Power, 1880–1924* (New York: Oxford University Press, 2013), esp. 31–32 and 52–53. For the debate over the 1921 and 1924 acts, see Mai Ngai, *Impossible Subjects and the Making of Modern America*, updated ed. (2004; repr., Princeton, NJ: Princeton University Press, 2014), 15–55.

of the world, but also to the various peoples of color who existed on the margins of the nation's racial landscape.

This anti-immigrant rhetoric in turn fueled the antilabor and antiradical crusades that became such a feature not just of the Red Scare era (1919–1920) but of the whole decade and were kept at the forefront of the national consciousness by the famous Sacco and Vanzetti Trial. The murder of a Massachusetts shoe factory guard and a clerk, allegedly by Italian-born anarchists Nicola Sacco and Bartolomeo Vanzetti, took place in 1920. Their trial lasted from 1921 to 1927, when they were finally electrocuted after years of appeals and protests from around the world. Their radicalism was clearly a factor in their conviction and eventual execution, and the separate crusades that emerged to defend and condemn them underscored the deep divides between American conservatives and radicals, and between older-stock Americans and new immigrants.

A wave of Christian fundamentalism further exacerbated the cultural conflicts of the decade as the literal truth of the Bible and the findings of modern science (specifically the theory of evolution), represented respectively by prosecuting attorney William Jennings Bryan and defense attorney Clarence Darrow, clashed dramatically in 1925 in the famous Scopes Trial in Dayton, Tennessee. Meanwhile, Christian fundamentalism experienced meteoric growth and massive media coverage in Los Angles. The conflicts between creationism and evolutionary science, drys and wets, urban-dwelling Catholic and Jewish immigrants, on one hand, and rural and small-town WASP Americans, on the other, between racial minorities and white Americans, all defined the American 1920s. A single infamous organization, the Ku Klux Klan, originally founded to reestablish white power structure in the post–Civil War South, reemerged in the 1910s and 1920s and spread across the nation and West, seeking to restore WASP supremacy and moral codes.

The country was becoming increasingly modern and urban. The 1920 Census suggested that for the first time in its history, the United States was home to more urban residents than rural ones (the statistical measure of urban classification is 2,500 or more). Regarding the pace of urbanization, the West was behind the Northeast, on a par with the Midwest, and well ahead of the South. Expanding cities, assembly line production, and remarkable developments in transportation and communication technology – the automobile, the airplane, the radio – were all markers of the new, faster-paced, America. The nation was considerably more diverse, too, than it had been even a generation before, because of the extensive immigration during the Progressive Era. The magnitude and sheer pace of these changes exacerbated tensions within the nation, as the majority culture adjusted to new realities and often sought to reconstitute what was generally perceived as a simpler, purer, and better past.[25] Indeed, Republican resistance to reapportionment in the House of Representatives was another manifestation of these cultural tensions playing out in the political sphere. The Republicans controlled the White House and both houses of Congress after the 1920 election and realized that heavy immigration and rural to urban migration favored the Democratic Party, so they refused to reapportion; it was the only time in the nation's history that the process was not enacted after a Census report.[26]

The Antiradical Crusade

The cultural conflicts that characterized the West and the nation during the 1920s were building during the war and immediate postwar years. The government-led and media-supported campaign for 100 percent Americanism began just as America entered the war and then generated even higher levels of public enthusiasm in the wake of the Bolshevik phase of the Russian Revolution in November 1917. The American antiradical movement was national in scope, but events in the West proved crucial to its development and to the Red Scare, which began in the fall of 1919. Earlier that year, in February 1919, the Seattle General Strike had captured the nation's attention because it featured an approach by labor not heretofore seen in the United States. The initial strike activity was in response to the shipyard workers' dangerous conditions, stagnant wages, and high cost of living (particularly housing); 35,000 of them walked off the job. Their action generated the support of workers in all sectors; 30,000 to 40,000 additional workers across the city, representing unions from the moderate American Federation of Labor (AFL) to the more radical Wobblies – Industrial Workers of the World (IWW) – joined them, and the strike became a comprehensive action with the potential to paralyze the city.[27] The press deemed the "general strike" un-American,

[25] Roderick Nash's argument along these lines in *The Nervous Generation: American Thought, 1917–1930* (1970; repr., Chicago: Ivan R. Dee, 1990) remains among the most convincing explanations for the many manifestations of cultural conflict in the 1920s. See also Lynn Dumenil, *The Modern Temper: American Culture and Society in the 1920s* (New York: Hill and Wang, 1995).

[26] Reapportionment would have benefited the Western states, since the region was growing at a faster rate than the nation, in large part because of migration from other American regions.

[27] Jeffrey A. Johnson, *They Are All Red Out Here: Socialist Politics in the Pacific Northwest, 1895–1925* (Norman: University of Oklahoma Press, 2008), 157; and Robert F.

and charges of Bolshevism were leveled against anyone who supported the action. During the brief strike, the strikers made all necessary provisions to ensure that vital city services were maintained; still, the media and government officials lambasted labor as communistic and anarchistic. Domestic radicalism became the primary issue of national concern in the wake of the Seattle developments, and the massively successful coordinated response against the strike by government and business was presented in the mainstream press, and largely accepted by the public, both regionally and nationwide, as heroic, patriotic, necessary, and not the least excessive.

Events in the state of Washington again took center stage that fall, and once again the IWW played an important role. On Armistice Day, November 11, 1919 – just a few days after the first of Attorney General A. Mitchell Palmer's notorious raids on the headquarters of radical organizations and arrests of hundreds of their members began in New York and 11 other cities on November 7 and 8 – the town of Centralia, Washington, exploded in a frenzy of anti-Wobbly violence and lawlessness. Members of the Centralia Protective Association (formed the previous October by the city's business interests) and the American Legion stormed the town's IWW meeting hall. During the much-debated series of events that followed, IWW members shot and killed three Legion members. The shooters were arrested, except for Wesley Everest, who fled the scene, pursued by a posse. Everest was finally captured after killing another Legionnaire during the pursuit. Upon apprehension, he was brutally beaten and locked up. A mob seized him from the Centralia jail, hung him (several times), shot his body to pieces, and delivered the battered corpse back to the facility to display before the imprisoned IWW members.

The major newspapers presented the "Centralia Massacre" as a brutal action by Bolshevist Wobblies against innocent, patriotic American veterans. Notably, many of the IWW members in the region, Everest included, were themselves veterans. In addition, the Central Protective Association had been formed with the express purpose of protecting the interests of big business; it was patriotic only insofar as its members purposefully wrapped their economic self-interest in the American flag. But such realities and complications found no place in the fast-developing landscape of violent antiradicalism. The events in Centralia sparked a wave of beatings and mass arrests of Wobblies on the West Coast, from

Ficken and Charles P. LeWarne, *Washington: A Centennial History* (Seattle: University of Washington Press, 1988), 86–87.

Seattle, Spokane, and Tacoma, Washington, to Oakland, California. The Centralia trial concluded the following March with seven IWW members receiving prison sentences ranging from 25 to 40 years. To the IWW and its sympathizers, the trial was a travesty of justice, since those convicted had acted in self-defense as a mob stormed their headquarters. Most conservatives and hyperpatriots were equally dissatisfied with the verdict, having clamored for convictions of first- (not second-) degree murder, and the accompanying death sentence.

A few months before the Centralia trial, the second wave of Palmer Raids took place. The November 1919 raids resulted in around 1,000 arrests, and the deportation to the newly established Soviet Union the following month of 249 suspected radicals on the US Army transport ship *Buford*, nicknamed the "Soviet Ark" by the media. Less than two months later, on January 2, 1920, Palmer orchestrated a series of actions in 33 cities in 23 states across the country, which included the arrest of more than 4,000 suspected radicals. Most detainees were held illegally, having not been charged with any crimes; many, it turned out, had no association whatsoever with radicalism.

There were virtually no arrests on January 2 in the West, but that was because the post-Centralia raids had already decimated the ranks of radical organizations in the region. Moreover, criminal syndicalism laws in the western states, directed at members of the IWW and other groups that advocated violence and sabotage to achieve their goals, were already leading to large numbers of arrests. In California, where past or present membership in the IWW became a criminal offense, an estimated 500 radicals were arrested between 1919 and 1921, and more than half were convicted. The Better America Federation (BAF), founded in May 1920, led the charge against radicals, labor unions, and progressives of all stripes in California, helping to destroy the IWW and preserve the open shop (workplaces where union membership is not required) in the southern part of the state, and playing an important role in creating the Los Angeles Police Department's infamous "red squad." Displaying an "extreme, intolerant nationalism," the BAF even sought the passage of a peacetime sedition act to muzzle ostensibly un-American opinions. The organization was unsuccessful in that particular venture, but nonetheless constituted a powerful antiradical force in the state in the early 1920s.[28]

[28] Edwin Layton, "The Better American Federation: A Case Study of 'Superpatriotism,'" *Pacific Historical Review* 30 (May 1961): 137–147, quote on 141.

The Red Scare hysteria began to dissipate nationwide by the spring of 1920, though it lingered a little longer in California and New York than elsewhere in the country. Palmer had predicted a massive wave of radical attacks on May Day (the first of the month) and the nation's largest cities prepared their defenses accordingly, but no such actions occurred and the attorney general's overreach was underscored and his reputation thereby damaged.[29] Palmer had hoped to secure the Democratic Party nomination for the 1920 presidential election, but the excesses of his Red Scare campaign undermined his candidacy. In the end, James Cox secured the nomination, but lacked the reputation or skills to mount an effective campaign against Republican candidate Warren G. Harding, who proved remarkably consistent in his outright avoidance of political issues. Harding seemed to express the popular will by calling for a return to "normalcy" and an end to the crusading fervor that had characterized both the reform efforts of the Progressive Era, the reactionary 100 percent Americanism campaign during 1917–1918, and the Red Scare. Harding secured more than 16 million votes to Cox's 9 million (Map 4.1). Socialist leader Eugene Debs also ran, but from his cell in the federal penitentiary in Atlanta, and gained 920,000 votes. He had been sentenced to a 10-year term in 1918 for violating the Espionage Act in one of his speeches (Harding released him on Christmas Day 1921). Republican candidates rode into office on Harding's coattails in 1920; the party gained 61 House and 10 Senate seats, ensuring comfortable majorities in both chambers. However, none of the candidates seemed to excite the public into mass participation; voter turnout at 49 percent was the lowest in the nation's history, before or since.[30]

The West proved receptive to Harding's message. In 1916, Republican candidate Charles Evans Hughes won a popular majority in just two western states, Oregon and South Dakota. In 1920, Harding won every state from the Plains to the Pacific aside from Texas. It had hardly been a western landslide, since Harding's margins of victory were quite slim across the region. Nonetheless, the West had certainly shifted back in favor of the Republicans in just a single four-year cycle. The major

[29] Coverage of the Seattle General Strike and of Centralia draws on Robert K. Murray, *The Red Scare: A Study in National Hysteria, 1919–1920* (1955; repr., New York: McGraw-Hill, 1964), 82–104, 166–189, 210–222, and 235. See also Shawn T. Daley, "Centralia, Collective Memory, and the Tragedy of 1919" (MA thesis, Portland State University, 2015).

[30] For coverage of the 1920 campaign, see John Milton Cooper, *The Pivotal Decades: The United States, 1900–1920* (New York: W. W. Norton, 1990), 365–373.

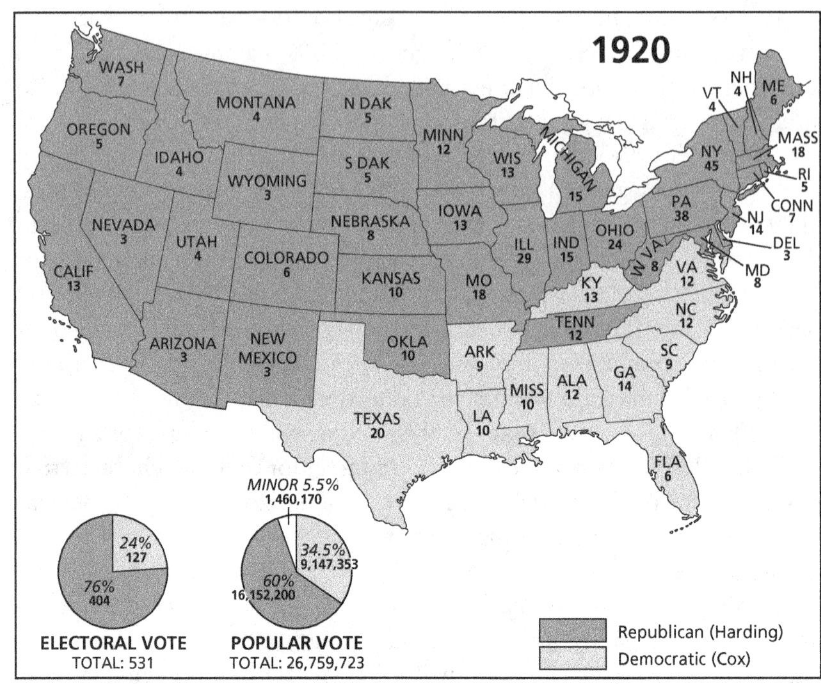

MAP 4.1 Electoral map, 1920.

parties had their fair share of both liberal and conservative leaders and constituencies in this period; today's clear divide in political ideology between Republican conservatism and Democratic liberalism was still a long way from emerging. Nonetheless, the Republican victory in the West certainly benefited from the growing conservatism in the region, which in turn was fueled by the influx of migrants from Iowa and other traditionally Republican Midwestern states. By the 1920 election, big business was in the ascendancy, big labor was on a downward slide, and the spirit of social justice reform that had been so vital a part of western Progressivism was dissipating fast, and along with it tolerance for ideas or people outside of the WASP mainstream.

Race Riots and Racial Policies

The United States fought the Great War with a segregated military and to maintain white majorities in mobilization camps the Army had to ship white draftees from the North and West to Georgia and Arkansas. Mistreatment of African American troops by white commanders and enlistees was pervasive across the country.[31] Meanwhile, the negative reaction of white Americans to the rising expectations of African Americans, their emerging middle class, and their mass migration to the North exploded in East Saint Louis in July 1917, when at least 40 African Americans were killed (estimates range as high as 200) by a white mob numbering 2,000. The mob burned down the black section of town, leaving 6,000 people homeless. In the summer and early fall of 1919, the enhanced expectations of equality among returning black servicemen, combined with growing white frustrations over the seemingly rapid pace of racial change and the backdrop of fear over radicalism, to spark a series of race riots in more than two dozen American cities, including the nation's capital; Knoxville, Tennessee; Chicago; and Elaine, Arkansas.[32] Additional riots occurred in the northeast Texas town of Longview, and in Omaha, Nebraska, where a white mob brutally lynched and mutilated an African American man, Will Brown, who was wrongfully accused and arrested for the rape of a young white woman, Agnes Loebeck. A force of more than 1,000 soldiers finally subdued the Omaha mob of nearly 4,000, which had earlier set the courthouse on fire and tried to hang the mayor for resisting its efforts to lynch Brown.

Tulsa, Oklahoma, suffered what was perhaps the single most deadly race riot in American history in the early summer of 1921. The black section of town, a 36-block area housing 10,000 people, the community's two hospitals, and all its churches, including the Mount Zion Baptist Church, which had just been built and opened a few weeks before, was burned to the ground and reduced to rubble by a white mob. The terrible violence in Tulsa followed the standard spurious charge that a black man had raped a white woman. Approximately 6,000 African Americans were arrested during the riot. The National Guard arrived in the early hours of June 1 to try to restore order. The official death count was 39, but estimates of fatalities range from that conservative figure to as high as 300. Almost all the victims were black.[33]

The efforts of the American majority culture to impose its power also shaped national policy toward Native peoples in the early 1920s. The Native American population of the United States had reached a new low of 248,253 in the Census of 1890 and continued to fall during the next

[31] Jennifer D. Keene, *Doughboys, the Great War, and the Remaking of America* (Baltimore: Johns Hopkins University Press, 2001), 82–104, esp. 85.

[32] Dumenil, *The Modern Temper*, 287–288.

[33] W. David Baird and Danney Goble, *Oklahoma: A History* (Norman: University of Oklahoma Press, 2008), 215–215.

1850	400,764	1910	265,683
1860	339,421	1920	244,437
1870	313,712	1930	332,397
1880	306,543	1940	333,969
1890	248,253	1950	343,410
1900	237,196		

FIGURE 4.3 Native American population in the United States, 1850–1950. Data from the US Census Office. Figures do not include Alaska Natives.

decade; the figure of 237,196 was recorded in 1900. There was some growth in the 1900s, with the number climbing to 265,683 by 1910, but the 1920 Census recorded a Native population of 244,437, lower than that of 1890. The decline was largely attributable to the 1918–1919 influenza epidemic but also to a lackluster effort by the Census Bureau to count Indians. By 1930, the Census suggested that the Native population had increased by around 90,000, to 332,397. Undercounting in 1920 explains some of the increase, but the Native population was indeed increasing in the 1920s, and the trend of demographic recovery has continued ever since.[34] This growth in numbers was an overridingly positive aspect of Indian nations' experience during the decade; however, the overall picture was deeply concerning for Native peoples (Figure 4.3).

On April 17, 1917, just 15 days after Woodrow Wilson's Declaration of War – a war that between 12,000 and 17,000 Native Americans served in – Indian Commissioner Cato Sells announced his "declaration of Policy in the Administration of Indian Affairs." Sells called for "reduced appropriations by the Government [for Indian people] and more self-respect and independence for the Indian," leading to "the ultimate absorption of the Indian race into the body politic of the Nation" and "the beginning of the end of the Indian problem."[35] The independence that Sells spoke of really amounted to freedom for the federal government from its responsibility to provide the necessary appropriations guaranteed in previous treaty negotiations with Native peoples. The shift in policy was as much

[34] Nancy Shoemaker, *American Indian Population Recovery in the Twentieth Century* (Albuquerque: University of New Mexico Press, 1999), 4.

[35] The Annual Reports of the Department of the Interior, II, 1917–1920, 3–4, quoted in Donald L. Parman, *Indians and the American West in the Twentieth Century* (Bloomington: Indiana University Press, 1994), 66. For more on Native American service in the US armed forces during World War I, see Steven Sabol, "'It Was a Pretty Good War, but They Stopped It Too Soon': The American Empire, Native Americans, and World War I," in *Empires in World War I: Shifting Frontiers and Imperial Dynamics in a Global Conflict*, ed. Andrew Tait Jarboe and Richard S. Fogarty (London: I. B. Taurus, 2014), 193–216, esp. 204.

an acceleration of the Bureau of Indian Affairs's (BIA) efforts to assimilate Native peoples into the American mainstream, through boarding schools, land allotments, and restrictions on indigenous cultural practices, as it was a truly new policy. Nonetheless, Sells's rhetoric heralded an era of heightened federal action and amounted to a declaration of war on Native sovereignty, lands, and cultural expression. The only positive aspects of this new initiative were its relative brevity and the strength of the organized opposition it prompted, which would lay the foundations for the Indian New Deal and the restoration of tribal sovereignty in the 1930s.

The real problem for Indian peoples in this period was twofold: the BIA began to more vigorously enforce restrictions on Native cultural expression, and the agency further facilitated the transfer of Indian lands and mineral rights to non-Native settlers in states such as California, Montana, Oklahoma, and Oregon. Western politicians, seeking new settlers and greater agricultural opportunities for those white Americans already in place, as well as for companies that were intent on exploiting Indian mineral resources, encouraged Sells to speed up the process of enabling Indians to part with their lands. Sells, in turn, convinced that reservation lands were underutilized by their owners and cognizant of the need for increased agricultural production during the Great War, eased restrictions on white access to those lands to enable leasing and purchasing. Thus, Thomas D. Campbell in 1918 managed to secure federal support for a massive wheat farming operation on 200,000 acres on the Crow Fort Peck, Blackfeet, and Shoshone reservations in Montana.[36]

The tide seemed to be shifting inexorably against Indian peoples when in 1922 an assault on New Mexico Pueblo Indian land rights resulted in the emergence of a powerful coalition of pro-Indian voices energized by the relentless efforts of reformer John B. Collier. New Mexico Republican Holm O. Bursum had introduced a bill in the US Senate to settle the claims of non-Indians residing on Pueblo lands. The Bursum Bill, which received the strong endorsement of Secretary of the Interior Albert B. Fall (himself formerly a Republican senator from New Mexico), would have reduced the 340,000 acres of Pueblo land holdings by 60,000 acres, eradicating the landownership and water rights of some 8,000 to 9,000 Indians in favor of those of about 12,000 non-Indians. The measure would have proven devastating for the Pueblo people immediately affected, and would have set an ominous precedent for the Pueblo nation, and indeed for all

[36] Parman, *Indians and the American West*, 67–69.

Indian peoples. But Collier's powerful rhetoric against the bill and his organization of the Pueblo people, along with the involvement of a range of Indian rights groups and the General Federation of Women's Clubs, led to its defeat and the subsequent passage of a compromise bill that better protected Pueblo land rights.[37]

In an article titled "Plundering the Pueblo Indians," in *Sunset Magazine* in January 1923, Collier praised the "fierce joy expressed in dance and song" that characterized the Pueblo people and declared that they "belong to the future as much as to the past," describing them as a "priceless part of America's cultural life."[38] The following month the new Indian commissioner, Francis E. Leupp, unimpressed by such pro-Indian sentiments, endorsed the recommendations of missionaries to limit Indian dances to one day-long dance per month and to prohibit the attendance at these dances of Indians under the age of 50. But Collier and the pro-Indian forces that had galvanized in opposition to the Bursum Bill also pushed back against BIA restrictions on Native cultural expression and managed to tap into an emerging vein of cultural relativism, with its appreciation for cultural diversity and faith in the possibilities for peaceful and productive coexistence of contrasting cultures.[39]

The American 1920s were clearly not notable for receptiveness to cultural difference, yet the decade marked a moment of positive transition with respect to white attitudes toward Indian cultures. As the controversy over Indian dances played out in the mid 1920s, President Coolidge signed the Indian Citizenship Act in June 1924, conferring full citizenship on all remaining Indian noncitizens.[40] While the legislation marked the high point of assimilationist efforts, it is important to note that it passed just a week after Congress had voted up the racist immigration quota act.[41]

[37] Brian W. Dippie, *The Vanishing American: White Attitudes and U.S. Indian Policy* (1982; repr., Lawrence: University Press of Kansas, 1991), 274–279; and Peter Iverson, *"We Are Still Here": American Indians in the Twentieth Century* (Wheeling, IL: Harland Davidson, 1998), 6–61.

[38] John B. Collier, "Plundering the Pueblo Indians," *Sunset Magazine* 50 (January 1923): 21–25, and 56, quoted in Iverson, *"We Are Still Here,"* 61.

[39] Cultural relativism had been inspired in part by the work of pioneering anthropologist Franz Boas. See Dippie, *The Vanishing American*, 280–284.

[40] The Five Civilized Tribes had gained citizenship in 1901, tens of thousands of others had gained citizenship through the allotment process set in motion by the Dawes Act (1887), and honorably discharged Indian veterans of the Great War were granted citizenship by Congress in 1919.

[41] Dippie makes this point in *The Vanishing American*, 195–196.

Meanwhile, workers for the Institute for Government Research, under the direction of Lewis Meriam and with the assistance of Omaha Indian and Yale University graduate Henry Roe Cloud, began in 1926 to compile a report on the conditions of Native peoples. The influential and lengthy (23,000-page) study, revealingly titled *The Problem of Indian Administration*, appeared in February 1928. The massively detailed Meriam Report chronicled the dispossession of Indians due to allotment; the excesses of the boarding school system, which had sought to eradicate Indian culture; the tragic impacts of the government's assimilation program; and the crushing poverty Indians experienced. Around 55 percent had per capita incomes below $200 per year, and only 2 percent had annual incomes greater than $500.[42] The document emphasized the need to "recognize the good in the educational and social life of the Indians in their religion and ethics . . . to develop it and build on it rather than to crush out all that is Indian" and concluded that "the Indians have much to contribute to the dominant civilization."[43] Thus, the efforts of Collier, Cloud, and other members of Meriam's staff, various Indian advocacy groups, and of Indians themselves set an important precedent for the changes that would come during the 1930s.

For Native peoples, the story of the 1920s had been one of federal assault, precipitating resistance on the part of Indians and enlightened white reformers, and ultimately the laying of foundations for indigenous tribal resurgence in the future. For Mexican-origin people in the West, the story was ultimately less positive. In 1910, there were more than 384,000 people of Mexican heritage in the United States, mostly residing in the southwestern states, from Texas to California. Of that number, nearly 222,000 had been born in Mexico, and a little more than 162,000 were US-born. The impact of the Mexican Revolution of the 1910s was evident in the 1920 Census, which recorded more than 738,000 Mexican-origin people, a near-doubling of that population. Over 486,000 of those counted were born in Mexico; 252,000 were born in the United States. The trend of migration from Mexico continued in the 1920s because of that nation's economic instability. By 1930, the Mexican-origin figure had nearly doubled again to over 1,488,000. The Census showed significant growth in the number born in Mexico, which was up to nearly

42 Donald L. Fixico, *Indian Resilience and Rebuilding: Indigenous Nations in the Modern American West* (Tucson: University of Arizona Press, 2013), 71.

43 Lewis Meriam et al., *The Problem of Indian Administration: Report of a Survey Made at the Request of Hubert Work, Secretary of the Interior, and Submitted to Him, February 21, 1928* (Baltimore, 1928), 21–22, quoted in Dippie, *The Vanishing American*, 299.

641,000 by 1930. However, the growth in the US-born, or Mexican American, population in the 1920s was massive – the figure reached nearly 848,000. Moreover, it is important to consider that these Census figures seriously undercounted the Mexican-origin population, in part because only first-generation US-born Mexicans were counted as being of Mexican origin.[44] Nonetheless, the numbers underscore the attraction of the adjacent border states of the Southwest (where more than 90 percent of the Mexican-origin population still resided as late as 1930), to Mexicans fleeing economic chaos, persecution, and violence.

Organized opposition to Mexican immigration emerged in earnest in the 1910s as the AFL and other unions feared that their efforts to bargain with employers would be undermined by the influx of lower-wage workers from south of the border. Also, as racist views gained increasing currency during the war and immediate postwar years, fueled by the alarmist tracts of eugenicists, opponents of Mexican immigration proclaimed that assimilation into American society was impossible, given the peasant and proletarian origins and racial characteristics of Mexicans, their proclivity for miscegenation, devotion to the Catholic faith and the Spanish language, and general barbarism. The concurrent arguments concerning assimilation and miscegenation were of course contradictory, yet the overall message was clear: Mexican migrants constituted, as one critic put it, "an invasion of Aliens." The agricultural recession at the beginning of the 1920s further fueled concerns over Mexican immigrant labor. However, western congressmen successfully lobbied on behalf of southwestern employers – including corporate farming interests – to secure an exemption to the 1924 National Origins Quota Act for Mexicans.[45]

Congress established the US Border Patrol just a few days after the 1924 immigration act to enforce that legislation. Mexican immigrants could travel to an official port of entry, pay the $18 head tax, submit to a health exam and literacy test, and enter the country legally, and large numbers did so. But there were perhaps as many as a million illegal border crossings into the United States from Mexico during the 1920s, and the underfunded Border Patrol could do little to prevent them. The United States had what essentially amounted to an open border prior to 1924,

44 Oscar J. Martinez, *Mexican-Origin People in the United States: A Topical History* (Tucson: University of Arizona Press, 2001), 13–14.

45 Kelly Lytle Hernández, *City of Inmates: Conquest, Rebellion, and the Rise of Human Caging in Los Angeles, 1771–1965* (Chapel Hill: University of North Carolina Press, 2017), 134.

and even up to 1929, enforcement of border migration was sporadic.[46] Meanwhile, Nativists in Congress continued to push for limits on Mexican immigration, legal and illegal, in the late 1920s. Spokesmen for Southwestern employers, responded to Nativist concerns over whether Mexicans were assimilable by arguing, disingenuously, that they were temporary visitors, birds of passage, not permanent settlers in the United States – fully 10 percent of the population of Mexico was living north of the border by 1929. A compromise between the two sides was reached in 1929 when Congress passed a bill sponsored by virulently racist South Carolina senator Coleman Livingston Blease that criminalized unregulated entry into the United States. The bill targeted Mexican-origin people by categorizing unlawful entry as a misdemeanor crime punishable by a $1,000 fine and/or up to a year in prison, followed by deportation. Repeat offences were considered felonies, subject to a $1,000 fine and/or up to two years in prison. By the end of the 1930s, tens of thousands of Mexicans had been imprisoned for immigration offenses.[47]

From the industrial and agricultural economies across the Southwest from California to Texas, and north into the sugar beet fields of Colorado, people of Mexican origin – whether in the country legally or not – provided the cheap labor that fueled the region's economic growth in the 1920s, all the while experiencing discrimination and exploitation. The weight of the anti-Mexican prejudice was illustrated in particularly disturbing fashion by the response of authorities in Los Angeles to a plague outbreak in the fall of 1924 – the last major outbreak of the disease in the country. The epidemic killed nearly 40 people, primarily of Mexican origin. The "Mexican district" in LA was subjected to a quarantine, which was quickly expanded to cover four additional districts, with guards enforcing restrictions on movement. Around 2,500 homes and other structures were razed to facilitate the eradication of the disease, with no compensation paid to owners and residents and no rebuilding of the destroyed section of the city. A massive rat-killing operation was

46 Sarah Deutsch, *No Separate Refuge: Culture, Class, and Gender on an Anglo-Hispanic Frontier in the American Southwest, 1880–1940* (New York: Oxford University Press, 1987), 119–126, quotation on 121; and Martinez, *Mexican-Origin People*, 26–28. See also Nugent, *Into the West*, 207. For enforcement efforts, see Kelly Lytle Hernández, *Migra! A History of the US Border Patrol* (Berkeley: University of California Press, 2010). Prior to the establishment of the US Border Patrol in 1924, immigration inspectors known as Line Riders policed the border with Mexico (from 1894), though their numbers were small; see James E. Dupree, "Line Riders, Masculinity, and Authority on the Mexican–American Border, 1882–1913" (MA thesis, University of Oklahoma, 2013).

47 Hernández, *City of Inmates*, 137–139.

also enacted to ensure the annihilation of the disease vectors. It amounted to "renewal as urban clearcutting," "a Southern California experiment with ethnic cleansing," and one that also targeted Russian, Chinese, and Japanese neighborhoods. But the city's Mexican-origin residents suffered the most from the orchestrated response to the plague by city authorities; a good number lost their jobs because employers feared they might be plague carriers, and those fears were nurtured by the city's actions, which reinforced racist stereotypes.[48]

The Second Klan in the West

The white supremacist Ku Klux Klan had first emerged in the South in 1866 in opposition to the Republican Party's efforts to improve conditions for newly freed slaves and spread across the whole region by 1870. Once the goal of reestablishing the white power structure was achieved in the wake of Reconstruction, the KKK went dormant for decades. The Klan was reborn in the 1910s and experienced massive growth in the first half of the 1920s. Like the antiradical crusade, the race riots, and the racial policies of the period, the organization was a clear manifestation of the growing cultural conflict in the United States. Also, like the coordinated and concerted antiradicalism of 1919–1920, the Klan proved to be a significant feature across much of the western landscape. At its peak around 1925, the Klan may have had anywhere from 1.5 million to 5 million members nationwide. There were women's auxiliary klans, junior klans for 12- to 18-year olds, and even "kiddie klaverns" for younger children. These auxiliary groups are included in the higher-end estimates of total Klan membership.[49]

48 The coverage and quotations are from William Deverell, *Whitewashed Adobe: The Rise of Los Angeles and the Remaking of Its Mexican Past* (Berkeley: University of California Press, 2004), 172–206, quotations on 188 and 191.

49 Kenneth T. Jackson, in *The Ku Klux Klan in the City, 1915–1930* (New York: Oxford University Press, 1967), 236, contends that Klan membership nationwide never exceeded 1.5 million at any given time; David M. Chalmers, in *Hooded Americanism: The History of the Ku Klux Klan*, 3rd ed. (Durham, NC: Duke University Press, 1987), 291, puts the national membership figure at over 3 million; Arnold S. Rice in *The Ku Klux Klan in American Politics* (Washington, DC: Public Affairs Press, 1962), 12, estimates 4 million; Nancy MacLean in *Behind the Mask of Chivalry: The Making of the Second Ku Klux Klan* (New York: Oxford University Press, 1994), 10, puts the figure at "perhaps as high as five million" by mid-decade; and David Kennedy, in *Freedom from Fear*, 15, estimates 5 million. Kathleen M. Blee, in *Women of the Klan: Racism and Gender in the 1920s* (Berkeley: University of California Press, 1991), estimates that the Women of the Ku Klux Klan (WKKK) had about half a million members. Jackson's low number and

The US Census Bureau recorded a national population figure of around 100 million for 1920; that number had risen to a little under 116 million by 1925. So, the Klan membership, whether 1.5 or 5 million, comprised a sizeable minority, and one that controlled numerous state legislatures, had elected governors in Colorado and Oregon, had representation in the US House of Representatives and Senate (including at one point both of Colorado's seats and one from Texas), and had influence in both major parties. The Klan effectively controlled many towns and even major cities across the country. For a few years in the early to mid 1920s, the nation endured a wave of xenophobic legislation, boycotts of non-WASP-owned businesses, and vigilante violence, all cloaked in the guise of 100 percent Americanism and proclaiming to be the ultimate expression of Christian righteousness and moral decency.

In its first incarnation, in the immediate wake of the Civil War, the Klan was antiblack and anti-Republican. The reborn Klan in the 1920s had a much broader brush of hate, though one that still included agitation against African Americans. The emerging black middle class was the Klan's primary target in Los Angeles. But the organization also targeted the Japanese in California and the Far West; Catholics, especially in the Northern Plains states and in Oregon; immigrants, especially Jews, but more broadly Southern and Eastern Europeans; Mexican Americans in the Southwest; as well as radicals, especially Wobblies, and even atheists. Meanwhile, across the nation, the Klan proclaimed to be the great defender of WASP morality and virtuous womanhood through its strong stands against alcohol, premarital sexual relations, marital infidelity, gambling, and other social transgressions. Klan activities ran the gamut from charitable fund-raising and legitimate political activities to night rides to terrorize non-WASP individuals and groups, and moral offenders – which Klan leaders disingenuously claimed were the work of imposters trying to tarnish the organization's reputation.

Based on the lower-end estimates (used here for all the western states), Klan membership peaked in Texas at around 200,000 in 1922, the year that Klansman Earl B. Mayfield won a seat in the US Senate and the organization gained control of the lower house of the state legislature. That year was also marked by numerous violent Klan attacks, including

the higher estimates are not necessarily incompatible, since, as Blee emphasizes, large numbers of people joined the Klan, were disillusioned by the gulf between "the image and reality of Klan life," and left the organization (4). So, the Klan may well have had as many as 5 million or even more dues paying members in the 1920s, but not at any given moment during the decade.

the whipping of a black Dallas bellhop and branding of his forehead with acid, and the stripping, beating, and tar and feathering of a white woman suspected of marital impropriety. The Klan was responsible for the flogging of at least 68 people in Dallas in that spring alone. In September 1923, a sizable crowd of 75,000 Klansmen gathered at the state fair in Dallas to hear the organization's Imperial Wizard Hiram Wesley Evans. But by then the Klan's power in Texas was starting to wane in the wake of the increasing public attention to its violent actions, and Klan candidates suffered major defeats in the 1924 elections, which saw Miriam "Ma" Ferguson elected to the governorship and Dan Moody to the attorney general's office on anti-Klan platforms.[50]

Texas's Southern Plains neighbor Oklahoma also showed significant enthusiasm for the Klan, its membership reaching 95,000 in the early 1920s, and perhaps exceeding 100,000 by 1923. In fact, the atmosphere following the horrifying Tulsa Race Riot in 1921 probably facilitated Klan recruitment in the state. One of those recruiters, Edwin ("Daddy") DeBarr, was the vice president of the University of Oklahoma, chair of the Department of Chemical Engineering, and the Grand Dragon of the state Klan. DeBarr's employer reprimanded him for fund-raising for the Klan on university time, but his transgressions were a minor part of the state's Klan activity. Oklahoma probably experienced more Klan violence than any other Plains state.[51]

Anti-Klan crusader Walter Witcher's *The Reign of Terror in Oklahoma* (1923) appeared during the height of the Oklahoma Klan crisis and chronicled a series of horrendous incidents of violence, including whippings, burning of women with acid, rape, and castration. The author also reprinted the report of the former secretary to the governor, who claimed that in a two-year period, the Oklahoma Klan had subjected 2,500 people to whippings. Witcher undoubtedly exaggerated the extent

[50] For more on the Texas Klan in the 1920s, see Charles C. Alexander, *The Ku Klux Klan in the Southwest* (1965; repr., Norman: University of Oklahoma Press, 1995); David M. Chalmers, *Hooded Americanism*, 39–48; and Douglas Hurt, *The Big Empty: The Great Plains in the Twentieth Century* (Tucson: University of Arizona Press, 2011), 47. Chalmers provides the figure of 200,000 for the Texas Klan; Jackson in *The Ku Klux Klan in the City*, provides a figure of 190,000 for Texas Klan membership. The originator and leader of the second Ku Klux Klan claimed a membership of 5 million in 1922, and an anti-Klan commentator in 1925 claimed a WKKK membership of 3 million (Blee, *Women of the Klan*, 20, 30). Both figures were exaggerated but help explain the high-end total membership figure of 8 million.

[51] David W. Levy, "The Rise and Fall of Edwin ('Daddy') DeBarr," *Chronicles of Oklahoma* 88 (Fall 2010): 288–315.

of Klan violence, though Klansmen did commit at least nine murders in the state. And the organization did for a time hold the reins of power, from the state legislature to the local level, where its agenda was violently enforced, and often against people innocent of any significant social or moral transgression.[52] After one particularly horrifying attack on a Jewish man in Tulsa, Governor Jack Walton stepped in to try to muzzle the Klan, imposing martial law in Tulsa and other parts of the state. Walton was derided by pro-Klan forces, and even by many opponents of the Klan, for his heavy-handedness and was quickly forced out of office by the Klan-controlled legislature. However, Walton's impeachment trial highlighted the Klan's violence and lawlessness, and the tide began to turn against the organization. Later that year, 1923, the Oklahoma state legislature became the first in the nation to "unmask" the Klan, outlawing the wearing of masks and hoods in public. Charges of graft and financial corruption within the Oklahoma Klan further hastened its demise, and after the 1926 elections, Klan influence in the legislature largely ended.[53]

Oklahoma's Plains neighbor to the North, Kansas, had a peak Klan membership in 1924 that ranged somewhere between 40,000 and 100,000. The Kansas Klan focused much of its attention on the state's African American, Jewish, and Catholic citizens by seeking to institute Jim Crow laws, limit employment opportunities, and boycott non-WASP-owned businesses. The organization also emphasized matters of moral stewardship, including advocacy for open Bibles in public schoolrooms, and punishment of gamblers, drinkers, and fornicators. Emporia had a Klan mayor, and Klan-endorsed candidates won in both the Republican and Democratic gubernatorial primaries in 1924.

The energetic and impassioned derision of governor Henry Allen and of legendary Kansas journalist and *Emporia Gazette* editor William Allen White helped generate public opposition to the Klan. White ran for governor in 1924, with no expectation of winning, but every intention of highlighting the Klan's corruption, violence, and hypocrisy, along with the Kansas State Republican Party's tacit cooperation. Launching his campaign, White declared, "The thought that Kansas should have a government beholden to this hooded gang of masked fanatics, ignorant and

[52] Walter C. Witcher, *The Reign of Terror in Oklahoma* (Fort Worth: W. C. Witcher, 1923), Huntington Library Rare Book Collection #350338, hereafter referred to as HEH RB. See also Hurt, *The Big Empty*, 48–49; Chalmers, *Hooded Americanism*, 49–55; and Alexander, *The Ku Klux Klan in the Southwest*, 104–105.

[53] Baird and Goble, *Oklahoma*, 186–188. See also Carter Blue Clark, "A History of the Ku Klux Klan in Oklahoma" (PhD diss., University of Oklahoma, 1976).

tyrannical in their ruthless oppression, is what calls me... into this disgraceful but necessary task." While the Republican Party candidate and possible Klan member Ben Paulson won the election, White secured a moral victory by prompting more Kansans to question the Klan's claims, methods, and purposes. The following January, the state supreme court ruled that the Klan could not operate without a charter, and the legislature upheld the ruling by denying an exemption for the organization. By 1927, the Klan was no longer a significant blot on the Kansas landscape.[54]

In Nebraska, the Klan was largely anti-Catholic, anti-Jewish, antiblack, and anti-Wobbly. Its membership probably peaked at around 25,000, though the national headquarters claimed 45,000 Cornhusker state members. The Nebraska Klan had little impact in the political arena and did not engage in the violent activities that marked the organization's presence on the Southern Plains. The press in the state largely opposed the Klan, and the chancellor of the University of Nebraska even threatened to expel any student who joined the organization.[55] In North and South Dakota, where the population still included large numbers of foreign-born and their children, the Klan, not surprisingly, made less headway. It certainly had a presence in both of those states, even gaining control of the school board in North Dakota in 1926. But by 1928, the Klan was a spent force on the far Northern Plains.[56]

North from Nebraska to the Canadian border, and across the Inter-Mountain West, Great Basin, and Southwest, only one state, Colorado, had significant Klan membership. Klan enrollment was negligible in about half of the western states: Utah, Idaho, and South Dakota each had only about 5,000 members, Arizona around 4,000, North Dakota and Montana 3,000 each, Nevada roughly 2,000, and Wyoming and New Mexico about 1,000 each. These nine states were also the region's most lightly populated ones. Their absence of significant Klan membership is partly explained by a combination of the large numbers of foreign-born and second-generation Americans of new immigrant (Southern and Eastern European) stock in some states, such as Montana and North Dakota, and the significant presence of Native peoples and Hispanics in Arizona and New Mexico – all groups that were thoroughly unreceptive to the Klan's WASP agenda. The relative absence of major cities in the

[54] William Allen White, *The Autobiography of William Allen White* (New York: Macmillan, 1946), quotation on 631; Chalmers, *Hooded Americanism*, 143–148. Jackson, *The Ku Klux Klan in the City*, 236, provides the 40,000 Kansas Klan membership figure; Hurt, in *The Big Empty*, 50–51, provides the figure of 100,000.

[55] Hurt, *The Big Empty*, 53. [56] Ibid., 54.

region also helps explain the Klan's failure to establish itself in the Inter-Mountain states. Klan recruiters, who themselves profited on a per capita basis, tended to invest less effort in lightly populated areas.[57]

Colorado, occupying about an eighth of the geographic space of the eight western states that lie between the Plains states and the Pacific Coast states, had nearly twice the number of Klan members (45,000) as the whole of the rest of that region combined (25,000), but it was also home to the region's largest metropolis, Denver, with over a quarter of a million residents in 1920. The Klan emerged in Denver in 1921 and, by the 1924 elections, had taken full control of the city and its Republican Party apparatus. One of its members, Clarence Morley, was elected to the governorship, and two Klan-friendly candidates were elected to the US Senate. Fully one in seven Denverites was a Klan member by 1925, and its ranks may have numbered as high as 60,000 if the Klanswomen and Junior Klansmen auxiliaries are included. Somewhere between 50,000 and 100,000 people attended the First Annual Klan Picnic at Lakeside Park, with a brass band and burning crosses providing aural and visual accompaniment to the day's proceedings.[58]

The Colorado Klan's message consisted of a large dose of anti-Catholicism, anti-Semitism, and antiblack sentiment, mixed with a pro–big business, antiregulation message, and a smattering of moral grandstanding, the most notable example featuring the Denver Grand Dragon Dr. John Galen Locke's kidnapping of a young man accused of premarital sexual relations with his girlfriend. The offender was given the choice of being wed to the woman right there and then in Locke's office or being castrated by the doctor. But Locke continued to overstep the bounds of propriety and embarrass the national and local Republican parties. His failure to pay federal taxes for 13 years, and resulting 10-day jail sentence, contributed to the growing debacle. Consequently, the Denver and Colorado Klan apparatus began to unravel. The Klan's ascendancy on the Front Range had been meteoric, and its demise was equally rapid; by late 1926, the organization was moribund in Colorado.[59]

57 Jackson, *The Ku Klux Klan in the City*, 186.

58 Jackson, ibid., 230, provides the more conservative estimate of the Lakeside Park crowd size; Chalmers, in *Hooded Americanism*, 131, provides the higher figure.

59 Chalmers, *Hooded Americanism*, 126–134; see also Robert A. Goldberg, *Hooded Empire: The Ku Klux Klan in Colorado* (Urbana: University of Illinois Press, 1981); Jackson, *The Ku Klux Klan in the City*, 215–231; and Carl Abbott, Stephen J. Leonard, and Thomas J. Noel, eds., *Colorado: A History of the Centennial State*, 4th ed. (Boulder: University of Colorado Press, 2005), 271–278.

The West Coast, like the Southern Plains and Colorado, was another bastion of western Klan strength, with perhaps 50,000 members each in California and Oregon, and another 25,000 to 40,000 in Washington. In the Golden State, the Klan was well established by 1922 and particularly strong in LA and Kern Counties, where its members mainly railed against Mexican immigrants and the Catholic Church, spreading the standard stories of young women imprisoned in church buildings for the pleasure of priests. The growing African American community was another major Klan target, as were alleged moral transgressors, and, by 1923 and 1924, it had also turned its attention to the matter of Japanese landownership. The influential Reverend Shuler offered his strong support to the organization in the state, railing against all minority groups, as well as moral delinquency.

In Los Angeles, the African American population grew by almost 150 percent in the 1920s, from 16,000 to 39,000, and the success of the black middle class in the city attracted the Klan's attention. The largest number of black migrants to Los Angeles came from Texas, while Louisiana, Arkansas and Oklahoma were well represented. A good number of migrants departed Tulsa after the terrible race riot there. Those same states were also the source of most of the Southern white migration to Los Angeles in this period, and this demographic reality only fueled racial tensions, particularly in East LA in the summer of 1921. That summer *The Birth of a Nation* was rescreened at LA's Garrick Theater and further inflamed the situation. The NAACP successfully lobbied to get the film withdrawn, and the *LA Times* and other regional newspapers lambasted the Klan as un-American. *Times* editor John Steven McGroarty energetically praised the city's African American community for its law-abiding qualities and denounced the Klan's mob mentality and unabashed racism.[60] In Anaheim, the Klan took over the city council in 1924, though its success there was short-lived. Antimask laws in the state legislature helped bring about the California Klan's decline, and by 1926, it had largely dissipated as a political force in the state.[61]

The Klan spread from California into Oregon in 1921, and Portland quickly emerged as the organization's primary stronghold in the state. "Grand Lecturer of the Pacific Northwest Domain" Reuben Herbert Sawyer spoke in the city's Municipal Auditorium to an estimated 6,000

[60] Douglas Flamming, *Bound for Freedom: Black Los Angeles in Jim Crow America* (Berkeley: University of California Press, 205), 196–202.

[61] Flamming, *Bound for Freedom*, 198; Chalmers, *Hooded Americanism*, 119–125; and Jackson, *The Ku Klux Klan in the City*, 186–193.

people in December 1921 on "The Truth about the Invisible Knights of the Ku Klux Klan." In keeping with official Klan protocol, Sawyer emphasized the Knights' charitable activities, including "hundreds of baskets of food [sent] to worthy families without regard to race, religion or color." But, as was the case in so many Klan speeches in the 1920s, the veil of decorum was soon lifted, and he descended into the inflammatory rhetoric that encapsulated the Klan's real fears and motivations: "We control Madmen, mad dogs and other mad beasts," he declared, and added that "the negro in whose blood flows the mad desire for race amalgamation is more dangerous than a maddened wild beast... he *must* and *will* be controlled."[62] African Americans comprised only 1 percent of the Portland population and were not the Klan's primary concern in the city. For the most part the Oregon Klan placed its special emphasis on prohibition enforcement, anti-Catholic legislation, and boycotts of Catholic-owned businesses.

The Oregon Klan's power grew considerably in 1922 and 1923. In the 1922 elections, William Pierce, a Klan member (albeit an undeclared one) was elected governor running as a Democrat in what had traditionally been a strongly Republican state. During the campaign, the Klan supported a controversial and highly divisive compulsory public school bill aimed in part at the Catholic schools in the state. The measure passed in 1922 by a very slim majority statewide, though two-thirds of voting Portlanders voted in favor. In early 1923, the Klan-friendly and appropriately named Kasper K. Kuble was elected speaker of the state House of Representatives. Under his leadership, an Alien Land Law was passed, directed, like the California and Washington laws that preceded it, against the Japanese and Chinese. By this time, the Portland Klan had reached a membership of between 9,000 and 15,000, and statewide the figure was somewhere between 15,000 and 35,000. The Oregon Klan never gained full control of the state's political machinery, and internal political divisions precipitated its decline by the middle of the decade. The compulsory public school measure was overturned by the Federal District Court in Oregon in 1924 and declared unconstitutional by the US Supreme Court the following year.[63]

[62] Reuben Herbert Sawyer (Grand Lecturer of the Pacific Northwest Domain), *The Truth about the Invisible Knights of the Ku Klux Klan* (Portland, OR: R. H. Sawyer, 1922, published by the Pacific Northwest Domain, No. 5, Invisible Empire, Knights of the Ku Klux Klan, Multnomah Hotel, Portland, Oregon): HEH RB 257348.

[63] Robert D. Johnston, *The Radical Middle Class: Populist Democracy and the Question of Capitalism in Progressive Era Portland* (Princeton, NJ: Princeton University Press, 2003), 218–247; Jackson, *The Ku Klux Klan in the City*, 196–214; Chalmers, *Hooded*

The Klan spread from Oregon into Washington and enrolled between 25,000 and 40,000 members in the early to mid 1920s. The organization had some influence in the major population centers of Seattle, Spokane, Walla Walla, and Tacoma, emphasizing anti-Catholicism and immigration restriction. A huge initiation ceremony just outside of Seattle in July 1923 celebrated the Klan as "the return of the Puritans in this corrupt, and jazz-mad age." The Klan introduced a school bill, modeled on the Oregon one and designed to eradicate parochial schools, but it was defeated in the 1924 election. Washington's Klan membership was not insignificant, but overall the Klan was less influential there than in its neighboring states to the south.[64] Much in line with the Klan experience in many other parts of the region and the nation, internal divisions brought about the Klan's demise in the Evergreen State. The organization also had a brief impact in western Canada, particularly in the province of Saskatchewan, where the arrival of immigrants from Southern and Eastern Europe raised the standard fears about Catholicism and prompted the recruitment of perhaps as many as 40,000 new Klansmen.[65]

Determining whether the West, based on the level of Klan membership and activity, was any more a bastion of reaction than other regions of the country – including the Midwest, the South, the Mid-Atlantic, and New England – requires parsing the region.[66] The whole Inter-Mountain West region (an eight-state area) – with the notable exception of Colorado – was one of the American regions least impacted by the Klan.[67] However, the Plains area stretching from Texas to Nebraska, with a conservatively estimated total membership of 350,000 Klan members, was, on a per capita basis, among the strongest centers of Klan activity in the country; though Texas was as southern as it was western.[68] The Pacific Coast States

Americanism, 85–91; and William G. Robbins and Katrine Barber, *Nature's Northwest: The North Pacific Slope in the Twentieth Century* (Tucson: University of Arizona Press, 2011), 73–75.

64 Chalmers, in *Hooded Americanism*, 218, puts the membership figure at 35,000 to 40,000 in Washington, and provides the quotation; Jackson, in *The Ku Klux Klan and the City*, 237, estimates the Klan membership in Washington at 25,000.

65 Chalmers, *Hooded Americanism*, 279–280.

66 In *The Ku Klux Klan and the City*, Jackson uses just three regional divisions: South, North (including the Midwest), and West.

67 Until recently, the scholarly consensus was that New England was another region that saw relatively little Klan activity, but Mark Paul Richard in *Not a Catholic Nation: The Ku Klux Klan Confronts New England in the 1920s* (Amherst: University of Massachusetts Press, 2015), shows otherwise.

68 Alexander's *The Ku Klux Klan in the Southwest* focuses on Texas, Oklahoma, Arkansas, and Louisiana; the author estimates a peak membership of perhaps half a million in that four-state region (54).

of California, Oregon, and Washington with a total Klan membership of around 125,000 comprised another significant regional Klan presence.

The Midwest, with Ohio, Indiana, and Illinois as the geographic center, was probably the country's most significant Klan stronghold. Ohio and Indiana, with an estimated 240,000 and 195,000 members, respectively, were the organization's largest state-based constituencies; Illinois, with 95,000, was also among the top five Klan membership states, and Michigan had an estimated 70,000 members. The South, not surprisingly, was another regional center for the Klan, and participation was particularly high in Georgia, Florida, Alabama, and Louisiana. Pennsylvania, with 150,000 members (the fourth largest Klan state), along with New York, 80,000, and New Jersey, 60,000 (both among the top 11 in membership), collectively ensured the Mid-Atlantic's inauspicious status as another region particularly receptive to the Klan's message of intolerance.

Notably, on a per capita basis of Klan members to residents, three of the six major centers of Klan support were in the West, broadly defined: Dallas, Denver, and Portland. The other three were Indianapolis, Dayton, and Youngstown. The Klan organizations in Los Angeles and Seattle, Oklahoma City and Tulsa, Houston, Fort Worth, and San Antonio were also influential.[69] The second Ku Klux Klan, then, was not an especially western phenomenon across all parts of the nation's largest geographic region. However, many of the West's rapidly expanding cities proved especially receptive to the Klan's aggressive nativism and rhetorical championing of social morality. The sheer pace of demographic growth and accompanying cultural diversity in these new western metropolises help explain the Klan's success in feeding public fears.[70]

As the Klan began to peak in numbers and influence in 1924, it had its greatest political impact on the Democratic Party. At the party's New York convention that year, politicians representing large urban areas with significant black, Jewish, and Catholic constituencies called for the convention to formally condemn the Klan. That resolution failed after a vote of 542 (opposed) to 541 (in favor), which underscored the Klan's influence within the party and the magnitude of the rift that divided its constituencies. The prohibitionist South's and the West's favored nominee for the presidency was Wilson's son-in-law, the prohibitionist and progressive William Gibbs McAdoo. McAdoo, a native Georgian, also

[69] Jackson, *The Ku Klux Klan in the City*, 236.

[70] Klan recruiters concentrated on the largest population centers, where the profits to be reaped were higher.

happened to be the Klan's favored candidate, in no small part because he had never criticized the organization. Alfred E. Smith, governor of New York, was the other main contestant for the nomination and represented the party's urban, immigrant, ethnic, wet, and decidedly non-WASP constituencies. The debate over the Klan exacerbated the divisions within the Democratic Party, which became so deep and heated that after 11 days and 102 ballots the convention was still unable to secure a two-thirds majority for either candidate. In the end, the Democrats picked a dark horse candidate, John Davis, inoffensive to both its core constituencies but unable to inspire enthusiasm among voters.

Davis not only faced the popular incumbent Calvin Coolidge, who had assumed the presidency after Harding had died in office in the summer of 1923, but also the Wisconsin reformer Robert La Follette, who ran as the candidate of the Progressive Party, with Senator Burton K. Wheeler of Montana as his vice presidential running mate. Coolidge won the election comfortably, with 15.7 million votes and 54 percent of the popular vote to Davis's 8.4 million and 28 percent of the popular vote. La Follette garnered about 4.8 million votes, less than 17 percent of the total, but a very strong showing for a third-party candidate. Davis won the 11 states of the Old Confederacy and Oklahoma. The West, aside from Texas and Oklahoma, voted for the Republican Party, and recently enfranchised women voters contributed to the GOP's gains in 1924, as they had in 1920, and would again in 1928[71] (Map 4.2).

The Progressive Party, drawing its support primarily from workers and farmers, performed better than the Democratic Party in a total of 12 states, including 9 western ones: California, Nevada, the Pacific Northwest states of Idaho, Oregon, and Washington, and the northwestern states of Montana, North and South Dakota, and Wyoming. The Progressives also outpolled the Democrats in Iowa, Minnesota, and La Follette's home state of Wisconsin. In fact, in the 17 western states, from the Plains to the Pacific, the Progressives' vote tally doubled that of the Democrats, and in California La Follette outpolled Davis by four to one.[72] These figures suggest that the legacies of municipal reform and social justice oriented Progressivism in the 1920s extended more deeply into the West than other American regions.

[71] Mona Morgan-Collins, "Votes for and by Women: How Did Women Vote after the Nineteenth Amendment?" Working Paper, 1–33, available at: www.lse.ac.uk/government/research/resgroups/PSPE/Working-papers/Mona-Morgan-Collins-Votes-For-and-by-Women.pdf accessed February 3, 2017.

[72] Parrish, *Anxious Decades*, 69–70, and Etulain and Malone, *The American West*, 85.

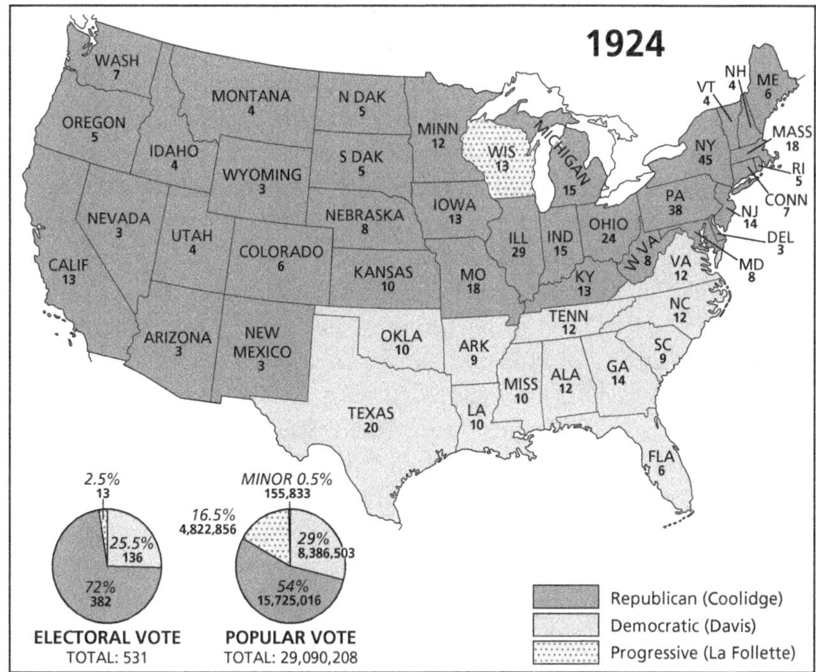

MAP 4.2 Electoral map, 1924.

In California, a generally reformist state government remained ascendant throughout the decade, opposed corporate control and supported publicly owned and operated utilities – public power – and expansion of social services. Public power initiatives were also a hallmark of progressive reform in the Pacific Northwest. Five of the six states that ratified the proposed constitutional amendment in 1924 prohibiting child labor were western ones: Arizona, California, Colorado, Montana, and Washington. Vestiges of Progressive Era activism clearly persisted in the 1920s. Though, as a whole, the 1920s, both in the nation and in the West, were marked more by reaction than substantive reform.[73]

The Klan on the national and western regional levels went into a quite steep decline in the wake of the 1924 election. The passage of the 1924 Johnson–Reed Immigration Act, or National Origins Quota Act, both validated the organization's nativist crusade and simultaneously took some of the wind out of its xenophobic sails by severely restricting the

[73] Nash, in *The American West in the Twentieth Century*, makes the case that the 1920s were a "period of muted reform," 106–116, quotation on 106.

numbers of new immigrants and Asians who could enter the country. If the immigrant "problem" was growing smaller, demographically, it might no longer warrant quite the same degree of hateful animus. In addition, the economy had seen significant improvement by mid-decade, even if the process was uneven (rural America still suffered from overproduction and attendant low commodity prices), and the anxieties and animosities that had accompanied the postwar recession were dissipating, thereby providing less fertile ground for Klan recruitment.

The other factor that induced the Klan's decline was the 1925 arrest and conviction of David Stephenson, the Grand Dragon of the Indiana Klan, on the charge of rape and murder of schoolteacher Madge Oberholtzer. Stephenson's brutal actions led many members to turn their backs on the organization in disgust. One of the key leaders of an organization that proclaimed to be the great upholder of prohibition and white Anglo-Saxon Protestant womanhood had turned out to be a drunken rapist. Moreover, the Klan's moralistic rhetoric appeared increasingly shallow and hypocritical as corruption, profiteering, and infighting, largely over money rather than principle, became increasingly evident within the organization by the mid 1920s.[74]

Nonetheless, the Klan mustered a mini-revival in 1928, inspired by opposition to the candidacy of Al Smith in the 1928 presidential election. Smith secured the Democratic nomination, despite the Klan's opposition to the perceived urban, immigrant, Catholic, wet takeover of the party. In a disastrous move, Smith promised to campaign for the repeal of the Eighteenth Amendment, despite the presence of prohibition as a core plank of his party's platform. It was no great surprise that the Anti-Saloon League endorsed Hoover, but it was a massive shock to the Democrats when Jane Addams did the same. Smith had managed to hit all the wrong notes in the campaign. He highlighted the one issue he should have assiduously avoided: prohibition.

Meanwhile, Smith failed to emphasize the core issues that would have energized his party's divided constituencies: WASP rural and small-town dwellers, on one hand, and urban dwellers of immigrant stock, on the other. Those issues included Treasury Secretary Andrew Mellon's tax policies, which favored the wealthy at the expense of wage earners, and the nation's restrictive tariff policies, which favored big business and disadvantaged the agricultural sector. Smith ended up sounding like a mouthpiece for corporate America, and meanwhile he was being

[74] For more on the Klan's decline, see MacLean, *Behind the Mask of Chivalry*, 184–188.

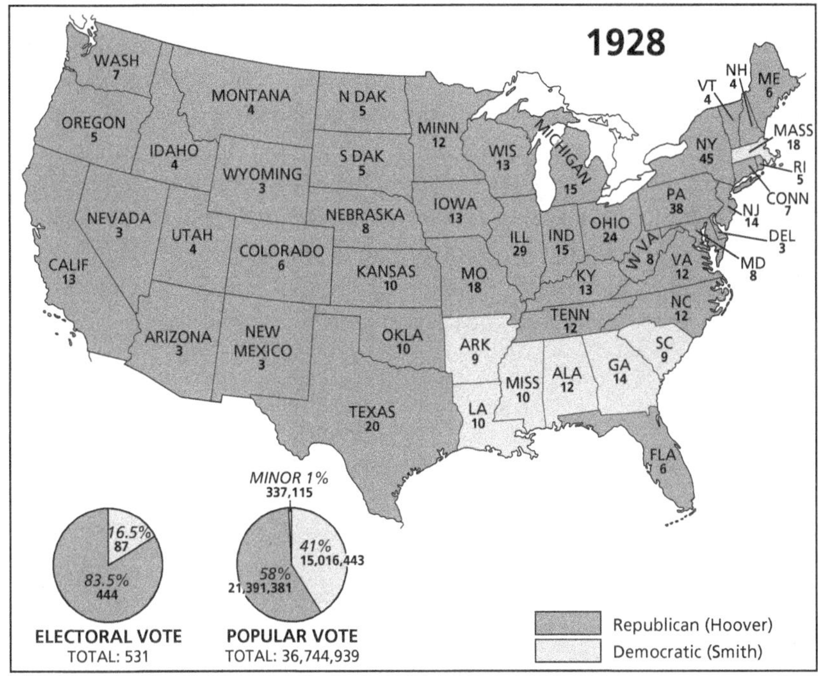

MAP 4.3 Electoral map, 1928.

lambasted by WASP Democrats for his purported devotion to alcohol and to Rome. The local Klan Klavern in Oklahoma City erected a burning cross when he showed up to speak there, and he was widely condemned by Methodist and Baptist ministers, particularly in the Southern Plains and the South. The leader of Oklahoma City's largest Baptist Church told his congregation, "If you vote for Al Smith, you're voting against Christ and you'll all be damned."[75]

Smith's opponent, Herbert Hoover, was the beneficiary of general prosperity under the two previous Republican administrations of the 1920s, and of the popularity of the incumbent, Coolidge. Hoover secured 21.4 million votes (58 percent) to Smith's 15 million (41 percent), carried 40 of the 48 states (including Smith's home state of New York), and 444 electoral votes, to Smith's 87. The whole of the West, including Texas and Oklahoma voted Republican (Map 4.3). Indeed, outside of the Plains states, only a mere smattering of counties (mainly in California, Colorado,

[75] For general coverage of the election and the quotation, see Parrish, *Anxious Decades*, 212–214.

and Nevada) went Democratic. Still, as comprehensive as the Republican victory was, Smith had done far better than Davis in the preceding election. More important, 1928 marked the start of a tremendously important trend, and one that endures into the present. Smith was the first Democratic candidate to win a plurality in the nation's 12 largest cities. His margin in those metropolises may only have been 30,000, but it marked a turnaround of about 1.3 million votes in urban support for the party. A new era was dawning for the Democratic Party, both in the West and the nation, one that would witness the coalescence of constituencies that had been deeply divided by the cultural conflicts of the 1920s.

5

From Safety Valve to Safety Net

> As long as we had free land . . . society chose to give the ambitious man free play and unlimited reward provided only that he produced the economic plant so much desired . . . In retrospect we can now see that the turn of the tide came with the turn of the century. We were reaching our last frontier; there was no more free land and our industrial combinations had become great uncontrolled and irresponsible units of power within the state . . . The day of enlightened administration has come.
>
> – Franklin Delano Roosevelt, Commonwealth Club Address, San Francisco, September 23, 1932

In the Frontier's Shadow

"The day of enlightened administration has come," Democratic presidential candidate Franklin D. Roosevelt boldly declared in San Francisco less than six weeks before the 1932 election, as the nation experienced a calamitous economic collapse. In the wake of the frontier's passing, FDR insisted, opportunities for individual economic rebirth had been largely extinguished, and corporations had established monopolies and seized control of the country. The federal government, he boldly declared, would now have to step in and replace the "safety valve" of available western lands with a safety net of social programs for those hit hardest by the depression. Thus, for FDR the end of the old western frontier explained the need for the New Deal, and by the end of the decade the New Deal had built a New West.

By 1930, the Depression had hit California, the Pacific Northwest, and the Great Plains; the Rockies and the Southwest were less affected by the economic downturn at first, but by 1932 were feeling its impact, too. The West remained a heavily agricultural region, and crop prices were plummeting. The value of California's agricultural output dropped by half from $750 million to $372 million between 1929 and 1932. During those years, farm incomes in the West were cut almost in half. In some parts of the region the decline was much worse. In Idaho, for example, where economic fortunes were tied to the wheat and potato crops, the average farm income dropped from $686 to $250; in Wyoming, it declined from $798 to $330. North and South Dakota suffered farm income declines of 64 percent and 68 percent respectively, the worst losses in the whole nation. On the Great Plains, the impact of mechanization and drought was driving people off the land in the early 1930s before the devastating Dust Bowl began in 1934; by the end of the decade as many as 700,000 people were displaced. No major agrarian sector avoided the economic collapse. The western cattle industry suffered as meat consumption declined nationwide. The Pacific Coast's fish industry also fell victim to declining prices.[1]

Core extractive industries in the West such as oil and mining suffered a steep decline because of the downturn in eastern manufacturing, as well as in the West's developing manufacturing sector. Businesses failed in the West at a higher rate than in the East, and income levels across the region (in nonagricultural as well as agricultural sectors) dropped sharply. Of the 20 states with the greatest decline in per capita income, 12 were western ones, and 7 were among the top 10. A third of the West's smaller banks went bankrupt. The West's heavy reliance both on agriculture and extractive industries made it particularly vulnerable, and by 1933 economy activity in the region had declined to less than half of the 1929 level. The western tourism industry suffered too as discretionary income dried up and visitation levels declined by half during those first years of the Depression.[2] Taking all these factors into consideration, the West was one of the nation's two hardest hit regions during the early 1930s. The

[1] Gerald Nash, The American West in the Twentieth Century: A Short History of an Urban Oasis (1973; repr., Albuquerque: University of New Mexico Press, 1985), 136–138; Leonard J. Arrington and Don C. Reading, "The New Deal Economic Programs in the Northern Tier States, 1933–1939," in *Centennial West: Essays on the Northern Tier States*, ed. William L. Lang (Seattle: University of Washington Press, 1991), 227–243, figures on 228–229; and William G. Robbins and Katrine Barber, *Nature's Northwest: The North Pacific Slope in the Twentieth Century* (Tucson: University of Arizona Press, 2011), 106.

[2] Nash, *The American West in the Twentieth Century*, 138; and Richard White, "*It's Your Misfortune and None of My Own*": *A New History of the American West* (Norman: University of Oklahoma Press, 1991), 463–464.

South was the other. The West was also the region that would benefit the most from the new era of federal activism that FDR promised.

Fittingly, FDR's campaign officially began in the West when he announced his candidacy in January 1932 in North Dakota. His selection as the Democratic Party nominee was secured on the fourth ballot when another prospective nominee William Gibbs McAdoo swung the California delegation to FDR's side, and John Nance Garner did the same for Texas, and got on board as the vice presidential candidate. Western support was vital to FDR's nomination. As the election neared, FDR's travels provided him with a clear picture of how the depression was devastating the region. In a series of key speeches FDR addressed western problems directly. In Topeka, Kansas in mid-September, he emphasized his plans to revive the agricultural economy. In Portland, the following week, he announced plans for government-funded and managed hydroelectric power. Two days later he delivered his campaign defining address in San Francisco.[3] FDR's campaign speeches were short on specifics, but clearly demonstrated his commitment to the western states' needs.

In the election, FDR swept the whole of the West, the South, and Midwest, as well as his home state of New York, and neighboring New Jersey, a total of 42 of the 48 states. He secured nearly 23 million votes (57 percent of the total) to Hoover's tally of under 16 million (40 percent). FDR also won 89 percent of the Electoral College votes (472 to Hoover's 59). Between 1928 and 1932 every western state had shifted into the Roosevelt camp, and would mostly remain there throughout his presidency (Map 5.1). But FDR's victory in the West was largely attributable to his personal appeal and marked no fundamental shift in a region where party allegiance had been weak since the Progressive Era.

The closed-frontier theme became an essential intellectual thread of FDR's developing New Deal and reflected his brain trust's central strategy in responding to the deepening crisis in early 1933. The notion of government replacing the frontier was articulated again and again by leading New Dealers. FDR and his key advisors insisted that the unrestricted individualism of an earlier era was a major factor contributing to the nation's economic woes, and that the recent combination of frontier contraction and corporate growth had unleveled the playing field. Under FDR the government expanded its regulation of the economy and

[3] Richard Lowitt, *The New Deal and the West* (Bloomington: Indiana University Press, 1984; republished in Norman by the University of Oklahoma Press, 1993), page numbers from the reprint, 1–7.

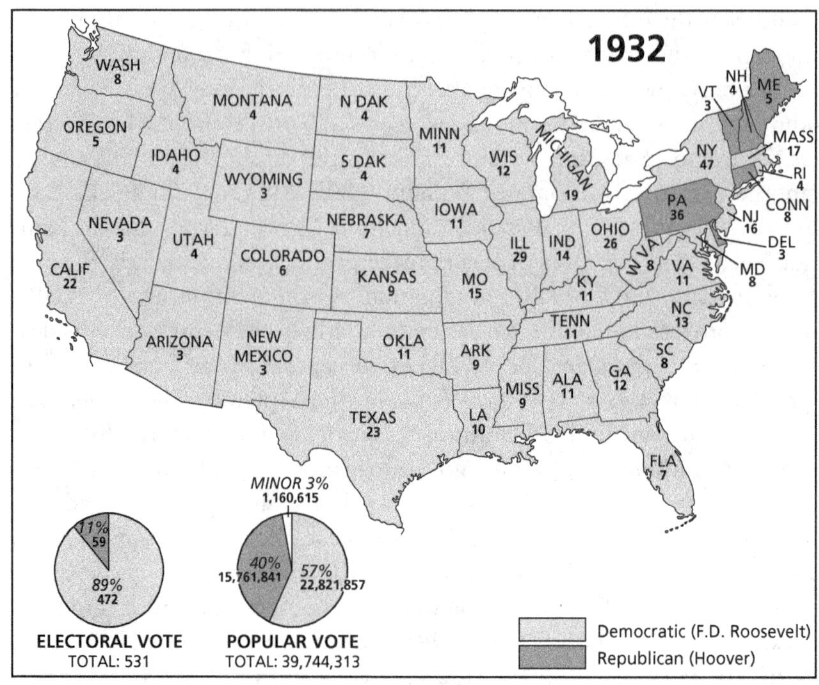

MAP 5.1 Electoral map, 1932.

attempted to establish financial security for its citizens in the postfrontier era.[4]

In response, to the new administration's rationale for its expanded role, conservative critics, including the recently defeated incumbent Herbert Hoover, insisted that frontiers of opportunity still abounded in the United States wherever individual initiative and entrepreneurship were left unhindered by state and federal regulations. Hoover made this point vehemently in his 1934 anti–New Deal jeremiad, *The Challenge to*

[4] For the closed-frontier theme and the New Deal, see David Wrobel, *The End of American Exceptionalism: Frontier Anxiety from the Old West to the New Deal* (Lawrence; University Press, of Kansas, 1993), 122–142; quotation from FDR's Commonwealth Club Address on 133. For the full text of FDR's speech, see www.americanrhetoric.com/speeches/fdrcommonwealth.htm accessed October 12, 2015. Much of the speech is reproduced in the opening chapter of FDR's book *Looking Forward* (New York: John Day, 1933), "Reappraisal of Values," 17–36.

The historian Frederick Jackson Turner, who declared the frontier closed in his famous 1893 essay, did not live to see FDR's articulation of the need for federal action in the postfrontier era (he passed away six months before the San Francisco speech), but he would have approved. In fact, FDR had been a student in Turner's course The Development of the West at Harvard in spring 1904, and that class concluded with the theme of the postfrontier future.

Liberty. Hoover declared, "[w]e have to determine now whether, under the pressures of the hour, we must cripple or abandon the heritage of liberty for some new philosophy which must mark the passing of freedom."[5] By 1938, Hoover was using the term "totalitarian" to characterize the Roosevelt presidency, and he adopted the term "totalitarian liberals" to describe New Dealers.[6] A generation later, in his autobiography, a still deeply embittered Hoover characterized the New Deal as both "sheer economic fascism," and as "the communal pole of thought."[7] Such rhetoric characterized Hoover's rather graceless postpresidential career, but also encapsulated the conservative fears that accompanied the growth of the New Deal state. In short, right wing anti–New Dealers contended, it was big government that was closing the frontier – a metaphorical frontier of individual opportunity and entrepreneurship – rather than rescuing the nation from the new economic realities accompanying the end of the western frontier.

The Book-of-the-Month Club highlighted the respective positions of the New Dealers and their conservative critics in the fall of 1934 when it chose both Hoover's *The Challenge to Liberty* and Secretary of Agriculture Henry A. Wallace's *New Frontiers* as featured selections. In making his case for government as the new frontier, the former progressive Republican Wallace declared, just as Roosevelt had done in San Francisco in 1932, that the United States was no longer a pioneer country, "Frontier free-booter democracy of the purely individualistic type" – i.e., laissez-faire capitalism – was no longer an appropriate ideology, and new "social machinery" was essential to the nation's health and well-being. Wallace dramatically announced that "[t]his machinery will carry out the Sermon on the Mount as well as the present social machinery carries out and intensifies the law of the jungle."[8] Thus, the western frontier, or, more precisely, the matter of its disappearance, served as an essential backdrop

5 Herbert Hoover, *American Individualism* (Garden City, NY: Doubleday Page, 1922); and *The Challenge to Liberty* (New York: Charles Scribner's Sons, 1934). The quotation is from Hoover's article, "The Challenge to Liberty," *Saturday Evening Post*, September 8, 1934, which comprised excerpts from the forthcoming book, which appeared later that month.

6 Herbert Hoover, "It Needn't Happen Here," *American Mercury* 50 (July 1940): 263–270, esp. 269.

7 Herbert Hoover, *The Memoirs of Herbert Hoover: The Cabinet and the Presidency, 1920–1933* (New York: Macmillan, 1951), 173.

8 Henry Wallace, *New Frontiers* (New York: Reynal and Hitchcock, 1934), 277 and 11. For discussion of the concurrent Book-of-the-Month Club listing, see George H. Nash, "Hoover's Forgotten Manifesto," October 2, 2014, available at: www.libertylawsite.org/2014/10/02/hoovers-forgotten-manifesto/ accessed September 24, 2015. Wallace was born in Iowa in 1888, when the state was generally considered to be part of the West.

to the New Deal, and the West became the favored site of some of the government's most profound transformations.

The New Dealers' closed-frontier argument generally emphasized a sharp break between the nineteenth-century past and the twentieth-century present, just as historian Frederick Jackson Turner had at the start of the depression of the 1890s. But there was another intellectual foundation of the New Deal that emphasized continuity between those two eras in the role of government, which also placed the West at the center of the argument. Historian Walter Prescott Webb highlighted the connection in 1937, insisting that "[t]he glamor of the frontier concealed the fact from homesteaders that they were all direct recipients of federal aid."[9] New Deal legal advisor and later head of the Securities and Exchange Commission, Jerome Frank, articulated this position in memorable fashion in a 1938 speech to the Harvard Business Club, declaring that the nineteenth century in America was "an era of the most stupendous pump-priming in the history of the modern world." Frank explained that the "individual private initiative" that developed the continent was in fact "stimulated and aided . . . by billions and billions of dollars of gifts from the government of the United States." Frank catalogued the process by which public lands, forests, and mineral resources were transferred to private ownership, making the settlement and development of the nation possible, and argued that the massive public works programs of the New Deal amounted to a new example of a long history of government underwriting of national growth and economic well-being. Frank went further still, insisting that this program of government stimulus "is the intelligent alternative to dictatorship."[10] By this time, FDR's critics on the right were portraying him as a dictator; newspaper magnate William Randolph Hearst began privately referring to the president as Stalin Delano Roosevelt.

Senator Lewis Schwellenbach from Washington State echoed Webb and Frank when he declared that it was "the spirit of the pioneer" that fueled the New Deal. Schwellenbach explained that federal largesse had underwritten nineteenth-century American expansion, but when it came

[9] Walter Prescott Webb, *Divided We Stand: The Crisis of a Frontierless Democracy* (New York: Farrar and Rinehart, 1937), quoted in Robert L. Dorman, *Hell of a Vision: Regionalism and the Modern American West* (Tucson: University of Arizona Press, 2010), 79.

[10] Jerome Frank, Address before the Harvard Business Club, December 8, 1938, quoted in Jason Scott Smith, *Building New Deal Liberalism: The Political Economy of Public Works, 1933–1956* (New York: Cambridge University Press, 2006), 118–119.

to "government bounties," "the real pioneers who grubbed and slaved and really developed the country got none of them." The railroads, timber companies, mining companies, and other big businesses, he added, had essentially run the government in that earlier era. The only difference between the government's role in the pioneer past and the Depression present, Frank, Schwellenbach and other supporters of FDR's programs argued, was that the federal government was now aiding "the people" rather than "the interests."[11] Whether the federal safety net was presented as an essential substitute for a landed frontier that no longer existed or as a vital continuation of the long tradition of federal underwriting of national development, or even as a dangerous step toward state socialism and the destruction of American individualism and self-reliance, the theme of westward frontier expansion and contraction stood at the center of the great debate between the New Dealers and FDR's conservative critics.

Building Western Regions

Right after his inauguration in early March 1933, FDR called Congress into emergency session for over three months, the famous First Hundred Days. The magnitude of the problems facing the nation was staggering. At least one in every four American workers was unemployed, only about a quarter of the unemployed were receiving any relief, and many millions more were underemployed since employers were reducing them to part-time workers.[12] Still, with large Democratic majorities to work with – 311 to 116 in the House and 60 to 35 in the Senate – and the Republicans deflated and divided, FDR pushed his agenda through Congress quickly.[13] The remarkable flurry of legislative activity that ensued amounted to the first phase of FDR's age of "enlightened administration." The measures of what would later become known as the First New Deal developed over the initial two years of FDR's administration and fell into five core categories.

[11] Lewis Schwellenbach, Address before the Jeffersonian Democratic Club of Virginia, May 4, 1940, and untitled speech, July 15, 1938, quoted in Smith, *New Deal Public Works*, 120–121. It would be more accurate to say that the New Deal in its first phase was providing for the people *as well as* the interests.

[12] Lawrence Levine, "The Historian and the Icon: Photography and the History of the American People in the 1930s and 1940s," in *Documenting America, 1935–1943*, ed. Carl Fleischhauer and Beverly W. Brannan (1988; repr., Berkeley: University of California Press, 2007), 15–42, esp. 19.

[13] James T. Patterson, *Congressional Conservatism and the New Deal: The Growth of the Conservative Coalition in Congress, 1933–1939* (Lexington: For the Organization of American Historians by University of Kentucky Press, 1967), 1–31.

Three of those categories of federal action had an enormous impact on the West: regional planning, relief programs, and rural/agricultural policies. The other two categories – regulation (of the banking industry and the stock market), and the coordinated economic recovery efforts of the National Recovery Administration (NRA) – were less significant for the region.

Regulatory policy for the banks and financial markets was national in scope and design and generally successful, though there was nothing particularly notable about its implementation in the West. However, western influence in the Senate led to the passage of the Silver Purchase Act of 1934, which provided a significant federal stimulus to the region's silver and related lead, zinc, and copper mining industries. The government added silver to the nation's monetary reserves and bought up most of the West's output, and at prices more than twice as high as the true market value.[14]

The NRA's influence nationwide was cut short after less than two years when the Supreme Court declared the agency unconstitutional in May 1935. Prior to that inauspicious end, George Creel, former progressive Mayor of Denver, head of the Committee on Public Information during World War I, and head of the NRA's Western Division, intervened during a strike among cotton pickers that began in California's San Joaquin Valley in the fall of 1933. His actions favored agribusiness over the workers who were clearly being exploited, and may have even helped precipitate the formation of the rigidly antilabor Associated Farmers of California the following spring. Creel's actions certainly encapsulated the left's common criticism of the early New Deal programs for being too oriented toward the needs of big business.[15] But for the most part the NRA had little lasting impact on the West, or in any other region. Creel resigned his NRA position in 1934 to mount a challenge to Upton Sinclair for the Democratic Party California gubernatorial nomination.[16]

In contrast, the New Deal's emphasis on regional planning and relief programs had an enormous impact on the West as well as the South. Matching in scope and scale the Tennessee Valley Authority's (TVA) controversial re-engineering of one of the South's poorest regions through

[14] Gerald Nash, *The Federal Landscape: An Economic History of the Twentieth-Century West* (Tucson: University of Arizona Press, 1999), 32–33.

[15] The New Deal's critics on the left are treated later in this chapter. Smith provides a useful overview of critiques of the New Deal from historians on the left in *Building New Deal Liberalism*, 1–20.

[16] Lowitt, *The New Deal and the West*, 176–177.

flood control, the introduction of a range of scientific farming techniques and, most significantly, the provision of hydroelectric power, the New Deal's dam projects on the Columbia River transformed the Pacific Northwest. Those projects brought a significant measure of prosperity to a region that had previously been economically underdeveloped and largely reliant on agriculture and extractive industry. The Pacific Northwest was relatively unknown as a region prior to the 1920s when railroad advertising grouped the states of Washington, Oregon and Idaho together for promotional purposes and began to use the regional label consistently.[17] New Deal regional planning built on those early foundations and helped to create a strong regional identity among residents of those states, as well as a growing sense nationwide of the Pacific Northwest as a coherent regional entity. The Pacific Northwest Regional Planning Commission (PNRPC), created by the federal government in 1934, played an important role in coordinating the region's economic development.[18]

As early as the 1920s, federal and state officials had begun to consider the damming of the Columbia River and the accompanying production of hydroelectric power as a pathway to regional development, but it was the massive infusion of New Deal funds that made those projects a reality. Construction on the Grand Coulee Dam in Washington State began in July 1933. Funded by the Public Works Administration (PWA) and built by the Bureau of Reclamation and two separate consortia of private construction companies, work on the 4,200-foot long and 450-foot high dam continued for nearly nine years. The dam became operational in June 1942. Journalist and later senator from Oregon Richard Neuberger famously described the structure as "the biggest thing on earth," and it was the largest concrete structure that had ever been built. It was also "the largest single reclamation project ever undertaken in the United States," covering some 2.5 million acres (twice the size of Delaware), including four large dams in addition to Grand Coulee, and including a total of more than 2,200 miles of main and tributary canals and nearly 3,500 miles of drains and waste channels.[19]

[17] John Findlay, "A Fishy Proposition: Regional Identity in the Pacific Northwest," in *Many Wests: Place, Culture, and Regional Identity*, ed. David M. Wrobel and Michael C. Steiner (Lawrence: University Press of Kansas, 1997), 37–70, esp. 51–52.

[18] For more on the PNRPC, see Dorman, *Hell of a Vision*, 101–102.

[19] Richard Neuberger, *Our Promised Land* (New York: Macmillan, 1939), quoted in Robert F. Ficken and Charles P. LeWarne, *Washington: A Centennial History* (Seattle: University of Washington Press, 1988), 121. Details on the dam are from Paul C. Pitzer, *Grand Coulee: Harnessing a Dream* (Pullman: Washington State University Press, 1994).

Work on the PWA-funded and US Army Corps of Engineers-built Bonneville Dam, near Portland, Oregon, began in 1934 and was completed in late September 1937. On that date, FDR delivered a speech at the massive new facility to mark the occasion and then pressed the button that turned on its two huge hydroelectric generators. A month earlier, the New Deal government created the Bonneville Power Association (BPA) to oversee the production and distribution of Columbia River-generated electrical power throughout the region.[20] In addition to its power production capacity, the Bonneville Dam made the Columbia River navigable for ocean-going vessels for 188 miles from the Pacific inland to the Dalles, providing a massive boost to commerce and regional development. The Bonneville project also made the costly provisions necessary to maintain salmon runs through a complex system of spillways, leading FDR to remark cynically in 1935 that he hoped "that the salmon will approve the spillways and find them really useful, even though they cost almost as much as the dam and the hydroelectric power development." Despite the efforts at salmon-run accommodation in the actual design and construction of the Bonneville Dam, and fish-run relocation efforts, which accompanied the Grand Coulee project, the cumulative consequences for salmon of these and subsequently built Columbia River dams have been devastating.[21]

The two massive dam projects had an overwhelmingly positive effect on unemployment and general economic well-being in the Pacific Northwest. During construction, Bonneville and Grand Coulee together directly employed tens of thousands of people and spurred the employment of many thousands more in those industries such as steel, concrete, and timber that provided the necessary building materials. The Columbia River projects ensured that Washington (right after lightly populated Nevada) led the region and the entire nation in total per capita level federal expenditures between 1933 and 1939. Once the BPA's hydroelectric facilities were operational, they provided the cheapest electricity in the country and much like the TVA in the South provided a vitally important yardstick for measuring and regulating the rates private electrical utility companies charged consumers.[22]

[20] For coverage of the Columbia River dam projects, see Lowitt, *The New Deal and the West*, 157–171, and Richard White, *The Organic Machine: The Remaking of the Columbia River* (New York: Hill and Wang, 1995).

[21] FDR quoted in Lowitt, *The New Deal and the West*, 159. White, in *The Organic Machine*, provides a more critical assessment than Lowitt of the dams' impact on salmon.

[22] White, *"It's Your Misfortune and None of My Own,"* 487. For more on the Bonneville and Grand Coulee Dams and the Bonneville Power Authority, see David P. Billington

The Columbia River dams were among the most significant of the New Deal's public works projects. The Far West was also the site of another of the most impressive and symbolically significant examples of New Deal regional development through public works projects, the Boulder Dam. The Six Companies, a consortium of large construction companies including the Henry J. Kaiser Company, built the dam on the Nevada border with Arizona. The structure provided flood control, irrigation, and hydroelectric power production, primarily for Arizona and California. The project, begun during the Hoover administration as a private initiative rather than a public power project (Hoover opposed public power), prompted the creation of the worker town of Boulder City, Nevada, and the growth of Las Vegas and Southern Nevada, as well as the continued growth and infrastructural development of Southern California. The dam also provided vital flood control for California's Imperial Valley, and enabled the irrigation of 2.5 million acres of land in Colorado, Utah and Wyoming, as well as in Arizona and California.[23]

Boulder Dam would have been built even if there had been no Great Depression or New Deal, but with FDR's election the massive construction initiative became an iconic public works project. The 727-foot high, 660-foot thick, and 1,244-foot long structure was completed with PWA funds in 1935 and operated by the Bureau of Reclamation. By June 1937, the dam's hydroelectric power-generating capacity was operational. The dam structures, with their striking art deco design, collectively served as a powerful symbol of the New Deal in the West, though the human toll of 112 fatalities during construction is worth remembering too.

When the British writer J. B. Priestley visited the recently constructed Boulder Dam in the winter of 1935–1936, he wrote glowingly about it: "[h]ere in this Western American Wilderness the new man, the man of the future, has done something, and what he has done takes your breath away." Stunned by the results of the New Deal's "collective planning," Priestley proclaimed, "[h]ere is the soul of America under socialism." When FDR dedicated the dam in late September 1935, while on a western tour, he certainly made no mention of collective planning or socialism, and no mention either of his inveterate critic Hoover, whose *The Challenge to Liberty* had appeared the previous year and accused him of practicing both. FDR did not invite the ex-president to the ceremony,

and Donald C. Jackson, *Big Dams of the New Deal Era: A Confluence of Engineering and Politics* (Norman: University of Oklahoma Press, 2006), 152–190.

[23] Lowitt, *The New Deal and the West*, 86.

and it would take until a few years after FDR's death in 1945 for Boulder Dam to be reassigned the original name Hoover Dam that Congress had ascribed in 1930.[24]

In addition to being the greatest beneficiary of the Boulder Dam, California was home to several of the largest of the New Deal's western public power and water projects. The All-American Canal project in California's Imperial Valley was initiated in 1928, but largely constructed in the 1930s by the Bureau of Reclamation and the Six Companies. The canal, which transports water from the Colorado River to the valley, was completed in 1942. The Central Valley Project (CVP) moved water from the northern part of the state to the more arid San Joaquin Valley in the south. Initially begun in 1933 and officially overseen by the Bureau of Reclamation beginning in 1937, the system of 20 dams and reservoirs and canals, supplied hydroelectric power and provided flood control, in addition to delivering a regulated water supply to the arid parts of the valley, including municipalities. The CVP included Shasta Dam, another of the major dam projects of the era, built between 1938 and 1945 across the Sacramento River.[25] In addition, the PWA provided substantial funding for private hydroelectric initiatives, including California's Hetch Hetchy Project in Tuolumne County, California, which expanded the O-Shaughnessy Dam, thereby increasing the capacity of the Hetch Hetchy Reservoir and ensuring San Francisco's growing municipal needs would be met.

The hydraulic imprimatur of the New Deal reached beyond the Pacific Northwest, Desert Southwest, and California to other parts of the West. Close to a thousand miles from the Hoover Dam, the Fort Peck Dam, stretches across the Missouri River in northeast Montana. The PWA project was begun in 1933 and completed in 1940. The massive earth filled structure – 250 feet high, 50 feet wide at the top and about a half-mile wide at the base, and more than 21,000 feet, or 3.68 miles, long – employed well over 10,000 workers by 1936, helping to revive Montana's economy. Tragically, six workers died in a landslide during construction

[24] Russell R. Elliott, with the assistance of William D. Rowley, *History of Nevada*, 2nd ed. (Lincoln: University of Nebraska Press, 1987), 277. For more on the construction of Boulder Dam, see Billington and Jackson, *Big Dams of the New Deal Era*, 133–151. For J. B. Priestley's quotation, see his *Midnight on the Desert: Being an Excursion into Autobiography during a Winter in America, 1935–1936* (New York: Harper and Brothers, 1937), 110–111 and 112–113.

[25] For the Central Valley Project, see Billington and Jackson, *Big Dams of the New Deal Era*, 272–288.

in 1938. By 1943 the dam was fully operational and generating hydroelectric power.[26]

Of similarly grand scale and significance, the Colorado-Big Thompson Project (C-BT) was begun under the auspices of the Bureau of Reclamation in 1938, with PWA funding, and completed at mid-century. One of the Bureau's most expansive projects, the C-BT comprised a huge system of tunnels and reservoirs to transfer water from the western slope to parched lands in eastern Colorado. In addition, the PWA provided funding for other major initiatives that were not managed and overseen by the federal government, including Oklahoma's Grand River Dam, the state's first hydroelectric facility, built between 1938 and 1941, and projects in Arizona, Idaho, Nebraska, and Utah. Between 1933 and 1943, the PWA financed $2 billion worth of projects in the West.[27] Together, these public power projects and public/private partnerships thoroughly transformed the economies of the West's subregions, and laid the infrastructural foundations for the massive development of the defense industry during the war years.

The Rural Electrification Administration (REA), another of the New Deal's signature regional development initiatives, brought modern comforts and conveniences to much of the rural West. The United States lagged behind Europe in the provision of electrical utility service to rural areas, largely because of the unwillingness of private companies to invest in the necessary infrastructure to bring light and power to remote locations. Through the establishment of rural cooperatives and the provision of loans from the REA, rural westerners received the electrical service that private companies refused to provide, or grossly overcharged for. Once the federal government got into the business of funding these rural cooperatives, critics complained that the state had no right to intervene in the private sector. The same arguments were leveled against the TVA, BPA and other federal hydroelectric projects, and like those initiatives, the REA made a major difference. Texas provides the best example, which was fitting given that the state's congressman Sam Rayburn was the sponsor of the original REA legislation. In 1935, when the REA was established, only 12.6 percent of all American farms had electricity, but in Texas the situation was far worse: only 2.3 percent of Texas farms had

[26] For the Fort Peck Dam, see Billington and Jackson, *Big Dams of the New Deal Era*, 211–230.

[27] Smith, *Building New Deal Liberalism*, 94. Lowitt provides the figure for PWA expenditures in Lowitt, *The New Deal and the West*, 223.

service. Three decades later only 2 percent of Texas farms were without electricity. The REA was entirely responsible for the remarkable shift. The agency financed 79 electrical distribution systems totaling more than 180,000 miles of utility lines, serving nearly half a million rural connections and impacting 246 of the state's 254 counties and 95 percent of its residents.[28]

Similar transformations occurred across much of the rural West. In Idaho, about 70 percent of farms were without electricity when the REA began its operations, but by 1939, 54 percent of farms had electrical service, and by 1954, fewer than 3 percent of the state's farms lacked electricity. In North Dakota, only 2.3 percent of farms had service in 1935, but by 1954 the number had risen to 90 percent. Just 3.4 percent of South Dakotans had electrical service in 1935, and the figure reached 90 percent by 1960. At the end of the 1920s less than 6 percent of Nebraska farms and ranches had electricity, but by the mid 1960s virtually all of them did, which was a fitting testament to Senator George Norris, one of the primary champions of the REA whose efforts were vital to the creation of the agency. In Wyoming, just 527 ranches and farms had electricity in 1935, but that number increased sixfold to 3,300 by 1939 because of the REA; the number in Montana more than doubled from 2,758 to 6,000. The REA eased the burdens of life in the rural West, just as it did in the rural South. In addition to electric light at the flick of a switch, electricity powered radios, telephones, water pumps, cooking ranges, refrigerators, washing machines, vacuum cleaners, and even milking machines. It was government enterprise that brought the rural West into the modern world.[29]

[28] For the national figure, see T. H. Watkins, *The Great Depression: America in the 1930s* (Boston: Little, Brown, 1993), 262. For Texas, Randolph B. Campbell, *Gone to Texas: A History of the Lone Star State* (New York: Oxford University Press, 2003), 389; and https://tshaonline.org/handbook/online/articles/dpr01 accessed January 12, 2016.

[29] Carlos A. Schwantes, *In Mountain Shadows: A History of Idaho* (Lincoln: University of Nebraska Press, 1991), 209; and Leonard J. Arrington, *History of Idaho*, 2 vols. (Moscow: University of Idaho Press, 1994), 2:62; Elwyn B. Robinson, *History of North Dakota* (Lincoln: University of Nebraska Press, 1966), 447; Herbert B. Schell, *History of South Dakota* (Lincoln: University of Nebraska Press, 1968), 304; James C. Olson and Ronald C. Naugle, *History of Nebraska*, 3rd ed. (Lincoln: University of Nebraska Press, 1997), 347–348; and Duane A. Smith, *Rocky Mountain Heartland: Colorado, Montana, and Wyoming in the Twentieth Century* (Tucson: University of Arizona Press, 2008), 143–144.

Restoring and Developing Western Lands

As the nation's most arid and ecologically fragile region, it was not surprising that the West became the primary site for these huge water engineering projects. But the region also disproportionately benefited from the New Deal's work relief initiatives. The Civilian Conservation Corps (CCC) is a particularly important example. In operation from 1933 to 1942, the agency employed between 2.5 and 3 million men, mostly young and unmarried, earning $30 a month, and required to send $25 of it home to help their families. They engaged mostly in manual labor geared to natural resource conservation and improvements to national and state parks. The Corps literally reengineered the nation's natural landscape, and especially the West's. Nationwide, fully 800 new state parks were developed; more than 10,000 small reservoirs were built, along with 46,000 vehicular bridges, 125,000 miles of new roads, and close to 600,000 additional miles of old roadway were improved; 28,000 miles of new hiking trails were built and another 100,000 miles of existing trails were improved; and nearly a million miles of fence were constructed.

When Priestley encountered a CCC camp in Sedona, Arizona, he remarked that "the fortunate young men . . . had some decent work to do for the good of their community, and they were being reasonably well sheltered and fed and paid in one of the most enchanting places on earth." He contrasted the "brown, husky [CCC] lads" with the "unemployed English youths who stand outside our labor exchanges and slushy street corners, just miserably kept alive by the dole." Priestley concluded, "I could not see that we could teach the Americans much about social services."[30] The CCC not only improved the health of its workers, it helped restore the health of watersheds, forests and eroded lands that had suffered from drought conditions, poor land management, and high demand for timber that had decimated the nation's natural resources in the 1920s and early 1930s. The CCC was probably the single most popular and least controversial of all the New Deal agencies.[31]

The CCC was national in scope. The law that created the agency provided for the purchase of over 20 million acres of private land, much

[30] Priestley, *Midnight on the Desert*, 295.

[31] Neil M. Maher, *Nature's New Deal: The Civilian Conservation Corps and the Roots of the American Environmental Movement* (New York: Oxford University Press, 2008), 3–15, 43, and 71; and John A. Salmond, *The Civilian Conservation Corps, 1933–1942: A New Deal Case Study* (Durham, NC: Duke University Press, 1967), 121–122.

of it in the East, to ensure locations for Corps camps across the nation. Nonetheless, the agency especially benefited the western states. Since the West was home to most of the nation's public lands, including national parks and forests, the agency's reforestation efforts proved particularly significant in the region. Moreover, FDR consciously targeted the Rocky Mountains and the Pacific Coast not just because of their high concentrations of national forest lands but also because he sought to augment his political base there. The president understood all too well that providing employment for local youth and a market for local businesses that supplied the CCC camps would garner public support.

The Corps also worked to prevent and combat forest fires, including the construction of the massive 600-mile "Ponderosa Way" firebreak along the base of the Sierra Nevada in California and the dispatching of 1,400 men to control a fire near Los Angeles in 1934 that might otherwise have devastated the city. In addition, CCC workers planted a shelterbelt (mostly on privately-held lands) across the Great Plains, from the Canadian border at North Dakota to the Texas panhandle, to reduce wind-driven soil erosion, part of the 2 billion trees that "Roosevelt's Tree Army" was responsible for planting. CCC workers labored to mitigate soil erosion on as much as 40 million acres of farmland. Those efforts were expanded after the 1934 Dust Bowl, when FDR increased the number of CCC camps in the Great Plains. Notably, the CCC also included an Indian Division, administered by the Bureau of Indian Affairs. The organization initially employed 14,400 young Indian men who engaged in natural resource conservation and development mainly on reservations and mostly in the western states; by 1942, more than 88,000 had worked for the Corps.[32]

While the CCC camps were evenly distributed across the nation's most heavily forested lands, from the Northeast, Appalachia, and the Mid-Atlantic to the Great Lakes, California, the Rockies, and the Pacific Northwest, the per capita expenditures tell a markedly different story, and one of distinct western advantage.[33] National per capita expenditures on the CCC from 1933 to 1939 were $19.50; for the Pacific Coast

[32] See Joel Jason Orth, "The Conservation Landscape Trees and Nature on the Great Plains" (PhD diss., Iowa State University, 2004); Maher, *Nature's New Deal*, 43–76; Salmond, *The Civilian Conservation Corps*, 121–134; and Donald L. Fixico, *Indian Resilience and Rebuilding: Indigenous Nations in the Modern American West* (Tucson: University of Arizona Press, 2013), 77–78.

[33] See the map of "Emergency Conservation Work Camps" in Maher, *Nature's New Deal*, 46–47.

states they were $28.50; and for the relatively lightly populated Rocky Mountain states the figure was $85.80, well over four times the national average.[34] The CCC funding proved important not just because it provided much-needed economic stimulus and facilitated natural resource restoration for fragile western ecosystems, but also because the agency was developing both the natural and built environments for the expansion of tourism and recreation in the West.[35] Thus, the Corps played an essential role in making western places more attractive for seasonal visitors and potential new residents seeking quality of life in the region's increasingly accessible and well-appointed natural wonderlands.

The CCC raised the ire of numerous ecologists and preservation organizations during the mid and late 1930s. The Corps's critics advocated radically reduced management of ecosystems, allowing for the self-restoration of natural landscapes; they found the Corp's methods too intrusive.[36] *Nature Magazine* criticized the CCC in 1935 for its "wild orgy of road-building" and proclaimed that the agency sought to "solve the wilderness problem in much the same way the Turks set about solving the Armenian problem – by annihilation." Such wilderness advocates promoted "nature without the handrails," wholly undeveloped spaces accessible to the natural enthusiast willing to expend the energy and effort to explore them, unassisted by all modern comforts and conveniences, and closed to everyone else.[37]

Yet, for any ecological shortcomings, the CCC had played an essential part in building a more thoroughly accessible and thus more democratic nature-scape across the country, but most memorably in the West. Consequently, the West's dramatic landscapes became the pleasure ground not just for privileged artists, writers, and wealthy travelers who could afford access in earlier eras, but for a significant segment of the American population starting in the 1930s, and even larger numbers in the post–World War II years. In 1933, annual visitation to the nation's national parks

34 White, *"It's Your Misfortune and None of My Own,"* 475.

35 CCC wages went back to worker's families, wherever they resided, so not all those funds stayed in the West, though that was the case for all regions.

36 Maher examines these critiques in *Nature's New Deal*, 165–180.

37 "A New Defender of the Wilderness," *Nature Magazine* 26 (September 1935): 188–179, quoted in Earl Pomeroy, *In Search of the Golden West: The Tourist in Western America*, 2nd ed. (1957; repr., Lincoln: Bison Books/University of Nebraska Press, 2010); Joseph L. Sax, *Mountains without Handrails: Reflections on the National Parks* (Ann Arbor: University of Michigan Press, 1980); and Paul Sutter, *Driven Wild: How the Fight against Automobiles Launched the Modern Wilderness Movement* (Seattle: University of Washington Press, 2002).

totaled 3.4 million; by 1940 that figure had almost quintupled, rising to 16.7 million. Four new national parks were added to the system during those years, bringing the total to 26, while the number of national monuments more than doubled, from 40 to 82. The Corps's imprint, handrails and all, along with FDR's impact as a deeply committed conservationist president remains vital and pervasive eight decades later.[38]

The Taylor Grazing Act of 1934 also contributed significantly to the New Deal's enduring legacy for the public lands. The long-gestating legislation largely ended the homesteading era after more than seven decades of operation. The act withdrew a total of 142 million acres of western lands from potential purchase under the Homesteading Act of 1862 and brought some protection to approximately 80 million acres of the nation's fragile semiarid grazing lands by managing them more systematically.[39] By 1939, more than 65 million acres of the withdrawn lands were organized into grazing districts, with local ranchers and state officials agreeing upon the district boundaries. All those districts remain in effect today, though stock growing interests have always dominated them, sometimes at the expense of soil conservation. Nonetheless, in combination with the federal Soil Conservation Service (SCS, formerly the Soil Erosion Service), the Taylor Grazing Act finally responded to the crisis of soil erosion on public lands. While the Taylor Act and the SCS were imperfect, they clearly improved upon the previous policy of no federal regulation at all, which had contributed to the environmental disaster.[40]

In addition to the big reclamation projects, the work of the CCC, the Taylor Grazing Act and the SCS, the first phase of the New Deal featured a concerted effort to help distressed farmers. The Agricultural Adjustment Administration (AAA) was created in 1933 and charged with the vital task of curtailing overproduction and thereby raising the prices of agricultural

[38] Otis L. Graham Jr., *Presidents and the American Environment* (Lawrence: University Press of Kansas, 2015), 116 and 138.

[39] Some new homesteading did occur in the region after the passage of the Taylor Grazing Act, but the new leasing and permit systems made it harder to stake new homestead claims; see Brian Q. Cannon, *Reopening the Frontier: Homesteading in the Modern West* (Lawrence: University Press of Kansas, 2009).

[40] For more on the Taylor Grazing Act (TGA), see US Department of Interior, Bureau of Land Management website: www.blm.gov/wy/st/en/field_offices/Casper/range/taylor .1.html accessed December 14, 2015; Carl Abbott, "The Federal Presence," in *The Oxford History of the American West*, ed. Clyde A. Milner, Carol A. O'Connor, and Martha A. Sandweiss (New York: Oxford University Press, 1994), 469–497, esp. 478; and Leisl Carr Childers, *The Size of the Risk: Histories of Multiple Land Use in the Great Basin* (Norman: University of Oklahoma Press, 2015), 15–53.

staples. This goal was, to a degree, successfully achieved through the work of the AAA's Domestic Allotment System, which essentially paid farmers to take portions of their land out of cultivation to reduce supply. The crop-reduction system began too late to have much effect in 1933, and 10 million acres of sprouting cotton were plowed back into the ground, and 6 million baby pigs and 200,000 pregnant sows slaughtered, all of which was hard to explain to millions of severely undernourished Americans. Children and the elderly were dying from malnutrition, yet the government was systematically destroying hogs and cotton to restore commodity prices.

Republican newspapers blamed a seemingly overbearing federal government for the debacle of food destruction, but the critics made no mention of the 100 million pounds of surplus pork that the Federal Surplus Relief Corporation distributed to the hungry. The Domestic Allotment System – together with the drought conditions that were already developing across the Plains in 1933 and 1934 and which reduced agricultural productivity – raised price levels. Cotton increased from 7 cents a pound to more than 12 cents in 1934, wheat from 38 cents a bushel to 86 cents, and corn, from 32 cents a bushel to 82 cents. Parity in the agrarian sector was never fully achieved during the 1930s, but because of crop-reduction programs and the federal credits they brought to farmers, the parity ratio (the measure of agricultural price levels to those in other sectors of the economy) did rise from a low of 58 in 1932 to 93 in 1937, before slumping to 81 in late 1941. In Idaho, for example, the AAA negotiated over 73,000 production control contracts, which collectively contributed to a rise in the total value of crop production from around $42 million in 1932 to about $75 million in 1935.[41]

Mechanization, in the form of tractors, which drove many sharecroppers and leaseholders off the land, along with the federal credits for crop reduction, particularly those given to larger farming interests on the Great Plains, further contributed to the displacement of poorer farmers who were thrown off the land as it was taken out of production. This was an unintended consequence of the AAA's efforts, but one that highlighted the tendency of some early New Deal programs (including the NRA)

41 David Kennedy, *Freedom from Fear: The American People in Depression and War* (New York: Oxford University Press, 1999), 204–207, and Parrish, *Anxious Decades*, 300–307. The Idaho statistic is from Michael P. Malone, "The New Deal in Idaho," *Pacific Historical Review* 3 (August 1969): 293–310; Arrington, in *History of Idaho*, provides a somewhat more conservative picture of increase in the value of agricultural goods, from $52 million in 1933 to $80 million in 1939 (68).

to seek recovery on a macro- economic scale through the single-minded goal of restoring price levels without fully considering the potential policy implications for the nation's most vulnerable farmers and farmworkers. It was perhaps the most regrettable irony of the First New Deal that some of those Great Plains families displaced by the AAA's program of limiting supply to raise prices ended up becoming part of the mass migrations to the Pacific Northwest and California.[42] Moreover, the Southern Plains exodus to the Golden State (see Chapter 6) would become one of the defining developments of the Depression decade.

The early efforts of the New Deal to bring relief and recovery effected some parts of the West less than others. For example, Oklahoma, under the heel of one of its most controversial and dictatorial governors, William, "Alfalfa" Bill, Murray, strongly resisted FDR's programs. Unsuccessful as a Democratic Party nominee for the presidency in 1932, Murray resented and despised FDR. The president, for his part, described Murray as "crazy as a bedbug." Oklahoma's poorest citizens suffered because of their governor's intransigence, which owed nothing to principle and everything to personal bitterness. Murray left office in 1934 and E. W. Marland, a strong supporter of Roosevelt, campaigned successfully to "Bring the New Deal to Oklahoma" and proceeded to fulfill his promise.[43]

In Oregon, Charles Henry Martin became governor in 1934 campaigning as a New Dealer, but quickly turned against public power and relief initiatives in the state, and railed against the pro-labor provisions of the NIRA. A thoroughgoing Social Darwinist, Martin's views made Hoover's opposition to government intervention on behalf of needy citizens seem moderate indeed. If a citizen had nothing to contribute to society, then Martin insisted that society had absolutely no obligations to that person. Thus, he supported a proposal to chloroform "the aged and feeble-minded wards of the state." He suggested cutting $300,000 from the state's budget by putting 900 of the 969 residents of the Fairview Home in Salem, a state facility for the mentally challenged, "out of their misery." Martin mobilized National Guard troops against striking workers in 1935 and

[42] Neil Foley, *The White Scourge: Mexicans, Blacks, and Poor Whites in Texas Cotton Culture* (Berkeley: University of California Press, 1997), 163–182

[43] W. David Baird and Danney Goble, *Oklahoma: A History* (Norman: University of Oklahoma Press, 2008), 227–228. Murray would seek the governorship again in 1938, but was unsuccessful.

1937, and he organized Red Squads to repress labor organizations. Martin also railed against the Social Security Act of 1935, declaring that it was "driving the country into national socialism." Oregon continued to secure more than its fair share of New Deal funding despite its governor, who was defeated in the Democratic primary in 1938. Charles Sprague, a liberal Republican who admired FR and supported public power and other key New Deal programs, succeeded Martin.[44]

In California, Republican Governors James Rolph (1931–1934) who died in office in 1934, and his successor, former Lieutenant Governor Frank Merriam (1934–1939), proved largely unreceptive to New Deal initiatives. Merriam did come on board at least to some small degree after the dramatic 1934 gubernatorial election, but California agribusiness proved another major source of opposition to federal programs.[45] California's resistance to the New Deal was in keeping with its brutal opposition to labor; the New Deal was supportive of labor's right to unionize and bargain collectively. Daily wages for California field workers averaged $2.55 in 1930, but by 1933 had dropped to $1.40, or 15 to 16 cents an hour. Thirty-seven strikes took place across the state in 1933. In the fall of that year, 12,000 cotton pickers in the lower San Joaquin Valley (mostly Mexicans and Filipinos, but also some African Americans and white Southern Plains migrants), organized by the Cannery and Agricultural Workers Industrial Union (CAWIU), went on strike. The action met with a violent response from local authorities; several strikers and sympathizers were gunned down. Sherriff's deputies even prevented the union from delivering food supplies to the striking workers and their families. The National Industrial Recovery Act (NIRA) provided no significant protections for agricultural workers. Nonetheless, the NRA did intervene to help broach a compromise, which provided for a small pay increase for the workers, but no formal recognition for the CAWIU. The federal government had not yet formally taken a side, but it was clearly leaning toward labor.[46]

44 Gary Murrell, *Iron Pants: Oregon's Anti–New Deal Governor* (Pullman: Washington State University Press, 2000), 158–159 and 186.

45 For more on California's political resistance to the New Deal, see Lowitt's chapter "California Is Different" in *The New Deal and the West*, 172–188.

46 Lori A. Flores, *Grounds for Dreaming: Mexican Americans, Mexican Immigrants, and the California Farmworker Movement* (New Haven, CT: Yale University Press, 2016), 32. See also Devra Weber, *Dark Sweat, White Gold: California Farm Workers, Cotton, and the New Deal* (Berkeley: University of California Press, 1994), esp. 79–111.

Then in San Francisco in the summer of 1934 militant Australian labor leader Harry Bridges, empowered by the NIRA, led a walk-out that turned horribly violent on July 5, "Bloody Thursday," when thousands of strikers faced 800 uniformed and armed police also employing tear gas and fire hoses. Two workers were killed and many more were severely injured. Workers across the city supported the longshoremen and a general strike followed; San Francisco was paralyzed. Governor Frank Merriam declared martial law, the National Guard was called in, and for two weeks the city seemed to be on the brink of even more violent clashes before the strikers submitted to arbitration. The resulting agreement met many of labor's demands. Nonetheless, the backdrop of systematic resistance to labor and, in the state legislature to New Deal programs, ensured a climate of "New Deal, No Deal" in California.[47]

California, Oklahoma, and Oregon were more the exceptions than the rule in the West, where the first phase of New Deal programs and the funds that accompanied them were generally accepted with enthusiasm. The governors of Colorado, Idaho, and South Dakota also expressed resentment over federal intervention in state affairs and resisted providing matching state funds, but such ethical qualms did not prevent them from spending federal dollars. Western state governments mostly welcomed New Deal programs, even as they worried about the potential for federal dependency; such concerns were fueled by the region's strong individualistic ethos. The president was aware of the need to draw the West into his coalition, despite the efforts of some westerners to bite (rhetorically at least) the federal hand that was feeding the region.

In the summer of 1934, upon returning from a trip to Hawaii, FDR toured the West, from Oregon and Washington across the northern tier to the Great Plains, and then back to DC. It was a brief trip – less than a week – but one filled with opportunities to highlight the work of the New Deal in the region, at the Bonneville and Grand Coulee Dams, at Glacier National Park and Fort Peck in Montana, and Devil's Lake, North Dakota. The results of congressional and gubernatorial races across the West the following fall underscored the region's growing enthusiasm for the president and his initiatives.[48] The Democrats gained two House seats

[47] Rick Wartzman, "New Deal, No Deal: The 1930s," in *A Companion to California History*, ed. William Deverell and David Igler (Malden, MA: Wiley Blackwell, 2008), 292–306, esp. 296–299.

[48] Lowitt, *The New Deal in the West*, 203–205.

in California and one in Wyoming, which more than offset Republican gains of a single seat in Nebraska and another in Oregon. In the Senate, the party held on to all its open seats.

The sweeping success of the programs of the First Hundred Days was evident nationwide in the results of the 1934 midterm elections. In a major exception to the common trend of congressional losses for the incumbent party, the Democrats added seats in both houses – nine in the Senate (all in nonwestern states) and nine in the House. The performance was even more remarkable considering the party's massive congressional gains in 1932 – 97 seats added in the House and 12 more in the Senate. Indeed, FDR's 1934 gains remain unmatched by either party in the more than eight decades since.[49] Voters were increasingly drawn to FDR in no small part because millions of them had been direct beneficiaries of the New Deal's direct relief efforts involving the distribution of food and money; work relief programs that provided much-needed jobs and the dignity that accompanied employment; and credit relief programs which helped refinance homes and farms, thus preventing foreclosures.

Reaction, Reform, and Overreach

For all its marked successes, the first phase of the New Deal was not without its critics. Those on the right, with ex-President Hoover in the lead, railed against the expansion of the federal government and its perceived assault on private enterprise, viewing the TVA, BPA, and other large regional development and public works initiatives as intrusive state socialism. Given the magnitude of the change in the federal government's role, it would have been surprising if conservatives had not responded in anger and frustration. However, the harshest criticism of FDR's initial efforts to provide economic relief and spur recovery came not from the right but the left and emphasized the New Deal's favoring of corporate interests over destitute, impoverished citizens.

[49] The only comparable midterm results since were the Democratic gain of five seats in the House in 1998 (zero gains in the Senate), most likely a response to the Republicans' overreach in trying to impeach President Bill Clinton; and the Republican gain of eight in the House and two in the Senate in 2002. The 2002 gains came in the wake of and were partly attributable to President George W. Bush's spirited response to the 9/11 attacks, standing in the rubble at the World Trade Center. Those results also stemmed from low Democratic voter turnout. Nonetheless, neither the 1998 nor the 2002 election saw gains nearly as significant as the Democratic Party's in 1934, and neither followed massive congressional gains in the previous presidential election.

Father Charles Coughlin, a Catholic priest in Detroit and initial supporter of the New Deal, was by 1934 condemning it as an unholy government alliance with big business and big banking, an effort to save capitalism, but not working people. Coughlin's rhetoric was also polemical, and horribly anti-Semitic. Nonetheless, his criticism of FDR as the servant of the bankers and corporate leaders appealed to those who had not yet directly benefited from the New Deal, and many had slipped through the webbing of the emerging federal safety net. Coughlin quickly emerged as the nation's second most popular radio personality, after his target, the president.[50] Meanwhile, in Louisiana, senator and former governor Huey P. Long was developing his "Share Our Wealth" program in 1934. Seeking to make "Every Man a King," Long proposed the appropriation and redistribution of large corporate gains, as well as high individual incomes and inheritances, to fund infrastructural developments, and housing, health care, jobs, free college education, veterans' benefits, aid to farmers, old age pensions, a 30-hour working week, and a guaranteed "household estate" of $5,000 and guaranteed annual income of $2,500 for all Louisiana families.[51] Long insisted he was no Socialist or Communist, but warned that without radical redistribution of wealth, revolution would be imminent. The United States Senate had no time for Long's radical program, but he formed the Share Our Wealth Society to promote it nationally and by summer 1935 there were 27,000 Share Our Wealth Clubs, with a total membership of 7.5 million. A Democratic National Committee–sponsored public opinion poll in spring 1935 suggested that as a third-party candidate Long could secure as many as 6 million votes, potentially enough to swing the election away from FDR and to a Republican candidate. Long's assassination in the Louisiana State Capitol in Baton Rouge, in September 1935, a month after he announced his presidential campaign, ended such possibilities. Still, Long, like Coughlin, had effectively channeled, and fueled public disappointment concerning the limitations of FDR's early New Deal programs.[52]

Long's Share Our Wealth clubs were most numerous and popular in Louisiana and the South more broadly, but they also spread across the

[50] For Coughlin, see Alan Brinkley, *Voices of Protest: Huey Long, Father Coughlin and the Great Depression* (New York: Alfred A. Knopf, 1982). Alonzo Hamby provides the comment about Coughlin as a populist of the right, in *Man of Destiny: FDR and the Making of the American Century* (New York: Basic Books, 2015), 216.

[51] Kennedy, *Freedom from Fear*, 238.

[52] For the Share Our Wealth clubs and Long's potential as a third-party candidate in 1936, see Brinkley, *Voices of Protest*, esp. 194–215.

Far West, including Utah, Arizona, Washington, and especially California. By way of contrast, Father Coughlin had little appeal in the West.[53] California had two progressive spokesmen of its own though who contributed mightily to the growing "thunder on the left" in 1934 and 1935. In the fall of 1933, Dr. Francis Townsend, a 67-year-old physician from Long Beach, announced a plan to address the heart-rending hardships experienced by older Americans, many of whom had lost their life savings when banks collapsed. Townsend advocated a government payment of $200 a month to every citizen aged 60 and older, with the stipulation that recipients spend those funds every month, thereby stimulating the economy, and not work, thereby relieving additional strains on the job market. The plan was to be financed through a 2 percent value added sales tax.

Townsend Clubs sprang up across California and the Far West, and more than 2 million people joined them – almost a fifth of the population over the age of 60. Townsend's supporters demanded a federal bill to implement his proposal, and 25 million people signed petitions supporting it. He had effectively mobilized another major constituency that was underserved by the New Deal. In January 1935 Townsend appeared on the cover of *Newsweek* and a California congressman introduced a bill containing Townsend's pension model, just as FDR was preparing his Social Security bill.[54] A few months later, LA radio commentator and former Share Our Wealth organizer for the Golden State, Robert Noble, began pushing his popular "Ham and Eggs" pension scheme for California, which proposed to pay $25 every Monday to every unemployed man or woman over the age of 50.[55]

Further contributing to the mounting pressure for an even more activist federal response to the economic collapse, one of the muckraking giants of the Progressive Era, Upton Sinclair, devised a plan to save the state of California. Author of the influential novel *The Jungle* (1906), Sinclair launched a campaign in 1934 to become the Democratic nominee for governor. He outlined his program – End Poverty in California, or EPIC – in a short book, *I Governor of California, and How I Ended Poverty* (1934), which became a bestseller. Modeled on the successful cooperatives that

[53] Ibid., 204–206.

[54] Kennedy, *Freedom from Fear*, 234–235; and Edwin Amenta, *When Movements Matter: The Townsend Plan and the Rise of Social Security* (Princeton, NJ: Princeton University Press, 2006), 1 and 120–121.

[55] Darren Dochuk, *From Bible Belt to Sun Belt: Plain-Folk Religion, Grassroots Politics, and the Rise of Evangelical Conservatism* (New York: W. W. Norton, 2011), 88–89.

had sprung up in Southern California, as well as Seattle and Denver, during the early Depression years, Sinclair's plan involved the overlaying of a cooperative-based nonprofit economy, or economy for use, on top of the existing capitalist one, which he predicted would eventually disappear. The state would reopen abandoned and foreclosed farms and shuttered factories, and put the unemployed to work in return for scrip payments that could be used to purchase food, clothing and other commodities from within the production for use system. King Vidor's critically acclaimed film, *Our Daily Bread*, which celebrated the virtues and benefits of life on an American collective farm, was released nationwide in October 1934, during the height of the gubernatorial campaign.[56]

Sinclair's bold plan was lauded by those on the left for its attentiveness to the needs of the unemployed and underemployed, the hungry and the destitute, and lambasted by conservatives for being socialistic. By August there were more than 1,000 EPIC Clubs operating in the state. Sinclair's efforts resulted in the registration of 350,000 new Democratic Party members, and for first time the Democrats outnumbered Republicans in California. At the end of the month, Sinclair won the Democratic primary with a 436,000-vote majority. Sinclair met with FDR in early September, but failed to get the president's endorsement for the fall election. FDR feared that Sinclair's radicalism would damage the Democratic Party and the New Deal nationally, particularly his effort to develop a Social Security program.

Whether the president's overt support would have swung the election away from Republican incumbent governor Merriam and toward Sinclair is debatable. The Longshoreman's strike and the resulting general strike in San Francisco that summer made the public nervous about labor radicalism and undercut Sinclair's support. The Republicans, through an organization called United for America, launched a comprehensive campaign against Sinclair. They were supported in their efforts by big business, big agriculture, organized religion, the press, Hollywood, and the University of California, all of which seized the opportunity to pay Sinclair back for his scathing treatments of them in his novels in the 1920s and early 1930s. With the help of newspaper giants William Randolph Hearst and Harry Chandler, and the Hollywood film industry, Sinclair was roundly condemned as a dangerous radical out to bankrupt the Golden State. Studio chiefs in Hollywood blocked the release of *Our Daily Bread* in

[56] John H. M. Laslett, *Sunshine Was Never Enough: Los Angeles Workers, 1880–1210* (Berkeley: University of California Press, 2012), 118–123.

the state, fearing that the film's positive portrayal of cooperatives would boost Sinclair's chances. The carefully coordinated and often shameless red-baiting campaign against Sinclair in the *LA Times* and other newspapers and in newsreels created by Louis B. Mayer and MGM Studios proved highly effective. It did not help that Sinclair informed reporters of how he had joked with Harry Hopkins that if elected on the EPIC platform half of the nation's unemployed would come to California and Hopkins would have to take care of them through New Deal programs. Fictitious newsreels were shot depicting tramps and vagrants pouring into the state to take advantage of welfare and work programs.[57]

FDR maintained his distance from Sinclair, and then, right before the election, the California Democratic Party establishment stuck a deal with Merriam to throw their support to him in return for his public announcement that upon reelection he would support New Deal programs in the state. The incumbent Merriam ended up winning the election quite comfortably, with 1,138,620 votes, close to 49 percent of the total, to Sinclair's 879,527, less than 38 percent. In addition, Raymond Haight, a third- party candidate running on the Commonwealth/Progressive Party ticket and offering a moderate alternative to Sinclair, garnered 13 percent of the vote. Haight's and Sinclair's vote totals together actually exceeded Merriam's, and Sinclair had done better than any other Democratic gubernatorial candidate in the state's history. Twenty-six EPIC candidates, including future governor Culbert Olson, were voted into the state legislature despite Sinclair's defeat. The EPIC campaign contributed to the forces pushing FDR to the left and, in an interesting twist, pressured California's leaders to stop blocking the implementation of at least some of the president's programs.[58]

Thus, the West, perhaps more than any other region, helped move FDR toward a more reformist agenda in the summer of 1935, when he called Congress back into emergency session for another three-month plus period, the Second Hundred Days. With the help of key western congressmen, such as Colorado representative Edward T. Taylor, who served as Acting House Floor Leader, and Arizona Senator Carl Hayden, who sat on the important Appropriations Committee, FDR pushed

[57] Kevin Starr, *Endangered Dreams: The Great Depression in California* (New York: Oxford University Press, 1996), 120–155, esp. 142–150; and T. H. Watkins, *The Great Depression: America in the 1930s* (Boston: Little, Brown, 1993), 238–239; Kennedy, *Freedom from Fear*, 225–227.

[58] Laslett, *Sunshine Was Never Enough*, 122; Watkins, *The Great Depression*, 239; and Starr, *Endangered Dreams*, 154.

through the extensive body of bills that has since come to be known as the Second New Deal. The Wagner Act placed the weight of the federal government more firmly behind the rights of labor to bargain collectively. In addition, the legislative session also saw passage of the Banking Act, the Wealth Tax Act, and the Social Security Act, along with a series of measures designed to assist the small farmers, leaseholders, sharecroppers and migrant workers hit hardest by the agricultural crisis. Through those various bold and controversial initiatives, FDR effectively stole the left's thunder. He implemented higher taxes on corporate gains, high incomes, and inheritances; subjected the banking industry to greater federal oversight than it had ever previously known; provided a system of old age and survivors' pension; and placed the government firmly behind organized labor. With these measures, FDR shifted the focus away from a tripartite alliance between the federal government, big business, and big labor, toward a decidedly more anti–big business program, one that addressed the needs of those hit worst by the depression.

This important development in the New Deal was evident in the establishment of the Works Progress Administration (WPA – renamed the Works Projects Administration in 1939) in April 1935, technically before the Second Hundred Days began. The WPA proved truly transformative for the American workforce and the nation's infrastructure, and it encapsulated the shift from the limited work relief efforts of the First New Deal to the concerted emphasis on work relief programs and other relief initiatives in the Second New Deal. Between July 1935 and July 1943, when the program ended, the WPA employed 8.5 million people, and at its peak in 1938 provided 3.3 million jobs. The agency built more than 67,000 miles of city streets, 500 water-treatment facilities, and nearly 20,000 miles of water mains, improved more than 8,000 city parks, built 12,800 playgrounds, built or improved close to 1,000 airports, constructed nearly 40,000 public buildings and improved an additional 85,000, including the expansion, or modernization of more than 40,000 schools. The WPA also laid more than 572,000 miles of rural roads, and built 78,000 new bridge and viaducts.[59] For all the criticism of the WPA at the time as a wasteful agency that provided nonessential labor (some joked that the acronym stood for We Piddle Around), it is worth considering that much of what it built remains essential to the nation's infrastructure four generations later. Moreover, the WPA played a tremendously important role in restoring dignity to the formerly unemployed.

[59] Smith, *Building New Deal Liberalism*, 107, 113–117.

Many western states benefited hugely from WPA funding. Between 1935 and 1941 WPA per capita funding averaged a little over $44 per person across all the states. The figure was considerably lower for Texas, at $26 per capita. In this regard the Lone Star State, where racial politics kept Democrats from supporting the more racially inclusive federal relief measures, was in keeping with most of the South, and an anomaly among western states. But Texas aside, WPA funding ranged across the western region from a high of $88 in Montana and $73 in Colorado (due to Taylor's efforts) to a low of $49 in Wyoming and $45 in Nebraska. Every western state, aside from Texas, did better than the national average. North and South Dakota, received $59 and $66 per capita, respectively. Their Southern Plains neighbors, Kansas and Oklahoma, received $45 and $48, respectively. The southwestern states of Arizona ($58) and New Mexico ($64) did quite well, as did California ($60), the Great Basin States, Utah ($58) and Nevada ($66), and the Pacific northwestern states, Idaho ($51), Oregon ($60), and Washington ($64). While the annual per capita expenditures were quite low, they had a significant impact on a region that had been hit terribly hard by the Depression. Remarkably, four western states – Montana, North Dakota, South Dakota, and Utah – received more money per capita from the WPA alone than they paid to the government in federal tax revenues between 1935 and 1940; Montana received twice as much. Two additional states, Arizona and New Mexico, received roughly the same amount in WPA funding per capita as they paid in taxes.[60]

From the lightly populated rural West to the region's largest metropolises, the WPA's impact on infrastructural development, employment, and general economic recovery was crucial. From iconic sites such as San Antonio's River Walk and the reconstructed Fort Gibson, Oklahoma (the terminus of the Cherokee Trail of Tears a century before), to San Francisco's Cow Palace, the Timberline Lodge at Mount Hood, Oregon, and Seattle's Woodland Park Zoo, to the rural roads, city streets

[60] For the WPA per capita expenditure figures by state, see Smith, *Building New Deal Liberalism*, 116–117. The national average is calculated by combining Smith's figures for each state, and dividing by the number of states (48); thus, it is an average of the state's per capita figures rather than an actual per capita average. For the overall western annual per capita WPA figure, see White, *"It's Your Misfortune and None of My Own,"* 475–476. For WPA per capita moneys versus per capita federal tax revenue for the years 1935–1940, see *Department of the Treasury, Internal Revenue Service, Statistics of Income, Individual Income Tax Returns, 1935–1940* (Washington, DC: Government Printing Office, 1936–1941).

and sidewalks, bridges, public parks, schools, and municipal buildings, the legacy of the WPA does not merely endure but remains ubiquitous in built environments across the West.[61]

In addition, the other massive New Deal work relief program, the Public Works Administration (PWA), established during the First Hundred Days, proved particularly beneficial to sparsely populated western states, including Montana, Nevada, and Wyoming. These and other western states were swing states that could be brought into the Democratic fold with relatively minimal expenditures. Thus, Nevada, forty-sixth in the nation in the total allocation of New Deal funds, ranked first on a per capita basis, receiving the massive sum of $352 per capita in PWA funds between 1933 and 1941, and another $66 per capita in WPA funds between 1935 and 1939. The Silver State also ranked first in per capita Civil Works Administration (CWA) and CCC funding, as well as federal loans.[62] The only other states in the country to exceed $100 per capita from the PWA were Arizona ($133) and Montana ($170), and the next highest figures were in Washington ($72), Oregon ($71), Nebraska ($68), New Mexico ($68), and Utah ($53). The territories of Alaska and Hawaii also benefited significantly from PWA funding, with per capita rates at $101 and $58, respectively, for 1933–1941. Idaho ($46) and Colorado ($43) also did quite well; California ($35) and Texas ($30) were close to the national average; though, notably, Texas received a massive total of 912 PWA projects and California received 807. South Dakota ($26), Kansas ($25), Oklahoma ($25), and North Dakota ($22) did less well when it came to per capita funding from the PWA.[63]

When the various New Deal stimulus programs are considered together, the West's disproportionately high funding levels are fully evident. The New Deal programs expended about $400 per person nationwide. Nevada, with its tiny population and massive Boulder Dam project and various other federal stimuli, received about $1,500 per capita. The Rocky Mountain states received an average of $716 per capita; Montana ranked second, Wyoming third, and Idaho fifth in total per capita federal expenditures. The Pacific Coast states, at $536 per capita, were well ahead of the national average, and the Great Plains states at $424,

[61] For more on the WPA's impact nationwide, see Nick Taylor, *American Made: The Enduring Legacy of the WPA: When FDR Put the Nation to Work* (New York: Bantam Dell, 2008).

[62] Smith, *Building New Deal Liberalism*, 115.

[63] Ibid., 91 and 116–117.

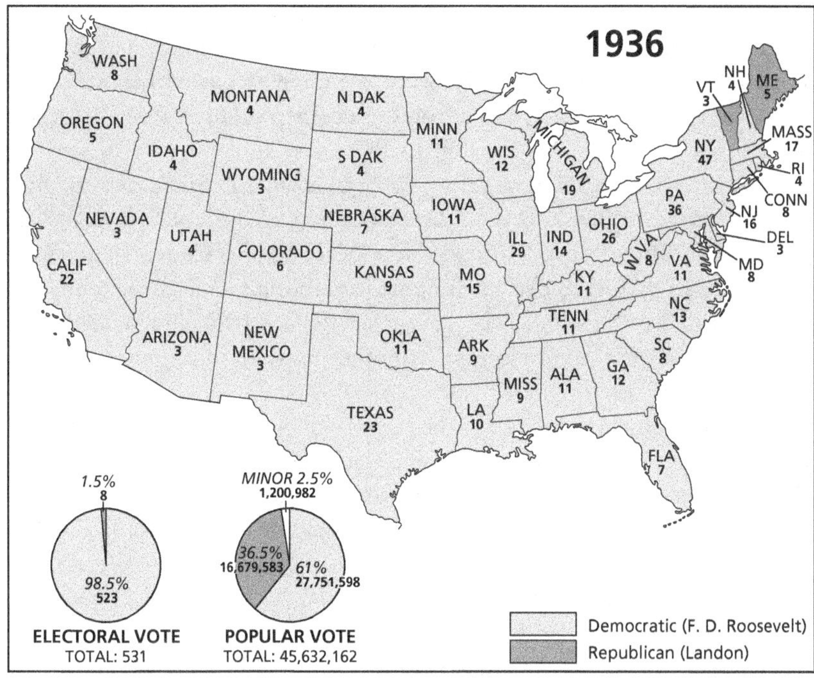

MAP 5.2 Electoral map, 1936.

were just a little above the national figure. The West was undeniably the government's favored region during the New Deal years.[64]

The economic benefits of the first flurry of New Deal programs pushed through Congress in early to mid 1933 were firmly in place by the time the sweeping reforms of the second wave of New Deal programs were being enacted in the summer of 1935. The 1936 election was a testament to FDR's popularity and the impact of those initiatives. It was, all measures considered, the most sweeping electoral victory in the nation's history. The president received almost 61 percent of the popular vote to 35 percent for his opponent, Kansas Governor Alf Landon. The vote in the Electoral College was 523 to 8 for the Democratic Party, which also won 46 of the 48 states (Landon secured just Vermont and Maine) (Map 5.2). The congressional majorities were the largest ever for either

[64] Figures from Arrington and Reading, "The New Deal Economic Programs in the Northern Tier States, 1933–1939," 238; Robbins and Barber, *Nature's Northwest*, 110; and Nash, *The Federal Landscape*, 39.

party. In the Senate, the Democrats had 76 seats to the Republicans 16, and in the House, it was 334 to 88. There was nothing particularly regional about the victory; FDR swept every region except for New England, and secured most of the votes even there. There was, however, a clear socioeconomic dimension to the 1936 landslide: 81 percent of Americans with an income below $1,000 voted for FDR, and 79 percent for those earning between $1,000 and $2,000 did, too. Those figures reflected the tangible assistance the New Deal had provided through direct relief, work relief, credit relief, support for labor and agriculture, and for the infirm, the aged and other groups.[65] There was a racial element, too, behind FDR's 1936 electoral triumph: he secured 71 percent of the African American vote.

Yet this high-water mark for the New Deal also marked the beginning of the decline of FDR's age of enlightened administration. The president's majorities were massive but unwieldy and included large numbers of newly elected conservative Southern Democrats who rode into office on the president's substantial coat tails but were often unreceptive to his programs. Also, FDR took his comprehensive victory as an unqualified mandate for further executive action, and in doing so over reached. This was evident in the failed Supreme Court Packing Plan in 1937, which faced strong opposition from powerful western senators including Nebraska's Burton K. Wheeler and Wyoming's Joseph O'Mahoney; and FDR's ill-conceived effort to purge intransigent Democrats from Congress during the 1938 Midterm elections. In addition, the president, partly due to pressure from fiscal conservatives in Congress, particularly those on the House and Senate Appropriations Committees, scaled back some of the New Deal relief programs to balance the budget, precipitating the so-called Roosevelt Recession of 1937–1938. These factors combined with FDR's growing identification with the labor movement, which was engaged in several violent strike actions led by the Congress on Industrial Organizations (CIO) in 1937, and his increasingly vehement anti–big business rhetoric, caused concern among segments of the middle class and stoked the fires of conservative opposition.

In the 1938 midterm elections, the Democrats lost 72 House seats and 7 more in the Senate. FDR's congressional majorities remained substantial, though the growing opposition of conservative Southern Democrats to the president's programs was further fracturing the party. The Democrats

[65] George Brown Tindall and David Emory Shi, *America: A Narrative History*, Brief 9th ed., vol. 2 (New York: W. W. Norton, 2013), 878–879.

suffered gubernatorial, congressional or state legislative setbacks in Colorado, Idaho, Kansas, Nebraska, North Dakota, Oregon, and Wyoming. The bright spots for the New Deal in the West remained Washington and the Southwest. One additional positive was California, whose governors had previously provided quite consistent opposition to FDR's programs, but where voters elected an enthusiastically pro-New Dealer and former EPIC candidate Olson in 1938, ending four decades of Republican Party dominance of the office.[66]

Despite these setbacks in FDR's second term, the New Deal's public works and regional planning programs efforts in the West were massively influential. Western writer Bernard DeVoto had described the West in a controversial 1934 *Harper's Magazine* article as a "plundered province," victimized by eastern corporations and essentially reduced to colonial status. Such charges underestimated the degree to which some western states (including California) had, as early as the Progressive Era, used the political system to place at least some regulatory pressure on corporate power. DeVoto also overlooked the extent of western internal economic development and urban growth by the end of the 1920s. By the time the *Harper's* article was published, the West, if the full largesse of federal support during the New Deal era is considered, was becoming as much a pampered province as a plundered one.

More accurately, the West was a region experiencing the manifold benefits of careful planning on the part of the federal government. The Bureau of Reclamation, Department of Agriculture, WPA, PWA, CCC, CWA, NYA and other agencies together had provided relief and recovery across the region. There was, no complete reversal of the economic crisis; however, a set of bold infrastructural innovations had laid the foundations for the growth in the agricultural, industrial and urban sectors during World War II. Federal stimulus proved more vital to the West's economic health and well-being during the New Deal than to that of any other region, though that legacy is not reflected in the resentment toward the federal government that characterized much of the West during the New Deal era and continues to eight decades later.[67]

[66] Lowitt, *The New Deal and the West*, 215; and Rick Wartzman, "New Deal, No Deal: The 1930s," in Deverell and Igler, *A Companion to California History*, 292–307.

[67] Bernard DeVoto, "The West: A Plundered Province," *Harper's* 169 (August 1934): 355–264. Lowitt, *The New Deal and the West*: Lowitt writes, "Federal largesse... became... an integral component of western life during the New Deal, more so than anywhere else in the United States" (218).

In late September 1937, as he concluded his speech at the dedication of the Bonneville Dam on the Columbia River in Oregon, FDR declared that "instead of spending, as some nations do, half their national income in piling up armaments and more armaments for purposes of war, we in America are wiser in using our wealth on projects like this which will give us more wealth, better living and greater happiness for our children."[68] It turned out that the infrastructure the New Deal had built across the West, with the Columbia and Colorado River Projects, and various other large-scale power projects that modernized the West, helped lay the foundations for the defense industry and the larger martial economy that would see the region become an increasingly vital player in national affairs during the Second World War and the Cold War that followed.

While the New Deal was in decline by the time FDR dedicated the Bonneville Dam, it was nonetheless during the second half of the decade and the second phase of New Deal programs, as we will see, that federal intervention in the West helped to expose the truly deplorable conditions for workers in the agricultural sector and bring some much-needed relief to certain segments of the population. Throughout the decade, the fault lines of race fractured the region, giving the lie to the comforting national memory of a country, its regions and its races, coming together in a spirit of mutual support and cooperation during hard times.

[68] FDR, Address at Bonneville Dam, Oregon, September 28, 1937.

6

Exposing the Promised Land

Their roots were all torn out. The only background they had was a background of utter poverty. It's very hard to photograph a proud man against a background like that because it doesn't show what he's proud about. I had to get my camera to register the things about those people that were more important than how poor they were – their pride, their strength, their spirit.[1]

– Dorothea Lange, c.1964

Racial Fault Lines in the Depression West

The racial fault lines of the 1930s ran deep and wide in the largely biracial landscape of the South, but were equally evident in the multiracial landscapes of the West. In the West, much like in the South, racial minorities became the first targets of white-dominated power structures, and increasingly so as economic conditions worsened.

The First New Deal for agriculture (1933–1935) sought to raise staple crop prices by limiting production, which primarily benefited farmers with extensive landholdings and corporate agricultural interests. Across Texas, and especially in the state's cotton growing regions, large landowners systematically exploited the Agricultural Adjustment Administration (AAA) acreage reduction program to great effect. They found ways to redefine the status of tenants and sharecroppers to ensure they did not

[1] Dorothea Lange, quoted in Michele Landis Dauber, *The Sympathetic State: Disaster Relief and the Origins of the American Welfare State* (Chicago: University of Chicago Press, 2013), 113; and Milton Meltzer, *Dorothea Lange: A Photographer's Life* (New York: Syracuse University Press, 2000), 97.

receive any significant part of the federal payments, and they often evicted those who complained to the Department of Agriculture or to local oversight boards. Landowners often replaced white tenants and sharecroppers with African Americans and Mexicans who were more vulnerable and exploitable. When tenants and croppers complained about the unfairness of the program's implementation, the federal government almost invariably decided not to risk the political fallout of intervening in local matters.[2]

Wages for people of color in parts of the West were so low that federal relief payments functioned as a disincentive for some seasonal workers to take on jobs, which in turn angered employers, who then lobbied the government to be less generous. The Federal Emergency Relief Administration (FERA) acquiesced to the racist demands of local communities and scaled the size of relief checks based on race. Tucson officials created separate categories of payments for Anglos, Mexican Americans, Native Americans, and Mexican immigrants. Texas relief payments for African Americans were set lower than for whites; in Houston, for example, African Americans received about $12.67 per month on average, around three-quarters of the average of $16.86 for white workers. Worse still, in Walker County, in east central Texas, just 13 of the more than 13,000 African American families received relief. In Phoenix, Arizona federal benefits were not systematically denied to minorities by local authorities: 51 percent of African Americans, compared with 59 percent of Mexican Americans and 11 percent of Anglos, were on relief. However, those figures do illuminate the severe poverty those racial minority groups experienced. In California and Colorado, an individual's refusal to take any agricultural job, no matter how low the wages, resulted in the termination of relief. When it came to work relief, the politics of race again prevailed in the region. In Texas, Mexican-origin people were often denied access to Works Progress Administration (WPA) and Civilian Conservation Corps (CCC) programs. In both Texas and Oklahoma, African Americans were often excluded from the CCC. Moreover, across much of the West, and particularly where populations of color were large, the white majority regularly complained that New Deal programs upset the established racial power structure by providing opportunities to those groups.[3]

[2] Neil Foley, *The White Scourge: Mexicans, Blacks, and Poor Whites in Texas Cotton Culture* (Berkeley: University of California Press, 1997), 163–182.

[3] Richard White, *"It's Your Misfortune and None of My Own": A New History of the American West* (Norman: University of Oklahoma Press, 1991), 474–475; Albert S.

Conditions for African Americans in the West during the Depression were dire. In the San Francisco Bay Area, rates of black unemployment and underemployment far exceeded those for white residents, and African American households were more likely to take in lodgers to make ends meet; well over a quarter did so. African American homeownership rates declined in virtually every major western city, and most significantly in Denver, Houston, Oakland, San Antonio, and Seattle. African Americans were the victims of racially restrictive housing covenants; explicit segregationist laws in the public schools in Arizona, Texas, and Oklahoma; de facto segregation for schoolchildren across most of the rest of the region; and restricted access to parks, beaches, swimming pools, movie houses and other public facilities. African American unemployment was nearly 40 percent in Houston in 1931, over 33 percent in Los Angeles; the rate was lower in Seattle (under 24 percent). The African American unemployment rate in most western cities dropped significantly by 1937, in no small part because of New Deal work relief programs.[4]

Disproportionately high rates of unemployment for African Americans in San Francisco did at least enhance eligibility for participation in New Deal work relief agencies such as the Civil Works Administration (CWA), WPA, and National Youth Administration (NYA). The federal government proved receptive to the situation, partly because of the influence of Mary McLeod Bethune, the NYA's national director of Negro affairs and one of the era's most important African American leaders. In Texas, future president Lyndon Baines Johnson, the state director of the NYA, proved well attuned and sympathetic to the economic needs of African Americans, who received a fair share of NYA positions. Also, while African American CCC workers certainly faced discrimination, including segregated dining facilities in some California camps, across most of the West they were generally not placed in segregated camps. In contrast, throughout the South, racially segregated CCC camps were the norm, and it proved enormously difficult for African Americans to

Broussard, *Expectations of Equality: A History of Black Westerners* (Wheeling, IL: Harlan Davidson/Cody, WY: The Buffalo Bill Historical Center, 2012), 84–93, esp. 86–87; and Quintard Taylor, *In Search of the Racial Frontier: African Americans in the American West, 1528–1990* (New York: W. W. Norton, 1998), 227–236, esp. 230.

4 Albert S. Broussard, *Black San Francisco: The Struggle for Racial Equality in the West, 1900–1954* (Lawrence: University Press of Kansas, 1993), 113–130, esp. 114–115 and 119; and Taylor, *In Search of the Racial Frontier*, 227–229 and 233. Omaha, with a slight increase in black home ownership rates during the 1930s, was the lone exception. In San Francisco, black unemployment rose from just over 18 percent to close to 27 percent between 1931 and 1937.

even get on the agency's rolls, especially in the first years of the program. Yet it was close to impossible for African Americans to gain employment with the Six Companies building the Boulder Dam. In 1933, there were only 14 African American workers among the 4,000 who labored on the project, and the number never exceeded 30; and those few workers suffered the indignity of separate housing, dining and recreational facilities.[5]

By the 1930s, Los Angeles, the nation's fastest-growing city, was home to the West's largest African American community. In 1900, LA had just 2,000 African American residents, but by 1920 that number had risen to close to 16,000, and to nearly 39,000 by 1930. By 1940, 25,000 new African American residents had arrived, hailing mostly from Dallas, Houston and New Orleans, increasing the community's size to nearly 64,000 (the pattern only accelerated in the 1940s, 1950s, and 1960s). By comparison, Oakland had an African American population of about 8,500 in 1940; Denver's was around 8,000; San Francisco's 5,000; and Seattle's 4,000.[6] In fact, during the 1930s, most of the African Americans residing west of the Great Plains were in LA. The city, like Chicago, was considered a promised land by African American migrants and to some degree it lived up to its reputation. Racial bias was hardly absent. Restrictive covenants segregated African American from white housing developments, and there was significant discrimination in the workplace, too. But the horrendous racial violence that African Americans were subjected to in the South was generally not a feature of their lives in Southern California. Around a third of African American Angelenos owned their own homes, evidence of the size and strength of an emerging middle class.

But the foundations of African American prosperity in LA were nothing if not fragile. Heavy reliance on service sector jobs, including as domestic servants and railroad porters, meant their positions were among the first to go when the Depression hit. The protections of organized labor did not extend as readily to African Americans in LA as to those residing in the industrialized cities of the North and Midwest, partly because of LA's fierce (and often extralegal) maintenance of the open

5 Broussard, *Black San Francisco*, 121, 123, and 126–127.

6 See Josh Sides, *L.A. City Limits: African American Los Angeles from the Great Depression to the Present* (Berkeley: University of California Press, 2003), 15; and www.nps.gov/nr/feature/afam/2010/afam_los_angeles.htm accessed December 30, 2015.

shop, but also because of the preference of many employers in the city's industrial sector for white and Mexican labor. Conditions deteriorated rapidly as the economic crisis deepened and by 1934 fully half of all African Americans in LA were unemployed. Still, African Americans in the Southland, as in the Bay Area, benefited from the opportunities provided by the CCC, CWA, NYA, and WPA. While those agencies, particularly the CCC, were marked by racial discrimination, they nonetheless provided opportunities for thousands of the city's black residents. Had California's governors James Rolph and Frank Merriam been more receptive to FDR's New Deal, the benefits for African Americans would have been greater still. However, if African American journalists such as Leon Washington in his "Don't Spend Where You Can't Work" campaign had been less persistent in their efforts to highlight and combat racial discrimination in the city, opportunities would surely have been more limited.[7]

In the end, the New Deal helped the African American population in LA and across the West, and the multiracial realities of that city and much of the larger region stretching from the Desert Southwest to the Pacific Northwest proved preferable to the biracial and virulently antiblack landscapes of the South and the Southern Plains. Conditions in the West's cities for African Americans were on a par with those of the Northern and Midwestern cities that African Americans were also migrating to from the South in huge numbers during the 1930s. Moreover, massive changes were on the horizon for African Americans already in the West, and for those who would migrate from the South to the West Coast's cities in huge numbers as the Depression finally faded and the defense industry expanded in the early 1940s.

Just as in the South, FDR's administration did not view itself as having a major role in the reconstruction of race relations in the West. The principle of racial justice was sacrificed time and again as FDR tried to hold his fragile Democratic coalition together and sustain support for New Deal programs. However, Eleanor Roosevelt was more attentive to the needs of African Americans than any previous First Lady, and the New Deal did provide a range of opportunities. By 1934, and especially by 1936, African Americans had found a new political home in the Democratic Party, in large part because it was providing some assistance during the economic crisis. But racism at the state and local levels remained a

[7] Sides, *L.A. City Limits*, 27–30.

barrier to African American advancement across the South and the West, and much of the rest of the country.[8]

One of the most tragic and lamentable examples of systematic racial bigotry in the Depression Era West was the so-called repatriation of Mexican Americans and Mexicans. At the start of the decade, the Mexican American population in the United States, mostly located in the Southwest, from Texas to California, numbered approximately 1.5 million. Anglo Americans argued that Mexicans were taking jobs away from whites, were draining relief funds, and illegally benefiting from services intended for citizens. Between 1929 and 1935, between 450,000 and 1 million people of Mexican origin, or about a third to two-thirds of the total number, and mainly from California, Texas, and Colorado, left the country for Mexico. In 1931 alone, an estimated 138,519 were pressured to leave the United States. Tens of thousands were forcibly rounded up and transported by rail to Mexican cities, and from there about 80 percent headed to small towns and villages where they faced dire circumstances; Mexico was still in the throes of revolutionary turmoil and economic instability. Roughly 40 percent of the "repatriated" were under 12 years of age, and most of those children were born in the United States.[9]

As an "involuntary mass migration," the repatriation of Mexican-origin people far exceeded in raw numbers the Indian removals of a century before. In the first years of the decade the Federal Bureau of Immigration, which became the Immigration and Naturalization Service (INS) in 1933, worked with the support of the American Federation of Labor, with Hoover's Secretary of Labor, William Dovak, and with local governments, to enforce the repatriation policy. The INS was directly responsible for 82,000 Mexican repatriations/deportations from 1929 to

[8] Harvard Sitkoff, *A New Deal for Blacks: The Emergence of Civil Rights as a National Issue*, 30th Anniversary ed. (New York: Oxford University Press, 2009); Douglass Flamming, *African Americans in the West* (Santa Barbara: ABC-CLIO, 2009), 150–158; and Ira Katznelson's chapter "Jim Crow Congress" in his *Fear Itself: The New Deal and the Origins of Our Time* (New York: Liveright/W. W. Norton, 2013), 156–194.

[9] Albert Camarillo, *Chicanos in California: A History of Mexican Americans in California* (San Francisco: Boyd and Fraser, 1984), 47–68, esp. 48–61; Walter Nugent, *Into the West: The Story of Its People* (New York: Alfred A. Knopf, 1999), 235–236; Camille Guerin-Gonzales, *Mexican Workers and American Dreams: Immigration, Repatriation, and California Farm Labor, 1930–1939* (New Brunswick, NJ: Rutgers University Press, 1994), 77–95; and Jorge Iber and Arnoldo DeLeon, *Hispanics in the American West* (Santa Barbara, CA: ABC/CLIO, 2006), 213–215.

1935, and Dovak announced that he intended to get rid of "400,000 illegal aliens," and thereby solve the unemployment problem and end the Depression. Moreover, Dovak had the enthusiastic support of President Hoover who in 1930 declared that Mexicans had played a role in bringing about the economic downturn.[10]

Coordinated efforts by the state government in Texas resulted in a one-third reduction in the Mexican-origin population of Texas. Between 1929 and 1939, around 250,000 people were deported from or left the state for Mexico under duress, and about 60 percent of those "repatriates" were American citizens. Federal judges in the state facilitated the deportation process by upholding almost all vagrancy violation charges leveled against detainees. For example, in South Texas at the height of the deportation efforts Judge F. M. Kennerly presided over 70 illegal immigration cases in a single 6-hour session, finding every person guilty – 59 of them were deported and the other 11 imprisoned. In El Paso, a main processing center for deportations, public officials and the press created a particularly dangerous climate for Mexican-origin people. In Malakoff, in northeast Texas, a Mexican labor center was bombed, and across the Southwest repatriation became a tool for Mexican union busting. In 1935 and 1936 Colorado's governor expelled Mexican sugar beet workers from the state and blockaded the border with New Mexico.[11]

Los Angeles's Anglo power structure was responsible for reducing the Mexican-origin population by 35,000, or fully one-third, during the decade. Police sweeps in the city were designed to strike fear into the Mexican-origin population and precipitate voluntary migration out of the county and the country. The LA County Welfare Department (LACWD), concerned about the availability of resources for white Californians, actively promoted repatriation by distributing flyers in Mexican neighborhoods proclaiming that both legal and illegal immigrants were subject to deportation, and by identifying Mexicans on relief, so immigration officials could more easily apprehend them. The LACWD also helped to organize more than a dozen deportation trains. In his important study, *North from Mexico* (1948), Carey McWilliams, who had been

[10] Abraham Hoffman, *Unwanted Mexican Americans in the Great Depression* (Tucson: University of Arizona Press, 1974), 174–175; and George J. Sánchez, *Becoming Mexican American: Ethnicity, Culture and Identity in Chicano Los Angeles, 1900–1945* (New York: Oxford University Press, 1993), 213.

[11] Foley, *The White Scourge*, 175; Oscar J. Martinez, *Mexican-Origin People in the United States: A Topical History* (Tucson: University of Arizona Press, 2001), 29–33; Hoffman, *Unwanted Mexican Americans*, 258; and Nugent, *Into the West*, 236.

championing the cause of the state's migrant farmworkers and exploited minority populations for more than a decade, pointed out that county officials in LA determined to the penny the expense of repatriating each trainload of Mexican repatriates: $77,249.29, versus $347,468.41 in relief spending, a savings of $270,219.12 per train. Meanwhile, the LA Welfare Department sought to reduce expenses at city hospitals by repatriating bedridden and terminally ill patients, including leprosy sufferer Genevieve Valencia, Frank Sepulveda who had tuberculosis, Fermin Quintero, who was paralyzed, and Narcisa Renteria, who was 86 years old. In Santa Barbara immigration officials simply herded Mexican farmworkers into the Southern Pacific Railroad depot, loaded them into sealed cars, and transported them across the border. California formally recognized the injustice of repatriation by passing an "Apology Act" in 2005, though no reparations accompanied the admission of culpability for systematic civil and human rights violations.[12]

In Arizona, by 1933 close to two-thirds of the Mexican-origin population had no steady employment. Noncitizens were the most vulnerable, since they were ineligible for early New Deal relief programs. The state's growing Anglo and African American populations brought more competition for agricultural labor, leading growers to drastically reduce wages. Some Mexican American workers refused to take jobs since their economic needs were better met by the relief rolls than by exploitative employers, but, as in California and Colorado, the state ordered the termination of relief payments for field hands who refused to work. As conditions for Mexican-origin migrant families worsened, a typhoid epidemic broke out in their camps and local authorities expelled the residents. While there were no formal repatriation programs in Arizona, an estimated 18,000 Mexicans and Mexican Americans left the state between

[12] Francisco E. Balderrama and Raymond Rodriguez, *Decade of Betrayal: Mexican Repatriation in the 1930s*, rev. ed. (1995; repr., Albuquerque: University of New Mexico Press, 2006), 9, 132, and 150–151; Camarillo, *Chicanos in California*, 49; Carey McWilliams, *North from Mexico: The Spanish-Speaking People of the United States* (1948; repr., New York: Praeger, 1990), 176; Douglas Monroy, *Rebirth: Mexican Los Angeles from the Great Migration to the Great Depression* (Berkeley: University of California Press, 1999), 147–151; Elliott Robert Barkan, *From All Points: America's Immigrant West, 1870s–1952* (Bloomington: Indiana University Press, 2007), 327–332; Nugent, *Into the West*, 236; John H. M. Laslett, *Sunshine Was Never Enough: Los Angeles Workers, 1880–1210* (Berkeley: University of California Press, 2012), 112; Sánchez, *Becoming Mexican American*, 214–215; and David Kennedy, *Freedom from Fear: The American People in Depression and War* (New York: Oxford University Press, 1999), 165.

1929 and 1937, because of the declining economic conditions and the climate of fear generated by Anglos.[13]

"Repatriation" figures fell quite significantly after 1932. The New Deal years were better for Mexican Americans than the preceding Republican ones. New Deal relief agencies prohibited the denial of relief funds based on legal status, and federal relief monies could not be used to transport noncitizens across the border. Federal works agencies were only open to citizens and those in the process of filing for citizenship, but this encouraged noncitizens to begin their paperwork rather than be pressured into repatriation, a policy that municipal agencies in cities such as Los Angeles were still pushing.[14] Repatriation was the most prominent feature of the landscape of racial discrimination that Mexican-origin people endured in the West during the 1930s, but not the only feature. The decade was marked by acute hardship. Awful conditions prevailed even after the repatriation movement slowed. Hispanos in northern New Mexico and Southern Colorado, for example, experienced reductions in their land base, which forced residents to become seasonal workers in Colorado's mines and sugar beet fields. As those opportunities declined, 8,000 workers lost their farms and ranches when they were unable to pay taxes.[15] Meanwhile, the Ku Klux Klan reemerged again in Colorado in 1936, distributing flyers in the sugar beet towns warning Mexicans to leave the state. While most Anglos in the Southwest did not resort to such outright threats and intimidation, they did voice the standard anti-Mexican stereotypes depicting disease, criminality, and sexual immorality more frequently during the Depression years.[16]

The large agricultural interests successfully lobbied the federal government to ensure that Mexican American laborers were pushed off the relief rolls when the picking seasons began. In reality, the federal support provided to impoverished workers, and the response of white growers

[13] Oscar J. Martinez, "Hispanics in Arizona," in *Arizona at Seventy-Five: The Next Twenty-Five Years*, ed. Beth Luey and Noel J. Stowe (Tucson: University of Arizona Press, 1987), 87–122, esp. 108–110.

[14] For repatriation figures, see Hoffman, *Unwanted Mexicans*, 174–175; and Nugent, *Into the West*, 236. For New Deal relief guidelines, see Sánchez, *Becoming Mexican American*, 221–222.

[15] Manuel G. Gonzales, *Mexicanos: A History of Mexicans in the United States* (Bloomington: Indiana University Press, 1999), 141, and Sarah Deutsch, *No Separate Refuge: Culture, Class, and Gender on an Anglo-Hispanic Frontier in the American Southwest, 1880–1940* (New York: Oxford University Press, 1987), 162–199.

[16] David Montejano, *Anglos and Mexicans in the Making of Texas, 1836–1986* (Austin: University of Texas Press, 1987), 225–234.

to those programs, in the Southwest Texas borderlands and across the greater Southwest underscored the oppressive and inhumane nature of the labor systems those workers and their families experienced.[17] While New Deal administrators often acquiesced to local racial prejudices against Mexican-origin people, just as they did with African Americans, the federal government's programs provided enough in the way of direct relief and work relief to help ensure that the Mexican American vote gravitated to the Democratic Party, where it has remained. This shift was evident, for example, in New Mexico, when Republican Senator Bronson Cutting crossed party lines to support FDR in the 1932 election and where the appointment of Democrat Dennis Chavez to the US Senate in 1935 helped cement Democratic hegemony in the state.[18]

Mexican-origin people in the West also improved their conditions through labor union activity, becoming major participants in the American Federation of Labor (AFL), and even more so in its offshoot union the Congress of Industrial Organizations (CIO) after 1935. They experienced forceful opposition to their efforts to improve conditions in agriculture and canneries, as well as factories. The Cannery and Agricultural Workers Industrial Union (CAWIU), along with other organizations such as La Confederación de Uniones de Campesinos y Obreros Mexicanos (CUMOM), participated in 37 major strikes in California during 1933, from the fields of the San Joaquin and Imperial Valleys to the coastal canneries and in a good number of cases secured wage increases. But by 1935 CAWIU was reeling from the state's prosecution of its leadership, and the Associated Farmers were pushing back against labor with a campaign of "open private warfare" against strikers. Meanwhile, President Roosevelt encouraged and facilitated unionization efforts, with Section 7a of the National Industrial Recovery Act in 1933, and even more so with the passage of the Wagner Act in the summer of 1935, and Mexican Americans, as they sought to advance their economic interests, increasingly became part of the multiethnic tapestry of the New Deal. They did so in no small part, too, because of the concerted efforts of Mexican-origin women workers, who faced both poor working conditions and sexual

[17] Deutsch, *No Separate Refuge*, 174–177; and Timothy Paul Bowman, *Blood Oranges: Colonialism and Agriculture in the South Texas Borderlands* (College Station: Texas A&M University Press, 2016), 143–144.

[18] Calvin A. Roberts and Susan A. Roberts, *New Mexico*, rev. ed. (Albuquerque: University of New Mexico Press, 2006), 171; and Earl Pomeroy, *The American Far West in the Twentieth Century* (New Haven, CT: Yale University Press, 2008), 343.

harassment on the job, but stood up defiantly, and often successfully, for their rights.[19]

For Native Americans, the 1930s brought tremendous hardship and some opportunity, though the picture varied widely across the West and from Indian nation to nation. In the summer of 1931, drought and swarms of grasshoppers destroyed crops in Nebraska, the Dakotas, and eastern Montana. Then, as winter set in, the Bureau of Indian Affairs (BIA) had the US Army deliver 55 train cars full of clothing and blankets, as well as food supplies to reservations on the Plains. Bitter winter conditions in Arizona and New Mexico that year necessitated an airplane drop of 300,000 pounds of food to the Navajo. Two-thirds of the families on Montana's Blackfeet reservation were on relief. The report of the Commissioner of Indian Affairs in 1932 showed a total Indian population of just over 320,000, with close to 200,000 or 62 percent residing in the four western states of Oklahoma, South Dakota, Arizona and New Mexico. At the dawn of the Indian New Deal, conditions were bleak in Indian country. In March 1933, Dr. Dirk Lay, a missionary on Arizona's Pima Reservation, wrote to the newly appointed BIA Commissioner John Collier to inform him that in one of the reservation's townships, where a third of the tribe resided, fully one-fourth of the Pimas had died of starvation over the past four and a half years.[20]

New Deal work programs such as the Indian CCC and the WPA provided much-needed support for reservation families, and direct relief payments were also vitally important. In addition, federal public health initiatives limited the spread of contagious diseases and lowered infant mortality rates. The Indian Reorganization Act (IRA), or Wheeler-Howard Act, of 1934, which Collier designed, was passed with well-meaning intentions toward the nation's Native peoples. The "Indian New Deal" was designed to end the policy of assimilation begun in 1887 with the Dawes Act and to promote Indian self-government, or "re-tribalization." The full title of the legislation provided a clear indication

19 Sánchez, *Becoming Mexican American*, 240–252; Camarillo, *Chicanos in California*, 53–55; and Vicki Ruiz, *Cannery Women/ Cannery Lives: Mexican Women, Unionization, and the California Food Processing Industry, 1930–1950* (Albuquerque: University of New Mexico Press, 1987).

20 Donald L. Fixico, *Indian Resilience and Rebuilding: Indigenous Nations in the Modern American West* (Tucson: University of Arizona Press, 2013), 74 and 76; and William G. Robbins and Katrine Barber, *Nature's Northwest: The North Pacific Slope in the Twentieth Century* (Tucson: University of Arizona Press, 2011), 107.

of its goals: "An Act to conserve and develop Indian lands and resources; to extend to Indians the right to form business and other organizations; to establish a credit system for Indians; to grant certain rights of home rule to Indians; to provide for vocational education for Indians; and for other purposes."[21]

Collier wrongly assumed that re-tribalization and an end to individual landholding would prove equally attractive to all the country's Indian nations and their diverse populations. The allotment process had proven disastrous for most Native people, but had worked quite well for some individuals and nations; for them, turning the clock back to the preallotment era of common landholding was not desirable. Levels of support for or opposition to the IRA also reflected the different needs of full blood and mixed blood Indians, of younger and older generations, and major differences across Indian country.[22]

During the decade that followed the introduction of the IRA legislation, a total of 258 Indian nations from across the United States held elections to determine whether to adopt the act. Virtually all the opposition to the IRA came from Indian nations in the West; New York State was the only exception. A total of 192 nations representing around 130,000 people eventually adopted the IRA, while 77 nations, representing over 86,000 people, including the 45,000 Navajo in the Southwest, and the Klamath and Crow in the Northwest, voted to reject it. The Navajo were incensed by the BIA's program to eliminate overgrazing and thereby restore the health of the range through reduction in the size of sheep, goat, and cattle herds. Since land erosion was not just impacting the carrying capacity of the land, but was causing sand and soil to wash into the Colorado River, potentially threatening Boulder Dam, federal officials demanded that the Navajo reduce herd sizes. The program went into effect in 1933 and continued until the late 1940s, resulting in the killing of hundreds of thousands of animals (more than half of the total herd sizes) and making it impossible for Collier to convince enough Navajo leaders of the benefits of any other federally directed program. The Navajos narrow defeat of the IRA was a major blow to Collier. Oklahoma's Indian nations were initially excluded from the IRA, but the Oklahoma Indian Welfare Act (OIWA) of 1936 extended many of the

[21] For the full title and text of the act, see https://tm112.community.uaf.edu/files/2010/09/The-Indian-Reorganization-Act.pdf accessed June 28, 2016.

[22] For a fuller discussion of the IRA, see ibid., 78–95, and Donald L. Parman, *Indians and the American West in the Twentieth Century* (Bloomington: Indiana University Press, 1994), 94–106.

act's provisions to them. Similar legislation that year did the same for Alaska's Native peoples.[23]

The Indian New Deal focused too much on idealizing the communal dimensions of Native culture and too little on the varied needs of Indian peoples across the West and the nation, and on individual reservations. Collier was deeply committed to helping Native Americans and promoting their cultures, but he was paternalistic, impatient, and at times heavy-handed in his administration of the Indian New Deal. Still, for all its failings, federal support for Indian self-government was in many ways preferable to the assimilationist policies that preceded the IRA and to the termination policy that succeeded it. The program might have proven more successful had its foundations not been systematically undermined in the wake of Collier's resignation in 1945. Despite its shortcomings, the IRA was inclusionary in design, and it was genuinely intended to improve conditions for Native Americans, and the same cannot be said for the termination policy. Native nations regained cultural and religious freedom during the 1930s, and often shaped the Indian New Deal to meet their needs.[24]

Depicting the Migrants' Plight

Beginning in the spring and summer of 1935, the New Deal entered a second phase that was more attentive to the plight of the poorest farm families. This shift in agricultural policy toward the needs of the desperate and displaced encapsulated the larger transition in the New Deal. The

[23] Fixico, *Indian Resilience and Rebuilding*, 85; Marsha Weisiger, *Dreaming of Sheep in Navajo Country* (Seattle: University of Washington Press, 2009); Richard White, *The Roots of Dependency: Subsistence, Environment, and Social Change among the Choctaws, Pawnees, and Navajos* (Lincoln: University of Nebraska Press, 1983), 251; Donald J. Parman, *The Navajos and the New Deal* (New Haven, CT: Yale University Press, 1976); Patricia Limerick, *The Legacy of Conquest: The Unbroken Past of the American West* (New York: W. W. Norton, 1987, 2006), 201–209; Kenneth R. Philp, *Termination Revisited: American Indians on the Trail to Self-Determination, 1933–1953* (Lincoln: University of Nebraska Press, 1999), 1–11; and Richard Lowitt, *The New Deal and the West* (Norman: University of Oklahoma Press, 1992), 128–129. For Oklahoma Indians, see Jon S. Blackman, *Oklahoma's Indian New Deal* (Norman: University of Oklahoma Press, 2013), 157; and Carter Blue Clark, "The New Deal for Indians," in *Between Two Worlds: The Survival of Twentieth Century Indians*, ed. Arrell M. Gibson (Oklahoma City: Oklahoma Historical Society, 1986), 72–84. For the full voting record on the IRA, see www.doi.gov/sites/doi.gov/files/migrated/library/internet/subject/upload/Haas-TenYears.pdf accessed January 12, 2016.

[24] Kennedy, *Freedom from Fear*, 379; White, *"It's Your Misfortune and None of My Own,"* 493; Fixico, *Indian Resilience and Rebuilding*, 95.

initial emphasis was on economic recovery and cautiously scaled relief programs. The second round of New Deal programs included an expansion of relief efforts, tighter regulation of big business, and a commitment to structural reform of the American economic system. This new focus was fully evident in FDR's Second Inaugural Address in January 1937 when he boldly reminded the nation of "the challenge to our democracy of ten millions of its citizens . . . who at this very moment are denied the greater part of what the very lowest standards of today call the necessities of life." FDR declared in one of the most memorable lines of any presidential address: "I see one-third of a nation ill-housed, ill-clad, ill-nourished," and insisted that "[t]he test of our progress is not whether we add more to the abundance of those who have much; it is whether we provide enough for those who have too little."[25]

The centerpiece of the Second New Deal for Agriculture was the Resettlement Administration, established in 1935 and administered by Rexford Tugwell. The agency provided loans to farmers for the purchase of feed, seed, fertilizer and equipment; emergency grants to purchase food, fuel, and clothing; assistance to displaced tenant farmers; and sanitary camps for migrant workers. The Resettlement Administration also sought to highlight the plight of distressed and dispossessed farm families through written reports and visual evidence that would move Americans to support further federal efforts on behalf of the rural poor. Conditions for tenant farmers and sharecroppers were so deplorable that Henry Wallace, after touring the cotton belt from Arkansas to the East Coast in 1935, remarked that a third of American farmers faced conditions that were so much worse than those experienced by European peasants "that the city people of the United States should be thoroughly ashamed."[26] Wallace's findings became part of a report that helped secure the passage of the Bankhead-Jones Farm Tenancy Act, which folded the Resettlement Administration into a new and expanded agency, the Farm Security Administration (FSA), in 1937.

It was the Resettlement Administration and then the FSA that financed the brilliant documentary films of Pare Lorentz, *The Plow that Broke the Plains* (1936), and *The River* (1938), that examined the problems

[25] FDR's Second Inaugural Address, January 20, 1937, available at: http://historymatters.gmu.edu/d/5105/ accessed December 17, 2015.

[26] Henry Wallace, quoted in John C. Culver and John Hyde, *American Dreamer: The Life and Times of Henry A. Wallace* (New York: W. W. Norton, 2000), 170.

of drought, soil erosion and flooding to demonstrate the need for federal action to restore the health of people and the land. More impactful even than Lorentz's powerful cinematic dramatizations of ecological disaster and federal response, was the remarkable pictorial record produced by the Resettlement Administration/FSA's Historical Section, which was directed by Roy Stryker and included Walker Evans, Dorothea Lange, Russell Lee, Arthur Rothstein, and Ben Shahn. Their work highlighted the pitiful circumstances of the rural poor, with special emphasis on the 300,000 to 425,000 migrants who flooded into California from the Southern Plains in the wake of the severe drought and Dust Bowl that devastated the region throughout the mid and late 1930s. The migrants were not just "burned out and blowed out," but in addition suffered plagues of crop destroying insects. They were also "tractored out," victims of mechanization in the region, which reduced the landowners' need for their labor as tenants and sharecroppers.[27] Around 400,000 farm families on the Great Plains lost everything during the 1930s, and in North Dakota and Montana at least half the farmers lost their properties between 1933 and 1937.[28] The migrants' westward exodus became a defining story of the Depression

The New Deal photographers emphasized the tragic circumstances, but also the decency, dignity, and determination of their desperately poor subjects. Their visual record was part of a larger rediscovery of the "common man" by writers, artists, and intellectuals during the 1930s. American intellectuals were alienated from the larger public during the 1920s because of the widespread (though short-lived) popular support for the Red Scare, the tremendous growth and widespread influence of the Second Ku Klux Klan, the rise of religious fundamentalism, the new national reality of prohibition, anti-immigrant sentiment and restrictive legislation, and various other manifestations of cultural intolerance. But as the business heroes of the 1920s such as Henry Ford became villains in the eyes of the public in the 1930s, so that public, after being vilified by intellectuals in the 1920s, was lauded by them in the 1930s for its fortitude and perseverance in the face of the Depression. That was the task of the FSA photographers: to present the rural poor as the noble face of a nation stoically enduring hard times and deserving help from their government.

[27] Foley, *The White Scourge*, 165.

[28] Gerald Nash, *The Federal Landscape: An Economic History of the Twentieth-Century West* (Tucson: University of Arizona Press, 1999), 27 and 29.

Many of the individual faces that conveyed the message with the greatest power and poignancy were found in the West.[29]

The most striking of all was Lange's photograph of Florence Owens Thompson, a 32-year-old woman from Oklahoma with three of her seven children in a squatters' camp in Nipomo, California. The famous "Migrant Mother" image, as it later became known, was the second of two photographs of Thompson to appear in the *San Francisco News* a few days apart in March 1936 (Figure 6.1). It was published with the headline "What does the 'New Deal' mean to this mother and her Children." The newspaper issued an accompanying editorial plea to "the conscience of California" to demand federal aid for "the nearly 2000,000 men, women, and children who move from valley to valley with the crops and live in wretched improvised shelters as they perform the labor on which our harvests depend." The editorial emphasized that the conditions the families faced "mock the American dream of security and independence and opportunity in which every child has been taught to believe." It also pointed explicitly to the "organized opposition of the agricultural section of the State Chamber of Commerce to the Resettlement Administration's efforts to build sanitary facilities for the migrants." This photograph, which achieved Lange's goal of capturing her subjects' "pride, their strength, their spirit," was more widely distributed than the first in newspapers nationwide. "Migrant Mother" generated public support for the destitute families, prompted the federal government to increase its relief efforts, and eight decades later remains the most recognizable image of the Great Depression.[30] Interestingly, Thompson's identity as a Cherokee Indian was largely unknown for more than four decades after her image captured the heart of the nation.

[29] Lawrence Levine, "The Historian and the Icon: Photography and the History of the American People in the 1930s and 1940s," in *Documenting America, 1935–1943*, ed. Carl Fleischhauer and Beverly W. Brannan (1988; repr., Berkeley: University of California Press, 2007), 15–42, esp. 33; John Raeburn, *A Staggering Revolution: A Cultural History of Thirties Photography* (Urbana: University of Illinois Press, 2006), 143–193; and Marion Elizabeth Rodgers, *Mencken: The American Iconoclast* (New York: Oxford University Press, 2005). Literary critic Malcolm Cowley captured the magnitude of this change in attitude in *Exile's Return: A Literary Odyssey of the 1920s* (New York: Viking, 1934).

[30] *San Francisco News* article, quoted in James R. Swenson, *Picturing Migrants: "The Grapes of Wrath" and New Deal Documentary Photography* (Norman: University of Oklahoma Press, 2015), 23–24; and see Richard Steven Street, *Everyone Had Cameras: Photography and Farmworkers in California, 1850–2000* (Minneapolis: University of Minnesota Press, 2008), 214–215.

FIGURE 6.1 Dorothea Lange, "Destitute pea pickers in California. Mother of seven children. Age thirty-two. Nipomo, California," 1936. The iconic "Migrant Mother" appeared in the *San Francisco News* on March 11; the image was reprinted in newspapers across the country and increased public sympathy and government support for California's migrant agricultural workers. Library of Congress, Prints and Photographs Division, FSA/OWI Collection, LC-DIG-fsa-8b29516 (digital file from original neg.).

The following month (April 1936), Rothstein's captivating shot of Arthur Coble and his two sons "Fleeing a Dust Storm" in Cimarron, in the far western corner of the Oklahoma panhandle, drew further attention to the human consequences of the ecological disaster on the Great Plains. Lee provided a moving photographic account of the journey of Oklahoma migrants to California in the summer of 1939, just a few months after the publication of John Steinbeck's then controversial novel *The Grapes of Wrath*, which chronicled the Joad family's journey. That summer, Lee took a series of photographs of the impoverished conditions in Oklahoma City's May Avenue migrant camps, which Henry Hill Collins described in his 1941 book *America's Own Refugees: Our 400,000 Homeless Migrants*: "so foul were these human habitations and so vast their extent," Hill wrote, "that some authorities reluctantly expressed the belief that Oklahoma City contained the largest and worst congregation of migrant hovels between the Mississippi River and the Sierras."[31] Speaking of Lee's work, Stryker later wrote, "[w]hen his photographs would come in, I always felt that Russell was saying, 'Now here's a fellow who is having a hard time but with a little help he's going to be all right.' And that's what gave me courage."[32] The West became the regional heart of those New Deal efforts to convince the American people that government had a systematic role to play in assisting and even protecting those who had been worst hit by the Depression.

In October of 1936, two and a half years before *The Grapes of Wrath* appeared, the progressive *San Francisco News* printed Steinbeck's controversial series of seven articles on the plight of California's migrants, "The Harvest Gypsies." The newspaper was nervous about publishing the author's shocking and impassioned reportage. Steinbeck insisted that only the support of the federal government in guaranteeing the rights of farm workers to organize and in prosecuting acts of "vigilante terrorism" sponsored by California agribusiness could guarantee the peaceful future of the state. He called for the direct intervention of the US attorney general since the nature and extent of violations of human dignity in the state had become so extreme. Steinbeck even went so far as to label the

[31] Henry Hill Collins, *America's Own Refugees: Our 40,000 Homeless Migrants* (Princeton, NJ: Princeton University Press, 1941), 259, quoted in Swenson, *Picturing Migrants*, 126.

[32] Roy E. Stryker and Nancy Wood, *In This Proud Land: America 1935–1943 as Seen in the FSA Photographs* (Greenwich, CT: New York Graphic Society, 1973), 8, quoted in Levine, "The Historian and the Icon," 33.

methods of the Associated Farmers "fascistic" and to declare, "California democracy is rapidly dwindling away."[33]

Most significantly though, "The Harvest Gypsies" articles highlighted the conditions of the migrants in a manner intended to generate deep empathy. They comprise one of the most powerful accounts of the human impact of the Depression in the West. Steinbeck described the suffering of one family (husband, wife, and three children) who built a fragile shelter from willow branches and weeds, paper, tin, and old carpet strips and slept on an old piece of carpet on the floor, folding it up over them. "The three year old child," Steinbeck wrote, "has a gunny sack tied about his middle for clothing. He has the swollen belly caused by malnutrition... He will die in a very short time. The older children may survive." More tragic still, Steinbeck reported, "Four nights ago the mother had a baby in the tent, on the dirty carpet. It was born dead, which was just as well because she could not have fed it at the breast; her own diet will not produce milk." "This woman's eyes," Steinbeck observed, "have the glazed, far away look of a sleep walker's eyes... The husband has lost even the desire to talk." But Steinbeck's point, as he described what happened to women and men as their "children have sickened and died, after the loss of dignity and spirit have cut [them] down to a kind of sub-humanity," is that "malnutrition is not infectious, nor is dysentery, which is almost the rule among the children." These were curable and correctible conditions, Steinbeck reminded his readers, and the fact of their persistence was not attributable to the failings of the parents, or to their cultural background, he asserted, but to the meanness and inhumanity of California's organized agricultural interests.[34]

In the *San Francisco News* articles, Steinbeck called for an expansion of the Resettlement Administration's sanitary camp system for migrant families and advocated the setting aside of state and federal lands to provide them with subsistence farms so they could grow their own food to supplement their wages as crop pickers. The women and children, he explained, would be able to tend those farms, and once again enjoy the fruits of education and geographic rootedness, while only the employable men traveled to meet the seasonal demands of California agriculture. Steinbeck suggested that the cost to the government of providing small plots of land, small houses, and schools for migrant families "would not

[33] John Steinbeck, "The Harvest Gypsies," in *"The Grapes of Wrath" and Other Writings, 19391–1941* (New York: Library of America, 1996), 991–1022, quotation on 1022.

[34] Ibid., 998–2000.

be that much greater than the amount which is now spent for tear gas, machine guns and ammunition, and deputy sheriffs."[35] That was the long-term vision, but in the short-term, Steinbeck visited the squatters' camps often as he worked on his larger novel designed to bring public attention to the migrants' plight. He said of his mission in crafting *The Grapes of Wrath*, "I'm trying to write history while it happens and I don't want to be wrong." The novel itself became a historical event – one of the most widely read, discussed and debated, banned and burned works of American literature.

In *The Grapes of Wrath* Steinbeck traced the displacement of the Joad family and other Southern Plains migrants due to drought, economic collapse, and mechanization; their tragic journey along Route 66 to California (during which Grandpa and Grandma both die); and the horrendous conditions they face when they reach their imagined paradise. Drawn in part by the widely-distributed handbills that announced plenty of work and good wages in California agriculture, the Joads arrive to find that they can barely earn enough to feed themselves, and that the growers' deception has placed them in the middle of a labor strike. After taking to the road once more they reach the Weedpatch Camp (the Arvin Farm Labor Center) near Bakersfield, one of the federal facilities for migrant workers established by the FSA, and they find some respite from the exploitative migratory labor system. Tom Joad asks the camp administrator – a character based on Steinbeck's friend Tom Collins, who ran the Arvin camp – "Why ain't they more places like this?" He then adds, "Ma's gonna like this place. She ain't been treated decent for a long time."[36] A government facility thus plays a central role in restoring the Joads' dignity in the novel.

Like the FSA photographers, Steinbeck was exposing California's failure to live up to its promise. But in going beyond the photographers' depictions of human suffering and noble endurance to chronicle the very nature of the exploitation that migrant workers and their families were facing and what could be done to help them – not just its tragic results – he became the target of a coordinated backlash from California agribusiness. The controversy reached new heights after John Ford's stirring and popular adaptation of *The Grapes of Wrath* starring Henry Fonda and Jane Darwell (as Tom and Ma Joad) was released to great critical and popular

[35] Ibid., 1020.

[36] John Steinbeck, *The Grapes of Wrath*, in *"The Grapes of Wrath" and Other Writings*, 516.

acclaim in April 1940, the same month that the best-selling novel was awarded the Pulitzer Prize. The film was nominated for seven Academy Awards and won two. Enemies of the book and later of the film engaged in actions that amounted to life imitating art imitating life, as they sought to repress a literary depiction of their own repression of migrant workers and their families.[37]

Eleanor Roosevelt visited a California migrant camp in April 1940, and testified before Congress on the conditions she witnessed (the first time a First Lady had ever offered congressional testimony). In addition, she informed a reporter, much to Steinbeck's satisfaction, that she had "never believed that *The Grapes of Wrath* was exaggerated." Later that same month Oklahoma singer, songwriter Woody Guthrie was in New Jersey recording his famous *Dust Bowl Ballads* album, which included "Tom Joad," a six-minute summation of Steinbeck's novel, and a suite of other songs charting the displacement, migration, and struggle of Oklahoma's refugees. Released in July 1940, *Dust Bowl Ballads* was Guthrie's most successful recording and provided one more layer of validation and promotion for *The Grapes of Wrath*. Steinbeck's novel received further support in the findings of Robert La Follette Jr.'s Senate Committee on Education and Labor, which held hearings in California in December 1939 and January 1940. The committee established that the migrants were suffering a "shocking degree of human misery" and that the Associated Farmers had engaged in "the most flagrant and violent infringement of civil liberties."[38] La Follette Jr.'s report, however, was not released until October 1942, by which time many of the migrants had found work in the rapidly expanding defense industry on the West Coast.

By the end of the decade, the FSA had built a total of 95 migrant camps, which provided temporary shelter, safety, and sanitary facilities for 75,000 people. Steinbeck's novel and the controversy surrounding it had played an important part in generating public sympathy for the nation's destitute migrants and prompting further government action on their behalf. The New Deal documentary photographers had played a vital role, too. Their visual record had brought national attention to the migrants' plight for four years prior to the publication of *The Grapes of Wrath*. In fact, by late 1939, Stryker's Historical Section had begun

[37] Rick Wartzman, *Obscene in the Extreme: The Banning and Burning of John Steinbeck's "The Grapes of Wrath"* (New York: Public Affairs, 2008). Henry Ford won the Academy Award for Best Director, and Jane Darwell won for Best Supporting Actress.

[38] Jackson Benson, *John Steinbeck, Writer: A Biography* (New York: Penguin Books, 1990), 422–423.

mounting exhibits nationwide that paired the photographs of Lange, Lee, Rothstein, Shahn and others with blocks of text from *The Grapes of Wrath* to underscore the accuracy of the novel's portrayal of conditions in Oklahoma, along the migrant trail, and in California. Steinbeck had succeeded in "writing history while it happens," and in crafting a literary work of enduring significance.[39] His fictional Joads became national symbols of human perseverance.

Many Californians, including some who were recent arrivals themselves, collectively derided migrants from the Southern Plains with the label "Okie," and Steinbeck laid bare this reactionary, dehumanizing brand of regionalism: "Them goddamn Okies got no sense and no feeling. They ain't human. A human being wouldn't live like they do. A human being couldn't stand to be so dirty and miserable. They ain't a hell of a lot better than gorillas," one gas station attendant says to another in the novel.[40] Steinbeck addressed another important dimension of the Depression in the western states: the disturbing backdrop of racist attitudes and actions toward the nonwhite agricultural workers who the white migrants were displacing. In charting this pattern of exploitation by California agribusiness interests, Steinbeck wrote: "the owners imported slaves, although they did not call them slaves: Chinese, Japanese, Mexicans, and Filipinos. They live on rice and beans, the business men said... And if they get funny – deport them."[41]

Steinbeck had suggested in 1936 that California agribusiness would find it much harder to push the Southern Plains migrants around. But this was not because the Okies were tougher or more drawn to collective labor action than the nonwhite migrants they were displacing. Rather, Steinbeck implied, because they were white the Okies' plight would engender greater sympathy nationwide. Journalist Carey McWilliams made the same argument in his best-selling indictment of California's migrant labor system, *Factories in the Field* (1939), published just a few months after *The Grapes of Wrath*. McWilliams provided fuller coverage of the exploitation of Chinese, Japanese, Filipino and Mexican fieldworkers and their families than Steinbeck, but also emphasized that "these despised 'Okies' and 'Texicans' were not another alien minority group (although

39 Swenson, *Picturing Migrants*, 139–156. For more detail on the FSA photographers, Steinbeck, and McWilliams, see Street, *Everyone Had Cameras*, 165–321.

40 Steinbeck, *"The Grapes of Wrath" and Other Writings*, 445.

41 Ibid., 457 for the *Grapes of Wrath* quotation; for the treatment of the Chinese, Filipinos, Japanese, and Mexicans in "The Harvest Gypsies," see 992–993.

they were treated as such)," and with their arrival "a day or reckoning approaches for the California farm industrialists."[42]

The day of reckoning that McWilliams warned of never arrived because World War II pulled the nation out of the Depression and drew the exploited white migrants into an expanding defense industry that offered not just full employment, but good wages and overtime, too. The previously prevailing racial landscape of California agricultural labor was restored. In the late 1930s, the white migrant underclass was descending into the worst depths of poverty and destitution. By the early 1940s, the Southern Plains migrants were raised into the California middle class by a level of Keynesian economic stimulus that the New Deal, even at its height, came nowhere close to matching. Many of them had resided in squatters' camps and, if they were fortunate, FSA camps, and were now property-holders, and would help form the foundations for modern California conservatism.[43] Within a year of the release of the movie version of *The Grapes of Wrath*, the terrible conditions it portrayed had largely disappeared, at least for Southern Plains migrant families, as workers entered the defense industry and the armed forces.[44]

Depression and Demography

African American migration to western cities, the expulsion, oppression, and resistance of Mexican-origin people, and the resurgence in Indian self-determination have all started to become part of the American memory of the 1930s. Similarly, the Southern Plains migration to California has long been burned into the national consciousness because of the New Deal photographers' and Steinbeck's and Ford's moving depictions. Lange's "Migrant Mother" and Steinbeck's Joads have achieved iconic status as the human faces of the exodus to the Golden State. But another significant and comparably sized intrawestern migratory shift – the exodus from the Northern Plains – remains largely unknown.

As the Pacific Northwest's federally stimulated recovery began in earnest by the mid 1930s, huge numbers of migrants from the Northern

42 Carey McWilliams, *Factories in the Field: The Story of Migratory Farm Labor in California* (1939; repr., Berkeley: University of California Press, 1999), 306.

43 See McWilliams, *Factories in the Field*; and James Gregory, *American Exodus: The Dust Bowl Migration and Okie Culture in California* (New York: Oxford University Press, 1989).

44 Dan Morgan, *Rising in the West: The True Story of an "Okie" Family in Search of the American Dream* (New York: Vintage Books, 1992), 134–151, esp. 135.

Plains moved to the region. During the 1930s, Washington, Oregon, and Idaho together gained approximately 460,000 new residents, with around 300,000 of them coming from the states of North and South Dakota and Nebraska; the peak year for the Northern Plains migration was 1936. Approximately two-fifths of the migrants came from North Dakota, two-fifths from South Dakota, and one-fifth from Nebraska. Like their counterparts to the South, they left their home states because of drought conditions, economic collapse, and insect infestations. In 1934, almost 10 million acres of crops failed in North Dakota. The value of farmland in the state had dropped from $41 an acre to $25 during the 1920s, and by the end of the 1930s was worth just $13 an acre. As the population moved out of the state 43 of its 53 counties saw a population decline, and the overall rural population declined by 17 percent, but at the same time the urban population of the state increased at the same rate. North Dakotans were leaving the state, or moving to its cities, and the same pattern played out across the Plains states.[45]

Grasshopper plagues, a devastating accompaniment to the drought and dust, afflicted the whole of the Great Plains for the entire period from 1931 to 1939 (aside from a single year, 1934), but northwestern Nebraska and the western Dakotas suffered the heaviest infestations. The grasshoppers destroyed crops and all other vegetation, and even consumed clothes hung out to dry. The sheer scale of the out-migrations reflects the severity of the conditions. South Dakota, for example, experienced a 7 percent population decline in the 1930s; its population of 693,000 fell by approximately 50,000. Oklahoma, the state that has become synonymous with the Depression era migration from the Southern Plains, suffered a 2.5 percent decline during the decade; the state's 1930 population of around 2.4 M dropped by about 60,000.[46]

Unlike the migrants from the Southern Plains, the Nebraskans and Dakotans did not face systematic exploitation and mistreatment when they arrived in the Pacific Northwest. In addition to the massive public power projects on the Columbia River, and in part because of them, the Pacific Northwest's timber industry was doing quite well as the Northern Plains economy collapsed. The relative economic stability of the host region helped ease the transition of Northern Plains' migrants. Because

[45] Rolland Dewing, *Regions in Transition: The Northern Great Plains and the Pacific Northwest in the Great Depression* (Lanham, MD: University Press of America, 2006); and Nugent, *Into the West*, 244.

[46] Dewing, *Regions in Transition*, 3, 18, and 27.

the population of the Pacific Northwest was aging at the time of the Great Depression, younger migrants were a welcome addition, unlike those arriving in California from the Southern Plains and other parts of America. The socioeconomic and educational levels of Northern Plains migrants paralleled those of the residents of the Pacific Northwest states. In contrast, Southern Plains migrants shared less in common with resident Anglo-Californians, who often demonstrated hostility toward "Okies." In addition, many residents of the Pacific Northwest had been born or maintained family roots in the upper Midwest, and thus were better connected to their new hosts. They did not experience the kind of social ostracism and systematic exploitation endured by their southern counterparts who migrated to California.[47]

The Plains migrations serve as the clearest example of how the Depression hit the West unevenly. The Plains states of South Dakota (−7 percent), North Dakota (−6 percent), Nebraska (−4.5 percent), Kansas (−4 percent), and Oklahoma (−2.5 percent) were the only ones in the country to suffer net population losses during the 1930s, and most of the people who left them headed westward.[48] Between 1935 and 1940, one farming region in southwestern Kansas made up of 16 counties lost 30.5 percent of its farmers; during those years, over 212,000 people left the Sunflower State. Moreover, the Plains states all received generous per capita funding from the New Deal; the exodus would almost certainly have been even greater had the levels of federal support been lower.

The Far West clearly saw significant population increase because of migration from the Great Plains states and other parts of the country: California's population increased by 1,230,000, or nearly 22 percent. In the Southwest, Arizona (14.5 percent) and New Mexico (25 percent) both grew at a healthy rate. In the Pacific Northwest, Idaho (18 percent), Oregon (14 percent), and Washington (11 percent) all made respectable gains. While the far western states experienced their slowest rate of population growth in the twentieth century, migration ensured that they grew at a faster rate than the nation. Despite some outmigration to California, Texas's population increased during the 1930s from approximately 5,825,000 to 6,415,000, an increase of around 9 percent.[49] Likewise, in

47 Ibid., 2–3.

48 These figures do not capture the full scale of the Plains migration to California and the Pacific Northwest, since those Plains states were experiencing natural population increase (more births than deaths) during the decade.

49 Nash, *The American West in the Twentieth Century: A Short History of an Urban Oasis* (1973; repr., Albuquerque: University of New Mexico Press, 1985), 137.

the Great Basin and the Rockies, growth rates were generally modest, but positive. Colorado's population grew by about 10 percent, Wyoming's by 11 percent, and Utah's by 8 percent, though Montana's increased by just 4 percent. Lightly populated Nevada had better fortune, in no small part because of the building of Boulder Dam; still, the Silver State, with a population increase of 21 percent, had just 110,000 residents by 1940.[50] With the exception of the Plains states from North Dakota to Oklahoma, all the West's subregions grew, and generally at a faster pace than the South, the Midwest, Mid-Atlantic, or Northeast.

There were some notable exceptions to the pattern of far western demographic growth exceeding levels nationwide: Florida experienced a population increase of well over 25 percent, while Washington, DC's, rate of over 30 percent was the nation's highest.[51] Florida's generally desirable climate, which attracted huge numbers of retirees, and DC's role at the geographic center of an expanding federal government explain those anomalies. Meanwhile, the nation experienced the slowest growth rate in its history during the 1930s, increasing by less than 9 million, from 122.8 million at the start of the decade to just 131.7 million by its close, a rate of just 7.2 percent (the rate was 16.1 percent in the 1920s and 14.5 percent in the 1940s). This very limited increase was largely due to fewer childbirths (a direct response to the economic hardships of the decade) and to negligible immigration. Considering this national trend, the population increases across the Far West become even more significant.

The demographic increase in the Far West was fueled largely by migration from other regions, but owed very little to immigration from other countries. Ten thousand Filipinos returned home between 1933 and 1935 because of the declining US economy, and a Filipino repatriation act in 1935 contributed to the departure of an additional 7,400. Just a few hundred Chinese and a few dozen Japanese immigrants arrived annually during the 1930s, and throughout the decade, Anglos violently repressed and sought to evict Japanese farmers from Oregon's Yakima Valley to California's Central Valley and Arizona's Salt River Valley. It is likely that more people from both China and Japan departed during the 1930s than arrived. Immigration to the United States from Europe was low,

[50] Alaska experienced healthy demographic increase, from 59,000 to over 72,000; as did Hawaii, from 368,000 to nearly 423,000.

[51] Florida grew by 400,000, from 1,468,000 to 1,897,000, while Washington, DC, jumped from around 487,000 to 663,000.

too, though several thousand Jewish refugees from Germany and Nazi-occupied Europe arrived in Southern California. That figure would have been considerably higher had Congress and the State Department been willing to loosen the immigration quotas and admit more refugees. The Jewish population of LA increased from 70,000 in 1930 to 130,000 in 1941. The Mexican population, as noted, declined massively because of the coordinated deportation initiatives, though by the latter part of the decade, the demand for Mexican field labor was again on the rise.[52]

With rural economies across the West in generally poor shape throughout the 1930s, it is no surprise that much of the region's demographic increases were a largely urban phenomenon. Los Angeles led the way, gaining more than 265,000 new residents and increasing from around 1.24 M at the start of the decade to over 1.5 M by its end, a 21.5 percent gain. The greater LA metro area had reached 2.9 M by 1940. This was nothing like the meteoric growth the city and metro area experienced in the 1920s and would experience again in the 1940s, but it was impressive nonetheless. San Diego's growth rate of 25.5 percent topped LA's. In contrast, Oakland saw only limited growth, and San Francisco experienced none. In the Mountain West, Denver grew by 11.5 percent. In the Southwest, Phoenix and Albuquerque saw the largest population increases, of 36 and 33.5 percent, respectively.[53]

In Texas, the agricultural depression fueled a migration from rural areas into Houston, which grew by an impressive 31.5 percent, increasing from around 292,000 at the start of the decade to 384,000 by its close – a higher rate of increase than for even San Diego or LA. Dallas, San Antonio, and Fort Worth all experienced steady growth, too. El Paso, in part because the city was an administrative center for the anti-Mexican repatriation initiatives, experienced a net loss of a few thousand during the decade.[54] The farm exodus in the Plains states fueled migration not just to Arizona and California, but to Oklahoma City and Omaha, the

[52] Nugent, *Into the West*, 239–241. For more on Filipino immigration and repatriation, and Jewish immigration to LA, see Barkan, *From All Points*, 269–280. Anti-Japanese movements in the 1930s West are discussed in Robert V. Hine and John Mack Faragher, *The American West: A New Interpretive History* (New Haven, CT: Yale University Press, 2000), 394–395.

[53] San Diego gained 55,000 new residents to top 200,000; Denver gained 34,000 to reach over 322,000; Phoenix's population topped 65,000 by decade's end; and Albuquerque's reached over 35,000.

[54] Dallas grew from around 260,000 to about 295,000 (13.5 percent); San Antonio from about 232,000 to roughly 254,000 (9.5 percent); and Fort Worth from about 163,000 to nearly 178,000 (9 percent). El Paso declined from 102,000 to 99,000.

former growing by over 10 percent to top 200,000 (though some of those new residents lived in the notorious May Avenue migrant camps).

The New Deal public works programs, and the generally desirable climates of the West Coast, Southwest, and parts of the Rockies, help explain the region's demographic growth. New Deal projects and programs were less of a pull factor in California (at least until Governor Frank Merriam became more receptive to them in the mid 1930s) than in other parts of the West, but the Golden State's agricultural and industrial economies and generally mild climates continued to attract migrants throughout the decade. The sustained movement of the national population in a westerly direction and toward urban centers during the Depression years helped ensure that a decent supply of labor would be in place as the defense industry began to expand exponentially in the early 1940s in the West's urban cores.

The rural South was home to the very worst, most desperately inhumane conditions during the Depression years, and the South may have been even worse hit in the 1930s than the West. But parts of the West, particularly the Southern Plains and California, received greater national attention, in part because the eroded topsoil of the Plains at times blackened the sky in the East, literally bringing with it the terrible reality of the Dust Bowl and generating national interest in the resulting exodus to the Golden State. In addition, the federal government's systematic highlighting of the ecological disaster on the Plains and of poverty across the West and efforts to combat both through the CCC, Resettlement Administration/FSA, and other agencies, placed the region at the center of the national consciousness. The New Deal brought recovery, relief, and reform to the nation, but it also helped to restore the promise of the West. The nation's westward demographic trajectory continued, even in the worst of times, in no small part because of federal interventions in the western economy. However, the benefits of FDR's enlightened administration were far from evenly spread across the West's racial and socioeconomic fault lines; yet they were at least spread to some degree, as work relief and other New Deal programs managed at least sometimes to cross the divides of color. The greater restoration of western opportunity would come with the war, though again, not in equal measure for all westerners.

7

The Landscape of War

> Let us no longer blind ourselves to the undeniable fact that the evil forces which have crushed and undermined and corrupted so many others are already within our own gates... We must be the great arsenal of democracy.
>
> – FDR, Radio Address, December 29, 1940

The Arsenal of Democracy

The Second World War had been raging in Europe for over a year when American voters went to the polls in November 1940. FDR was reelected to an unprecedented third term as president on the promise of neutrality and the achievements of the New Deal, with nearly 85 percent of the Electoral College vote, a comfortable 5 million vote margin, and 55 percent of the popular vote to Republican Wendell Willkie's less than 45 percent. The Democrats lost three seats in the Senate, gained five in the House, and remained firmly in control of both chambers. But cracks were forming in the Roosevelt coalition in the wake of the Supreme Court Packing Plan, the Roosevelt Recession of 1937–1938, the president's failed purge effort in the 1938 midterms, and his growing identification with an increasingly assertive labor movement. Those fissures were most evident in the isolationist Midwest and Great Plains. FDR had swept the West in 1932 and 1936 but lost the three Northern Plains states (the Dakotas and Nebraska) as well as Kansas and Colorado in 1940 (Map 7.1). Still, for the most part, the Far West and the nation, especially after the fall of France in June 1940, still preferred the steady hand of Roosevelt, who had steered the nation through eight years of the Depression.[1]

[1] David Kennedy, *Freedom from Fear: The American People in Depression and War, 1929–1945* (New York: Oxford University Press, 1999), 454–464.

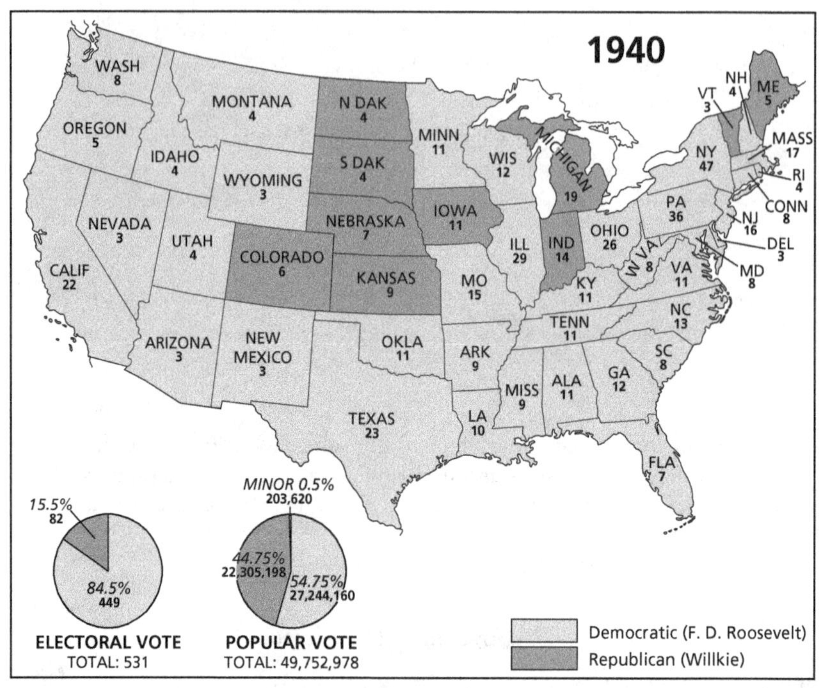

MAP 7.1 Electoral map, 1940.

On November 6, 1939, a month after German forces defeated the Polish army, Congress approved and FDR signed the Cash and Carry bill, a major modification of the Neutrality Acts of 1935–1937. The new law allowed Britain and other nations at war to purchase nonmilitary goods from the United States. The measure helped to jump-start industrial production and pull the United States out of the Depression. "We must be the great arsenal of democracy," Franklin Roosevelt declared in a radio fireside chat at the end of 1940, a full year before the nation entered the war, and just a few months after 16 million American men had been placed on the draft rolls through the Selective Service and Training Act. In March 1941, the president persuaded Congress to pass the Lend Lease Bill. It enabled the United States to provide Britain with the military equipment it needed to continue to wage the war against Germany, which by then controlled most of Western Europe. The German invasion of the Soviet Union began in June 1941, and that fall the Lend Lease program was expanded to help supply the Soviets' military needs. The defense industry was thus moving into high gear well before the nation formally entered the war in December.

In early January 1942, less than a month after the Japanese attack on Pearl Harbor and the United States's entry into the war, the president announced that the Allied nations required an "overwhelming . . . a crushing superiority of equipment in any theater of the world war." FDR's hope for the Allies was fully realized. The aircraft industry provides one of the most striking examples. American workers built almost 48,000 aircraft in 1942, and nearly 86,000 in 1943. By 1944, the arsenal of democracy was in peak production, building more than 96,000 planes. Even as the war began to wind down in 1945, the United States produced around 50,000 planes. For most of the war, the United States was building more planes than the Soviet Union, Britain, and the countries of the British Commonwealth combined. Moreover, the Allies were outproducing the Axis powers by a factor of 2:1, or 3:1, and in 1942, and 1943, close to 4:1.[2] When the D-Day landings took place on June 6, 1944, the Germans had a meager 319 aircraft available on the Western Front; the Allies were able to employ 12,837 planes, or 40 times as many.[3] Wars are won on battlefields of course, but victories are also secured through the productive capacity of industrial plants and the effective mobilization of civilian personnel, and this was certainly the case during World War II, when American workers built more than 300,000 planes, over 88,000 tanks, and 3,000 merchant ships, known as Liberty ships. The US defense industry exceeded FDR's ambitious war production targets; his hope that the nation would become an unparalleled giant of martial production was realized with greater speed and scale than he had imagined possible.[4] The American workplace proved vital to the defeat of Nazism and Japanese imperialism.

Becoming the arsenal of democracy involved massive federal investment that in turn had a tremendous impact on national demography, and especially the flow of people to the Far West. Americans had migrated in large numbers to the West beyond the Plains in the 1930s, but the scale of the movement in the 1940s was much more pronounced. Likewise, the difference in scale between the federal stimulus of the Depression years and that of the war years was striking. The federal budget in 1945 was over $100 billion, more than 11 times the size of the 1939 figure of

[2] Paul Kennedy, *The Rise and Fall of the Great Powers: Economic Change and Military Conflict from 1500 to 2000* (New York: Random House, 1987), 352–353.

[3] Ibid., 354.

[4] Kennedy, *Freedom from Fear*, 618; and Gerald D. Nash, *The Great Depression and World War II: Organizing America, 1933–1945* (New York: St. Martin's Press, 1979), 136.

$9 billion. This massive increase resulted from a near-doubling of the gross national product from $91 billion to $166 billion; a doubling of the federal income tax burden after the passage of the Revenue Act of 1942; the creation of 17 million new jobs through the war effort (and all the resulting taxable income); and from the government's willingness to raise the federal debt, which increased fivefold to $260 billion during the war years. While the Roosevelt Recession of 1937–1938 had demonstrated that FDR was a reluctant Keynesian at best, the necessities of war turned him into a thoroughgoing practitioner, willing to engage in massive deficit spending to meet the Allies' military needs.[5]

The Second New Deal's "Big Bill," as FDR called it, the Emergency Relief Appropriation Act of 1935, which was the largest peacetime spending bill in the nation's history, had provided $4.8 billion to fund the programs of the Works Progress Administration all across the country.[6] However, during the four years the nation was involved in World War II, the federal government expended around $70 billion building the martial economic infrastructure of the West alone, or close to 15 times as much as the Big Bill. The United States spent over $4 billion just on military bases between 1940 and 1945. Roughly half of all federal expenditures in the entire West during the war went to California and the state accounted for fully 10 percent of all federal funds in those years, though only around 7 percent of the national population resided there. By 1945 those federal expenses accounted for fully 45 percent of California's personal income, which marked a massive change: in 1930 the figure had been only 5 percent, and even after the New Deal spending of the 1930s, had risen to just 10 percent by 1940. Federal investments in the Golden State were thus disproportionate to per capita spending nationwide by the government.[7]

[5] Richard White, *"It's Your Misfortune and None of My Own": A New History of the American West* (Norman: University of Oklahoma Press, 1991), 496; Kennedy, *Freedom from Fear*, 624; and Charles C. Alexander, "The United States: The Good War?," in *Allies at War: The Soviet, American, and British Experience, 1939–1945*, ed. David Reynolds, Warren F. Kimball, and A. O. Chubarian (New York: St. Martin's Press, 1994), 285–305, esp. 286.

[6] George Brown Tindall and David Emory Shi, *America: A Narrative History*, Brief 9th ed., vol. 2 (New York: W. W. Norton, 2013), 875.

[7] Carl Abbott, *How Cities Won the West: Four Centuries of Urban Change in Western North America* (Albuquerque: University of New Mexico Press, 2008), 171. In mid-1940, California's population comprised 5.2 percent of the national population, and that figure rose to fully 7 percent by mid-1945, yet the state received 10 percent of all federal expenditures during the war years. See www.dof.ca.gov/html/FS_DATA/STAT-ABS/documents/B1.pdf accessed March 2, 2016. See also Ric Dias, "The Great Cantonment: Cold War Cities in the American West," in *The Cold War American West, 1945–1989*,

While the full weight of the New Deal stimulus had come late to California, largely because of the opposition of Republican governors, the wartime stimulus more than made up for lost time and engendered no opposition.

During the 1944 election campaign against Republican Thomas Dewey, FDR proclaimed that he was retiring "Dr. New Deal" and turning all attention to "Dr. Win the War." For much of the West though, and certainly for the West Coast states, it must have seemed that the federal supports of the 1930s were not being replaced, but rather ramped up to unprecedented new levels. Federal resources rolled in a westerly direction, along with civilian migrants and military personnel. During the 1930s and 1940s, the West, the American region that self-identified as the great bastion of rugged individualism and independence, was the recipient of significantly higher levels of federal support and investment than the nation. The last regional descendant of the much-lauded frontier process was first in line at the federal trough and in many regards, considerably more federally reliant than self-reliant. In fact, the region's federally underwritten industry of war was like a second Homestead Act, drawing people to the Far West just as the landmark 1862 measure had brought settlers to the Prairies, Plains and Inter-Mountain West.

Like the defense industry, the West's extractive industries proved vital to the war effort. Western mines produced more than 90 percent of the nation's mineral needs, and half of its oil supplies. Washington, California, and Oregon were together responsible for 40 percent of the US timber yield. Meanwhile, western agricultural production ramped up to meet the needs of the European allies. Between 1941 and 1945 the West produced more than two-thirds of the nation's fruit and vegetables, and wheat, and more than half of its other staple grains such as corn and oats. However, this growth in agricultural productivity was increasingly the result of agribusiness expansion across the region. Larger landholdings rather than small family farms had traditionally characterized California agriculture and the state's "factories in the field" only got larger during the war years.[8]

ed. Kevin J. Fernlund (Albuquerque: University of New Mexico Press, 1998), 71–85, figure for spending on military bases on 74.

[8] Gerald D. Nash, *The American West Transformed: The Impact of the Second World War* (Bloomington: Indiana University Press, 1985), 198–200; and Michael P. Malone and Richard W. Etulain, *The American West: A Modern History, 1900 to the Present* (Lincoln: University of Nebraska Press, 2007), 27.

The Demography and Economy of War

The West and the nation experienced extraordinary demographic changes during World War II and the early Cold War years: 8 million people flocked to new opportunities in the West's mushrooming martial economy, roughly half of them to the war production centers on the Pacific Coast. "They were begging for workers," Norman Cantrell, a former Texan and California migrant worker recalled, adding that "you were bombarded" with job offers.[9] From 1940 to 1945, the number of women in the workforce rose from 11.9 million to 18.6 million because of the expanding defense industry. During the 1940s, the US population increased from just under 132 million to almost 151 million, a rate of 14.5 percent, or double the 7.2 percent rate in the 1930s. The 1940s growth rate was even more impressive since World War II reduced the stream of immigration from overseas to a trickle from 1940 to 1945. Moreover, during the 1940s, the combined population of the three Pacific Coast states increased at more than triple the national rate. This level of migration-driven population growth and economic transformation has been compared to the California Gold Rush, though World War II mostly accelerated the well-established demographic trends of previous decades, rather than creating new ones, as the Gold Rush had done.[10]

California saw the most dramatic growth in the West and the nation, gaining around 3.7 million new residents, rising from 6.9 million in 1940 to 10.6 million in 1950, an increase of over 53 percent (by 1962, it was the nation's most populous state). Around a million of those new Californians resulted from natural population increase in the early baby boom years, beginning in 1941. The other more than 2.5 million new residents were 1940s migrants to the Golden State; around 1.5 million of them arrived between 1940 and 1944.[11] Oregon and Washington

[9] Richard Etulain, *Beyond the Missouri: The Story of the American West* (Albuquerque: University of New Mexico Press, 2006), 362.

[10] Nash, *The American West Transformed*, vii; see also Nash's *World War II and the West: Reshaping the Economy* (Lincoln: University of Nebraska Press, 1990); and his *The Federal Landscape: An Economic History of the Twentieth-Century West* (Tucson: University of Arizona Press, 1999); Walter Nugent, *Into the West: The Story of Its People* (New York: Knopf, 1999), 257; and R. Douglas Hurt, *The Great Plains during World War Two* (Lincoln: University of Nebraska Press, 2008), 128, for women in the workforce.

[11] For more on the baby boom's early beginnings in 1941 (1946 is generally cited as the starting date for the phenomenon), see Nugent, *Into the West*, 271–272. For California

saw population growth during the 1940s that was not quite as impressive as California's, but still virtually unparalleled anywhere else in the country. Oregon increased by over 39 percent to more than 1.5 million, while Washington's population reached 2.38 million, a rate of more than 37 percent.[12] White European migrants from the Plains states of North and South Dakota, Nebraska, and Kansas, along with African American sharecroppers and tenant farmers from the South, and workers from the manufacturing centers of New York and other eastern states, all flocked to the Pacific Coast as war production kicked into high gear within just weeks after the attack at Pearl Harbor. In just the first two months of 1942, 1 million people moved to the three West Coast states, fully half of them heading to the greater LA metro area.[13]

The next highest regional growth rate in the nation after California and the Pacific Northwest was in the Desert Southwest, where Arizona grew by half, Nevada by almost half, New Mexico by more than 28 percent, and Utah by 25 percent. The other demographic giant of the larger western region (and of the South, too) was Texas, which grew by over 20 percent during the 1940s, reaching 7.7 million. In the interior Northwest, Wyoming and Colorado saw population increases of 16 percent and 15 percent, respectively. Thus, the population of the whole massive L-shaped region comprising the Pacific Coast and the Greater Southwest (from Washington down to Southern California and across to Texas) grew at a faster rate than the nation.[14] Florida, which grew by 46 percent in the 1940s, was an exception to this trend of far western dominance in population growth. But aside from the Sunshine State, where shipbuilding operations and military installations accounted for most of the population gain (and migrating retirees played a part, too), the only places outside of the West that approximated even the lower end of the impressive scale

migration figures, 1940–1944, see Marilynn S. Johnson, *The Second Gold Rush: Oakland and the East Bay in World War II* (Berkeley: University of California Press, 1993), 8.

12 During the 1940s, the media paid great attention to the Far West's demographic growth; see, for example, Jay Walz, "Americans Go West, But to Factory, Not Farm," *New York Times*, October 10, 1948, E7.

13 Richard Lingeman, *Don't You Know There's a War Going On? The American Home Front, 1941–1945* (1970; repr., New York: Nation Books, 2003), 69; and Maury Klein, *A Call to Arms: Mobilizing America for World War II* (New York: Bloomsbury Press, 2013), 537.

14 Wyoming's population dropped from 246,000 to 232,000 between 1940 and 1945; see Hurt, *The Great Plains during World War Two*, 385. Hurt's figure is a little lower than the official US Census Bureau figure of 250,742 for Wyoming, since he does not include the military population temporarily stationed in the state.

of far western regional growth were the Great Lakes state of Michigan (21 percent) and the coastal states of Virginia (24 percent), Maryland (29 percent), Delaware (19 percent), and Washington, DC (21 percent), where the federal bureaucracy grew in tandem with the war effort. Thus, some of the Atlantic Coast states clearly benefited from the growing martial economy, as did Texas on the Gulf Coast and bicoastal Florida. But it was the Far West, and particularly the West Coast, that constituted the leading edge of the decade's demographic growth.[15]

However, western population growth was thoroughly uneven during the 1940s. Parts of the region grew at the expense of others. Idaho, Montana, Kansas, Nebraska, and South Dakota all experienced anemic growth. Oklahoma and North Dakota joined Arkansas and Mississippi as the only states to suffer a net population loss during this era of general growth nationwide. Thus, a total of seven noncoastal western states stretching from the Plains to the Rockies, with their minimal population growth, or even loss in a few cases, served as a sobering counterbalance and contributor to the story of meteoric growth in the geographic hubs of the new martial West: the Pacific Coast, and Desert Southwest. Still, the entire western region, from the Plains to the Pacific, saw an overall demographic increase of 26 percent during the 1940s, a rate far exceeding that of the South, Northeast, and Midwest.[16]

The West had earlier served as a national bellwether for the crisis of the 1890s, for some of the most laudatory and lamentable aspects of Progressive Era reform, for the cultural conflicts of the 1920s, and the government transformations and racial tensions of the Depression years. In keeping with tradition, the West during World War II comprised the leading edge of the demographic volatility, accelerated urban and industrial expansion, movement from farm to city, as well as the sweeping social and political changes that accompanied those population shifts. The changes in the West were greater in the 1940s than in any previous decade. Still, they rested on the foundations of demographic, urban, and infrastructural growth established throughout the previous four decades and particularly during the New Deal years.

The trend toward increased urbanization was the most pronounced of the West's demographic shifts. When the twentieth century began, about

15 These figures are for the whole decade of the 1940s. Some states outside of the Far West saw quite rapid growth during the World War II years and slower growth during the second half of the decade.

16 Demographia, "US Population by State from 1900," available at: http://demographia.com/db-state1900.htm.

a quarter of the region's residents lived in towns of 2,500 or more and were thus, technically speaking, urban dwellers. By 1930, more than half of the West's population resided in urban centers, but the West was still a little behind the national curve; the 1920 Census showed that the United States had become more urban than rural. However, by the time the nation entered World War II, the West was fast becoming the country's most urban region. Ten years later, the rate of urban demographic growth had further accelerated, fueled in large part by a nationwide farm exodus. During the war years, the nation's farm population declined by almost 17 percent (not including the 1.5 million farm dwellers who joined the armed forces), with 900,000 people heading to the cities annually. By 1950, the number of individually or family-owned and -operated farms in the United States had declined by a more than a million from the 1900 figure of around 5.74 million, while the national population had doubled during those years, from 76 million to over 152 million. Family farms were being replaced by larger agribusiness ventures.[17]

Texas was well above the national rate of demographic increase, yet nowhere close to the levels of growth in the Pacific Coast states. However, the movement from farm to city continued unabated in the Lone Star State in the 1940s and the state's gains paralleled those in the West Coast's cities. Dallas grew by 47.5 percent, San Antonio by 50 percent, Houston by 55 percent, and Fort Worth by 57 percent.[18] On the California Coast, Los Angeles added close to half a million new residents, growing by almost one-third and reaching nearly 2 million. San Diego's growth rate of 64.5 percent was even more impressive. Meanwhile the metropolitan areas surrounding Southern California's two mushrooming major cities were also booming as the region experienced huge suburban expansion.[19] Oakland (27.5 percent) and San Francisco (22 percent) grew at healthy rates, albeit at lower ones than their Southern California

[17] Lingeman, *Don't You Know There's a War Going On?*, 67. See also US Census Bureau, "Changes in Agriculture, 1900 to 1950," 70, available at: www2.census.gov/prod2/decennial/documents/41667073v5p6ch4.pdf accessed July 18, 2016. During the Depression years, 375,000 people a year left the farms for the cities; during the 1920s, the figure was markedly higher – 600,000 per year – but still only two-thirds as large as the annual rural to urban exodus of the World War II years.

[18] See Figure 4.2.

[19] At the start of the 1940s the population of LA comprised 54 percent of the population of LA County, but by 1950, that figure had dropped to 47.5 percent. For Los Angles city and county figures, see "County Population 1850–2010 – Los Angeles Almanac," available at: www.laalmanac.com/population/po02.htm accessed February 2, 2016.

urban counterparts. The West's metropolitan and urban growth was not confined to the Pacific Coast states and Texas: for example, Las Vegas nearly tripled in size, Albuquerque grew by a remarkable 173 percent, Phoenix grew by more than a third, and Denver increased by almost a quarter.[20] Largely because of the growth of the martial economy, the West by 1950 was home to 7 of the nation's 25 largest cities: Los Angeles (third largest), San Francisco (eleventh), Houston (fourteenth), Seattle (nineteenth), Dallas (twenty-second), Denver (twenty-fourth), and San Antonio (twenty-fifth). The trend of western urban growth leading the nation has continued unabated ever since: in 2016, 13 of the nation's 25 largest cities were in the West (6 in Texas and 4 in California), along with 11 of the 25 largest metropolitan areas.

The massive public works projects of the New Deal provided the infrastructural foundations for what followed in the war years. In fact, the lingering depression offered some advantages as the United States shifted its economy and its workforce toward the needs of war. When Germany defeated France in mid June 1940, there were still nearly 9 million Americans out of work. The country was already well on the path to becoming the arsenal of democracy when the Japanese attacked Pearl Harbor, Hawaii, 18 months later; but even by that late date more than 3 million Americans remained unemployed. During the Depression years, the productive capacity of American industrial plants was massively underutilized. So, as the nation entered the war, the process of conversion from peacetime production to a martial economy was far less complicated than it had been during World War I, when the nation had full employment and its plants were already at optimal capacity. The war rescued the American economy from the Depression, but the Depression, paradoxically, prepared the economy for its remarkably rapid and successful conversion to a war footing.[21]

[20] Seattle's growth rate in the 1940s was 27 percent, and Spokane's was 33 percent. See Etulain, *Beyond the Missouri*, 306; and Nugent, *Into the West*, 257. All the western states, aside from North Dakota, Montana, Oregon, and Alaska, exceeded the national rate of rural–urban change during the 1940s, and for most of the West the level of increase was considerably higher. Arizona went from 35 percent urban in 1940 to 44 percent urban in 1950, Texas from 45 percent to 63 percent. California was already 71 percent urban in 1940 and was 81 percent urban by 1950; see Abbott, *How Cities Won the West*, 178.

[21] Kennedy, *Freedom from Fear*, 616–617.

Nowhere was that transition to martial production more pronounced than in the Far West. The patterns of migration to the region during the Depression years and, in previous decades, facilitated the continued movement of families there during wartime; with friends and family in place the prospect of relocation was less daunting. Moreover, all the massive New Deal hydroelectric projects were either fully operational or nearing completion when the nation entered the war. The Pacific Northwest was unable to consume even a fraction of the power-generating capacity of the Columbia River by the end of the New Deal years, which raised concerns that the hydroelectric infrastructure had been massively overbuilt. However, as the US defense industry geared up, that newly established power resource ensured that the region became home to six of the seven aluminum plants the government built during the war to support the aircraft industry. Fully 84 percent of the power that supplied wartime production in the West came from federal projects. The shipbuilding, aircraft, and armaments industries drew on the human resources, the hydroelectric power supply, and the raw resources of the region – including minerals and timber – to quickly develop the region's industrial capacity.[22]

Nonetheless, despite these advantages, meeting the growing demand for workers in the West's rapidly expanding war industry remained complicated. Military needs had to be balanced with those of agricultural and industrial production, and the new array of available employment opportunities made it difficult to keep workers in certain sectors. For example, western ranchers had difficulty keeping their operations staffed, and this affected American beef production. Jobs in war plants paid $80 to $100 a week and ranch hands, who were accustomed to salaries of about half that much, were lured away.[23]

The arsenal of democracy faced the conundrum of how to maintain the individual rights of citizens while at the same time meeting the needs of the nation during wartime. The British Ministry of Labor and National Service had the power to effectively direct human resources toward the military, industrial, and agrarian sectors of the economy as needed, and it did so. In Germany and the Soviet Union, the level of state control was far greater still. But despite all the federal agencies that FDR's administration created to manage the war effort, the United States never came close to imposing even Britain's level of top-down economic management of its

[22] White, "*It's Your Misfortune*," 499; and Nash, *The American West Transformed*, 197.
[23] Klein, *A Call to Arms*, 542.

civilian population.[24] The discrepancy was explained by the reality that the war impacted the United States far less than it did Britain. Britain had been at war for 27 months before its Atlantic cousin entered and had suffered constant bombing raids from the German Luftwaffe. The general mobility of the American population was also a factor. Americans had pulled up roots and migrated to other parts of the country, mostly in a westerly direction, for centuries before the demographic transformations wrought by World War II. The defense industry magnet thus continued an established pattern rather than starting a new one.

Nevertheless, migration to the centers of wartime production did not occur without prompting. Henry J. Kaiser, who had headed up the Six Companies construction conglomerate that built the Boulder Dam and other major New Deal era projects, became a major player in the West Coast shipbuilding industry when he landed a federal contract in 1940 to build 30 merchant ships for the British.[25] During the war, he played a vital role in American shipbuilding. Kaiser was among the many corporate entrepreneurs who advertised nationwide for workers, and by providing day care facilities and health care services as well as good wages, and even chartering "Liberty Trains," attracted them from across the country. Kaiser literally delivered 38,000 workers to the West by rail to meet his ambitious production schedules. His Los Angeles Calship yard broke the world record for production by building 15 Liberty ships in June 1942, a ship every second day.[26] More than 200,000 African Americans headed to the West from the South during the war, and by the end of the decade another 79,000 arrived; Kaiser actively recruited African American workers. In addition, the federal government helped initiate a bracero program that brought approximately 170,000 Mexican workers to the West between 1942 and 1945. They came mainly to meet needs in the agricultural sector but also to provide railroad track maintenance as Americans entered the armed services and defense industry jobs.[27]

[24] Ibid., 545.

[25] Douglas Flamming, *African Americans in the West* (Santa Barbara, CA: ABC/CLIO, 2009), 163.

[26] Arthur C. Verge, "The Impact of the Second World War on Los Angeles," *Pacific Historical Review* 63 (August 1994): 289–314, Liberty ship numbers on 303; and Mark S. Foster, *Henry J. Kaiser: Builder in the Modern American West* (Austin: University of Texas Press, 1989), 68–89.

[27] George W. Pierson examined this feature of American life in *The Moving American* (New York: Alfred A. Knopf, 1973). For the figures on African American and Mexican migration to the region, see Nash, *The Federal Landscape*, 43 and 48; Nugent, *Into the* West, 256; Flamming, *African Americans in the West*, 164; and Quintard Taylor,

Kaiser and other industrialists took over the role that the railroads and state and local chambers of commerce and immigration bureaus had played in the late nineteenth and early twentieth centuries, heralding the economic opportunities in the West to attract new migrants. The federal government, through the War Manpower Commission, helped channel the flow of Americans to the West's centers of wartime production where they were most needed, and federal loans to the nation's leading industrialists played an important role, too. Kaiser, for example, borrowed nearly $100 million from the Reconstruction Finance Corporation (RFC) to build a steel mill at Fontana, east of Los Angeles; the RFC loaned Kaiser a total of $300 million to finance his defense industry operations. Federal funding accounted for fully 90 percent of the capital that financed the defense industry in the West.[28] The government was essentially underwriting the nation's largest industrialists during the war in much the same way that it had bankrolled the expansion of the transcontinental railroads generations earlier through generous subsidies and grants of land. These massive federal incentives for corporations helped guarantee the levels of martial production necessary to win the war; by contrast, federal welfare for railroad magnates in the post–Civil War era was less essential to national interests.[29]

The government built the West in a systematic fashion through regional development initiatives in the 1930s and was now providing financial supports that enabled industrialists to profit enormously from the new martial economy at virtually no personal risk. Then, after the war ended and the process of reconverting the existing industrial infrastructure to peacetime production began, the government minimized the risks for those same entrepreneurs by offering them generous incentives to purchase the defense plant facilities it had built for them during the war, and to do so for a mere fraction of their actual value – generally only about 10 cents on the dollar. Thus, the US Steel Corporation, Kaiser, and other private interests enjoyed federal assistance in complementary phases, and on a staggering scale.[30]

West Coast metropolitan and industrial growth went hand in hand. Shipbuilding operations in California, Oregon, and Washington

In Search of the Racial Frontier; African Americans in the American West, 1528–1990 (New York: W. W. Norton, 1998), 251–277.

[28] Klein, *A Call to Arms*, 537–539.

[29] See Richard White, *Railroaded: The Transcontinentals and the Making of Modern America* (New York: W. W. Norton, 2011).

[30] Klein, *A Call to Arms*, 537–539.

cumulatively employed 200,000 workers and accounted for more than half the ships built during the war. Kaiser's Bay Area plant in Richmond, California, operated three shifts of 16,000 workers each. The aircraft industry on the West Coast employed more than 300,000 people and was responsible for almost half the planes built in the United States during the war years, with eight California facilities stretching from LA to San Diego accounting for 243,000 of that number. Dallas–Fort Worth and Wichita also received lucrative aircraft contracts; Wichita's population grew by almost half during the 1940s. A burgeoning chemical industry operated in LA, Seattle, and Portland. Portland also became the center of Pacific northwestern aluminum production. The Denver Ordinance Plant, operated by the Remington Arms Company, was one of the largest weapon-making facilities in the country, employing 20,000 workers at its peak. The Rocky Mountain Arsenal, located in the Denver metropolitan area, produced chemical weapons and employed another 15,000 people. Henderson, Nevada, drawing on the water resources from the recently constructed Boulder Dam, became the center of magnesium production, employing 14,000 workers who helped fuel the growth of the Las Vegas Strip at a time when neighboring Las Vegas was home to only around 10,000 residents.[31]

In addition to the industrial magnets for new migrants, a series of new military bases were established and they drew civilian workers at about the same rate as military personnel. There were 10 bases in Utah alone, employing 60,000 civilians and accommodating 60,000 servicemen and -women. Between 1940 and 1944, close to 50 Army airfields were established in California for defense and pilot training. In the 1930s, there were fewer than 100,000 servicemen and -women stationed in the West. During the war, 15 million Americans served in the armed forces and, not surprisingly, given the significance of the Pacific theater, well over half that number were stationed in the West at one time or another. Many of those military personnel relocated to the West with their families after the war, which helps explain the continued strong demographic growth of the region in the second half of the 1940s. Every state from the Plains to the Pacific, with the exceptions of Montana and Oregon, had at least

[31] Klein, *A Call to Arms*, 537–538; White, *"It's Your Misfortune,"* 500; and Lingeman, *Don't You Know There's a War Going On?*, 69. In Las Vegas, the El Rancho opened in 1941, the Last Frontier in 1942, the Flamingo in 1946, the Thunderbird in 1948, and the Desert Inn in 1950.

one major military base, and the latter state was home to Kaiser's massive Vanport shipyard.[32]

East of Los Angeles, the Desert Training Center, established in January 1942 and covering 16,000 square miles, was the largest military training facility in the world, and serviced over a million US troops during the war. The Navy significantly expanded its facilities at San Diego and Long Beach and built more than 60 air stations nationwide for personnel training and plane maintenance, many of them in California and Texas and one in Norman, Oklahoma. Nevada benefited from the establishment of Nellis Air Force Base, near Las Vegas, and New Mexico received three Air Force bases. Washington was home to Fort Lewis, originally built in 1917, and expanded by the Works Progress Administration (WPA) in 1938 to include an Air Force base. The facility became a training site that accommodated up to 37,000 troops during the war. Idaho received an Air Force base and a naval base. Fort Carson was built near Colorado Springs and accommodated close to 40,000 Army personnel, as well as 12,000 Axis POWs. On the Southern Plains, Texas gained two Army bases – Fort Bliss and Fort Hood – and several Air Force bases, and Oklahoma saw the establishment of Fort Sill. The contiguous West (not including Alaska and Hawaii) was home to 54 military bases in total prior to World War II. During the war, 93 additional bases were established across the region. Another 91 bases were added during the Cold War years, though most of them after 1950. Not surprisingly, Alaska and Hawaii, with their immense strategic importance, were also vital parts of the new martial landscape. The 1950 Census showed there was a member of the armed forces for every 4.3 civilians in Alaska.[33]

Federal funding of war-related science initiatives proved vital to the development of the new western military–industrial complex. In late 1942 the Department of War, on the advice of project director J. Robert

[32] The Utah figure is from Klein, *A Call to Arms*; the figure for servicemen and -women stationed in the West is from Nash, *The Federal Landscape*, 43–44; David W. Mills, in *Cold War in a Cold Land: Fighting Communism on the Northern Plains* (Norman: University of Oklahoma Press, 2015), puts the figure at more than 10 million (181).

[33] Arthur Verge, "World War II," in William Deverell and Greg Hise, *A Companion to Los Angeles* (Malden, MA: Blackwell, 2010), 311–321, esp. 315; Abbott, *How Cities Won the West*, 179. For numbers of military bases, see Timothy M. Chambless, "Pro-Defense, Prof-Growth, and Anti-Communism: Cold War Politics in the American West," in Fernlund, *The Cold War American West*, 101–117, chart of military bases on 102; for Fort Carson, see Stephen J. Leonard and Thomas J. Noel, *Colorado: A History of the Centennial State*, 4th ed. (Boulder: University of Colorado Press, 2005), 305.

Oppenheimer, selected remote Los Alamos, northwest of Santa Fe, New Mexico, as the location for the Los Alamos National Laboratory, the central site for the Manhattan Project. Thousands of employees worked at the secret facility developing the atomic bomb and, later, the hydrogen bomb. Meanwhile, the US Army Corps of Engineers and the DuPont Corporation identified Hanford, Washington, as the ideal site for plutonium production, based on its ample supply of clean water and hydroelectric power from the Grand Coulee Dam. The facility was established in 1943 and quickly became home to more than 50,000 workers and their families. By late 1944, the world's first production reactor was operational at Hanford and plutonium was being processed at the site. Within a few months, two more reactors had been built and plutonium was being shipped to Los Alamos.

The first atomic bomb was tested near Alamogordo, New Mexico, in July 1945. Just a few weeks later, the atomic bombs were dropped on Hiroshima on August 6 and Nagasaki on August 9, 1945, ending the war. The following summer, the work of Hanford found its way to the Marshall Islands when atomic bombs were exploded at Bikini Atoll. During 1947, as the Cold War with the Soviet Union began to develop, Hanford became the sole producer of weapons-grade plutonium for the nation's nuclear program, and five more reactors were added at the site. Meanwhile, in 1946, the US Air Force selected San Diego–based contractor Convair to build a new missile; this initiative eventually resulted in the Atlas Intercontinental Ballistic Missile (ICBM). Also, in the late 1940s, the West emerged as the center of the aerospace industry, with major facilities in California and Texas as well as Seattle and Wichita. In 1951, the West's martial landscape was further expanded when the Atomic Energy Commission established the Nevada Test Site, north of Las Vegas, as the primary site for aboveground atomic tests (Map 7.2).[34]

World War II and the Cold War also had a significant impact on higher education in the West, helping turn some of the region's universities, including the California Institute of Technology and the University of California at Berkeley, into world-class research institutions. The government invested close to $100 million in western universities during the

[34] John M. Findlay and Bruce Hevly, *Atomic Frontier Days: Hanford and the American West* (Seattle: University of Washington Press, 2011), xi–xii; and Hill Williams, *Made in Hanford: The Bomb That Changed the World* (Pullman: Washington State University Press, 2011), xiv–xv; and Gerald D. Nash, *A Brief History of the American West since 1945* (New York: Harcourt, 2001), 10–11.

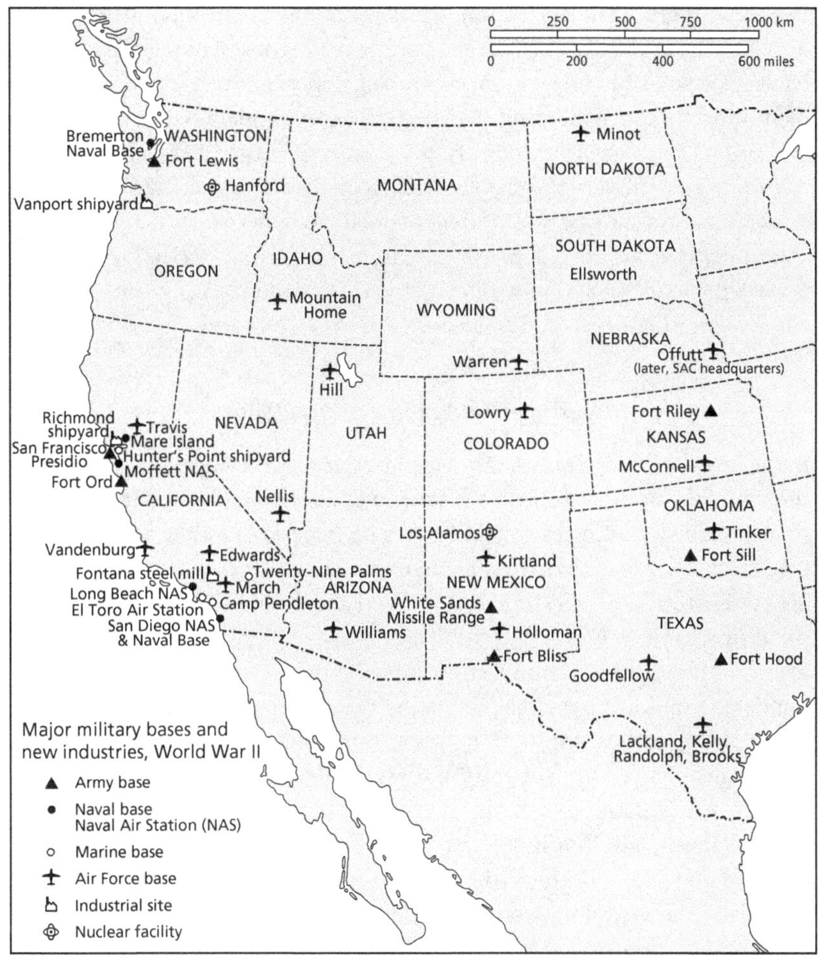

MAP 7.2 Major military bases and new industries, World War II. From Walter Nugent, *Into the West: The Story of Its People* (New York: Alfred A. Knopf, 1999), 256. George Colbert, cartographer.

war years, which exceeded the amount those institutions had spent on scientific research for their entire existence prior to the war. That federal stimulus helped ensure the region's long-term global competitiveness in science and technology. In addition, the Servicemen's Readjustment Act of 1944, better known as the GI Bill, provided low cost mortgages and small business loans to returning veterans, and underwrote a massive expansion of higher education in the United States by providing tuition coverage and living expenses for those who wished to pursue degrees.

By 1946, there were more than 2 million students enrolled in American universities, and fully half were GI Bill beneficiaries. Among the growing college population were 60,000 women and 70,000 African American men and women (including veterans). The expanded access to colleges and universities was particularly pronounced in the western states. For example, the University of New Mexico had 1,600 students before the war began and 24,000 soon after it ended; Arizona State Teachers' College quickly grew into a major research institution, becoming Arizona State University (ASU) in 1958; and various military programs boosted enrollment at colleges and universities across Colorado.[35]

Wartime and Postwar Party Politics

In the arena of American electoral politics, it was business as usual during the war. Elections were held on schedule, as they had since the nation's founding, a sign of just how insulated the American public was from the true horrors of war that were being experienced by civilians and soldiers across Eastern and Western Europe and the Pacific World. Still, as the midterm elections loomed in the fall of 1942, Americans were concerned in the wake of their nation's entry into the war. The United States made important military gains in the Pacific theater at the Battle of the Coral Sea in May and at Midway in June, but the full significance of those engagements was not yet fully understood. The Republicans gained 9 seats in the Senate (4 of them in western states: Nebraska, Oklahoma, South Dakota, and Wyoming) and 47 in the House, though the Democrats retained control of both chambers.

During the next congressional session, a coalition of Republicans and conservative Southern Democrats dismantled many of the New Deal's signature agencies, such the WPA, Civilian Conservation Corps, and National Youth Administration, and radically defunded others, including the Farm Security Administration and Rural Electrification Administration. Since the war was bringing full employment to the nation, and high rainfall had returned to the Plains, boosting agricultural productivity, the New Deal agency closures were more symbolic than economically significant. The dissolved and defunded agencies had served their purpose, while

[35] White, *"It's Your Misfortune,"* 502; and William E. Davis, "History of Higher Education in the Southwest: Arizona, Colorado, Nevada, New Mexico, and Utah," in *Higher Education in the American West: Regional History and State Contexts*, ed. Lester Goodchild et al. (New York: Palgrave Macmillan, 2014), 137–177, esp. 141 and 158.

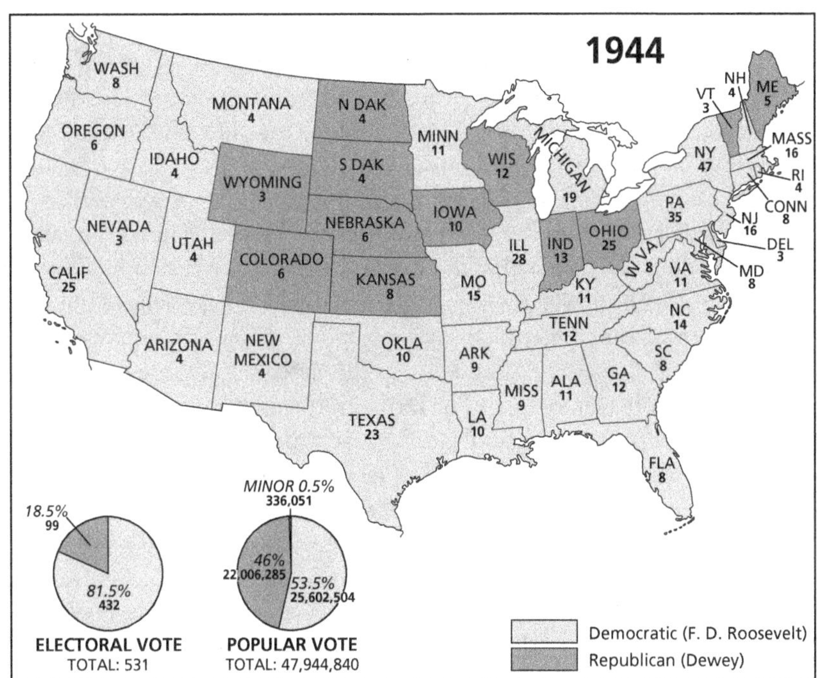

MAP 7.3 Electoral map, 1944.

other signature initiatives, such as Social Security and banking reform, continued to provide safeguards for the public and the economy.[36]

Military successes in North Africa and Sicily in 1943 and on the Italian mainland in 1944, the successful D-Day invasion of Normandy in June 1944, and the turning of the tide in the Pacific theater meant that by the time of the presidential election in fall 1944, the expectations of an Allied victory were high. The backdrop of military success overseas and full employment at home decided the 1944 presidential election. FDR won a fourth term in office with a comfortable 3.6 million vote victory, an impressive 81.5 percent of the Electoral College vote, and a popular vote margin of 53.5 percent to Republican Thomas Dewey's 46 percent. In addition to the five western states FDR had failed to hold in 1940, he also lost Wyoming and suffered larger losses in the Midwest than in 1940 (Map 7.3).

The Democratic Party prevailed across most of the western region, albeit a little less convincingly than in FDR's previous victories. Yet, it

[36] Kennedy, *Freedom from Fear*, 783.

is difficult to draw any definitive region-specific lessons from the 1944 election. The president and his party generally secured victory in those western states, experiencing the heaviest federal investment in the defense industry and the heaviest in-migration, and for the most part lost in those states that saw only limited economic and demographic growth or actual population loss. However, Colorado, which grew demographically at a slightly higher rate than the nation and received more than its fair share of defense dollars, remained in the Republican camp, which it had joined in the 1940 election. Meanwhile, Oklahoma, which experienced population loss, and Montana, which saw only a tiny population increase and lost significant numbers of residents to the defense industries in Seattle, continued to vote Democratic. The Democratic hold on the West was sustained for one more presidential election cycle after FDR's four successive victories in the region, but the cracks in the party's regional dominance were starting to appear by 1944 as political tides shifted.

When Americans went to the polls in the 1946 midterm elections, the nation was experiencing rising inflation and labor unrest. Workers across the country had been dedicated to the war effort and engaged in only minimal strike actions. With the war won, labor sought improved contracts and conditions, but large segments of the public disapproved. The Harry S. Truman administration faced the difficult task of reconverting the wartime economy to peacetime production without causing a recession. In retrospect, reconversion played out quite successfully, though at the time the process appeared disorganized and the general perception was that taxes were too high, the economy was overregulated, labor strife was too pervasive, and the Republicans would do a better job of managing the economy.

The Democrats had controlled the White House and both houses of Congress since 1932, but 1946 witnessed a broad Republican realignment. The GOP gained 55 seats in the House and 12 more in the Senate, securing control of both houses (Senate, 51–45; House, 246–188) for the first time since 1928. The massive Democratic majorities from the 1936 election had been overturned. While the Democrats managed to hold on to their seats in the South, outside of that region, 40 percent of party incumbents lost their congressional races. California accounted for seven of the new House seats for the Republicans, and Washington for three more. Republican candidates also defeated incumbent Democratic senators in Washington, Idaho, Montana, Nevada, and Utah; therefore, the Far West accounted for nearly half the GOP's gains in that chamber. Despite all the New Deal era and wartime building of the West – all of it done with the Democrats in control of the legislative process at the national level – the political carry-over was transitory indeed. The built environment of the West was transformed, but its political culture was not. After the 1946 elections, the Republicans also controlled most state governorships around the country. The Republican-dominated Congress pushed back against Harry Truman's Fair Deal – an expansion of FDR's New Deal programs – most significantly with the passage (over Truman's veto) of the Taft–Hartley Act, which limited the rights of workers to organize and bargain collectively.

In the 1948 election, Truman, who had survived the efforts of his party to drop him as the nominee, campaigned against what he called the "do nothing 80th Congress," while at the same time lambasting the Republicans for their assault on labor and ordinary Americans and their support for big business and the wealthy. The campaign included a two-week whistle-stop western train tour in June that took the president from Chicago to the Pacific Northwest, down the coast to Los Angeles, and across the Southwest to Kansas City. Painting the Republicans as the party of the rich and the enemy of the middle class proved a winning strategy, and one that most successful Democratic presidential candidates have employed ever since. Despite the improving economy after a recession in 1946 and 1947, Truman's victory was largely unexpected. He secured 49.5 percent of the popular vote to his Republican opponent Dewey's 45 percent, even though two third parties, the Progressives and the Dixiecrats (Southern States Rights Party), pulled votes away from the Democratic ticket. Truman won 10 of the 11 western states beyond the Great Plains (losing only Oregon), along with the Plains states of Texas and Oklahoma, though he lost the Dakotas, Nebraska, and Kansas. In all, the incumbent secured 98 Electoral College votes in the West, while Dewey won just 28 (Map 7.4). In addition, the Democrats regained control of the House, picking up 75 new seats (just 9 of them in the West) and gaining 9 seats in the Senate (3 of them in the West: Idaho, Oklahoma, and Wyoming). The quick recovery of the Democrats in the West suggests that for all that party's long-term investment in western (and national) infrastructure, short-term developments – such as public anger over the Taft–Hartley Act – and well-orchestrated and energetic campaigns, like Truman's, often decide elections.

The 1950 midterm elections occurred in the shadow of the Korean War that had begun in June and increasing allegations of Communism within the State Department. With Truman's popularity again subsiding, the Democrats lost 28 House seats to the Republicans (6 of them in the

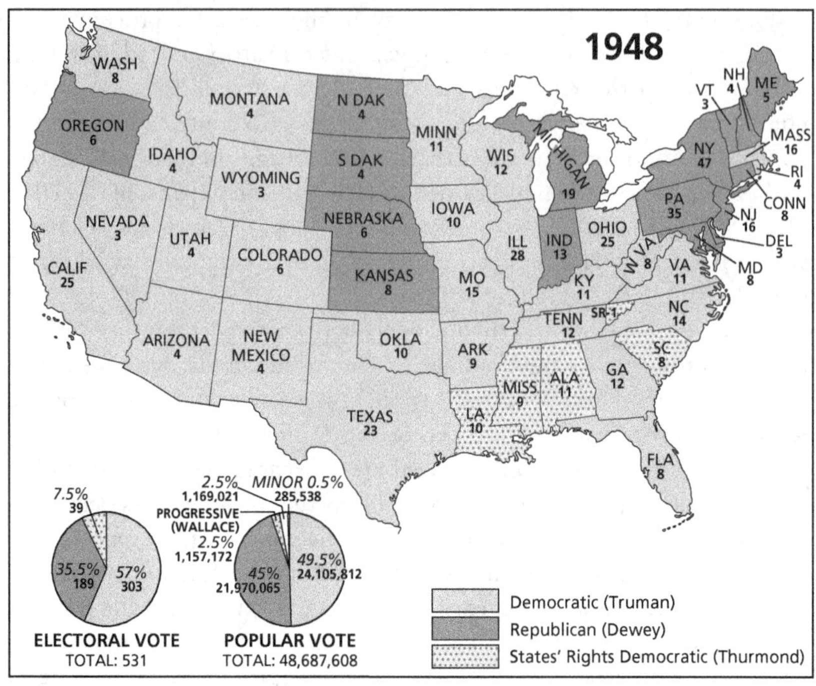

MAP 7.4 Electoral map, 1948.

West) and 5 Senate seats (3 of them in the West: California, Idaho, and Utah). The next Republican candidate, Kansas native Dwight Eisenhower (whom the Democrat Party had tried to enlist as its candidate), swept the whole of the West in 1952 and 1956. Largely in the Democratic camp during the New Deal years, the West had transitioned toward the Republican Party during the war and early Cold War years and by the 1950s had become a Republican regional stronghold. The West would remain a Republican stronghold in presidential elections through 1988, except for Lyndon Johnson's near-sweep of the region in 1964, when his opponent Barry Goldwater won only his home state of Arizona.

The West was a bellwether of national political trends in the 1940s and stood at the leading edge of economic and demographic growth, including urbanization and suburbanization. The region's defense industry, built on the infrastructural foundations of New Deal public works projects, proved vital to the war effort and drew workers and their families from across the country, including the western Plains states. Most significantly, the West more than any other American region had developed into a landscape of war, tightly regulated by the federal government and characterized by military bases, airfields, conventional weapons ranges, atomic testing, and federal support for university-based research initiatives. By mid-century the pattern was evident – the West had emerged as the nation's most martial region (and continued to expand in the second half of the century), as well as its most metropolitan and culturally diverse one. Those characteristics were most evident in the western places that experienced the most sweeping demographic and economic change – the Pacific Coast, the Desert Southwest, and Texas. But it was those regions that were also now heavily dependent on continuing high levels of federal expenditure in the defense sector. Western congressional representatives had lobbied hard to secure the federal contracts that built the martial infrastructure of the West, but now the continued economic well-being of their constituencies depended upon the maintenance of federal funding streams for the defense sector. Moreover, those regions most transformed by the war also experienced the worst of the racial tensions that accompanied the western boom of the 1940s.

8

The Good War?

> When we talk of freedom of opportunity for all nations, the mocking paradoxes in our own society become so clear that they can no longer be ignored. The nation now possesses, however, the will and the physical unity and the power to achieve what it should have achieved fifty years ago – total democracy in the United States.
>
> – Carey McWilliams, *Brothers under the Skin* (1943)

War and Social Dislocation

By early May 1945, the German forces in Europe capitulated, and by mid-August, the Japanese surrendered and the war in the Pacific was won. Alfred Eisenstaedt's iconic photograph of a US Navy man kissing a white uniformed woman during the Victory over Japan Day (VJ Day) parade in New York's Times Square on August 14, 1945, encapsulates American public memory of the Second World War as the "Good War." The economy boomed both in the industrial and agrarian sectors. The average weekly wage grew from $25.20 to $45.39 between 1940 and 1945, an increase of 72 percent. Parity with other sectors of the economy was no longer a concern for farmers as war-torn Europe's demands for American food expanded. In addition to the economic good fortune, popular memory suggests that World War II fostered greater unity on the home front and a more developed sense of national purpose than any previous American war. The notion of the Good War is in many ways convincing; yet, like the identities of the subjects in Eisenstaedt's photograph, it is also contested, and events in the American West highlight its complications. The Far West was the geographic heart of the arsenal of democracy, and its history illustrates both the broad possibilities and the restricted horizons of America's democratic promise during the war.[1]

The economy of war in the West was built at such speed that social divisions, disruptions, and dislocations were virtually inevitable. As western cities became boomtowns because of the defense industry, school systems and other municipal services were overwhelmed. As larger numbers of women moved into the workforce and the military, where 400,000 served during World War II, and as millions of men entered the armed services, levels of parental supervision were compromised. The increased freedom that many young people experienced often had adverse effects: juvenile delinquency was on the rise, along with the rate of sexually transmitted diseases. Some contemporary observers blamed the rise in juvenile delinquency on the movement of women from "the kitchen" into the "defense plants." But the centrality of fathers to stable family structures was considered equally important. Montana senator Burton Wheeler went so far as to introduce a bill exempting fathers from the draft, and in arguing for the measure, he cited Los Angeles as a prime example of social dysfunction. He quoted from a report by FBI director J. Edgar Hoover warning of a "complete breaking down of morale and morals of the boys and girls in this country" in the absence of married men in the home. Still, Wheeler's measure would have disqualified 6 million men from the service rolls, and that was not acceptable to the military. Meanwhile, police forces were strained as experienced officers entered military service, and military police had to step in to help combat crime. These developments were by no means unique to the West, but they were more pronounced in the region since the pace of migration and urban growth was so accelerated.[2]

1 Eleven different men later claimed to be the sailor in Eisenstaedt's photograph, and three women claimed to be the nurse. For wages, see Michael C. C. Adams, "The 'Good War' Myth and the Cult of Nostalgia," *Midwest Quarterly* 40 (Autumn 1998): 59–74, quotation on 59. For the Good War theme, see Charles C. Alexander, "The United States: The Good War?," in *Allies at War: The Soviet, American, and British Experience, 1939–1945*, ed. David Reynolds, Warren F. Kimball, and A. O. Chubarian (New York: St. Martin's Press, 1994), 285–305, esp. 296–297 and 305; Roger W. Lotchin, *The Bad City in the Good War: San Francisco, Los Angeles, Oakland, and San Diego* (Bloomington: Indiana University Press, 2003); and Studs Terkel, *"The Good War": An Oral History of World War II* (New York: Pantheon Books, 1984).

2 Robert L. Griswold, *Fatherhood in America: A History* (New York: Basic Books, 1993), 167–169; Richard Lingeman, *Don't You Know There's a War Going On? The American Home Front, 1941–1945* (1970; repr., New York: Nation Books, 2003), 87–90; Katherine F. Lenroot, testimony in Wartime Health and Recreation, Hearings before a subcommittee of the Committee on Education and Labor, US Senate, part I, Washington,

Meeting the housing needs of new migrants was a primary concern. While city planners and officials generally welcomed the building of homes to expand the property tax base, local communities across the West and the nation resisted the construction of permanent high occupancy housing units (apartment buildings) to accommodate newly arrived war industry workers. Concerned by the potential for reduced property values, homeowners lobbied for temporary units, and as a result many war workers resided in substandard conditions, even as they were fortunate to move out of their cars and the tents and makeshift shanties that sprung up in and around the cities near the wartime production centers. In Richmond, California, some Kaiser shipyard workers endured living conditions as poor as the Hoovervilles of the 1930s before government stepped in to address their housing needs. The pattern played out in cities across the Far West that experienced heavy migration of new workers and their families. There was nothing particularly distinctive about the failure of western municipalities to meet the needs of new residents, or in the commitment to protect property values; but since urban growth rates were highest in the West, those patterns were more prevalent. The same held true regarding rates of juvenile delinquency. The urban Far West attracted migrants on a greater scale than other parts of the country and thus experienced more social disruption.[3]

Vanport City, Oregon, dubbed Kaiserville, was hastily constructed by the federal government in the late summer and fall of 1942 to house workers in Kaiser's Portland-area shipbuilding operations, where a 24-hour production schedule was maintained. Vanport City's nearly 10,000 apartments and small houses – more than 600 wooden buildings in total – soon became home to 42,000 residents, and in 1943 the massive government housing project (reportedly the world's biggest at the time) was Oregon's second-largest city. With African Americans comprising roughly 40 percent of Vanport City's population, it was also the largest minority concentration in the state. The federal government oversaw everything in Vanport, including apartments, stores, day care centers, and transportation. Some viewed the instant federal city as the embodiment of the New Deal welfare state run amok. Others saw Vanport's existence as vital to

1994, 100–115, cited in Richard Polenberg, ed., *America at War: The Home Front, 1941–1945* (Englewood Cliffs, NJ: Prentice Hall, 1968), 143–148; and Arthur Verge, "World War II," in William Deverell and Greg Hise, *A Companion to Los Angeles* (Malden, MA: Blackwell, 2010), 311–321, esp. 319.

[3] Lotchin, *The Bad City in the Good War*, 188; and Lingeman, *Don't You Know There's a War Going On?*, 81.

the maintenance of racial boundaries and property values in Portland and were happy to see the ramshackle encampments of workers who had employment but no proper accommodations relocated away from the municipal limits.[4]

Vanport's very existence was a testament to the demographic and social strains the war brought to western cities. Those pressures were illuminated in the most tragic fashion just a few years later, on May 30, 1948, when Vanport's population, then just half its wartime peak production size (despite an influx of GI Bill veterans to the brand-new Vanport Extension Center college campus), was not given sufficient warning as the waters of the Columbia River rose. A makeshift dike failed, the town was completely flooded, and 15 people drowned. The federal government failed to handle the emergency appropriately, accepted no responsibility for the disaster, and provided no compensation to the former residents, who were now once more part of the problem of overcrowding in Portland. Race was a factor in Vanport's initial creation and almost certainly played a part, too, in the federal government's slow response to the disaster.[5]

Race Relations on the Western Home Front

The influx of African Americans to western cities from 1940 to 1970 was part of a Second Great Migration away from the white-dominated and economically underdeveloped South. During the 1940s, the West's African American population grew by 443,000, or 33 percent, though the rates of demographic increase on the West Coast were considerably higher. California proved the most popular destination, with 338,000 new African American residents in the state by decade's end, an increase of 272 percent. Seattle's African American population expanded fourfold, from less than 4,000 to close to 16,000 in the 1940s; San Francisco saw

4 Carl Abbott, *How Cities Won the West: Four Centuries of Urban Change in Western North America* (Albuquerque: University of New Mexico Press, 2008), 174–175; Heather Fryer, *Perimeters of Democracy: Inverse Utopias and the Wartime Social Landscape in the American West* (Lincoln: University of Nebraska Press, 2010), 1–2, 68–71; Gordon B. Dodds, *The College That Would Not Die: The First Fifty Years of Portland State University, 1946–1996* (Portland: Oregon Historical Society Press and Portland State University, 2000), 2–4; and Jewel Lansing, *Portland: People, Politics, and Power, 1851–2001* (Corvallis: Oregon State University Press, 2003), 341.

5 Fryer, *Perimeters of Democracy*, 225–232; and Dodds, *The College That Would Not Die*, 18–22.

an enormous 800 percent jump, from less than 5,000 to well over 43,000 in the same period.[6]

Racial discrimination had initially limited the numbers of African Americans employed in the West Coast's defense plants; white migrants (and residents) secured the vast majority of jobs from 1940 to 1943. But during 1942, as more workers entered the military, as production targets increased to meet the Allies' needs, and as the walls of job discrimination were breached, the economic opportunities for African Americans in Los Angeles expanded rapidly. In June 1941, there were exactly four African American production workers in the entire Southern California aircraft industry. By the summer of 1943, 10,000 to 12,000 African Americans were arriving in the city each month, comprising at that point around 50 percent of all new arrivals, and the production line jobs opened for them. LA's African American population was approximately 54,000 in 1940; by April 1944, it had more than doubled, reaching nearly 119,000; and by 1950, the number had risen to 171,000. The African American migration to LA and other Pacific Coast cities, while primarily a southern phenomenon, also included an exodus from the Southern Plains states of Texas and Oklahoma. The Sooner State's African American population declined by over 23,000, or 14 percent, during the 1940s.[7]

The enhanced employment opportunities for African Americans in the war industry resulted from not only economic necessity but also the efforts of leaders such as A. Philip Randolph. His threatened mass march on Washington in the summer of 1941 to protest racial discrimination in hiring prompted FDR to issue Executive Order 8802, which pressured defense companies to end the practice. The following spring, FDR used Executive Order 9346 to create the Fair Employment Practices

[6] Quintard Taylor, *In Search of the Racial Frontier; African Americans in the American West, 1528–1990* (New York: W. W. Norton, 1998), 251–277, esp. 251–254.

[7] Flamming, *African Americans in the West*, 165; Abbott, *How Cities Won the West*, 175; Quintard Taylor, *The Forging of a Black Community: Seattle's Central District, from 1870 through the Civil Rights Era* (Seattle: University of Washington Press, 1994); and *In Search of the Racial Frontier*, 251–277; Albert S. Broussard, *Black San Francisco: The Struggle for Racial Equality in the West, 1900–1954* (Lawrence: University Press of Kansas, 1993), 133. See also Josh Sides, *L.A. City Limits: African American Los Angeles from the Great Depression to the Present* (Berkeley: University of California Press, 2002); Verge, "The Impact of the Second World War on Los Angeles," *Pacific Historical Review* 63 (August 1994): 289–314, African American employment and migration figures on 301 and 303; and Nugent, *Into the West: The Story of Its People* (New York: Knopf, 1999), 269.

Commission (FEPC) to monitor hiring at defense plants. In addition, the "Double V" campaign, through which African American organizations emphasized their dedication to defeating fascism overseas and Jim Crow at home, also helped to shift public attitudes. Still, it took hard work by the NAACP and by local organizations in the centers of war production, such as the Negro Victory Committee in LA, to persuade the War Manpower Commission to actively enforce Executive Order 8802. For example, a coordinated campaign by African Americans against the Los Angeles Railway (LARY) in 1943 and 1944 resulted in the hiring of African Americans as drivers and conductors.[8]

Increasing job opportunities constituted the good news for African Americans migrating to the West Coast, often in segregated railroad cars. However, they experienced discrimination from white workers and supervisors, severe housing shortages and thoroughly substandard accommodations upon arrival. LA's well-established racial covenants restricted the African American population to the already crowded Central Avenue, West Jefferson, and Watts neighborhoods, so new arrivals moved into "Little Tokyo," the area vacated by the interned Japanese-origin population.[9] In Richmond, Oakland, Seattle and other wartime production centers that attracted large numbers of African American migrants, the story paralleled LA's. There were expanding employment opportunities, but also significant wage discrepancies; African American workers in Kaiser's plants and other facilities earned lower wages than their white counterparts, but considerably higher wages than they had in the South. White-dominated labor unions such as the Boilermakers maintained discriminatory policies. And housing shortages prevailed, though they were partially alleviated by government housing projects. In Seattle, by 1945 over 10,000 African Americans crowded into a neighborhood that had accommodated 3,700 in 1940. The overcrowded conditions in San Francisco's Fillmore district and in what had formerly been Japantown were similarly acute.[10]

[8] Flamming, *African Americans in the West*, 171–175; Verge, "The Impact of the Second World War on Los Angeles," 301; Kevin M. Kruse and Stephen Tuck, eds., *Fog of War: The Second World War and the Civil Rights Movement* (New York: Oxford University Press, 2012), 88; and Sides, *L.A. City Limits*, 62.

[9] Gretchen Lemke-Santangelo, "Four Migrant Stories: African American Women in Wartime California," in *The Human Tradition in California*, ed. Clark Davis and David Igler (Wilmington, DE: Scholarly Resources, 2002), 147–160, esp. 151; and Verge, "The Impact of the Second World War on Los Angeles," 304-305.

[10] Flamming, *African Americans in the West*, 165–171; William G. Robbins and Katherine Barber, *Nature's Northwest: The North Pacific Slope in the Twentieth Century* (Tucson:

There was also an important gender dimension to the West Coast migration of African Americans from the South. Large numbers of young African American women were moving to San Francisco, LA, and other coastal cities. Female African American migrants outnumbered their male counterparts by almost two to one and filled vital roles in defense plants, as did white, Mexican-origin, and Native American women. Around 500–600 Chinese American women also worked in defense industry plants in the Bay Area. By 1943, women made up fully 40 percent of the workforce in California's aircraft plants and 46 percent in Seattle's Boeing plants. The numbers of women in shipbuilding production work were much lower, but their glass ceiling was shattered in April 1942 when Kaiser's Oregon Shipbuilding Company hired its first two woman welders. Desperate to keep women on the job in the face of the competing demands of home life for mothers, the federal government stepped into the childcare business. With the Lanham Act, Congress authorized nearly $52 million for childcare (with an additional $26 million in state matching funds) to support more than 3,000 facilities that served 600,000 children; most of those funds went to California.[11]

For all the advantages that the new martial landscape in the West offered to African Americans, the pervasive discrimination in the workplace and restricted access to decent housing provided sobering correctives. In the fall and winter of 1942–1943, the 8,000 strong members of the all-white Butte Miners' Union, in defiance of Executive Order 8802, engaged in a walk-out, refusing to work alongside 39 furloughed black soldiers who had been sent to Butte by the War Department to help mine copper, a vital wartime commodity. In the summer of 1943, a terrible race riot, perpetrated by white shipyard workers in the African American section of Beaumont, Texas, left three African Americans and one white resident dead, left 400 more people injured, and forced 2,500 African Americans to flee the city. Most never returned. Another riot in Oakland the following summer between white sailors and African

University of Arizona Press, 2011), 118; Taylor, *The Forging of a Black Community*, 169; and *In Search of the Racial Frontier*, 266–267.

[11] Sheila McManus, *Choices and Chances: A History of Women in the U.S. West* (Wheeling, IL: Harlan Davidson, 2011), 277–288; and Laura E. Woodworth-Ney, *Women in the American West* (Santa Barbara, CA: ABC-CLIO, 2008), 267; Andrew Rolle and Arthur Verge, *California: A History*, 7th ed. (Wheeling, IL: Harlan Davidson, 2008), 323; Robbins and Barber, *Nature's Northwest*, 119; Verge, "World War II," 316; and Nugent, *Into the West*, 269.

Americans resulted in one death. The painful irony that the United States was waging a war against Nazi racism with a segregated military which tolerated and even encouraged discrimination against African American servicemen resulted in additional violent episodes across the West.[12]

On July 17, 1944, at Port Chicago, north of San Francisco, 202 African American Navy men were among the 320 who died in a massive explosion while loading ammunition ships; nearly 400 more were injured, again mostly African Americans. When, a few weeks later, several hundred surviving African American naval personnel refused to load ammunition ships at a nearby facility until safety conditions were improved, they were pressured into resuming their work. Fifty men who were considered the ringleaders of the resistance were prosecuted for mutiny and sentenced to 15 years' detention and dishonorably discharged. The men were quietly released and reinstated in 1946, largely because of the NAACP's lobbying efforts. The Port Chicago explosion was a horrific event, and racism played a central part in it. At Fort Lawton, Seattle, in August 1944, African American soldiers' frustration precipitated a riot. Angered by unfair work assignments and by their exclusion from the city's bars while Italian prisoners of war were allowed supervised visits to those same establishments, they murdered an Italian POW. Twenty-three African Americans were found guilty and imprisoned.

Terrible as the tragedies at Port Chicago and Fort Lawton were, conditions were worse for African Americans on the military bases and in the communities of the South than they were in the West. Moreover, conditions for the civilian population were clearly superior, both economically and socially, in the West. Nonetheless, the gains that African Americans secured in the region during the war and early postwar years were the result of their relentless lobbying for civil rights and economic opportunity. Black migration to the West had strengthened civil rights organizations such as the NAACP and by mid-century several western states, including California, New Mexico, Oregon, and Washington, had passed fair employment practices statues. Moreover, the struggle against restricted housing covenants also gained momentum in the immediate postwar years, and nowhere more so than in Los Angeles. Between 1945 and 1948, black residents of LA filed more lawsuits against restricted

[12] Matthew L. Basso, *Meet Joe Copper: Masculinity and Race on Montana's Home World War II Front* (Chicago: University of Chicago Press, 2013), 160–161.

covenants than the rest of the nation combined, with NAACP attorney Loren Miller leading the effort.[13]

Conditions for Mexican-origin people across the West also belied the Good War stereotype. The repatriation movements of the late 1920s and 1930s, and the criminalization of unsanctioned border crossings after 1929, had exemplified the degree to which Mexicans and Mexican Americans were deprived of civil and human rights in the West. The Good War ethos was tragically absent in Los Angeles for five days in early June 1943 when 200 roving, bat-wielding sailors and other military personnel, incensed by false reports that a white woman had been assaulted by zoot suiters, were ferried around in convoys by city taxi drivers, and attacked Mexican youth, beating them, stripping them of their distinctive clothing, and leaving them lying in the streets, where LAPD officers then arrested the victims for disturbing the peace (no servicemen were convicted). The LAPD was thoroughly ill disposed toward Mexican youth and had in fact been arguing for years that Mexican-origin people were inherently prone to criminality. The LAPD had launched a major crackdown against "Mexican" youth in August 1942, which resulted in the wrongful conviction of a dozen innocent young men on trumped up murder charges in the infamous Sleepy Lagoon case, and in the mass arrest of more than 600 young Mexican American men in a single night.[14]

The so-called Zoot Suit Riots, highlighted the deep racial tensions in LA, and the LAPD along with the *LA Times* and other area newspapers in the region, were in no small part responsible for fueling the flames of racial discord through damning depictions of Mexican youth culture and

[13] Taylor, *The Forging of a Black Community*, 167; and *In Search of the Racial Frontier*, 265–266, and 271; Flamming, *African Americans in the American West*, 181–184; and *In Search of the Racial Frontier*, 252 and 270; Kimberly L. Phillips, *War! What Is It Good For? Black Freedom Struggles and the U.S. Military from World War II to Iraq* (Chapel Hill: University of North Carolina Press, 2012), 32 and 48; Kevin Starr, *Embattled Dreams: California in War and Peace, 1940–1950* (New York: Oxford University Press, 2002), 118–121; and Verge, "World War II," 319.

[14] Eric Avila, "Social Flashpoints," in Deverell and Hise, *A Companion to Los Angeles*, 95–109, esp. 101–102; Louis Alvarez, *The Power of the Zoot: Race Culture and Resistance during World War II* (Berkeley: University of California Press, 2008); Kevin Leonard, *The Battle for Los Angeles: Racial Ideology and World War II* (Albuquerque: University of New Mexico Press, 2006), 147–197; and "Making Multiculturalism: Immigration, Race, and the Twentieth Century," in Deverell and Hise, *A Companion to Los Angeles*, 339–257, esp. 346–348; Sânchez, *Becoming Mexican American: Ethnicity, Culture, and Identity in Chicano Los Angeles, 1900–1945* (New York: Oxford University Press, 1993), 265–269; Starr, *Embattled Dreams*, 101–111.

false reports of beatings of sailors by zoot suiters. The story captivated readers across the nation. On June 11, the *Washington Daily News*, a small North Carolina newspaper, carried the headline "Zoot Suiters Run for Cover, but Their 'Cholitas' Carry On." The article proceeded to describe the role of "Dark-eyed young Mexican women packing razors in the tops of their black mesh stockings," indiscriminately attacking civilian women, and vowing to fight servicemen and the police "until one side or the other is wiped out."[15]

The news media's failure to report fairly and accurately on the attacks by white servicemen on Mexican youth, and the willful failure of the LAPD to protect victims rather than encourage perpetrators, should come as no surprise given the long history of racial stereotyping of Mexican-origin people in California and the Southwest. The great wonder was that no one died during the five days of violence. The federal government, responding to a request from the Mexican consulate, finally mobilized the military to stop the violence, barring Navy men from downtown LA. There were several positive developments in the wake of the violence: Governor Earl Warren launched an investigation into the riots, and First Lady Eleanor Roosevelt emphasized the role that racial discrimination had played in initiating the violence. The events of early June 1943 also prompted minority churches and organizations to make various efforts to cooperate across racial lines to counter racial prejudice.[16]

The Zoot Suit Riots were a defining moment for Mexican-origin people in Los Angeles and across California and the Southwest during the war, but they were by no means the only important development. Just as the lamentable repatriation policy needs to be considered along with the struggle of Mexican-origin people to organize and bargain collectively in pursuit of their economic interest in the 1930s, the awful anti-Mexican rioting had its positive counterpart in the struggles of Mexican American communities to secure civil rights during and after the war. Mexican American rights organizations such as the League of United Latin American Citizens (LULAC), offering a sort of parallel to the African American Double V campaign, forcefully argued that the United States's Good Neighbor Policy toward Mexico and other Latin American countries could only be successful if the government addressed the matter of

15 William C. Payette, "Zoot Suiters Run for Cover, but Their 'Cholitas' Carry On," *Washington Daily News*, June 11, 1943.

16 Albert Camarillo, *Chicanos in California: A History of Mexican Americans in California* (San Francisco: Boyd and Fraser, 1984), 65–68; Leonard, "Making Multiculturalism," 348.

discrimination at home. In addition, the Mexican American Movement (MAM), formed in 1934, largely by high school students, was, by the early 1940s, lobbying hard to encourage Mexican and Mexican American youth to seek social advancement through education and to push back against segregated schools, swimming pools, and other public facilities prominent across California and much of the Southwest.[17]

MAM's efforts provided a foundation for Mexican American GI's to build on when they returned from their service. They were the most decorated ethnic group during the war and experienced a disproportionate number of casualties on the battlefield. They came home eager to ensure that the four freedoms their nation had purportedly fought for were extended to their own communities. In 1948, Dr. Hector P. Garcia founded the American GI Forum (AGIF) to address the matter of segregation as it impacted Mexican American veterans. AGIF's first case involved the burial of a Mexican American veteran Felix Longoria who had died in service in the Philippines, but had been denied burial in a white-owned Texas funeral home. Dr. Garcia lobbied Senator Lyndon B. Johnson, who secured burial of Longoria's remains in Arlington National Cemetery. In addition, Mexican American communities, with the help of LULAC, won landmark school desegregation cases in *Mendez v. Westminster Independent School District* (Orange County, California) in 1947, and *Delgado v. Bastrop Independent School District* (near Austin, Texas) in 1948.[18]

While both cases preceded the better-known 1954 *Brown v. Board of Education* case, they were not focused on the segregationist precedent of *Plessy v. Fergusson* (1896), which ruled that separate but equal conditions were appropriate for different races under the Fourteenth Amendment. Instead, the Mendez and Delgado cases revolved around the absence of specific legislation in California and Texas, respectively, providing for separation within a race, and Mexican American children were classified as Caucasian (white). California's Ninth Circuit Court had declared in its Mendez case ruling: "Nowhere in any California law is there a suggestion that any segregation can be made of children within

[17] For more on Mexican American efforts to combat job discrimination during the war, see Emilio Zamora, *Claiming Rights and Righting Wrongs: Mexican Workers and Job Politics during World War II* (College Station: Texas A&M University Press, 2009).

[18] Sánchez, *Becoming Mexican American*, 255–266; Camarillo, *Chicanos in California*, 69–74; and Carlos K. Blanton, *The Strange Career of Bilingual Education in Texas* (College Station: Texas A&M University Press, 2004), 112–114.

one of the great races." Thus, California and Texas had both violated the Fourteenth Amendment equal protection rights of Mexican Americans. Notably though, Governor Earl Warren, in the wake of the Mendez decision, signed into law the repeal of those California statutes that did provide for segregated facilities in that state, and was serving as the chief justice of the Supreme Court when it handed down the *Brown* decision. Meanwhile, the Delgado decision initiated a successful decade-long struggle in Texas, led by LULAC and the American GI Forum of Texas, to end segregation in the state's public schools.[19]

Civil rights reform did not comprise the only rising tide for Mexican-origin people in the 1940s. The demography and economy of war had provided enhanced opportunities for skilled and semiskilled labor for Mexican-origin women and men in the defense industry and, for women especially, in a wide range of clerical positions that had been largely closed to them previously. Indeed, wartime labor needs were so great that the repatriation policies of the 1930s were literally reversed a decade later as the United States worked with the Mexican government to develop the bracero labor program to bring temporary workers into the country to perform vital tasks. In addition to providing farm and railroad labor, some braceros worked in industry. The bracero program was formalized in August 1942, and the war years comprised its first phase. US records show that around 4,000 Mexican workers entered the United States in 1942, during the first few months of the program. Then, between 1943 and 1945, an average of nearly 55,000 per year arrived (official Mexican records show around 100,000 a year for those three years). The bracero program was scaled back from 1946 to 1948, but expanded again at the end of the decade when US records show 107,000 braceros arriving in 1949. The numbers grew massively during the 1950s. By the second half of that decade, well over 400,000 braceros were coming to the United States each year. While the wartime braceros worked mainly in California, the program expanded both demographically and geographically in the postwar years. By 1953, 87 percent of the cotton pickers and 74 percent of the cowboys in Texas were bracero laborers. By 1963, 39 percent of braceros were working in Texas and 25 percent in California. The program, which remained in place until 1964, provided the United States with a vital labor supply during the war years and the subsequent

[19] Elliott Robert Barkan, *From All Points: America's Immigrant West, 1870s–1952* (Bloomington: Indiana University Press, 2007), 422.

two decades of postwar economic growth; around 4.5 million bracero contracts were issued over the whole period.[20]

The Mexican government barred Texas from the original bracero agreement, because of that state's long and violent history of discrimination against Mexicans. The ban was lifted in 1947 after the Lone Star State's Good Neighbor Commission worked hard to get back in Mexico's good graces, in part by ensuring some protections for bracero laborers. During the years of the Texas bracero ban, Texas growers successfully lobbied the US government for what essentially amounted to an "open border" for Mexican farm laborers to enter the state for a period of one year. In response, the Mexican government pressured the United States to limit this new alternative to the official bracero program, since it offered no protections to workers against discrimination. The two governments tangled over the matter of contract labor and illegal immigration, with Texas agribusiness pushing the Immigration and Naturalization Service (INS) to turn a blind eye during the war years to the entry of "wetback" or undocumented workers.[21] The history of Mexican immigration and migration to the United States during the 1940s, documented and undocumented, contracted and uncontracted, warrants careful consideration in the present when facile arguments about "illegal aliens" fail to consider the complicated and at times even convoluted story of governments, corporations, and, most importantly, millions of human beings negotiating the border as both "transnational subjects" and largely "unprotected subjects," working 10- to 14-hour days for a dollar an hour.[22]

For Native Americans, the war years were marked by minimal demographic growth, from around 334,000 to 343,500, together with significant economic opportunity and heavy migration to the urban centers of war production. The Civilian Conservation Corps Indian Division provided vocational training that prepared participants to secure skilled jobs

[20] Manuel García y Griego, "The Importation of Contract Laborers to the United States, 1942–1964," in Between Two Worlds: Mexican Immigrants in the United States, ed. David G. Gutiérrez (Wilmington, DE: Scholarly Resources, 1996), 45–85, figures from 49–50; Camarillo, *Chicanos in California*, 75–76; and Nugent, *Into the West*, 304.

[21] Griego, "The Importation of Contract Laborers," Texas policy, 52–55.

[22] Deborah Cohen, *Braceros: Migrant Citizens and Transnational Subjects in the Postwar United States and Mexico* (Chapel Hill: University of North Carolina Press, 2011); and Lori A. Flores, *Grounds for Dreaming: Mexican Americans, Mexican Immigrants, and the California Farmworker Movement* (New Haven, CT: Yale University Press, 2016), 5 and 49. The wage figures provided are for braceros in California fields in the 1940s.

in the war industry. In addition, about 12,000 Native women worked in the war industry. By the end of the war about 7 percent of the West's Native people lived in urban areas, and by the end of the decade that number had doubled. The 1940s marked the start of a long period of Native migration away from reservations; by 1943, 46,000 had moved, many of them for the first time. In addition to work in the centers of wartime industrial production, mining, farming, and ranching operations expanded and military installations required civilian labor. Navajos, for example, played a primary role in the construction of ordnance depots at Fort Wingate, New Mexico, and Bellemont, Arizona, beginning in 1941, and some stayed on as workers after the completion of the sites. About a quarter of those who left reservations seeking employment were women. Moreover, as men left to take up jobs and military service, opportunities for Native women in tribal government and the tribal economy expanded.[23]

Eligible for selective service in the wake of the Indian Citizenship Act of 1924, around 25,000 Native people joined the military during the war, including 800 women. Unlike African Americans, Native Americans fought in racially integrated units, though some of those units, such as the Oklahoma-based Thunderbird Forty-Fifth Division, were heavily Native American in composition. More than 400 Navajo code talkers eventually served as radio operators, generally working in pairs within combat units, utilizing their language to create a communications system indecipherable by the enemy. Their efforts proved vital to American military success. There were numerous other examples of distinguished Native service. For example, Ira Hayes, a Pima Indian, was among the small group of Marines who raised the US flag at Iwo Jima. The wartime experience, both in the armed services and in war-related industries, brought Native peoples into greater contact with other cultures.[24]

The advantages World War II brought to Indian peoples need to be weighed against some of the setbacks for the Indian Reorganization Act

[23] Donald L. Parman, *Indians in the American West in the Twentieth Century* (Bloomington: Indiana University Press, 1994), 107–111; and Paivi Hoikala, "The Hearts of Nations: American Indian Women in the Twentieth Century," in *Indians in American History: An Introduction*, 2nd ed., ed. Frederick E. Hoxie and Peter Iverson (Wheeling, IL: Harland Davidson, 1998), 253–276, esp. 260–261.

[24] Parman, *Indians in the American West*, 111–115; Donald L. Fixico, *Indian Resilience and Rebuilding: Indigenous Nations in the Modern American West* (Tucson: University of Arizona Press, 2013), 97; and Alvin M. Josephy Jr., "Modern America and the Indian," in Hoxie and Iverson, *Indians in American History*, 198–217, esp. 205.

with its emphasis on Indian self-determination and cultural revival. The American wartime emphasis on cultural unity was not accompanied by much sensitivity to the needs of racial minorities, and certainly featured little regard for Indian separateness and cultural autonomy. The Bureau of Indian Affairs (BIA) suffered a major budget cut during the war. By the end of the war, John Collier, the chief architect of the Indian New Deal, and the BIA commissioner, resigned out of frustration with the pushback against Indian rights and self-governance and accompanying demands, often from those seeking land and minerals, to break up reservations and thereby force Indians to assimilate. Collier's critics, many of them western congressional representatives, argued that his BIA policies were keeping Indians dependent, preventing their assimilation, and wasting taxpayer money. Moreover, for all the economic gains that reservation Indians made during the war years from livestock and timber sales and land leases, they remained thoroughly impoverished. The BIA estimated in 1945 that a third of reservation families were surviving on incomes of less than $500 a year, and most of the rest earned less than $1,000.[25]

The Indian Claims Commission Act of 1946 enabled Indian nations to seek financial redress for land cessions that had occurred prior to 1894, and by the end of the 1940s a few Indian nations, such as the Utes, had managed to secure significant settlements from Congress. But political conservatives considered the Claims Commission's work in resolving Indian grievances not as an admission of the failure of the United States to live up to its promises, but as a step toward government withdrawal from its responsibility for Indian welfare. By the second half of the 1940s, those conservative critics of the Indian New Deal were in the ascendancy and federal Indian policy began to transition away from self-determination and cultural renewal to "termination," urban relocation, and a renewed emphasis on assimilation. The BIA and the IRA were under constant attack from western politicians, including Montana's Senator Burton K. Wheeler, Oklahoma's Elmer Thomas, and South Dakota's Harlan J. Bushfield. The critics' primary motivation was opening Indian lands to development, but they framed their arguments ideologically. In the heated atmosphere of the emerging Cold War they charged that reservations were thoroughly antithetical to American values of individualism and self-reliance and even communistic in nature. In 1953 Congress

[25] Josephy, "Modern America and the Indian," 205; Parman, *Indians in the American West*, 116–117.

approved the termination policy, ending federal responsibilities to Indian nations.[26]

Meanwhile, the West's booming postwar economy, which included an expansion of roads, dams and hydroelectric infrastructure, as well as military facilities, provided a wide range of new nonreservation job opportunities for Native people. The late 1940s marked the beginning of an urban relocation program. The initiative started in the wake of terrible suffering among Navajos during the winter of 1947–1948. The military airlifted supplies to keep sheep and horses alive, and the government began to address the matter of overpopulation on the reservation by encouraging residents to move to jobs and housing, primarily in Denver, Salt Lake, and Los Angeles. Urban relocation provided opportunities for many Indians, but also a difficult transition to nonreservation life for some. The tragic fate of the war hero Ira Hayes encapsulated the downside of urban relocation. Hayes moved to Chicago in 1953 as part of the BIA's new program, then to Los Angeles, but failed to adjust to city life, began drinking heavily, and returned to Arizona, where he died from exposure and alcoholism in 1955. Urban relocation was marked by success stories, too, as Native people gained a wide range of academic and job skills, with a good number eventually returning to their reservations and enriching those communities with their newly acquired expertise. All in all, the 1940s brought a mixture of new economic opportunities, difficult social adjustments, and dwindling federal support, and some notable civil rights advances for Native Americans. For example, in 1947 a federal court forced Arizona and New Mexico to extend Social Security public assistance programs for seniors, children, and the blind, to Native people.[27]

For Japanese-origin people in the West, the story was considerably less mixed. When their experience is taken into consideration, the notion of the Good War is stretched to its very limits and beyond. In the immediate

[26] Parman, *Indians in the American West*, 123–129; and Donald L. Fixico, *Termination and Relocation: Federal Indian Policy, 1945–1960* (Albuquerque: University of New Mexico Press, 1986), 21–44.

[27] Fixico, *Termination and Relocation*, 3–4; Fixico, *Indian Resilience and Rebuilding*, 98; Parman, *Indians in the American West*, 125–126 and 128; and for an emphasis on the more positive impacts of Indian urban relocation, see Douglas K. Miller, "Urban Relocation and American Indian Initiative, 1940s–1960s," *Ethnohistory* 60 (Winter 2013): 51–76; and "Reservation Limits: American Indian Urbanization and Uplift in the Twentieth Century" (PhD diss., University of Oklahoma, 2014).

aftermath of the Japanese attack on Pearl Harbor, the fate of the West Coast's Japanese and Japanese Americans hung in the balance. Dehumanizing anti-Japanese sentiment and restrictive policies – most notably school segregation and the alien land laws – stretched back to the beginning of the century. Japanese submarine attacks on American merchant shipping along the Pacific Coast, from Washington to California in late December 1941 through the first months of 1942, including the shelling of an oil depot near Santa Barbara, contributed to the atmosphere of fear, anger, and distrust. But the rapid relocation and internment of 110,000 Nisei (first-generation Americans) and Issei (Japanese-born) that General John DeWitt called for, and President Roosevelt agreed to, was not the only option open to the government.[28]

Within days of the attack, writer John Steinbeck sent a memorandum to William Donovan, newly appointed Coordinator of Information, and Donovan sent the communication on to FDR. Steinbeck recommended a precise course of government action toward Japanese-origin people on the West Coast involving the administering of a loyalty test. Steinbeck contended that virtually all Issei (Japanese-born) and Nisei (American-born) were unquestionably loyal to the United States, and anyone who was not would refuse to take the test and could be interned or deported. The plan was far from perfect; the administering of a loyalty test exclusively to any racial group is thoroughly undemocratic. Nonetheless, Steinbeck became the first writer of note to oppose relocation and internment and his proposal, which had developed out of his close association with Japanese-origin people, surely would have proven far better for the nation and for its most vulnerable minority population than the lamentable course that was adopted.

At the start of the war, around three-quarters of the nation's approximately 127,000 Japanese-origin people resided in California and anti-Japanese groups including the Native Sons of California, Native Sons of the Golden West, and American Legion chapters lobbied hard for their removal. Earl Warren, the state's attorney general, who was running for the governorship, was influenced by the organized anti-Japanese sentiment. In early February 1942, incumbent governor Culbert Olson, talking to Japanese American editors, displayed the depths of West Coast racism when he proclaimed that he could determine the loyalty of German or Italian Americans simply by looking at them, but could not do so "with the inscrutable Orientals, and particularly the Japanese." Olson

[28] Starr, *Embattled Dreams*, 34–65.

encouraged the group to "Promise to give up your freedom, if necessary, to prove your loyalty." Meanwhile, General De Witt, after much indecision, began to define the Japanese as an "enemy race" and recommended to the War Department a swift "evacuation [from the Pacific Coast] of all persons of Japanese ancestry," a course favored by Secretary of War Henry L. Stimson. Soon thereafter, DeWitt declared, "A Jap is a Jap and that's all there is to it." Such publicly expressed sentiments helped shape opinion in California and across the country. According to a national survey in 1942, 93 percent of Americans advocated removal of the Issei, and 59 percent approved the removal of the Nisei. Yet, there were no documented instances of espionage or sabotage by people of Japanese ancestry in the United States.[29]

FDR signed Executive Order 9066 in February 1942, authorizing the removal of all Japanese and Japanese Americans from the West Coast. A Public Proclamation issued in early March 1942 urged those of Japanese ancestry to relocate voluntarily to the interior western states, and nearly 5,000 did so, with around 2,000 heading to Colorado (mostly to Denver) and around 1,500 to Utah. When some of the voluntary evacuees reached state borders, police turned them away. In April the War Relocation Authority (WRA) met with the governors of all mainland western states (excluding California and Texas) to encourage them to permit more Japanese Americans to relocate there, but only Colorado governor Ralph Carr offered to cooperate. Had the interior western states proved more receptive to voluntary relocation, the nation might still have avoided the debacle of internment. In the end, the political leadership and majority population of the West Coast demanded evacuation, the nation supported those demands, and the rest of the West acquiesced.[30]

Starting in late March, the process began of placing around 110,000 persons of Japanese ancestry in 16 "assembly centers," mostly racetracks, county fairgrounds, and migrant labor camps. The largest was the Santa Anita Race Track in Arcadia, California, where close to 19,000 people

[29] John Howard, *Concentration Camps on the Home Front: Japanese Americans in the House of Jim Crow* (Chicago: University of Chicago Press, 2008), 14; Rolle and Verge, *California*, 319; Governor Olsen quoted in Barkan, *From All Points*, 373–374, and General DeWitt, 374; and Walter L. Gary, Y. Okihiro, and Julie Sly, "The Press, Japanese Americans, and Concentration Camps," *Phylon* (1983): 66–83, reprinted in Walter L. Hixson, ed., *The American Experience in World War II*, vol. 10, *The American People at War: Minorities and Women in the Second World War* (New York: Taylor and Francis, 2003), 222–239, esp. 234.

[30] Barkan, *From All Points*, 376.

MAP 8.1 World War II Japanese American internment camps. From Walter Nugent, *Into the West: The Story of Its People* (New York: Alfred A. Knopf, 1999), 262. George Colbert, cartographer.

were forced to live in horse stables converted into barracks, sleeping on straw-filled mattresses. Evacuees residing on or near the Oregon Coast were held at the Portland Livestock Exposition Center. From the assembly centers, the 40,000 Issei and 70,000 Nisei children and grandchildren (Sansei) were removed by the War Relocation Authority (WRA) to eight internment camps on federally owned or managed sites in the interior West – Tule Lake and Manzanar in California, Poston and Gila River, both on Native American lands in Arizona, Heart Mountain in Wyoming, Minidoka in Idaho, Topaz in Utah, and Granada (Camp Amache) in

Colorado – and two additional camps in Arkansas, Rohwer and Jerome (Map 8.1). General DeWitt's announcement of the completion of the Japanese evacuation from the West Coast came on June 7, ironically the very same day that US naval forces achieved victory at the Battle of Midway (June 4–7), and any real possibility of a Japanese invasion of the West Coast or Hawaii ended. The Japanese in Hawaii were not interned, in part because anti-Japanese sentiment there was not pervasive and the population was viewed as loyal to the United States, but mostly because their numbers were much larger and their role in the economy more vital.[31]

The internment camps, with the exception of the two in Arkansas, were located in remote desert areas, subject to extremes of temperature. When she first arrived at Heart Mountain, camp resident Amy Uno Ishii recalled that "[we] looked up there at the camp that was to be our home... [and] most of the people who got off the train shed tears like you've never seen before... no trees, nothing green." Most of the camps were in windswept areas where the ground cover had been removed to make way for the barrack-style buildings. Monica Sone remembered, "We felt as if we were standing in a gigantic sand-mixing machine as the sixty-mile gale lifted the loose earth up into the sky, obliterating everything."[32] Families were crowded into buildings that were surrounded by barbed wire and overseen by armed guards. The government used inoffensive terms to describe the process, including "assembly centers," "relocation camps," and "evacuation," but the reality was that most of the nation's Japanese and Japanese Americans were "removed" from their homes and "confined" in far-away locations on the unsubstantiated suspicion that they might prove disloyal. It was the largest, worst, and most systematic violation of civil rights in twentieth-century America. Notably, the United States's internment story has a parallel in Canada where 22,000 Japanese Canadians were removed from the West Coast of British Columbia in

[31] General John DeWitt, Final Report, Japanese Evacuation from the West Coast, 1942 (Washington, DC: Government Printing Office, 1943), vii; Verge, "World War II," 313–314; Nugent, *Into the West*, 260–261; Robbins and Barber, *Nature's Northwest*, 120; and Barkan, *From All Points*, 376.

[32] Amy Uno Ishiio, in *Japanese American World War II Evacuation Oral History Project, Part I: Internees*, ed. Arthur A. Hansen (Westport, CT: Meckler, 1991), 80 and 67; and Monica Sone, *Nissei Daughter* (1953; repr., Seattle: University of Washington Press, 1979), 177; both quoted in Patricia Nelson Limerick, "Disorientation and Reorientation: The American Landscape Discovered from the West," in Limerick, *Something in the Soil: Legacies and Reckonings in the New West* (New York: W. W. Norton, 2000), 186–213, quotations on 204–205.

spring 1942 and confined in remote interior locations. The government confiscated their property, providing compensation, and Japanese Canadians were then required to fund their own removal expenses, and thousands were deported to Japan after the war.[33]

About 30,000 of the United States's interned Japanese had left the camps by the end of the war. Some had been released to areas where farm labor was in short supply, but most, around 22,000, entered the US Army in 1943 and 1944, serving bravely in units such as the 442nd Regimental Combat Team and the Hundredth Infantry Battalion (which included large numbers of Hawaiian, as well as mainland Japanese Americans). The 442nd became the most decorated US military unit and their service helped nurture a more receptive atmosphere for Japanese and Japanese Americans in the immediate postwar years. Nonetheless, the transition from camp life to reintegration into postwar American society proved difficult.

The internment order was finally rescinded on January 2, 1945, though a good number of Nisei had been released and relocated to the East and Midwest during the previous year. The order was delayed by the 1944 elections and accompanying concerns that it would hurt FDR's reelection campaign. Some former internees were welcomed back to the West Coast by church and civic organizations and by neighbors, who in certain cases had been good stewards of homes, businesses, and other property; but most did not experience such good fortune. For example, the several hundred Japanese and Japanese Americans who returned to California's Central Valley were met by violence, including shootings and acts of arson, and there was an unsuccessful effort to insert an alien land law into the state constitution in 1946. Some former internees remained in the areas to which they had been relocated. A good number migrated to Denver and Salt Lake, as well as to various other cities outside the West, including Chicago and New York. A little over 96 percent of the Japanese American population resided in the western states in 1940, including 88.5 percent in the Pacific Coast states. By 1950, that figure had dropped to around 82 percent in the West, with 69.5 percent in the Pacific Coast states. Because of the experience of relocation and the difficulty

[33] Greg Robinson, *By Order of the President: FDR and the Internment of Japanese Americans* (Cambridge, MA: Harvard University Press, 2001), 3–5; and *A Tragedy of Democracy: Japanese Confinement in North America* (New York: Columbia University Press, 2009), vii–viii and 5; and Tetsuden Kashima, *Judgment without Trial: Japanese American Imprisonment during World War II* (Seattle: University of Washington Press, 2003), 8–11.

of returning to communities on the West Coast, Japanese-origin people became the only group in the country that experienced net migration away from the West to other parts of the United States in the 1940s. Eighteen hundred dual citizens decided to return to Japan after the war.[34]

In addition to the difficult and often dehumanizing ordeal of internment and the immediate postinternment experience, it is important to remember that during the short time between the issuing of the relocation order and their transportation to the temporary confinement centers in the spring and summer of 1942, the Issei and Nisei in most cases could not sell their homes, vehicles, and other property at anything other than fire-sale prices and could only take to the camps those belongings they could carry. In 1948, Congress appropriated $38 million under the Japanese Claims Act to compensate Japanese American citizens who lost property because of internment. The appropriation was woefully insufficient. The 26,568 claims filed totaled $148 million, and the estimates of the full property losses from internment range from $350 million to over $3 billion. Still, the Claims Act did at least amount to the first official recognition that relocation violated the civil rights of American citizens. The famous 1944 Supreme Court Case challenging the constitutionality of internment, *Korematsu v. US*, had ended in a 6–3 decision in favor of the government.[35]

National recognition of the most lamentable aspect of the Good War in the West has come a long way in the decades since. Fred Korematsu, who had resisted internment, was awarded the Presidential Medal of Freedom in 1998 by President Bill Clinton. Earlier, in 1980, Congress established the Commission on Wartime Relocation and Internment of Civilians (CWRIC) and in 1983 the CWRIC issued its lengthy report on the injustices suffered by Japanese and Japanese Americans, recommending a reparations payment of $20,000 to each person. In 1988, President Ronald Reagan signed a bill providing for that amount (a total of

[34] Douglas Mark Dye, "The Soul of the City: The Work of the Seattle Council of Churches During World War II" (PhD diss., Washington State University, 1997); Nugent, *Into the West*, 264; and "Japanese American Population, by Census Region and selected States, 1940 and 1950," US Census Bureau.

[35] Brian Masaru Hayashi, *Democratizing the Enemy: The Japanese American Internment* (Princeton, NJ: Princeton University Press, 2004), 214; *Personal Justice Denied: Report of the Commission on Wartime Relocation and Internment of Civilians* (Seattle: The Civil Liberties Public Education Fund and University of Washington Press, 1997; originally published in two volumes by the Government Printing Office, Washington, DC, 1982 and 1983), 118.[34] Kennedy, *Freedom from Fear: The American People in Depression and War, 1929–1945* (New York: Oxford University Press, 1999), 783.

$1.2 billion), and in 1992 President George H. W. Bush declared Manzanar, in California's Owens Valley, a National Historic Site, signed a companion bill to the 1988 one, providing for an additional $400 million to ensure all internees received reparations, and issued a formal apology. He declared, "The interment of Americans of Japanese ancestry was a great injustice and it will never be repeated." The Minidoka National Historic Site in south central Idaho was established in 2001. Public memory of World War II as the good war has clearly been complicated and compromised by a deeper public understanding of the injustices of Japanese relocation and internment.

The Cold War, the West, and the Rebirth of American Exceptionalism

During the global war against Nazi totalitarianism and Japanese imperialism, and more particularly as the full horrors of the Holocaust became evident to the American public, the contours of American thought shifted away from the relativism of the interwar years toward a more absolutist understanding of the world. In this dualistic framing, the totalitarian evils of Nazism and Soviet Communism were juxtaposed against the United States as the force of good, the global defender of democracy, freedom, and God. Those parts of the national experience that contradicted this new narrative – the irony of a segregated military waging a war to secure the four freedoms, the forced internment of Japanese and Japanese Americans without evidence of disloyal acts, discrimination against African Americans and Mexican-origin people on the home front, and the abrogation of federal responsibility to Native peoples – were conveniently left out of the story. Thus, the "Good War" narrative evolved and expanded through the stark contrast drawn between democracy and totalitarianism, and a conscious silence concerning the many racial stains on the national record.[36]

The impact of World War II and the developing Cold War on American thought was evident in the writings in the second half of the 1940s by historian, literary critic, novelist, and devoted westerner Bernard De Voto and historian Arthur Schlesinger Jr. on the causes of the American Civil

[36] Theologian Reinhold Niebuhr, in his clear delineation of the forces of good and evil in the world through works such as *The Nature and Destiny of Man* (2 vols., 1941 and 1943) and *The Children of Light and the Children of Darkness* (1944), had helped rediscover and repopularize the notion of sin for a new generation of Americans and, in doing so, had helped lay the intellectual foundations for the turn toward absolutism.

War. Responding to the then prevailing revisionist argument that the Civil War could and should have been avoided and was begun by hotheaded and extremist ideologues on both sides, Schlesinger wrote, "To say there 'should' have been no abolitionists in America before the Civil War is about as sensible as to say there 'should' have been no anti-Nazis in the nineteen-thirties or that there 'should' be no anti-Communists today."[37] The Civil War increasingly came to be viewed not as an avoidable tragedy but as a vital crusade against evil. In the 1940s American intellectuals and politicians paralleled fascism, and later Communism, with slavery; all three systems came to be viewed as cancerous growths that had to be rooted out for the good of democracy and humanity. Thus, the United States's efforts in both World War II and the early Cold War years came to be viewed as parts of a larger Good War narrative. But it was not just the story of national redemption through the abolition of slavery that encapsulated the shift in American thought; the story of the American frontier also played a vital role.

In the same year that Schlesinger Jr. developed his absolutist argument linking the national past to the present, 1949 – a year marked by the victory of the Communist forces and establishment of the People's Republic of China, and by the Soviet Union's first test of an atomic bomb – historian Ray Allen Billington's influential and widely used textbook *Westward Expansion: A History of the American Frontier* appeared. Billington provided an even larger framing of the national heritage and its connection to the contemporary scene, and placed the western frontier at the center of the story. He began his account of the nation's westward movement on the Atlantic Coast in the early seventeenth century and concluded it in 1890, the moment when the Census Bureau declared the frontier process over. Billington essentially provided the historical detail to augment the frontier framework that Frederick Jackson Turner had presented more than a half-century before. But unlike Turner's 1893 essay, *Westward Expansion* was no lament; instead, it was a triumphalist heralding of American exceptionalism as nurtured through the frontier process of exploration, settlement, and social development.

The westward march of European Americans across the continent, in Billington's reckoning, had shaped the nation's democratic and

37 Arthur Schlesinger Jr., "The Causes of the Civil War: A Note on Historical Sentimentalism," *Partisan Review* XVI (October 1949), 970–981; and *A Life in the 20th Century: Innocent Beginnings, 1917–1950* (Boston: Houghton Mifflin, 2000), 445–449.

individualistic foundations, and those foundations would serve it well in its mid-twentieth-century moment of crisis. The publication of the study was timely indeed. *Westward Expansion* appeared at a critical moment in the expanding Cold War, just as American scholars were juxtaposing their nation's democratic heritage with that of its new nemesis, the Soviet Union. Billington's textbook helped re-cement the idea of American frontier settlement as a largely positive process, and America as an empire of liberty, not a traditional empire of conquest and colonialism. Billington drew a direct line from the distant American frontier past to the Cold War present and the nation's role as the force of light in the new bipolar world with its two great superpowers. Meanwhile, the first generation of American Sovietologists drew a direct line from the authoritarian Ivan the Terrible, Tsar of All the Russias (1547–1584), to the totalitarian Joseph Stalin. Thus, a brutal Russian heritage explained the Soviet present and the benign frontier heritage explained the American present at mid-century. This reborn triumphalist, frontier-centric American exceptionalism remained a core feature of American rhetoric during the long Cold War era.

It was during this period that Alexis de Tocqueville's *Democracy in America* (2 vols., 1835–1840), which emphasized the distinctiveness of the nation's democratic institutions and practices, was repeatedly republished (in 1945, 1946, 1947, 1948, 1951, and 1953) and emerged as one of the core texts of American exceptionalism.[38] This was also the moment when the American Studies movement emerged, and American scholars in history, literature, economics, political science, philosophy, sociology, and other disciplines emphasized the distinctiveness of the nation's cultural heritage, focusing on the common values Americans shared and playing down the fractures that had divided Americans during the course of their history.[39] In addition, during the 1940s, the western movie genre grew in significance and embodied the theme of the nation's struggles against the forces of evil in the world. Director John Ford's classic *My Darling Clementine* (1946) recounted the famous gunfight at the OK Corral, but more significantly, it was a story about rebirth in the West, one

[38] The Henry Reeve text of Tocqueville's *Democracy in America* (originally published in 2 vols., 1835 and 1840) was published in New York by Alfred A. Knopf in 1945, 1953, 1954, and 1956. Oxford University Press also reprinted the Reeve text in 1947 and 1959.

[39] See John P. Diggins, *The Rise and Fall of the American Left* (New York: W. W. Norton, 1992), 187–200.

that provided viewers with hope about the nation's place in the postwar world.[40]

The rebirth of the American frontier heritage in the late 1940s, unlike the closed-frontier concerns of the 1890s, was marked by a cautious optimism about the postfrontier and postwar future. Ford's brilliant western, *The Searchers* (1950), starring John Wayne and chronicling a seven-year journey across the West in search of two white girls taken by Comanche Indians after a brutal raid on a settler cabin, captured the tensions of the Cold War present, including the deep racism the nation needed to overcome. But the movie closed on a hopeful note suggesting that the nation's high ideals would secure its future. One of the girls is rescued and Wayne's character, Ethan, finally overcomes his racial hatred.[41] The movie perhaps served as a palliative for the nation as it struggled to come to grips with the racial complications that complicated the Good War and Cold War narratives.

California writer Carey McWilliams's noble vision articulated during World War II, of "overcoming the mocking paradoxes in our own society" and achieving "total democracy," was not close to fulfillment in the American West or the nation by the end of the 1940s. In those early Cold War years, the American government loudly and confidently proclaimed the nation's role as the defender of freedom and democracy around the globe but failed to guarantee those rights to many of its own citizens. Nonetheless, it was this very paradox that had helped highlight the need for change and force the government to live up to the rhetoric of the Good War, and would continue to do so as the West and America entered the second half of the twentieth century.[42]

[40] Richard Aquila, *The Sagebrush Trail: Western Movies and Twentieth-Century America* (Tucson: University of Arizona Press, 2015), 140–142.

[41] Ibid., 131–138.

[42] Carey McWilliams, *Brothers under the Skin* (Boston: Little, Brown, 1943), 7 and 295; and Mary Dzudziak, *Cold War Civil Rights* (2000; repr., Princeton, NJ: Princeton University Press, 2011).

Coda: The West at Mid-Century

By 1950, three generations had passed since the Census Bureau had declared the western frontier closed in 1890. Yet the frontier heritage became a touchstone during the New Deal years, when Franklin Roosevelt and key members of his cabinet emphasized the idea of a federal safety net to replace the safety valve. That heritage was revived again during the early Cold War years as the nation sought to define itself as the product of a benign and thoroughly democratic process of westward expansion, in stark contrast to its Soviet adversary. Moreover, the American West, with all its demographic dynamism, economic vitality, political innovation, and racial and cultural diversity and tension, had remained as consistently pivotal to the nation's development in the first half of the twentieth century as it had been in the nineteenth.

As the United States became increasingly marked by urbanization, industrialization, and immigration, as well as agrarian discontent, industrial violence, political corruption, and sectional tensions, in the 1890s, the closing of the frontier seemed to explain the various crises and even the nation's path to empire as the century ended. As the new century dawned, the future of the nation seemed bound up with the future of the West. As the era of Progressive reform unfolded, with all its complications and contradictions, Theodore Roosevelt seemed to encapsulate western frontier virtues as well as modern reform impulses. Demographic growth in the West was accompanied by that region's pace-setting role in the areas of environmental stewardship, and direct democracy reform, including women's suffrage. Unfortunately, the nativist underpinnings of

Progressivism also found their full expression in parts of the West as alien land laws and other race-based policies were enacted. Moreover, those strands of intolerance were woven more deeply into the regional cultural fabric after American entry into World War I and during the postwar Red Scare and the 1920s, as evidenced in the crushing of the IWW, the Bisbee deportation, and the passage and extensive utilization of criminal anti-syndicalist laws. The increased level of cultural conflict in the 1920s was manifested most clearly in the rise of the Ku Klux Klan nationwide, and the organization proved particularly influential in Texas and Oklahoma, on the West Coast, and in Colorado.

The West remained at the leading edge of national affairs in the 1930s and 1940s in no small part because of the federal government's massive infrastructural investments in the region. The imprint of federal agencies such as the Works Progress Administration, Public Works Administration, and Civilian Conservation Corps was disproportionately evident in the West, and much of the built environment the government provided remains a vital part of western landscapes, from massive dams to local municipal buildings, schools, parks, sidewalks, and stadiums. That federal imprint only grew larger during World War II and the immediate postwar years as the government turned the West into martial landscape of production and military bases. By investing so heavily in the region in the 1930s and 1940s, the federal government ensured that the West would continue to shape the course of the nation in the second half of the twentieth century and into the twenty-first. The region's remarkable patterns of demographic and economic growth, including metropolitan expansion, and its political and cultural influence on the nation have endured into the present.

The regional future looked bright in 1950. Yet, the story of western expansion and development was as much a cautionary tale as a promising one. The West remained the most significant regional focus of the expanding conservation and wilderness preservation movements, and the West's national parks became increasingly popular tourist attractions in an era of economic growth and increased discretionary income, as well as coordinated park promotional efforts. The parks hosted 17 million visitors in 1940 (most of them in the West), and that number had more than tripled to 56 million by 1955. The massive increase in visitors placed an enormous strain on park landscapes and on the NPS mission to both conserve and provide for public enjoyment of those natural wonderlands, and the dilemma has only grown more acute since. In 1964, when the national population stood at 192 million, 80 million people visited the parks; in 2015, the parks' visitation figure exceeded 307 million, and the national population numbered 320 million.[1]

But the dilemma of how to manage the nation's most spectacular landscapes in the face of their growing popularity and the expanding national population (as well as increasing visitation by tourists from across the globe) was just the tip of the environmental stewardship iceberg in the American West. Nuclear testing, uranium and plutonium mining, and excessive dam building had damaged the region's fragile physical landscapes, as well as its residents. At mid-century, almost 22,000 people were living in Richland, Washington, the town closest to the Hanford plutonium site, and around 10,000 each in the adjacent towns of Pasco and Kennewick. Hanford workers especially, but all area residents, were endangered by plutonium dust in the air, and plutonium isotopes in the water, the food supply, and, ultimately, their bodies, causing premature aging, birth defects, and cancer.[2] A tunnel collapse at the Hanford site in early May of 2017, serves as the most recent reminder of the dangers that accompany the storage of contaminated radioactive materials, and of the enduring legacy of the Cold War in the West.[3]

At mid-century, the West's cultural landscapes were also scarred. Japanese internment had taken its toll on individuals, families, and communities, and new social organizations had to be built and old ones restored when the camps closed. The New Deal's emphasis on tribal self-government and cultural renewal for Native peoples was succeeded by the new "termination" emphasis of the early Cold War years. Mexican Americans and African Americans, for all the economic opportunities that the martial West provided, continued to struggle for something more than second-class citizenship across the region. The mass deportation of 1.3 million undocumented Mexicans by the Immigration and Naturalization Service's "Operation Wetback" between 1954 and 1957 reflected Cold War fears of alien subversion, as well as long-standing prejudice against Mexican-origin people. Meanwhile, the bracero program hit its numerical peak of nearly half a million in 1956, as agribusiness operations from Texas to California secured the cheap labor they needed

[1] Otis L. Graham Jr., *Presidents and the American Environment* (Lawrence: University Press of Kansas, 2015), 183.

[2] Kate Brown, *Plutopia: Nuclear Families, Atomic Cities, and the Great Soviet and American Plutonium Disasters* (New York: Oxford University Press, 2013).

[3] Lindsey Bever and Steven Mufson, "Tunnel Collapses at Hanford Nuclear Waste Site in Washington State," *Washington Post*, May 9, 2017, accessed at: www.washingtonpost.com/news/post-nation/wp/2017/05/09/tunnel-collapses-at-hanford-nuclear-waste-site-in-washington-state-reports-say/?utm_term=.82ae0b90f935.

at the very same time that border security tightened and deportation numbers skyrocketed.[4]

The landscape of race in the West at mid-century was complicated indeed. California finally overturned its 1850 antimiscegenation law in 1948. The scope of the law had expanded over nearly a century to prohibit marriage between white persons and "Negros, mulattos, Mongolians, and Malays." In taking so long to negate such legislation, the Golden State seemed thoroughly retrogressive by comparison with Kansas, New Mexico, and Washington, which had all repealed their antimiscegenation statutes between 1859 and 1868. However, California was ahead of Arizona, Colorado, Idaho, Montana, Nebraska, Nevada, North Dakota, Oregon, South Dakota, Utah, and Wyoming, where such laws continued to remain on the books after 1950. In Oklahoma and Texas, antimiscegenation laws persisted until the Supreme Court ruling in *Loving v. Virginia* in 1967. In the matter of legality of marriages across racial lines, the West was more progressive than the South, but less progressive than the rest of the nation – all while the West led the nation regarding racial and ethnic diversity.

Southern California at mid-century was the regional epicenter of a developing conservative movement – influenced by the migration of "plain folk religious migrants" who headed from Oklahoma, Texas, and Arkansas to the Greater Los Angeles metropolitan area in the 1930s and 1940s – that has continued to shape American politics ever since.[5] California, and particularly the Bay Area, were also at the leading edge of student radicalism and countercultural protest in the 1960s and 1970s and quickly developed a reputation as bellwethers of the American left. The West, a political lightweight region in 1900 (aside from the Senate, where representatives from lightly populated western states wielded disproportionate influence), by mid-century had grown in political significance. Notably, the region has been the birthplace or home state of most of the nation's presidents since mid-century: Dwight Eisenhower, Lyndon Johnson, Richard Nixon, Ronald Reagan, George H. W. Bush, George W. Bush, and Barack Obama.

At mid-century, the western film remained one of Hollywood's most popular cinema and television genres, bolstering the nation's reborn frontier-centric exceptionalism. At the beginning of the 1950s, Knotts

[4] Lori A. Flores, *Grounds for Dreaming: Mexican Americans, Mexican Immigrants, and the California Farmworker Movement* (New Haven, CT: Yale University Press, 2016), 78–79.

[5] See Darren Dochuk, *From Bible Belt to Sun Belt: Plain-Folk Religion, Grassroots Politics, and the Rise of Evangelical Conservatism* (New York: W. W. Norton, 2011).

Berry Farm in Buena Park, California, was transitioning into a Wild West–themed amusement park. In 1955, Disneyland was established in Anaheim, California, with Frontierland, its reconstructed Wild West landscape, proving one of its most popular attractions. Frontier City theme park opened in Oklahoma City in 1958. The modern urban West was embracing the old western past. By 1957, Los Angeles had become the new home of the Brooklyn Dodgers and San Francisco the new home of the New York Giants, developments that further underscored the westward tilt in American popular culture.

And the West remained, as it had been throughout the first half of the twentieth century, the fastest-growing American region demographically, with the greater Southwest, from Texas to California, leading the way. California's population of 10.6 million in 1950 had grown to 15.7 million a decade later; Texas's 7.7 million had grown to almost 9.6 million. The populations of the Pacific Northwest states (Oregon, Washington, and Idaho) and Rocky Mountain states (Colorado, Utah, Montana, and Wyoming) expanded at an impressive rate, too. The Plains states of Oklahoma (which lost population), Kansas, Nebraska, North Dakota, and South Dakota did far less well in the 1950s, a continuation of the patterns of the 1930s and 1940s. By 1959, Alaska and Hawaii had gained statehood and joined the Union, and the West.[6]

[6] Western States Population, 1950–1960

State	Population in 1950	Population in 1960
Alaska	128,643	266,167
Arizona	749,587	1,302,161
California	10,586,223	15,717,204
Colorado	1,325,089	1,753,947
Hawaii	499,794	632,772
Idaho	588,637	667,191
Kansas	1,905,299	2,178,611
Montana	591,024	674,767
Nebraska	1,325,510	1,411,330
Nevada	160,083	285,278
New Mexico	681,187	951,023
North Dakota	619,636	632,446
Oklahoma	2,233,351	2,328,284
Oregon	1,521,341	1,768,687
South Dakota	652,740	680,514
Texas	7,711,194	9,579,677
Utah	688,862	890,627
Wyoming	290,529	330,066

At the close of the nineteenth century the West was conquered and colonized, but still sparsely populated and economically underdeveloped; yet, at the very same time, Americans worried that the western frontier was closed and the nation faced a dangerous postfrontier future. A half-century later, and in no small part due to massive support from the federal government, the West stood at the leading edge of national demographic developments, as well as many economic, political, and cultural ones. The West had not by any means led the nation in all respects during the first half of the twentieth century. The Northeast and Midwest, for example, saw more social justice reform than the West during the Progressive Era. But the impressive flow of the national population westward constituted a migratory stream that spoke volumes about where the nation's greatest economic and social opportunities were to be found. The government continued to develop the West from 1900 to 1950, just as it had underwritten geographic expansion, conquest, and settlement throughout the nineteenth century, and the demographically expanding West continued to play a central role in directing economic, political, and cultural trends in the nation.

America at mid-century was a nation nurtured on the ideals of the western frontier, as represented in popular culture. The West as a region, though, had been nurtured more in the first half of the twentieth century by federal largesse than by frontier ideals. Federal support, from the Homestead Act to massive railroad subsidies and military campaigns that defeated indigenous resistance, played a vital part in western development during the so-called frontier era. The conservation and reclamation initiatives of the early twentieth century, together with the New Deal programs of the 1930s and the federally sponsored war production and military infrastructure of the 1940s, continued the tradition and forged the modern West. Nonetheless, the frontier past – with its emphasis on hyperindividualism and self-reliance, as well as whiteness – remains an ideological wellspring for many western politicians. The rhetoric of rugged, frontier individualism has increasingly become a core characteristic of the western political ethos, one encapsulated in the cowboy culture embrace of Barry Goldwater and presidents Reagan and George W. Bush. Meanwhile, the real West's remarkable cultural diversity and the overwhelming degree to which its economic and political power and demographic growth were products of government activism are ignored or rejected by champions of the frontier western heritage. Such voices steadfastly deny that there was anything enlightened about the federal efforts that transformed the West and thereby helped the region to transform the nation. The West's measurable federal heritage, the actual source of much of its growing political and economic power and influence, is still decried by many, while, the opaquer frontier heritage remains a fountainhead for individualistic visions of the regional and national future. That is the paradox of history and memory in America's West.

Bibliography

Primary Sources

Beveridge, Albert. "The March of the Flag." Campaign Speech, September 16, 1898.

Bryan, William Jennings. Democratic National Convention Acceptance Speech, Indianapolis, IN, August 8, 1900.

Chipman, N. P. "Territorial Expansion: The Philippines – The Oriental Problem." *Overland Monthly and Out West Magazine* XXXIV (December 1889): 491–502.

"Territorial Expansion – II: The Philippines – The Oriental Problem." *Overland Monthly and Out West Magazine* XXXV (January 1900): 23–32.

Collier, John B. *Department of the Treasury, Internal Revenue Service, Statistics of Income, Individual Income Tax Returns, 1935–1940*. Washington, DC: Government Printing Office, 1936–1941.

"Plundering the Pueblo Indians." *Sunset Magazine* 50 (January 1923): 21–25 and 56.

Cowley, Malcolm. *Exile's Return: A Literary Odyssey of the 1920s*. New York: Viking, 1934.

De Tocqueville, Alexis. *Democracy in America*. New York: Vintage Books, 1945.

DeWitt, John. *Final Report, Japanese Evacuation from the West Coast, 1942*. Washington, DC: Government Printing Office, 1943.

Garland, Hamlin. *Jason Edwards: An Average Man*. Boston: Arena, 1892.

Main Travelled Roads. Boston: Arena, 1891.

Gleed, Charles S. "The True Significance of Western Unrest." *Forum* (October 1893): 251–261.

Hoover, Herbert. *American Individualism*. Garden City, NY: Doubleday Page, 1922.

The Challenge to Liberty. New York: Charles Scribner's Sons, 1934.

"It Needn't Happen Here." *American Mercury* 50 (July 1940): 263–270.

The Memoirs of Herbert Hoover: The Cabinet and the Presidency, 1920–1933. New York: Macmillan Co., 1951.

Hough, Emerson. "The Settlement of the West: A Study in Transportation, III: Across the Waters." *Century Illustrated Magazine* 63 (January 1902): 318–355.

Irwin, Will, ed. *Letters to Kermit from Theodore Roosevelt, 1902–1908.* New York: Charles Scribner's Sons, 1946.

Jefferson, Thomas. *The Writings of Thomas Jefferson*, ed. H. A. Washington, vol. 2. Washington, DC: Taylor and Maury, 1854.

Landman, J. H. *Human Sterilization: The History of Sexual Sterilization.* New York: Macmillan, 1932.

Lighton, William R. "Where Is the West?" *Outlook* 74 (July 1903): 702–704.

McWilliams, Carey. *Brothers under the Skin.* Boston: Little, Brown, 1943.

Factories in the Field: The Story of Migratory Farm Labor in California. Boston: Little, Brown, 1939.

Miller, J. K. "Are the People of the West Fanatics?" *The Arena* XIII (June 1895): 92–97.

Niebuhr, Reinhold. *The Nature and Destiny of Man.* New York: Charles Scribner's Sons, 1949.

Parish, John Carl. "The Persistence of the Westward Movement." *The Yale Review* XV (April 1926): 461–477.

Personal Justice Denied: Report of the Commission on Wartime Relocation and Internment of Civilians. Seattle: The Civil Liberties Public Education Fund and University of Washington Press, 1997; originally published in two volumes by the Government Printing Office, Washington, DC, 1982 and 1983.

Post, Emily. *By Motoring to the Golden Gate.* New York: Appleton, 1916.

Priestley, J. B. *Midnight on the Desert: Being an Excursion into Autobiography during a Winter in America, 1935–1936.* New York: Harper, 1937.

Roosevelt, Franklin Delano. Second Inaugural Address, January 20, 1937.

Roosevelt, Theodore. *Campaigns and Controversies: The Works of Theodore Roosevelt*, National ed., Col. XIV. New York: Charles Scribner's Sons, 1926.

The Life and Times of Thomas Hart Benton. New York: Houghton Mifflin, 1887.

"The Menace of the Demagogue." Speech before the American Republican College League, Chicago, IL, October 15, 1896.

The New Nationalism. New York: Outlook, 1911.

Ranch Life and the Hunting Trail. New York: Houghton Mifflin, 1889.

"The Rough Riders" and "An Autobiography." New York: Library of America, 2004.

The Winning of the West, Volume I: From the Alleghenies to the Mississippi, 1769–1776. New York: G. P. Putnam's Sons, 1889.

Roosevelt, Theodore, and George Bird Grinnell, eds. *American Big-Game Hunting: The Book of the Boone and Crockett Club.* New York: Forest and Stream, 1893.

Schlesinger, Arthur, Jr. "The Causes of the Civil War: A Note on Historical Sentimentalism." *Partisan Review* XVI (October 1949): 970–981.

Steinbeck, John. *The Grapes of Wrath and Other Writings, 1939–1941.* New York: The Library of America, 1996.

Turner, Frederick Jackson. "Sections and Nation." *Yale Review* 12 (October 1922): 1–21.

"The Significance of the Frontier in American History," in *Annual Report of the American Historical Association for the Year 1893* (Washington, DC: Government Printing Office, 1894), 199–227.

"The Significance of the Section in American History." *Wisconsin Magazine of History* 8 (March 1925): 255–280.

"The Significance of the Frontier in American History" and Other Essays, ed. John Mack Faragher. New York: Henry Holt, 1994.

Wallace, Henry. *New Frontiers*. New York: Reynal and Hitchcock, 1934.

White, William Allen. *The Autobiography of William Allen White*. New York: Macmillan, 1946.

Wilson, Woodrow. "The Making of the Nation." *Atlantic Monthly* LXXX (1897): 1–14.

Woods, Robert A., and Albert J. Kennedy. *Handbook of Settlements*. New York: Charities Publication Committee/Russell Sage Foundation, 1911.

Secondary Works

Books

Abbott, Carl. *How Cities Won the West: Four Centuries of Urban Change in Western North America*. Albuquerque: University of New Mexico Press, 2008.

The Metropolitan Frontier: Cities in the Modern American West. Tucson: University of Arizona Press, 1993.

Abbott, Carl, Stephen J. Leonard, and Thomas J. Noel, eds. *Colorado: A History of the Centennial State*. Boulder: University of Colorado Press, 2005.

Acuna, Rodolfo. *Occupied America: A History of Chicanos*. 5th ed. New York: Pearson and Longman, 2004.

Adams, David Wallace. *Education for Extinction: American Indians and the Boarding School Experience*, 1875–1928. Lawrence: University Press of Kansas, 1995.

Alexander, Charles C. *The Ku Klux Klan in the Southwest*. Norman: University of Oklahoma Press, 1995.

Alvarez, Louis. *The Power of the Zoot: Race Culture and Resistance During World War II*. Berkeley: University of California Press, 2008.

Amenta, Edwin. *When Movements Matter: The Townsend Plan and the Rise of Social Security*. Princeton, NJ: Princeton University Press, 2006.

Andrews, Thomas. *Killing for Coal: America's Deadliest Labor War*. Cambridge, MA: Harvard University Press, 2008.

Aquila, Richard. *The Sagebrush Trail: Western Movies and Twentieth-Century America*. Tucson: University of Arizona Press, 2015.

Armitage, Susan, and Elizabeth A. Jameson, eds. *The Women's West*. Norman: University of Oklahoma Press, 1987.

Arrington, Leonard J. *History of Idaho*, 2 vols. Moscow: University of Idaho Press, 1994.

Avila, Eric. *Popular Culture in the Age of White Flight: Fear and Fantasy in Suburban Los Angeles*. Berkeley: University of California Press, 2006.

Baird, W. David, and Danney Goble. *Oklahoma: A History*. Norman: University of Oklahoma Press, 2008.

Bakken, Gordon Morris. *The World of the American West*. New York: Routledge, 2011.

Balderrama, Francisco E., and Raymond Rodriguez. *Decade of Betrayal: Mexican Repatriation in the 1930s*. Albuquerque: University of New Mexico Press, 2006.

Barkan, Elliott. *From All Points, America's Immigrant West: 1870s–1952*. Bloomington: Indiana University Press, 2007.

Basso, Matthew L. *Meet Joe Copper: Masculinity and Race on Montana's Home World War II Front*. Chicago: University of Chicago Press, 2013.

Beale, Howard K. *Theodore Roosevelt and the Rise of America to World Power*. Baltimore: Johns Hopkins University Press, 1956.

Benson, Jackson. *John Steinbeck, Writer: A Biography*. New York: Penguin Books, 1990.

Benton-Cohen, Kathleen. *Borderline Americans: Racial Division and Labor War in the Arizona Borderlands*. Cambridge, MA: Harvard University Press, 2009.

Billington, David P., and Donald C. Jackson. *Big Dams of the New Deal Era: A Confluence of Engineering and Politics*. Norman: University of Oklahoma Press, 2006.

Blackman, Jon S. *Oklahoma's Indian New Deal*. Norman: University of Oklahoma Press, 2013.

Blanton, Carlos K. *The Strange Career of Bilingual Education in Texas*. College Station: Texas A&M University Press, 2004.

Blee, Kathleen M. *Women of the Klan: Racism and Gender in the 1920s*. Berkeley: University of California Press, 1991.

Blodgett, Peter, ed. *Motoring West, Volume 1: Automobile Pioneers, 1900–1909*. Norman: Arthur H. Clark, 2015.

Bold, Christine. *The Frontier Club: Popular Westerns and Cultural Power, 1880–1924*. New York: Oxford University Press, 2013.

Bowman, Timothy Paul. *Blood Oranges: Colonialism and Agriculture in the South Texas Borderlands*. College Station: Texas A&M University Press, 2016.

Brands, H. W. *T.R.: The Last Romantic*. New York: Basic Books, 1997.

Brantlinger, Patrick. *Dark Vanishings: The Discourse on the Extinction of Primitive Peoples, 1830–1930*. Ithaca, NY: Cornell University Press, 2003.

Brechin, Gray. *Imperial San Francisco: Urban Power, Earthly Ruin*. Berkeley: University of California Press, 1999.

Brinkley, Alan. *Voices of Protest: Huey Long, Father Coughlin and the Great Depression*. New York: Alfred A. Knopf, 1982.

Brosnan, Kathleen. *Uniting Mountain and Plain: Cities, Law, and Environmental Change along the Front Range*. Albuquerque: University of New Mexico Press, 2002.

Broussard, Albert. *Black San Francisco: The Struggle for Racial Equality in the West, 1900–1954*. Lawrence: University Press of Kansas, 1993.

Expectations of Equality: A History of Black Westerners. Wheeling, IL: Harlan Davidson/Cody, WY: The Buffalo Bill Historical Center, 2012.

Brown, Kate. *Plutopia: Nuclear Families, Atomic Cities, and the Great Soviet and American Plutonium Disasters*. New York: Oxford University Press, 2013.

Bryant, Keith. *Culture in the American Southwest: The Earth, the Sky, the People*. College Station: Texas A&M University Press, 2001.

Butler, Anne M., and Michael J. Lansing. *The American West: A Concise History*. Malden, MA: Blackwell, 2008.

Camarillo, Albert. *Chicanos in a Changing Society: From Mexican Pueblos to American Barrios in Santa Barbara and Southern California, 1848–1930*. Cambridge, MA: Harvard University Press, 1979.

Chicanos in California: A History of Mexican Americans in California. San Francisco: Boyd and Fraser, 1984.

Campbell, Randolph B. *Gone to Texas: A History of the Lone Star State*. New York: Oxford University Press, 2003.

Cannon, Brian Q. *Reopening the Frontier: Homesteading in the Modern West*. Lawrence: University Press of Kansas, 2009.

Capozzola, Christopher. *Uncle Sam Wants You: World War I and the Making of the Modern American Citizen*. New York: Oxford University Press, 2008.

Chalmers, David M. *Hooded Americanism: The History of the Ku Klux Klan*. Durham, NC: Duke University Press, 1987.

Childers, Leisl Carr. *The Size of the Risk: Histories of Multiple Use in the Great Basin*. Norman: University of Oklahoma Press, 2015.

Chinard, Gilbert. *Thomas Jefferson: The Apostle of Americanism*. Boston: Little, Brown, 1929.

Cohen, Deborah. *Braceros: Migrant Citizens and Transcontinental Subjects in the Postwar United States and Mexico*. Chapel Hill: University of North Carolina Press, 2011.

Collins, Michael L. *That Damned Cowboy: Theodore Roosevelt and the American West, 1883–1898*. New York: Peter Lang, 1989.

Cooper, John Milton, Jr. *Pivotal Decades: The United States, 1900–1920*. New York: W. W. Norton, 1990.

Cronon, William, ed. *Uncommon Ground: Rethinking the Human Place in Nature*. New York: W. W. Norton, 1995.

Cronon, William, George Miles, and Jay Gitlin, eds. *Under an Open Sky: Rethinking America's Western Past*. New York: W. W. Norton, 1993.

Culver, John C., and John Hyde. *American Dreamer: The Life and Times of Henry A. Wallace*. New York: W. W. Norton, 2000.

Daniels, Roger. *Guarding the Golden Door: American Immigration Policy and Immigrants since 1882*. New York: Hill and Wang, 2004.

Dauber, Michele Landis. *The Sympathetic State: Disaster Relief and the Origins of the American Welfare State*. Chicago: University of Chicago Press, 2013.

Davis, Clark, and David Igler, eds. *The Human Tradition in California*. Wilmington, DE: Scholarly Resources, 2002.

Davis, Mike. *City of Quartz: Excavating the Future in Los Angeles*. New York: Verso, 1990.

Ecology of Fear: Los Angeles and the Imagination of Disaster. New York: Henry Holt, 1998.

Deloria, Philip. *Indians in Unexpected Places*. Lawrence: University Press of Kansas, 2004.

Deloria, Philip, and Neal Salisbury, eds. *A Companion to Indian History*. Malden, MA: Blackwell, 2002.

Deutsch, Sarah. *No Separate Refuge: Culture, Class, and Gender on an Anglo-Hispanic Frontier in the American Southwest, 1880–1940*. New York: Oxford University Press, 1987.

Deverell, William, ed. *A Companion to the American West*. Malden, MA: Blackwell, 2004.

Railroad Crossing: Californians and the Railroad, 1850–1910. Berkeley: University of California Press, 1994.

Whitewashed Adobe: The Rise of Los Angeles and the Remaking of Its Mexican Past. Berkeley: University of California Press, 2004.

Deverell, William, and Greg Hise, eds. *A Companion to Los Angeles*. Malden, MA: Blackwell, 2010.

Deverell, William, and Anne F. Hyde. *The West in the History of the Nation*. Vol. 2. *Since 1865*. Boston: Bedford/St. Martin's, 2000.

Deverell, William, and Tom Sitton, eds. *California Progressivism Revisited*. Berkeley: University of California Press, 1994.

Dewing, Rolland. *Religion in Transition: The Northern Great Plains and the Pacific Northwest in the Great Depression*. Lanham, MD: University Press of America, 2006.

Diggins, John P. *The Rise and Fall of the American Left*. New York: W. W. Norton, 1992.

Dippie, Brian. *The Vanishing American: White Attitudes and U.S. Indian Policy*. Lawrence: University Press of Kansas, 1991.

Dochuk, Darren. *From Bible Belt to Sun Belt: Plain-Folk Religion, Grassroots Politics, and the Rise of Evangelical Conservatism*. New York: W. W. Norton, 2011.

Dodds, Gordon B. *The College That Would Not Die: The First Fifty Years of Portland State University, 1946–1996*. Portland: Oregon Historical Society Press and Portland State University, 2000.

Dorman, Robert L. *Hell of a Vision: Regionalism and the Modern American West*. Tucson: University of Arizona Press, 2010.

Revolt of the Provinces: The Regionalist Movement in America, 1920–1945. Chapel Hill: University of North Carolina Press, 1993.

Dumenil, Lynn. *The Modern Temper: American Culture and Society in the 1920s*. New York: Hill and Wang, 1995.

Duncan, Dayton. *Miles from Nowhere: Tales from America's Contemporary Frontier*. New York: Viking, 1993.

Edmunds, R. David, ed. *The New Warriors: Native American Leaders since 1900*. Lincoln: University of Nebraska Press, 2001.

Egan, Timothy. *The Worst Hard Time: The Untold Story of Those Who Survived the Great American Dust Bowl.* Boston: Houghton Mifflin, 2006.

Elliott, Russell R., with the assistance of William D. Rowley. *History of Nevada.* Lincoln: University of Nebraska Press, 1987.

Etulain, Richard W. *Beyond the Missouri.* Albuquerque: University of New Mexico Press, 2006.

Conversations with Wallace Stegner on Western History and Literature. Salt Lake City: University of Utah Press, 1983.

Re-imagining the Modern American West: A Century of Fiction, History, and Art. Tucson: University of Arizona Press, 1996.

Etulain, Richard W., and Michael P. Malone. *The American West: A Modern History, 1900 to the Present.* Lincoln: University of Nebraska Press, 2007.

Etulain, Richard W., and Ferenc M. Szasz, eds. *The American West in 2000: Essays in Honor of Gerald D. Nash.* Albuquerque: University of New Mexico Press, 2003.

Etulain, Richard W., et al., eds. *The American West in the Twentieth Century: A Bibliography.* Norman: University of Oklahoma Press, 1994.

Fernlund, Kevin J., ed. *The Cold War American West, 1945–1989.* Albuquerque: University of New Mexico Press, 1998.

Ficken Robert E., and Charles P. LeWarne. *Washington: A Centennial History.* Seattle: University of Washington Press, 1988.

Fiege, Mark. *Irrigated Eden: The Making of an Agricultural Landscape in the American West.* Seattle: University of Washington Press, 1999.

The Republic of Nature: An Environmental History of the United States. Seattle: University of Washington Press, 2012.

Findlay, John. *Magic Lands: Western Cityscapes and American Culture after 1940.* Berkeley: University of California Press, 1992.

Findlay, John M., and Bruce Hevly. *Atomic Frontier Days: Hanford and the American West.* Seattle: University of Washington Press, 2011.

Fite, Gilbert C. *American Farmers: The New Minority.* Bloomington: Indiana University Press, 1981.

Fixico, Donald L. *Indian Resilience and Rebuilding: Indigenous Nations in the Modern American West.* Tucson: University of Arizona Press, 2013.

ed. *Rethinking American Indian History.* Albuquerque: University of New Mexico Press, 1997.

Termination and Relocation: Federal Indian Policy, 1945–1960. Albuquerque: University of New Mexico Press, 1986.

The Urban Indian Experience in America. Albuquerque: University of New Mexico Press, 2000.

Flamming, Douglas. *African Americans in the West.* Santa Barbara, CA: ABC-CLIO, 2009.

Bound for Freedom: Black Los Angeles in Jim Crow America. Berkeley: University of California Press, 2005.

Fleischhauer, Carl, and Beverley W. Brannan, eds. *Documenting America, 1935–1943.* Berkeley: University of California Press, 2007.

Flores, Lori A. *Grounds for Dreaming: Mexican Americans, Mexican Immigrants, and the California Farmworker Movement*. New Haven, CT: Yale University Press, 2016.

Foley, Neil. *The White Scourge: Mexicans, Blacks, and Poor Whites in Texas Cotton Culture*. Berkeley: University of California Press, 1997.

Foster, Mark S. *Henry J. Kaiser: Builder in the Modern American West*. Austin: University of Texas Press, 1989.

Fryer, Heather. *Perimeters of Democracy: Inverse Utopias and the Wartime Social Landscape in the American West*. Lincoln: University of Nebraska Press, 2010.

Fulton, William. *The Reluctant Metropolis: The Politics of Urban Growth in Los Angeles*. Rev. ed. Baltimore: Johns Hopkins University Press, 2001.

Gerber, David A. *American Immigration A Very Short Introduction*. New York: Oxford University Press, 2011.

Gibson, Arrell M., ed. *Between Two Worlds: The Survival of Twentieth Century Indians*. Oklahoma City: Oklahoma Historical Society, 1986.

Goins, Charles Robert, and Danney Goble, eds. *Historical Atlas of Oklahoma*. Norman: University of Oklahoma Press, 2006.

Goldberg, Robert A. *Hooded Empire: The Ku Klux Klan in Colorado*. Urbana: University of Illinois Press, 1981.

Gomez, Arthur R. *Quest for the Golden Circle: The Four Comers and the Metropolitan West*. 1994; repr., Lawrence: University Press of Kansas, 2000.

Gonzales, Manuel G. *Mexicanos: A History of Mexicans in the United States*. Bloomington: Indiana University Press, 1999.

Goodchild, Lester, et al. *Higher Education in the American West: Regional History and State Contexts*. New York: Palgrave Macmillan, 2014.

Gould, Lewis L. *The Spanish-American War and President McKinley*. Lawrence: University Press of Kansas, 1982.

Graham, Otis L., Jr. *Presidents and the American Environment*. Lawrence: University Press of Kansas, 2015.

Greene, Jerome. *American Carnage: Wounded Knee, 1890*. Norman: University of Oklahoma Press, 2014.

Gregory, James. *American Exodus: The Dust Bowl Migration and Okie Culture in California*. New York: Oxford University Press, 1989.

The Southern Diaspora: How the Great Migrations of Black and White Southerners Transformed America. Chapel Hill: University of North Carolina Press, 2005.

Griswold, Robert L. *Fatherhood in America: A History*. New York: Basic Books, 1993.

Guerin-Gonzales, Camille. *Mexican Workers and American Dreams: Immigration, Repatriation, and California Farm Labor, 1930–1939*. New Brunswick, NJ: Rutgers University Press, 1994.

Gutiérrez, David G., ed. *Between Two Worlds: Mexican Immigrants in the United States*. Wilmington, DE: Scholarly Resources, 1996.

ed. *The Columbia History of Latinos in the United States, 1960–Present*. New York: Columbia University Press, 2004.

Walls and Mirrors: Mexican Americans, Mexican Immigrants, and the Politics of Ethnicity. Berkeley: University of California Press, 1995.
Hamby, Alonzo. *Man of Destiny: FDR and the Making of the American Century*. New York: Basic Books, 2015.
Harris, Charles H., III, and Louis R. Sadler. *The Plan de San Diego: Tejano Rebellion, Mexican Intrigue*. Lincoln: University of Nebraska Press, 2013.
Hayashi, Brian Masaru. *Democratizing the Enemy: The Japanese American Internment*. Princeton, NJ: Princeton University Press, 2004.
Hernández, Kelly Lytle. *City of Inmates: Conquest, Rebellion, and the Rise of Human Caging in Los Angeles, 1771–1965*. Chapel Hill: University of North Carolina Press, 2017.
Migra! A History of the US Border Patrol. Berkeley: University of California Press, 2010.
Herring, George C. *From Colony to Superpower: U.S. Foreign Relations since 1776*. New York: Oxford University Press, 2008.
Higham, Carol L., and William H. Katerberg. *Conquests and Consequences: The American West: From Frontier to Region*. Wheeling, IL: Harland Davidson/Cody, WY: Buffalo Bill Historical Center, 2009.
Hine, Robert V., and John Mack Faragher. *The American West: A New Interpretive History*. New Haven, CT: Yale University Press, 2000.
Hise, Greg. *Magnetic Los Angeles: Planning the Twentieth-Century Metropolis*. Berkeley: University of California Press, 1997.
Hixson, Walter L. *The American Experience in World War II*. Vol. 10. *The American People at War: Minorities and Women in the Second World War*. New York: Taylor and Francis, 2003.
Hoffman, Abraham. *Unwanted Mexican Americans in the Great Depression*. Tucson: University of Arizona Press, 1974.
Howard, John. *Concentration Camps on the Home Front: Japanese Americans in the House of Jim Crow*. Chicago: University of Chicago Press, 2008.
Hoxie, Frederick. *A Final Promise: The Campaign to Assimilate the Indians, 1880–1920*. Lincoln: University of Nebraska Press, 1984.
Parading through History: The Making of the Crow Nation in America, 1805–1935. Cambridge: Cambridge University Press, 1995.
Hundley, Norris. *The Great Thirst: Californians and Water – A History*. Berkeley: University of California Press, 2001.
Hunner, Jon. *Inventing Los Alamos: The Growth of an Atomic Community*. Norman: University of Oklahoma Press, 2004.
Hurt, R. Douglas. *The Big Empty: The Great Plains in the Twentieth Century*. Tucson: University of Arizona Press, 2011.
The Great Plains during World War Two. Lincoln: University of Nebraska Press, 2008.
Problems of Plenty: The American Farmer in the Twentieth Century. Chicago: Ivan Dee, 2002.
ed. *The Rural West since World War II*. Lawrence: University Press of Kansas, 1998.
Hurtado, Albert L., and Peter Iverson, eds. *Major Problems in American Indian History*. 2nd ed. Boston: Houghton Mifflin, 2001.

Hyde, Anne F. *An American Vision: Far Western Landscape and National Culture, 1820–1920*, New York: New York University Press, 1990.

Iber, Jorge, and Arnoldo DeLeon. *Hispanics in the American West.* Santa Barbara, CA: ABC/CLIO, 2006.

Igler, David. *Industrial Cowboys: Miller and Lux and the Transformation of the Far West, 1850–1920.* Berkeley: University of California Press, 2001.

Immerman, Richard H. *Empire for Liberty: A History of American Imperialism from Benjamin Franklin to Paul Wolfowitz.* Princeton, NJ: Princeton University Press, 2010.

Issel, William, and Robert W. Cherny. *San Francisco, 1865–1932: Politics, Power, and Urban Development.* Berkeley: University of California Press, 1986.

Iverson, Peter. *Dine: A History of the Navajos.* Albuquerque: University of New Mexico Press, 2002.

"We Are Still Here": American Indians in the Twentieth Century. Wheeling, IL: Harland Davidson, 1998.

Jackson, Kenneth T. *Crabgrass Frontiers: The Suburbanization of the United States.* New York: Oxford University Press, 1985.

The Ku Klux Klan in the City, 1915–1930. New York: Oxford University Press, 1967.

Jameson, Elizabeth. *All That Glitters: Class, Conflict, and Community in Cripple Creek.* Urbana: University of Illinois Press, 1998.

Jameson, Elizabeth, and Susan Armitage, eds. *Writing the Range: Race, Class, and Culture in the Women's West.* Norman: University of Oklahoma Press, 1997.

Johnson, Benjamin Heber. *Revolution in Texas: How a Forgotten Rebellion and Its Bloody Suppression Turned Mexicans into Americans.* New Haven, CT: Yale University Press, 2003.

Johnson, Jeffrey A. *They Are All Red Out Here: Socialist Politics in the Pacific Northwest, 1895–1925.* Norman: University of Oklahoma Press, 2008.

Johnson, Marilynn S. *The Second Gold Rush: Oakland and the East Bay in World War II.* Berkeley: University of California Press, 1993.

Johnston, Robert D. *The Radical Middle Class: Populist Democracy and the Question of Capitalism in Progressive Era Portland.* Princeton, NJ: Princeton University Press, 2003.

Kashima, Tetsuden. *Judgement without Trial: Japanese American Imprisonment during World War II.* Seattle: University of Washington Press, 2003.

Katznelson, Ira. *Fear Itself: The New Deal and the Origins of Our Time.* New York: Liveright/W. W. Norton, 2013.

Keene, Jennifer D. *Doughboys, the Great War, and the Remaking of America.* Baltimore: Johns Hopkins University Press, 2001.

Kennedy, David M. *Freedom from Fear: The American People in Depression and War.* New York: Oxford University Press, 1999.

Over Here: The First World War and American Society. 25th Anniversary ed. New York: Oxford University Press, 2004.

Kennedy, Paul. *The Rise and Fall of the Great Powers: Economic Change and Military Conflict from 1500 to 2000.* New York: Random House, 1987.

Kerstetter, Todd M. *Inspiration and Innovation: Religion in the American West.* Malden, MA: Wiley Blackwell, 2015.

Kirby, Jack Temple. *Darkness at the Dawning: Race and Reform in the Progressive South.* Philadelphia: Lippincott, 1972.

Klein, Maury. *A Call to Arms: Mobilizing America for World War II.* New York: Bloomsbury Press, 2013.

Kropp, Phoebe S. *California Vieja: Culture and Memory in a Modern American Place.* Berkeley: University of California Press, 2006.

Kruse, Kevin M., and Stephen Tuck, eds. *Fog of War: The Second World War and the Civil Rights Movement.* New York: Oxford University Press, 2012.

Lamar, Howard R. *The New Encyclopedia of the American West.* New Haven, CT: Yale University Press, 1998.

Lang, William L., ed. *Centennial West: Essays on the Northern Tier States.* Seattle: University of Washington Press, 1991.

Lansing, Jewel. *Portland, People, Politics, and Power, 1851–2001.* Corvallis: Oregon State University Press, 2003.

Laslett, John H. M. *Sunshine Was Never Enough: Workers, 1880–1910.* Berkeley: University of California Press, 2012.

Lay, Shawn, ed. *The Invisible Empire in the West: Toward a New Historical Appraisal of the Ku Klux Klan of the 1920s.* Urbana: University of Illinois Press, 1991.

Lee, Erika. *At America's Gates: Chinese Immigration during the Exclusion Era, 1882–1943.* Chapel Hill: University of North Carolina Press, 2006.

Lee, Erika, and Judy Yung. *Angel Island: Immigrant Gateway to America.* New York: Oxford University Press, 2010.

Leonard, Kevin. *The Battle for Los Angeles: Racial Ideology and World War II.* Albuquerque: University of New Mexico Press, 2006.

Leonard, Stephen J., and Thomas J. Noel. *Colorado: A History of the Centennial State.* Boulder: University of Colorado Press, 2005.

Limerick, Patricia. *The Legacy of Conquest: The Unbroken Past of the American West.* Reprint, New York: W. W. Norton, 2006.

Something in the Soil: Legacies and Reckonings in the New West. New York: W. W. Norton, 2000.

Limerick, Patricia, Clyde A. Milner II, and Charles Rankin, eds. *Trails: Toward a New Western History.* Lawrence: University Press of Kansas, 1991.

Lingeman, Richard. *Don't You Know There's a War Going On? The American Home Front, 1941–1945.* New York: Nation Books, 2003.

Link, William A. *The Paradox of Southern Progressivism, 1880–1930.* Chapel Hill: University of North Carolina Press, 1997.

Lotchin, Roger W. *The Bad City in the Good War: San Francisco, Los Angeles, Oakland, and San Diego.* Bloomington: Indiana University Press, 2003.

Fortress California, 1910–1961: From Welfare to Warfare. New York: Oxford University Press, 1992.

The Way We Really Were: The Golden State in the Second Great War. Urbana: University of Illinois Press, 2000.

Louter, David. *Windshield Wilderness: Cars, Roads, and Nature in Washington's National Parks.* Seattle: University of Washington Press, 2006.

Lowitt, Richard. *The New Deal and the West.* Bloomington: Indiana University Press, 1984.

Luebke, Frederick, ed. *European Immigrants in the American West: Community Histories.* Albuquerque: University of New Mexico Press, 1998.

Luey, Beth, and Noel J. Stowe, eds. *Arizona at Seventy-Five: The Next Twenty-Five Years.* Tucson: University of Arizona Press for the Arizona State University Public History Program and Arizona Historical Society, 1987.

MacLean, Nancy. *Behind the Mask of Chivalry: The Making of the Second Ku Klux Klan.* New York: Oxford University Press, 1994.

Madley, Benjamin. *An American Genocide: The United States and the California Indian Catastrophe.* New Haven, CT: Yale University Press, 2016.

Maher, Neil M. *Nature's New Deal: The Civilian Conservation Corps and the Roots of the American Environmental Movement.* New York: Oxford University Press, 2008.

Malin, James C. *The Contriving Brain and the Skillful Hand in the United States.* Ann Arbor, MI: Edwards Brothers, 1955.

Martinez, Oscar J. *Mexican-Origin People in the United States: A Topical History.* Tucson: University of Arizona Press, 2001.

Matsumoto, Valerie J. *Farming the Home Place: A Japanese American Community in California, 1919–1982.* Ithaca, NY: Cornell University Press, 1983.

Matsumoto, Valerie J., and Blake Allmendinger, eds. *Over the Edge: Remapping the American West.* Berkeley: University of California Press, 1999.

McFarland, Philip. *Mark Twain and the Colonel: Samuel L. Clemens, Theodore Roosevelt, and the Arrival of a New Century.* Lanham, MA: Roman and Littlefield, 2012.

McGerr, Michael. *A Fierce Discontent: The Rise and Fall of the Progressive Movement in America.* New York: Free Press, 2003.

McGirr, Lisa. *The War on Alcohol: Prohibition and the Rise of the American State.* New York: W. W. Norton, 2015.

McManus, Sheila. *Choices and Chances: A History of Women in the U.S. West.* Wheeling, IL: Harlan Davidson, 2011.

McWilliams, Carey. *North from Mexico: The Spanish-Speaking People of the United States.* 1848; repr., New York: Praeger, 1990.

Mead, Rebecca. *How the Vote Was Won: Woman Suffrage in the Western United States, 1868–1914.* Albany: New York University Press, 2004.

Meinig, D. W. *The Shaping of America: A Geographical Perspective on 500 Years of History.* Vol. 4. *Global America, 1915–2000.* New Haven, CT: Yale University Press, 2004.

Meltzer, Milton. *Dorothea Lange: A Photographer's Life.* New York: Syracuse University Press, 2000.

Miles, Tiya, and Sharon P. Holland, eds. *Crossing Waters, Crossing Worlds: The African Diaspora in Indian Country.* Durham, NC: Duke University Press, 2006.

Mills, David W. *Cold War in a Cold Land: Fighting Communism on the Northern Plains.* Norman: University of Oklahoma Press, 2015.

Milner, Clyde A., II, ed. *A New Significance: Re-envisioning the History of the American West.* New York: Oxford University Press, 1996.

Milner, Clyde A., II, Anne M. Butler, and David Rich Lewis, eds. *Major Problems in the History of the American West.* 2nd ed. Boston: Houghton Mifflin, 1997.

Milner, Clyde, II, Carol A. O'Connor, and Martha Sandweiss, eds. *The Oxford History of the American West.* New York: Oxford University Press, 1994.

Moehring, Eugene. *Resort City in the Sunbelt: Las Vegas, 1930–2000.* 2nd ed. Reno: University of Nevada Press, 2000.

Urbanism and Empire in the Far West, 1840–1890. Reno: University of Nevada Press, 2004.

Molina, Natalia. *Fit to Be Citizens? Public Health and Race in Los Angeles, 1879–1939.* Berkeley: University of California Press, 2006.

Monroy, Douglas. *Rebirth: Mexican Los Angeles from the Great Migration to the Great Depression.* Berkeley: University of California Press, 1999.

Montejano, David. *Anglos and Mexicans in the Making of Texas, 1836–1986.* Austin: University of Texas Press, 1987.

Morgan, Dan. *Rising in the West: The True Story of an "Okie" Family in Search of the American Dream.* New York: Vintage Books, 1992.

Morgan, H. Wayne, and Anne Hodges Morgan. *Oklahoma: A Bicentennial History.* New York: W. W. Norton, 1977.

Morris, Edmund. *Colonel Roosevelt.* New York: Random House, 2010.

The Rise of Theodore Roosevelt. New York: Coward, McCann, and Geoghegan, 1979.

Theodore Rex. New York: Random House, 2001.

Mowry, George. *The California Progressives.* Berkeley: University of California Press, 1951.

Murray, Robert K. *The Red Scare: A Study in National Hysteria, 1919–1920.* New York: McGraw-Hill, 1964.

Murrell, Gary. *Iron Pants: Oregon's Anti–New Deal Governor.* Pullman: Washington State University Press, 2000.

Nash, Gerald D. *The American West in the Twentieth Century: A Short History of an Urban Oasis.* New York: Prentice Hall, 2003.

A Brief History of the American West since 1945. New York: Harcourt Brace, 2001.

Creating the West: Historical Interpretations, 1890–1990. Albuquerque: University of New Mexico Press, 1991.

The Federal Landscape: An Economic History of the Twentieth-Century West. Tucson: University of Arizona Press, 1999.

The Great Depression and World War II: Organizing America, 1933–1945. New York: St. Martin's Press, 1979.

World War II and the West: Reshaping the Economy. Lincoln: University of Nebraska Press, 1990.

Nash, Gerald D., and Richard W. Etulain, eds. *Researching Western History: Topics in the Twentieth Century.* Albuquerque: University of New Mexico Press, 1997.

eds. *The Twentieth-Century West: Historical Interpretations*. Albuquerque: University of New Mexico Press, 1989.

Nash, Roderick. *The Nervous Generation: American Thought, 1917–1930*. Chicago: Ivan R. Dee, 1990.

Wilderness and the American Mind. 5th ed. New Haven, CT: Yale University Press, 2014.

Naske, Claus M., and Herman E. Slotnick. *Alaska: A History*. Norman: University of Oklahoma Press, 2011.

Ngai, Mai. *Impossible Subjects and the Making of Modern America*. 2004; repr., Princeton, NJ: Princeton University Press, 2014.

Nicolaides, Becky M. *My Blue Heaven: Life and Politics in the Working-Class Suburbs of Los Angeles, 1920–1965*. Chicago: University of Chicago Press, 2002.

Niehardt, John G., and Black Elk. *Black Elk Speaks: Being the Life Story of a Holy Man of the Oglala Sioux*. Albany: State University of New York Press, 2008.

Nugent, Walter. *Habits of Empire: A History of American Expansion*. New York: Alfred A. Knopf, 2008.

Into the West: The Story of Its People. New York: Alfred A. Knopf, 1999.

Progressivism: A Very Short Introduction. New York: Oxford University Press, 2010.

O'Mara, Margaret Pugh. *Cities of Knowledge: Cold War Science and the Search for the Next Silicon Valley*. Princeton, NJ: Princeton University Press, 2005.

Olson, James C., and Ronald C. Naugle. *History of Nebraska*. Lincoln: University of Nebraska Press, 1997.

Ostler, Jeff. *The Plains Sioux and U.S. Colonialism, from Lewis and Clark to Wounded Knee*. New York: Cambridge University Press, 2004.

Painter, Nell Irving. *Exodusters: Black Migration to Kansas after Reconstruction*. New York: W. W. Norton, 1976.

Parman, Donald L. *Indians and the American West in the Twentieth Century*. Bloomington: Indiana University Press, 1994.

The Navajos and the New Deal. New Haven, CT: Yale University Press, 1976.

Parrish, Michael E. *Anxious Decades: America in War and Depression, 1920–1941*. New York: W. W. Norton, 1992.

Pascoe, Peggy. *Relations of Rescue: The Search for Female Authority in the Modem West, 1874–1939*. New York: Oxford University Press, 1990.

Patterson, James T. *Congressional Conservatism and the New Deal: The Growth of the Conservative Coalition in Congress, 1933–1939*. Lexington: For the Organization of American Historians by University of Kentucky Press, 1967.

Peck, Gunther. *Reinventing Free Labor: Padrones and Immigrant Workers in the North American West, 1880–1930*. Cambridge: Cambridge University Press, 2000.

Petrik, Paula. *No Step Backward: Women and Family on the Rocky Mountain Mining Frontier, 1865–1900*. Helena: Montana Historical Society Press, 1987.

Philp, Kenneth R. *Termination Revisited: American Indians on the Trail to Self-Determination, 1933–1953*. Lincoln: University of Nebraska Press, 1999.

Philips, Charles, and Alan Axelrod et al., eds. *Encyclopedia of the American West.* 4 vols. New York: Simon and Schuster/Macmillan, 1996.

Phillips, Kimberly L. *War! What Is It Good For? Black Freedom Struggles and the U.S. Military from World War II to Iraq.* Chapel Hill: University of North Carolina Press, 2012.

Pierson, George W. *The Moving American.* New York: Alfred A. Knopf, 1973.

Pisani, Donald. *From the Family Farm to Agribusiness: The Irrigation Crusade in California and the West, 1850–1931.* Berkeley: University of California Press, 1984.

Water and the American Government: The Reclamation Bureau, National Water Policy, and the West, 1902–1913. Berkeley: University of California Press, 2002.

Pitzer, Paul C. *Grand Coulee: Harnessing a Dream.* Pullman: Washington State University Press, 1994.

Polenberg, Richard, ed. *America at War: The Home Front, 1941–1945.* Englewood Cliffs, NJ: Prentice Hall, 1968.

Pomeroy, Earl. *The American Far West in the Twentieth Century.* New Haven, CT: Yale University Press, 2008.

In Search of the Golden West: The Tourist in Western America. 2nd ed. Lincoln: Bison Books/University of Nebraska Press, 2010.

The Pacific Slope: A History of California, Oregon, Washington, Idaho, Utah, and Nevada. New York: Alfred A. Knopf, 1965.

Raban, Jonathan. *Bad Land: An American Romance.* New York: Pantheon, 1996.

Raeburn, John. *A Staggering Revolution: A Cultural History of Thirties Photography.* Urbana: University of Illinois Press, 2006.

Reisner, Mark. *Cadillac Desert: The American West and Its Disappearing Water.* New York: Viking Press, 1986.

Reynolds, David, Warren F. Kimball, and A. O. Chubarian, eds. *Allies at War: The Soviet, American and British Experience, 1939–1945.* New York: St. Martin's Press, 1994.

Rice, Arnold S. *The Ku Klux Klan in American Politics.* Washington, DC: Public Affairs Press, 1962.

Richard, Mark Paul. *Not a Catholic Nation: The Ku Klux Klan Confronts New England in the 1920s.* Amherst: University of Massachusetts Press, 2015.

Richardson, Heather Cox. *Wounded Knee: Party Politics and the Road to an American Massacre.* New York: Basic Books, 2010.

Riebsame, William, et al., eds. *The Atlas of the New West.* New York: W. W. Norton, 1997.

Righter, Robert W. *The Battle over Hetch Hetchy: America's Most Controversial Dam and the Birth of American Environmentalism.* New York: Oxford University Press, 2005.

Riley, Glenda. *Taking Land, Breaking Land: Women Colonizing the American West and Kenya, 1840–1940.* Albuquerque: University of New Mexico Press, 2003.

Robbins, William G. *Colony and Empire: The Capitalist Transformation of the American West.* Lawrence: University Press of Kansas, 1994.

Robbins, William, and Katherine Barber. *Nature's Northwest: The North Pacific Slope in the Twentieth Century*. Tucson: University of Arizona Press, 2011.

Roberts, Calvin A., and Susan A. Roberts. *New Mexico*. Albuquerque: University of New Mexico Press, 2006.

Robinson, Elwyn B. *History of North Dakota*. Lincoln: University of Nebraska Press, 1966.

Robinson, Greg. *A Tragedy of Democracy: Japanese Confinement in North America*. New York: Columbia University Press, 2009.

By Order of the President: FDR and the Internment of Japanese Americans. Cambridge, MA: Harvard University Press, 2001.

Rodgers, Marion Elizabeth. *Mencken: The American Iconoclast*. New York: Oxford University Press, 2005.

Rolle, Andrew, and Arthur Verge. *California: A History*. 7th ed. Wheeling, IL: Harlan Davidson, 2008.

Rothman, Hal. *Devil's Bargains: Tourism in the Twentieth-Century American West*. Lawrence: University Press of Kansas, 1998.

Neon Metropolis: How Las Vegas Started the Twenty-First Century. New York: Routledge, 2002.

Ruiz, Vicki. *Cannery Women/Cannery Lives: Mexican Women, Unionization, and the California Food Processing Industry, 1930–1950*. Albuquerque: University of New Mexico Press, 1987.

From Out of the Shadows: Mexican Women in Twentieth-Century America. New York: Oxford University Press, 1998.

Salmond, John A. *The Civilian Conservation Corps, 1933–1942: A New Deal Case Study*. Durham, NC: Duke University Press, 1967.

Sánchez, George J. *Becoming Mexican American: Ethnicity, Culture and Identity in Chicano Los Angeles, 1900–1945*. New York: Oxford University Press, 1993.

Sax, Joseph L. *Mountains without Handrails: Reflections on the National Parks*. Ann Arbor: University of Michigan Press, 1980.

Schell, Herbert B. *History of South Dakota*. Lincoln: University of Nebraska Press, 1968.

Schackel, Sandra K., ed. *Western Women's Lives: Continuity and Change in the Twentieth Century*. Albuquerque: University of New Mexico Press, 2003.

Schlesinger, Arthur, Jr. *A Life in the 20th Century: Innocent Beginnings, 1917–1950*. Boston: Houghton Mifflin, 2000.

Schlissel, Lillian, and Catherine Lavender, eds. *The Western Women's Reader*. New York: Harper Perennial, 2000.

Schlissel, Lillian, Vicki Ruiz, and Janice Monks, eds. *Western Women, Their Land, Their Lives*. Albuquerque: University of New Mexico Press, 1988.

Schwantes, Carlos A. *Coxey's Army: An American Odyssey*. Lincoln: University of Nebraska Press, 1985.

Going Places: Transportation Redefines the Twentieth-Century West. Bloomington: Indiana University Press, 2003.

In Mountain Shadows: A History of Idaho. Lincoln: University of Nebraska Press, 1991.

The Pacific Northwest: An Interpretive History. Lincoln: University of Nebraska Press, 1989.
Shaffer, Marguerite P. *See America First: Tourism and National Identity, 1880–1940*. Washington, DC: Smithsonian Institute Press, 2001.
Shoemaker, Nancy. *American Indian Population Recovery in the Twentieth Century*. Albuquerque: University of New Mexico Press, 1999.
Sides, Josh. *L.A. City Limits: African American Los Angeles from the Great Depression to the Present*. Berkeley: University of California Press, 2003.
Sitkoff, Harvard. *A New Deal for Blacks: The Emergence of Civil Rights as a National Issue*. New York: Oxford University Press, 2009.
Sklar, Robert. *Movie-Made America: A Cultural History of American Movies*. Rev. ed. New York: Vintage, 1994.
Slotkin, Richard. *Gunfighter Nation: The Myth of the Frontier in Twentieth-Century America*. New York: Atheneum, 1992.
Smith, Duane A. *Rocky Mountain Heartland: Colorado, Montana, and Wyoming in the Twentieth Century*. Tucson: University of Arizona Press, 2008.
Smith, Jason Scott. *Building New Deal Liberalism: The Political Economy of Public Works, 1933–1956*. New York: Cambridge University Press, 2006.
Smith, Sherry. *Reimagining Indians: Native Americans through Anglo Eyes, 1880–1940*. New York: Oxford University Press, 2000.
Spiro, Jonathan Peter. *Defending the Master Race: Conservation, Eugenics, and the Legacy of Madison Grant*. Lebanon, NH: University of Vermont Press/University Press of New England, 2009.
Starr, Kevin. *Embattled Dreams: California in War and Peace, 1940–1950*. New York: Oxford University Press, 2002.
Endangered Dreams: The Great Depression in California. New York: Oxford University Press, 1996.
Inventing the Dream: California through the Progressive Era. New York: Oxford University Press, 1985.
Material Dreams: Southern California through the 1920s. New York: Oxford University Press, 1991.
St. John, Rachel. *Line in the Sand: A History of the Western U.S.–Mexico Border*. Princeton, NJ: Princeton University Press, 2011.
Stoll, Steven. *The Fruits of Natural Advantage: Making the Industrial Countryside in California*. Berkeley: University of California Press, 1998.
Street, Richard Steven. *Beasts of the Field: A Narrative History of California Farmworkers, 1769–1913*. Stanford, CA: Stanford University Press, 2004.
Everyone Had Cameras: Photography and Farmworkers in California, 1850–2000. Minneapolis: University of Minnesota Press, 2008.
Stryker, Roy E., and Nancy Wood. *In This Proud Land: America 1935–1943 as Seen in the FSA Photographs*. Greenwich, CT: New York Graphic Society, 1973.
Sutter, Paul. *Driven Wild: How the Fight against Automobiles Launched the Modern Wilderness Movement*. Seattle: University of Washington Press, 2002.
Sutton, Matthew Avery. *Aimee Semple McPherson and the Resurrection of Christian America*. Cambridge, MA: Harvard University Press, 2007.

American Apocalypse: A History of Modern Evangelicalism. Cambridge, MA: The Belknap Press of Harvard University Press, 2014.

Swenson, James R. *Picturing Migrants: "The Grapes of Wrath" and New Deal Documentary Photography*. Norman: University of Oklahoma Press, 2015.

Szasz, Ferenc Morton. *The Day the Sun Rose Twice: The Story of the Trinity Site Nuclear Explosion, July 16, 1945*. Albuquerque: University of New Mexico Press, 1984.

Religion in the Modern American West. Tucson: University of Arizona Press, 2000.

Takaki, Ronald. *Strangers from a Different Shore: A History of Asian Americans*. Boston: Little, Brown, 1989.

Taylor, Nick. *American Made: The Enduring Legacy of the WPA: When FDR Put the Nation to Work*. New York: Bantam Dell, 2008.

Taylor, Quintard. *The Forging of a Black Community: Seattle's Central District from 1870 through the Civil Rights Era*. Seattle: University of Washington Press, 1994.

In Search of the Racial Frontier: African Americans in the American West, 1528–1900. New York: W. W. Norton, 1998.

Terkel, Studs. *"The Good War": An Oral History of World War II*. New York: Pantheon Books, 1984.

Thomas, Evan. *The War Lovers: Roosevelt, Lodge, Hearst and the Rush to Empire, 1898*. Boston: Little, Brown, 2010.

Tindall, George Brown, and David Emory Shi. *America: A Narrative History*. Vol. 2. New York: W. W. Norton, 2013.

Titus, A. Constandina. *Bombs in the Backyard: Atomic Testing and American Politics*. 2nd ed. Reno: University of Nevada Press, 2001.

Townsend, Kim. *Manhood at Harvard: William James and Others*. New York: W. W. Norton, 1997.

Travis, William R. *New Geographies of the American West: Land Use and the Changing Patterns of Place*. Washington, DC: Island Press, 2007.

Truett, Samuel. *Fugitive Landscapes: The Forgotten History of the U.S.–Mexico Borderlands*. New Haven, CT: Yale University Press, 2006.

Tyrell, Ian. *Crisis of the Wasteful Nation: Empire and Conservatism in Theodore Roosevelt's America*. Chicago: University of Chicago Press, 2015.

Udall, Stewart L. *The Quiet Crisis*. New York: Holt, Rinehart, and Winston, 1983.

Utley, Robert M. *The Last Days of the Sioux*. New Haven, CT: Yale University Press, 2004.

Vargas, Zaragosa, ed. *Major Problems in Mexican American History*. Boston: Houghton Mifflin, 1999.

Walsh, Margaret. *The American West: Visions and Revisions*. Cambridge: Cambridge University Press, 2005.

Wartzman, Rick. *Obscene in the Extreme: The Banning and Burning of John Steinbeck's "The Grapes of Wrath."* New York: Public Affairs, 2008.

Watkins, T. H. *The Great Depression: America in the 1930s*. Boston: Little, Brown, 1993.

Weber, Devra. *Dark Sweat, White Gold: California Farm Workers, Cotton, and the New Deal*. Berkeley: University of California Press, 1994.

Weisiger, Marsha. *Dreaming of Sheep in Navajo Country*. Seattle: University of Washington Press, 2009.

White, Richard. *"It's Your Misfortune and None of My Own": A New History of the American West*. Norman: University of Oklahoma Press, 1991.

The Organic Machine: The Remaking of the Columbia River. New York: Hill and Wang, 1995.

Railroaded: The Transcontinentals and the Making of Modern America. New York: W. W. Norton, 2011.

The Roots of Dependency: Subsistence, Environment, and Social Change among the Choctaws, Pawnees, and Navajos. Lincoln: University of Nebraska Press, 1983.

White, Richard, and John M. Findlay, eds. *Power and Place in the North American West*. Seattle: University of Washington Press, 1999.

Whitehead, John S. *Completing the Union: Alaska, Hawaii, and the Battle for Statehood*. Albuquerque: University of New Mexico Press, 2004.

Whitfield, Stephen J. *A Companion to 20th-Century America*. Malden, MA: Blackwell, 2004.

Wiese, Andrew. *Places of Their Own: African American Suburbanization in the Twentieth Century*. Chicago: University of Chicago Press, 2004.

Williams, Hill. *Made in Hanford: The Bomb That Changed the World*. Pullman: Washington State University Press, 2011.

Witt, John Fabian. *The Accidental Republic: Crippled Workman, Destitute Widows, and the Remaking of America Law*. Cambridge, MA: Harvard University Press, 2004.

Woodworth-Ney, Laura E. *Women in the American West*. Santa Barbara, CA: ABC-CLIO, 2008.

Worster, Donald. *Dust Bowl: The Southern Plains in the 1930s*. 25th Anniversary ed. New York: Oxford University Press, 2004.

Rivers of Empire: Nature, Aridity, and the Growth of the American West. New York: Oxford University Press, 1985.

Under Western Skies: Nature and History in the American West. New York: Oxford University Press, 1992.

Wrobel, David M. *The End of American Exceptionalism: Frontier Anxiety from the Old West to the New Deal*. Lawrence: University Press of Kansas, 1993.

Global West, American Frontier: Travel, Empire, and Exceptionalism from Manifest Destiny to the New Deal. Albuquerque: University of New Mexico Press, 2013.

Promised Lands: Promotion, Memory and the Creation of the American West. Lawrence: University Press of Kansas, 2002.

Wrobel, David M., and Patrick T. Long. *Seeing and Being Seen: Tourism in the American West*. Lawrence: University Press of Kansas, 2001.

Wrobel, David M., and Michael C. Steiner, eds. *Many Wests: Place, Culture, and Regional Identity*. Lawrence: University Press of Kansas, 1997.

Yoo, David. *Growing Up Nisei: Race, Generation, and Culture among Japanese Americans of California, 1924–1949*. Urbana: University of Illinois Press, 2000.

Young, Elliott. *Alien Nation: The Chinese Migration in the Americas from the Coolie Era through World War II*. Chapel Hill: University of North Carolina Press, 2014.

Yung, Judy. *Unbound Feet: A Social History of Chinese Women in San Francisco*. Berkeley: University of California Press, 1995.

Zamora, Emilio. *Claiming Rights and Righting Wrongs: Mexican Workers and Job Politics during World War II*. College Station: Texas A&M University Press, 2009.

Articles and Essays

Adams, Michael C. C. "The 'Good War' Myth and the Cult of Nostalgia." *Midwest Quarterly* 40 (Autumn 1998): 59–74.

DuBois, Ellen, and Robert W. Cherny, eds. "Women Suffrage: The View from the Pacific." Special Issue. *Pacific Historical Review* 69 (November 2000).

Layton, Edwin. "The Better American Federation: A Case Study of 'Superpatriotism.'" *Pacific Historical Review* 30 (May 1961): 137–147.

Levy, David W. "The Rise and Fall of Edwin ('Daddy') DeBarr." *Chronicles of Oklahoma* 88 (Fall 2010): 288–315.

Lew-Williams, Beth. "Before Restriction Became Exclusion: America's Experiment in Diplomatic Immigration Control." *Pacific Historical Review* 83 (February 2014): 24–56.

Malone, Michael P. "The New Deal in Idaho." *Pacific Historical Review* 3 (August 1969): 293–310.

Miller, Douglas K. "Urban Relocation and American Indian Initiative, 1940s–1960s." *Ethnohistory I* 60 (Winter 2013): 51–76.

Philp, Kenneth R. "Termination: A Legacy of the Indian New Deal." *Western Historical Quarterly* 14 (April 1983): 165–180.

Sabol, Steven. "'It Was a Pretty Good War, But They Stopped It Too Soon': The American Empire, Native Americans, and World War I." In *Empires in World War I: Shifting Frontiers and Imperial Dynamics in a Global Conflict*, ed. Andrew Tait Jarboe and Richard S. Fogarty, 193–216. London: I. B. Taurus, 2014.

Verge, Arthur C. "The Impact of the Second World War on Los Angeles." *Pacific Historical Review* 63 (August 1994): 289–314.

Wrobel, David, ed. "Forum: The American West Enters the Twenty-First Century: Appraisals on the State of a Field." *Historian* 66 (Fall 2004): 437–564.

Dissertations and Theses

Clark, Carter Blue. "A History of the Ku Klux Klan in Oklahoma." PhD diss., University of Oklahoma, 1976.

Daley, Shawn T. "Centralia, Collective Memory, and the Tragedy of 1919." MA thesis, Portland State University, 2015.

Dupree, James E. "Line Riders, Masculinity, and Authority on the Mexican–American Border, 1882–1913." MA thesis, University of Oklahoma, 2013.

Dye, Douglas Mark. "The Soul of the City: The Work of the Seattle Council of Churches during World War II." PhD diss., Washington State University, 1997.

Miller, Douglas K. "Reservation Limits: American Indian Urbanization and Uplift in the Twentieth Century." PhD diss., University of Oklahoma, 2014.

Orth, Joel Jason. "The Conservation Landscape: Trees and Nature on the Great Plains." PhD diss., Iowa State University, 2004.

Working Papers

Morgan-Collins, Mona. "Votes for and by Women: How Did Women Vote after the Nineteenth Amendment?" Working Paper. www.lse.ac.uk/government/research/resgroups/PSPE/Working-papers/Mona-Morgan-Collins-Votes-For-and-by-Women.pdf.

Index